OUR CONSTITUTION
An Introduction to India's Constitution
And Constitutional Law

Some Other Books by the Author

Constitutional Law of India (2 Vols.)
Parliamentary Procedure, Law, Privileges, Practice and Precedents
History of the Parliament of India (2 Vols)
Our Political System
Concise Encyclopedia of Indian Constitution
Blueprint of Political Reforms
Anti-Defection Law and Parliamentary Privileges
Constitution Making Since 1950
Citizen and the Constitution
Indian Constitution: Conflicts & Controversies
Our Parliament
History of Parliamentary Democracy
Parliamentary Wit and Humour
The Speaker's Office
The Politics of Defection
History of the Freedom Movement
The Politics of Power
Political System and Institution Building under Jawaharlal Nehru
Jawaharlal Nehru, the Constitution and the Parliament
The Citizen and Judicial Reforms
Constitutional Reforms
National Resurgence through Electoral Reforms
Constitution of India – Review and Reassessment

India—The Land and the People

OUR CONSTITUTION

An Introduction to India's Constitution And Constitutional Law

SUBHASH C. KASHYAP

nbt.india
एकः सूते सकलम्
NATIONAL BOOK TRUST, INDIA

Cover shows Dr. B.R. Ambedkar, Chairman, Drafting Committee of the Constitution of India, at work.

ISBN 978-81-237-0734-1

First Edition 1994; First Reprint 1995
Second Edition 1995; Reprints 1997, 1999, 2000
Third Revised Edition 2001; Reprints 2002, 2004
Fourth Revised Edition 2005; Reprints 2007, 2008, 2009, 2010 (twice)
Fifth Revised Edition 2011
Reprints 2011, 2013, 2014, 2015, 2017, 2019 (twice), 2021, 2023,
2024, 2025, 2026 (twice) (*Saka* 1948)

₹ 355.00
Published by the Director, National Book Trust, India
5 Institutional Area, Vasant Kunj, New Delhi-110070
Website : www.nbtindia.gov.in

CONTENTS

Preface

A celebrated author was once asked about the time taken by him in writing one of his well-known treatises. He replied that as for the actual writing it took him only one and a half years but in order to be able to write it during that period he needed the background, study and experience of a whole lifetime. Something similar, in all humility, can be said about the present work.

I have been a student of the Constitution of India and constitutional law for the last six decades *i.e.* right from its commencement in 1950. Also, after my working on the five volumes of *The Framing of India's Constitution* (IIPA), I always wanted to write a modest book on the Constitution of India as it had grown and worked and as it had been interpreted since 26 January 1950. But, all these many years, while I wrote extensively and published many titles in the field of politics, law, government and parliament, the Constitution project somehow got pushed to a lower priority. Only very recently, in 2008, I was at last able to complete the project and publish my 2-Volume, 4000-page treatise on the *Constitutional Law of India*.

The credit for the completion and publication of this handy introduction to the Constitution and Constitutional Law of India goes entirely to the National Book Trust, India. I had to work really hard to ensure that the work did not become bulky, that it did not assume scholarly pretensions, that it remained factual and objective and readable by the interested general public. For this purpose, I also avoided making extensive source referencing, giving footnotes etc. But I have done my best to ensure that nothing of relevance or importance is left out. So far as case law is concerned, I have generally confined myself to selected Supreme Court judgements. Also, while as a student of India's political system and constitutional law, I hold some strong views on certain constitutional controversies, I have tried to scrupulously avoid stressing them in the present work and reserved them for other works of a somewhat different nature.

Already, there are several voluminous and multi-volume works and some popular guide-books on our Constitution. But there has been a long-felt need for a concise but comprehensive and authoritative study. It is hoped that the present book meets this need. Not only students of political science and constitutional law but also lawyers and citizens wanting to understand the Constitution and know something about the politico-constitutional system under which we live find it useful.

Apart from the text of the Constitution itself and the Constituent Assembly Debates, I have depended heavily on the various law reporters and benefitted from works on the Constitution by several scholars. I am grateful to all of them.

Last, but not the least, I have made full use of my own earlier writings. I acknowledge my debt to all the other friends and family members who directly or indirectly helped me in completing this work.

The first edition of this work appeared in 1994. That it became necessary in less than one year to bring out a reprint and then the second, third and fourth revised editions and several reprints of each shows that the book has been widely welcomed. Also, the concluding chapter of the book had suggested the need for a review of the working of the Constitution. It was most gratifying that a National

Commission to Review the Working of the Constitution was at last appointed in 2000. Its Report was submitted in 2002 and several of its important recommendations have since got implemented.

The Hindi version of this book independently written by me has been equally well received. The book has been translated into several other Indian languages also. I am deeply beholden to the readers and the publishers – the National Book Trust, India.

The present edition which is the fifth, has been fully and substantially revised and updated in the light of valuable comments from the readers, latest developments and constitutional amendments including all those enacted till October 2009. It is hoped that the readers would find this revised edition more useful.

Subhash C. Kashyap

Kashyap Chauraha
62, Sainik Farms
New Delhi – 110062

Table of Cases

1

INTRODUCTION

What is a Constitution?

Constitution of a country lays down the basic structure of the political system under which its people are to be governed. It establishes the main organs of the state—the legislature, the executive and the judiciary, defines their powers, demarcates their responsibilities and regulates their relationships with each other and with the people.

In a democracy, sovereignty vests in the people and ideally the people govern themselves. But, with the growing complexities of administration and the size of the nation-states, direct democracy is no more feasible. In the modern representative democracies, people exercise their inalienable right to decide how and by whom they should be governed. The very first and the most fundamental application of their sovereignty by the people is in giving to themselves a constitution which outlines the ground rules under which certain powers are transferred to different organs of the state and are to be exercised by them.

In a federal polity, constitution *inter alia* delineates, delimits and distributes powers between the organs of the state at federal or union level on the one hand and those at the level of the states, provinces or the units on the other.

The Constitution of a country may also be described as its foundational law which ordains the fundamentals of its polity and on the alter of which all other laws and executive acts of the state are to be tested for their validity and legitimacy.

Every constitution represents the vision and values of its founding fathers and is based on the social, political and economic ethos and faith and aspirations of the people.

It is wrong to regard a country's constitution as a mere inert document. For, constitution is not only what is written in the text of the constitution. Constitution is a living organism of functioning institutions. It keeps constantly growing, evolving. Every constitution gets meaning and content only from the manner in which and the people by whom it is operated, the effects it acquires from how it is interpreted by courts of the land and the conventions and practices that grow around it in the actual process of its working.

Constitutional Law

Constitutional law would normally cover and connote the fundamental law of the land as contained in the provisions of the constitution. More particularly, it is concerned with the basic features of the framework of the distribution of powers between the organs of the state and between the union and the units. However, modern constitutional law, specially in free representative democracies, lays the greatest emphasis on fundamental human rights and the relationship between the individual citizens and the state. Also, the sources of constitutional law include not only the text of the constitution but also constitutional case law, conventions and a number of statutes enacted under certain constitutional provisions.

Constitutionalism

The concept of constitutionalism is that of a polity governed by or under a constitution that ordains essentially limited government and rule of law as opposed to arbitrary, authoritarian or totalitarian rule. Constitutional government, therefore, should necessarily be democratic government. Also, constitutionalism is a natural concomitant of a written constitution inasmuch as a written constitution is bound to define and delimit the powers and functions of various organs of the state and a government under a written constitution can only be limited government. But, it is certainly conceivable that some countries—there have been many examples—may have written constitutions which are not really democratic. It can be said that they have constitutions but not constitutionalism. Also, there are instances where there is no written constitution but constitutionalism prevails.

Constitution of India

Our present Constitution—the first Constitution of India framed and given to themselves by the people of India—was adopted by the Constituent Assembly on 26 November 1949. It came into full operation with effect from 26 January 1950. The Constitution as originally adopted had 22 parts, 395 articles and 8 schedules. Its present text is as amended from time to time. During the last 60 years, there have been as many as 94 amendments. From 8 the number of schedules has now gone up to 12 and the number of articles has increased from 395 to 448. A number of new articles (*e.g.* 31A, 31B, 31C, 39A, 43A, 48A, 51A, 134A, 139A, 224A, 233A, 239A, 239AA, 239AB, 239B, 243A to 243ZG, 244A, 258A, 268A, 290A, 300A, 312A, 323A, 323B, 338A, 350A, 350B, 361A, 361B, 363A, 371A to 371I, 372A, 378A, 394A) and new Parts (*e.g.* Parts IVA, IXA, XIVA) have been added to the Constitution and several articles (*e.g.* articles 31, 238, 242, 259, 278, 291, 306, 314, 362, 379 to 391) or even full Parts (*e.g.* Part VII) of the Constitution have been repealed by constitutional amendments, but following the standard practice in this regard and to facilitate referencing, the existing nos. of articles, Parts or Chapters have not been changed.

Sources of the Constitution

The sources of the Constitution of India are diverse and many. These are both indigenous and foreign. The founding fathers made it very clear that they were not writing on a clean slate. They took a conscious decision not to make a complete departure from the past, but to build on the existing structure and experience of institutions already established. Even otherwise, the Constitution of India had had an organic growth. It evolved through the interaction between various demands for representative responsible governmental institutions during the nationalist struggle for independence and the small doses of constitutional reforms grudgingly conceded by the British rulers from time to time. Howsoever rudimentary in form in the early stages, the process of political institution building—particularly the legislatures—in the modern sense of the term can be gauged from as early as the late 1920s onwards. In fact, the sources of some of the provisions of the Constitution can be traced back to the beginnings of the East India Company and the British rule in India.

Reference to organisation of village panchayats under the Directive Principles was clearly inspired by Mahatma Gandhi and the ancient Indian institutions of self-government. The 73rd and 74th Constitution Amendment Acts have since tried to give greater meaning and content to them.

Demand for some of the fundamental rights was made as early as in 1918 at the Bombay session of the Indian National Congress. The Commonwealth of India Bill, finalized by the National Convention in 1925 embodied a specific "declaration of rights" like equality before law, freedom of speech, assembly and religion etc. A resolution passed at the Madras session of the Congress in 1927 reiterated the demand for fundamental rights. The Motilal Nehru Committee appointed in 1928 by the All Parties Conference in its report declared that the first concern of the people of India was to secure justiciable fundamental human rights. Interestingly, ten of the nineteen fundamental rights incorporated in the Nehru Committee Report appeared in the Constitution of India substantially unchanged. The Karachi Congress Resolution of 1931 contained a specific enumeration not only of fundamental rights but also of fundamental duties. Several of the social and economic rights mentioned in the 1931 resolution found expression in the Directive Principles of the Constitution and a chapter on fundamental duties which did not find a place in the original Constitution got included later by the Constitution (Forty-second) Amendment Act in 1976.

A parliamentary system with a government responsible to Parliament, safeguards for minorities and a federal polity contained in the Constitution could also be said to have had their sources in the 1928 Nehru Committee Report.

Finally, nearly 75 per cent of the Constitution can be said to be a reproduction of the Government of India Act, 1935 with suitable adaptations and modifications. The basic structure of the polity and provisions regulating Union-State relations, declaration of Emergency etc. were largely based on the 1935 Act. Besides the indigenous sources, the Constituent Assembly had before it several models of foreign constitutions. Thus, the concept of Directive Principles was borrowed from the Irish Constitution. Parliamentary system with ministerial responsibility to the legislature came from the British and provisions making the President, the Executive head of the State and the Supreme Commander of the armed forces and the Vice-President, the *ex-officio* Chairman of the Council of States were based on the U.S. model. The Bill of Rights enshrined in the U.S. Constitution could also be said to have inspired our Fundamental Rights.

The Canadian Constitution *inter alia* influenced the federal structure and the provisions relating to Union-State relations and the distribution of powers between the Union and the States. The Concurrent List in the Seventh Schedule, provisions regarding Trade, Commerce and Intercourse, Finance Commission and parliamentary privileges were modelled presumably on the Australian Constitution. The Emergency provisions were influenced *inter alia* by the Constitution of the German Reich. For understanding the ambit and scope of provisions like those pertaining to the issue of writs and parliamentary privileges one has still to go to the British Constitution.[1]

Interpretation of the Constitution

The normal rules applicable to interpretation of statutes are equally valid in the field of constitutional interpretation. The interpretation clause—article 367—*inter alia* clarifies that the General Clauses Act shall apply to the interpretation of the provisions of the Constitution. But the Constitution is the fundamental and the supreme law which creates the Legislature and under which all the laws of the land are to be enacted and draw their legitimacy. Under what is called the Doctrine of Liberal Interpretation, therefore, the Constitution has to be interpreted liberally and not in a narrow sense.[2] Also, besides the general rules, there are some special rules for interpretation of the Constitution.

Every provision of the Constitution has to be so construed as to give meaning and relevance to every word used. It has been held by the Supreme Court that unless otherwise indicated, every word is supposed to have been used in its normal or ordinary connotation and should be given the plain common sense meaning.[3]

The purpose of interpretation is to ascertain the intent of the framers. But, this has to be ascertained from the actual words used in the text. If the language of a constitutional

---

1. For a fuller study and a Statement of various sources of provisions of the Constitution, see Subhash C. Kashyap, *Constitutional Law of India*, Universal, New Delhi, 2008, Vol.I.
2. *Goodyear India v. State of Haryana*, AIR (1990) SC 781.
3. *Kesavanand Bharti v. State of Kerala* (1973) 4 SCC 225.

provision is clear and unambiguous, things like the spirit of the Constitution or the views of the Constitution-makers expressed in the Constituent Assembly debates are irrelevant in interpretation. If, however, the vagueness of the language admits of more than one interpretation these can be considered for purposes of clarification.[1]

The Constitution must be read as a whole with due weight given to every part. Where two provisions appear to be in conflict, under the Principle of Harmonious Construction, the meaning which gives effect to both the provisions and ensures their smooth and harmonious operation should be accepted.[2]

Under what is called 'Doctrine of Severability', if a part of the provision is found to be invalid, the validity of the remaining part need not be affected if it can be separated from the impugned part and can stand on its own.[3]

According to the Doctrine of Prospective Overruling adopted by our Supreme Court, an interpretation given by the court and the law declared by it may not be given retroactive operation *i.e.* the validity of past acts may not be affected.[4]

---

1. *Menon v. State of Bombay*, AIR 1951 SC 128; *Gopalan V. State of Madras*, AIR 1950 SC 27.
2. See *Venkataramana v. State of Mysore*, AIR 1958 SC 255, *State of Madras V. Champakam*, (1951) S.C.R. 525, *Gopalan v. State of Madras*, (1950) S.C.R. 88.
3. *Gaya Pratap Singh v. Allahabad Bank*, AIR 1955 SC 765, *Gopalan v. State of Madras*, (1950) S.C.R. 88.
4. *Golak Nath v. State of Punjab*, AIR 1967 SC 1643.

2

CONSTITUTIONAL HISTORY

The edifice of the constitution of a country is always built on the foundations of its past. To understand any constitution in existence and operation, therefore, it is essential to know its background and history.

Constitutional Government in Ancient India

The concepts of democracy, representative institutions, limitations on the arbitrary powers of the rulers, and rule of law were not alien to India in the hoary past. The concept of the supremacy of *Dharma* was hardly different from the rule of law, constitutionalism or limited government. The rulers in ancient India were bound by *Dharma*, no one was above *Dharma*. Enough evidence has come to light to show that republican forms of government, representative deliberative bodies and local self-government institutions existed in many parts of ancient India and democratic thinking and practices permeated different aspects of the life of the people right from the Vedic age (circa 3000–1000 B.C.).

The *Rigveda* and the *Atharvaveda* mention the *Sabha* (General Assembly) and the *Samiti* (House of Elders). The *Aitareya Brahmana*, Panini's *Ashtadhyayi*, Kautilya's *Arthashastra*, the *Mahabharata*, inscriptions on Ashoka's pillars, the Buddhist and Jain texts of the period and the *Manusmriti* all bear witness to the existence of several functioning republics during the post-Vedic period of Indian history. After the *Mahabharata* particularly, large empires gave way to a number of small republican states. *Jatakas* make many references to how these republics functioned. The members met in *Santhagar*. Representatives were elected in open assembly. They selected their *Gopa* who became King and ruled with the help of a Council of Ministers.

In the 4th century B.C., the republican federation known as the *Kshudrak Malla Sangha* offered strong resistance to Alexander. Near Patliputra (Patna), there was Vaishali, the Capital of Lichchavis. The state was a republic governed by an assembly with an elected President called *Nayak*. Unfortunately, we know little of the details of the constitution of these republics. The Greek scholar Megasthenes has left records of popular assemblies that were preserved in the South and which restrained the power of Kings. Kautilya's *Arthashastra* also records that autocracy or the Divine Right of Kings had no place in ancient Indian polity. The power of the Indian King was hedged in by safeguards against abuse and limited by liberties and powers of other public authorities and interests. He was, in fact, a limited or a constitutional monarch. Manu and the *Mahabharata* say that an unjust and oppressive ruler should be killed by his own subjects like a street dog gone mad. *Nitisara* (Science of Polity) of Shukracharya written in the tenth century is a book on constitution. It deals with the organization of the central government as well as village and town life, of the King's Council and of various departments of government. The King was to act on the opinion of the majority of the people. To quote Dr.B.R. Ambedkar:

> It is not that India did not know what is Democracy. There was a time when India was studded with republics, and even where there were monarchies, they were either elected or limited. They were never absolute. It is not that India did not know Parliaments or Parliamentary Procedure. A study of the Buddhist *Bhikshu Sanghas* discloses that not only there were Parliaments—but the

Sanghas knew and observed all the rules of Parliamentary Procedure known to modern times. They had rules regarding seating arrangements, Motions, Resolutions, Quorum, Whip, Counting of Votes, Voting by Ballot, Censure Motion, Regularization, *Res Judicata*, etc. Although these rules of Parliamentary Procedure were applied by Buddha to the meetings of the *Sanghas*, he must have borrowed them from the rules of the political assemblies functioning in the country in his time.

Panchayati Raj Institutions

While the democratic institutions like the republican states, elective kingship, the *Sabha* and the *Samiti* later disappeared, representative bodies at the village level like the *Gram Sanghas, Gram Sabhas* or *Panchayats* survived and continued to function and flourish right through the rule of many Hindu and Muslim dynasties and till the advent of the British rule.

Advent of the British (1600–1765)

The British came to India to trade. It was on 31 December 1600 that the East India Company formed by some merchants of London secured from Queen Elizabeth a royal charter. The Charter granted to the company monopoly rights for trade with India and some areas of South East Asia for an initial period of 15 years. It laid down the constitution, powers and privileges of the company. Each year all the members of the company were to elect one governor and 24 one man committees. The management of the Company was entrusted to these 25 men in England. Subsequently, these committees came to be called Directors and the Court of Directors was born. The Governor and company could make laws for ensuring good governance of the company, regulating its business and maintaining discipline among its servants. But the legislative power of the company was very limited. They could not make any laws contrary to the laws, conventions and precedents in Britain.

The powers and privileges of the company were enlarged by each subsequent charter. By the year 1700, the company had established its factories (trading centres) and chief settlements at Bombay, Madras and Calcutta. By the Charter of 1669, the island and port of Bombay were entrusted to the company at an annual rental of Sterling Pounds 10. Simultaneously, the company was given the power to make necessary laws and issue ordinances for the good government of Bombay and its residents. Thus, for the first time in 1669 the company acquired the authority to rule over a definite territory and its people. From a mere trading company, it became a ruler. In 1677 the company was given the right to issue its own coins. The 1683 Charter empowered the company to declare war and enter into treaties subject to the proviso that the company itself could not assume sovereign powers over any territory. Whatever territories were acquired by the company or came under its control, were all for the British Crown with the company acting as its representative.

The Charter of 1726 empowered the Governors-in-Council of the three Presidencies of Bombay, Madras and Calcutta to make bye-laws, rules and ordinances in conformity with English laws and subject to approval by the Court of Directors. English laws were expressly introduced and Mayor's Courts established in the three Presidencies by the 1726 Charter.

Taking advantage of the weakening central authority, disintegration of the Mughal Empire and disturbed conditions all over the country after Aurangzeb's death (1707), the company gradually emerged as the dominant power. The victory of the company at the Battle of Plassey in 1757 against Sirajuddaulla, Nawab of Bengal, clinched the issue and the foundations of British rule in India were laid.

In 1764 the combined forces of Mughal Emperor Shah Alam and the Nawabs of Oudh and Bengal were defeated by the company at the Battle of Buxar. This left the company in full control over Bengal. In 1765, Shah Alam entrusted the Diwani of Bengal, Bihar and Orissa to the company which meant that the company acquired full powers of land revenue collection and administration of civil justice while the responsibility of administration, maintenance of law and order and criminal justice remained with the Nawab. The dyarchy which prevailed during 1765–1772 proved disastrous and led to the appointment of an inquiry committee by the British House of Commons. The committee recommended the need for regulating the activities of the company. The result was the Regulating Act of 1773.

The Company Rule (1773–1858)

Regulating Act of 1773**:** The 1773 Act is particularly important in India's constitutional history inasmuch as it was the beginning of the efforts at British parliamentary control over the company administration in India. The administration of territories under the company rule was no more a private affair of the traders of the company. The Regulating Act of 1773 for the first time presented a written Charter for company rule in India and acknowledged the political and administrative responsibilities of the company. This Act was also perhaps the first step in the direction of consolidation of British rule and centralization of administration in India. The Act established a Supreme Court at Calcutta, brought the three erstwhile independent and separate Presidencies generally under the control of the Governor-General of Bengal with his four newly appointed councillors, and brought about fundamental reforms in the composition of the Court of Directors in England.

Pitt's India Act**:** The 1773 Act suffered from several shortcomings in the matter of practical operation. The Amending Act of 1781 tried to remedy these. However, the next major Act was the Pitt's India Act of 1784. Under this Act, the East India Company's Court of Directors was left with responsibilities in matters of trade and commerce only while for political matters the British Government appointed a Board of Control of six members. This Board was empowered to superintend, direct and control all operations of the civil and military government of British possessions in India.

***Charter Acts of 1793 & 1813*:** The Charter Acts of 1793 and 1813 renewed the Company's Charter each time for a further period of 20 years. The 1813 Act, however, deprived the company of the monopoly of trade in India. While the powers of the three Councils of Madras, Bombay and Calcutta were enlarged, they were also subjected to greater control of the British Parliament. All regulations made by the three Councils were thereafter required to be laid before Parliament.

***Charter Act, 1833*:** The first faint beginnings of constitution-making during the British rule in India are to be found in the Charter Act of 1833. This Act introduced an element of institutional specialisation in the government of the British territories in India by differentiating the law making meetings of the Governor-General-in-Council from its executive meetings. The superintendence, direction and control of the whole civil and military government of all the British territories and revenues in India was expressly vested in "the Governor-General-of-India-in-Council". For the first time, thus, the Governor-General's Government was known as the "Government of India" and his Council as the "Indian Council". The Act introduced centralization in the legislative spheres as well. The Council was enlarged for legislative work by the addition of a Law Member in addition to the existing three. The Governor-General-of-India-in-Council was now vested, subject to certain restrictions, with the exclusive power of legislation for the whole of the British territories in India.

Charter Act, 1853: The last of the Charter Acts, the Charter Act of 1853 made important changes in the machinery for Indian legislation. Though the Governor-General's Council was continued as the one legislative authority competent to enact laws for the whole of British India, so many alterations were made in its character and composition that "the system was entirely changed".

The Council was enlarged for legislative purposes by the addition of six special members who were expressly debarred from sitting and voting in the Council, "except at meetings thereof for making laws and regulations". These members were called Legislative Councillors. The Council now consisted of twelve members including the Governor-General, the Commander-in-Chief, four representatives of the local Governments of Madras, Bombay, Calcutta and Agra. The legislative functions of the Council were clearly demarcated from its executive functions and their special nature emphasized by the express requirements of Section 23 of the Act that the powers of making laws or regulations, vested in the Governor-General-in-Council, were to be exercised only "at meetings of the said Council".

From the Company to the Crown (1858–1918)

The Act of 1858**:** The Revolt of 1857—described as the Indian Mutiny by the British historians and as the First War of Independence by the Indians—was the first organised attempt to overthrow the British rule in India after it was firmly established. The Revolt which was eventually suppressed gave a death blow to the system of East India Company's rule in India. A new Act was passed by the British Parliament after much discussion of the principles which should form the basis of a new policy. This Act finally became "The Act for the Good Government of India" of 1858. Under this Act all the Indian territories then "in possession of the Company" became vested in the Crown and were to be governed directly "by and in the name" of the Crown, acting through a Principal Secretary of State (for India). The Act of 1858 was, however, largely confined to the improvement of the administrative machinery by which the Indian

Government was to be superintended and controlled in England. It did not alter in any substantial way the system of Government that prevailed in India.

***Indian Councils Act of 1861*:** Soon after, it was deemed necessary by the Government to initiate a policy reform of the Indian administration and to consider ways and means of establishing closer contacts with the public opinion in the country and taking non-officials—both European and Indian—into the counsel of the Government "with a view to obtaining timely expression of the feelings and sentiments of the members of the outside public concerning measures proposed to be taken by Government".

The Indian Councils Act of 1861 is an important landmark in the constitutional history of India. It is important for two main reasons. First, it enabled the Governor-General to associate representatives of the Indian people with the work of legislation by nominating them to his expanded Council. Secondly, it decentralised the legislative powers of the Governor-General's Council and vested them in the Governments of Bombay and Madras.

The Executive Council of the Governor-General was enlarged by the addition of a fifth member who was to be a jurist and for purposes of legislation by the addition of not less than six and not more than twelve additional members, at least half of whom were to be non-officials. Although not expressly provided for in the Act, the non-official element of the legislative council could include Indians. Actually, in 1862, the Governor-General, Lord Canning, appointed three Indians—the Maharaja of Patiala, the Raja of Benares and Sir Dinker Rao—to the newly constituted Legislative Council. For the first time since the beginning of British rule in India, Indians were being associated with the work of legislation.

The 1861 Act suffered from many defects. Also, it did not satisfy Indian aspirations. It made the Governor-General all powerful. The non-official members could hardly play any effective role. No questions could be asked and the budget could not be discussed. The political and economic situation in the country steadily deteriorated. There was acute scarcity of foodgrains and a severe famine in 1877. The discontent was widespread and the situation explosive. The repression that followed the 1857 revolt had created strong feelings against the British. These were further deepened by the strong opposition by the Europeans and Anglo-Indians to the Ilbert Bill which had sought to remove all invidious distinction between European and Indian members of the Civil Services.

Birth of Indian National Congress: The Indian National Congress was started in 1885 by Mr. A.O. Hume, an Englishman. At its very first session held in Bombay on 28 to 30 December 1885, presided over by W.C. Bonerjee, the Congress demanded reform and expansion of the Legislative Councils. Thereafter, this demand was reiterated at every successive Congress session. It only became more and more emphatic from year to year. The Congress considered the reform of the Councils "at the root of all other reforms". Speaking on the subject at the fifth session of the Congress (1889), Surendranath Bannerjee said: "If you get that, you get everything else. On it depends the entire future of the country and the future of our administrative system". The resolution adopted at the 1889 session of the Congress went to the extent of suggesting a skeleton scheme for the reform and reconstitution of the Governor-General's Council and Provincial Legislative Councils to be incorporated in a bill to be introduced in the British Parliament. The scheme, *inter alia,* demanded enfranchisement of all male British subjects in India above 21 years of age and also voting by ballot.

The Indian Councils Act, 1892: In 1891, the Congress reiterated its conviction that India could not be governed well until her people were allowed, through their elected representatives, a potential voice in the legislatures. The passage of the Indian Councils Act, 1892, was mainly influenced by the resolutions of the Indian National Congress adopted in its sessions in 1889 to 1891. Under the 1892 Act, the number of additional members in the Governor-General's Council was increased to be "not less than ten and not more than sixteen" (instead of the erstwhile minimum of six and maximum of twelve). Similarly, the number of additional members in the Provincial Legislative Councils was also increased.

In addition to their legislative functions, the Councils were now allowed to hold a discussion on the annual financial statement or the Budget with certain conditions and restrictions. Members of the Councils were also permitted to ask questions on matters of public interest under prescribed rules imposing several conditions.

The Act of 1892 was certainly an improvement on the 1861 Act insofar as it brought in a representative element in the Legislative Council and relaxed to some extent the restrictions on the working of the Council by expanding its functions. The entry of the "elected" Members marked the beginning of the new era in the life of the Council.

***Swaraj as the Goal*:** At its session in 1906, the Congress declared its goal to be "Swaraj" which to the 'moderates' meant parliamentary self-government within the British empire and to the 'extremists' independence. It also demanded the immediate expansion of the Legislative Councils to "secure a larger and truly effective representation of the people and a large control over the financial and executive administration of the country".

Minto-Morley Reforms: In the wake of the growing strength of the extremists in the national movement and the relentless campaign continued by the moderates in the Indian National Congress for greater and more effective representation of Indians in running the affairs of the country, the then Secretary of State for India, Lord Morley, and the then Viceroy, Lord Minto, jointly worked out certain constitutional reform proposals during the years 1906 1908. These came to be popularly known as the Minto-Morley reform proposals and aimed at the expansion of the Legislative Councils and the enlargement of their powers and functions, the appointment of Indian members on the Executive Councils, the creation of such Councils where they did not exist, and the further development of local self-government.

The Indian Councils Act, 1909: The Act of 1909 as supplemented by the regulations framed under it made provisions to further enlarge the councils and make them more representative and effective by expanding their functions. The number of members were doubled or more than doubled. The maximum number of additional members of the Indian Legislative Council (Governor-General's Council) was raised from 16 (under the Act of 1892) to 60 (excluding the Executive Councillors who were *ex-officio* members).

The Act recognised the principle of indirect election. It was, however, decided that in the circumstances of India, territorial representation was not suited to the people and that representation by classes and interests was the only practicable method of embodying the elective principle in constituting the Indian Legislative Councils. Nomination was, however, retained (a) for the appointment of official members, and (b) for the appointment of non-official members to supplement the elected members so as to provide representation that seemed impracticable to provide by election. The elected members were to be returned by constituencies, such as municipalities, district and local boards, universities, chambers of commerce and trade associations, and groups of persons such as land holders or tea planters. The regulations created non-official majorities in all the Provincial Legislative Councils, but maintained an official majority in the Central Legislative Council. The regulations also provided for separate electorates and separate representation for the Muslim community. For the first time, thus, the pernicious principle of communal representation was introduced.

The reforms introduced by the Act afforded no answer, and could afford no answer, to the demand for responsible government, since the Councils set up thereunder lacked responsibility which was the savour of popular government.

Montagu's Declaration: On 20 August 1917 Mr. Montagu, the then Secretary of State for India, made a historic statement in the House of Commons. The statement, for the first time in India's chequered history under British rule, promised the establishment of "responsible government" in India.

The Montford Report (1918): The report on Indian Constitutional Reforms known as the Montagu-Chelmsford or Montford report prepared jointly by Mr. Montagu, Secretary of State for India, and Lord Chelmsford, the Viceroy of India, was published in July 1918.

Without paying any heed to the demand for the status of self-governing dominions, the report had most mischievously made the concessions conceded by the Congress to the League on separate communal electorates under the Lucknow Pact of 1916 between the Congress and the League as the basis for Montagu-Chelmsford Reforms.

Nationalist Movements and Growth of Representative Institutions (1919–1940)

***Government of India Act, 1919*:** The Government of India Act, 1919 based on the Montagu-Chelmsford Report, sought to make it abundantly clear that the British were prepared to concede only "the gradual development of self-governing institutions, with a view to progressive realisation of responsible Government". The time, manner and pace of each advance of constitutional progress was to be determined only by the British Parliament and not based on any self-determination by the people of India.

As supplemented by rules made under it, the 1919 Act introduced many important changes in the Indian constitutional system as it was established under the Act of

1909. In the case of the legislature at the Centre, the erstwhile Indian Legislative Council was replaced by a bicameral legislature consisting of a Council of State (Upper House) and a Legislative Assembly (Lower House). Even though some power of nominating members was retained, each House was to have an elected majority.

Members were to be elected directly by constituencies delimited by the Rules framed under the Act. The franchise was considerably enlarged. The electoral qualifications prescribed varied widely and were based on communal affiliation and residence and property credentials.

Dyarchy: The novel system of dyarchy was introduced by the 1919 Act in eight major Provinces which were known as "Governor's Provinces". As a preliminary to the introduction of partially responsible government in the Provinces, it was necessary to demarcate the sphere of work of the Provincial governments. The Act, accordingly, provided for rules being made for classification of subjects of administration as 'Central' and 'Provincial', for the devolution of authority in respect of Provincial subjects to local governments; and for the allocation of revenues and other moneys to those governments. The detailed classification of subjects into 'Central' and 'Provincial' was carried out by what were known as the 'Devolution Rules'.

***Shortcomings of the 1919 Act*:** The Act of 1919 had many shortcomings. It did not fulfill the demand for responsible government. Also, the Provincial Legislatures could not discuss Bills in a number of subject areas without the clearance of the Governor-General. Even though theoretically, the Central Legislature remained supreme and competent to legislate over the whole field, and notwithstanding any allocation of powers between the Centre and the Provinces, "the previously highly centralised government" was not intended to be converted into a federal one and the constitution of British India continued to be that of a Unitary State.

Above all, the system of dyarchy in the provinces was a dismal failure. The Governor dominated. In the absence of the power of the purse, the Ministers could not effectively implement their policy. Also, the Ministers were not collectively responsible to the Legislature and were only individually appointed advisers to the Governor.

The Congress and Indian opinion remained unreconciled and pressed for further reforms to make the administration more representative, responsible and responsive. World War I was over and there was an air of general expectation. But, what came were the special legislative proposals for repressive measures known as the Rowlatt Bills. These were passed despite widespread opposition. Satyagraha, Non-cooperation and Khilafat Movements for Swaraj under Gandhiji's leadership followed.

The Simon Commission: Under the 1919 Act, a Commission was scheduled to be appointed in 1929 to inquire into and report on the working of the Act and make further recommendations for reforms. In view of the discontent, the Indian Statutory Commission—the Simon Commission—was appointed in 1927 *i.e.* two years before schedule. However, its all white composition hurt Indian sentiments further.

Resolution on Purna Swaraj: The Congress was gradually veering round accepting complete independence as its goal. At the Calcutta session, however, it was decided to give one last opportunity to the British to concede Dominion Status within a year. After the rejection of the demand for a Dominion Status, the 1929 Lahore Session of the Congress adopted a resolution on *Purna Swaraj* or complete independence. A Civil Disobedience Movement began with a call to break the Salt Tax law and Gandhiji's Dandi March to reach the sea.

Round Table Conferences and the White Paper: Finally, the Government decided to hold a Round Table Conference in London in November 1930 to consider constitutional reforms. It was followed by two more such Conferences.

After three Round Table Conferences, the British Government published a White Paper in March 1933 containing an outline of a new constitution. The scheme contained provisions for a federal set up and provincial autonomy. It proposed dyarchy at the Centre and responsible governments in the Provinces.

The British Parliament constituted a Joint Committee of the two Houses to further consider the Government's Scheme formulated in the White Paper. The Joint Committee with Lord Linlithgo as its Chairman had Conservative members in majority. Representatives of British India and of the Princely States were invited to give evidence before the Committee as witnesses. The Joint Committee submitted its report in November 1934 which reiterated that Federation would be established only when at least 50 per cent of the princely states were prepared to join it.

On the basis of the Report, a bill was prepared which was introduced in the British Parliament on December 19, 1934. After its having been passed by the two Houses and Royal assent being given to it on August 4, 1935, it became the Government of India Act, 1935.

***Government of India Act, 1935*:** The most remarkable feature of the Government of India Act, 1935 was that it envisaged a 'federation of all-India', consisting of the British provinces and the Indian states willing to join it. Till the Round Table Conference of 1930 India was a completely unitary state and whatever powers the Provinces had were given to them by the Centre. That is, the Provinces were only agents of the Centre. The 1935 Act for the first time provided for a federal system which would consist of not only the Governors' Provinces of British India but also the Chief Commissioners' provinces and the princely states. It finally sought to break up the unitary system under which British India had hitherto been administered. The principle of the constitution of 1919 had been decentralisation rather than federation. Under the new Act the Provinces were for the first time recognized in law as separate entities, exercising executive and legislative powers in their own field, in their own right, free in normal circumstances from Central control, in that field.

The Act separated Burma from India and two new provinces of Orissa and Sind were created. Keeping the proposed scheme at the Centre in view, the eleven Governors' Provinces were fully 'liberated' from the 'superintendence, direction and control' of the Central Government and the Secretary of State except for certain specific purposes. The Provinces in other words were invested with 'a separate legal personality'. The scheme of provincial autonomy envisaged by the Act provided for an executive and a legislature in every Province. The provincial legislatures were given many new powers. The Council of Ministers was to be responsible to the Legislature which could remove it by passing a vote of no-confidence. The Legislature could exercise some control over the administration through Questions and Supplementaries. Nearly 80 per cent of the demands for grants could not however be assented to or rejected by the Legislature. In the legislative field, the legislature could also pass laws on subjects included in the Concurrent List, though in case of divergence, the Federal law would prevail over the Provincial law.

The federal part of the constitutional scheme under the Government of India Act, 1935 was most impractical. The Provinces did not accept the scheme of the Federation and since the condition of half of the States joining the Federation could not be fulfilled, the 'Federation of India' contemplated by the 1935 Act remained unborn and the federal part of the Act could not be implemented.

Elections for the provincial legislatures under the Government of India Act, 1935 were held in February, 1937.

The Congress once again won a resounding success at the polls. In all, the Congress captured 715 out of the 836 general seats. The Muslim League showed up badly even in the seats reserved for Muslims and in Muslim majority provinces. It failed to secure absolute majority in any province. In fact, it could capture only 51 of the 482 Muslim seats.

The Congress secured absolute majority in Madras, United Provinces, Bihar, Central Provinces and Orissa and won about half of the total seats in Bombay. In Assam and North-West Frontier Province, it emerged as the largest party. In Punjab, the Unionist Party obtained clear majority. Several minor groups emerged in Bengal and Sind.

The Government of India Act, 1935 occupies a very important and permanent position in the constitutional history of India. The Act had endeavoured to give a written constitution to the country. Although the people of India or their representatives had no hand in the creation of this document, and it suffered from several serious drawbacks, it cannot be denied that it was on the whole and in some respects a progressive step.

After centuries, the Indians got an opportunity for assuming some responsibility in running the administration of their country. Popular Ministries were formed in the Provinces by elected representatives responsible to the Legislatures. Words like Premier and Ministers were used for the first time and recognition was given to the precedence of the Premier. There were occasions when differences between the Governors and Ministers cropped up, but the Governors more or less respected the responsibilities and powers of the Ministers in the Congress Provinces and did not interfere in the day-to-day administration. The Ministers too discharged their duties with great ability, impartiality and dedication which earned them laurels and respect. Even the British administrators were surprised and influenced by the display of administrative ability and acumen by Indian Ministers.

Towards Independence (1942–1947)

The popular Ministries lasted only two years. All the Congress Ministries resigned in 1939 in protest to India being made a party to the Second World War without consulting the legislatures in India. In 1940 the Muslim League passed its Pakistan resolution.

The Cripps Mission: While the Second World War was passing through a crucial stage, it was felt that willing cooperation of the Indian public opinion would be an asset. Cabinet Minister Sir Stafford Cripps was accordingly sent in March 1942. The Cripps Mission, however, was a failure. Its proposals were turned down by all the political parties even though on different grounds. His proposals had conceded Dominion Status and the right of Indians to frame a Constitution in their Constituent Assembly, after the War. However, the Provinces were to have an option to accept or walk out of the new Constitution. The Muslim League rejected these proposals because its demand for partition of the country on communal grounds was not conceded, while the Congress found them unacceptable because they opened up possibilities of dividing India into many small bits and did not seek to transfer any really effective power to representative Indian hands during the War. Gandhiji condemned the proposals as a "post-dated cheque".

***Quit India Movement*:** The Congress Working Committee passed a resolution at Wardha in July, 1942 demanding the withdrawal of the British from India. It was adopted by the All India Congress Committee at Bombay on 8 August, 1942. In his speech before the Committee, Gandhiji declared that it was a decision "to do or die". Arrest of Congress leaders was followed by a country-wide agitation.

***Wavell Plan*:** Meanwhile, Lord Wavell replaced Lord Linlithgow as Viceroy. Under the 'Wavell Plan', pending the framing of a constitution by the Indians themselves and as an interim arrangement, the Executive Council was to be Indianized with the inclusion of Indian political leaders on the basis of parity between Muslims and caste Hindus with one representative each of the depressed classes and Sikhs. The only Non-Indians on the Council were to be the Viceroy and the Commander-in-Chief. The War portfolio was to continue with the Commander-in-Chief, but that of External Affairs was to be under the charge of an Indian member.

Simla Conference: The Viceroy convened a Conference of Indian leaders at Simla. The Conference was held from 25 June to 14 July 1945. The talks failed because while the Congress insisted on a united India, the Muslim League was not prepared to budge from its demand of Pakistan.

Elections and Cabinet Mission: Elections to the Central Legislative Assembly in India which were overdue were held in the last quarter of 1945. Elections to the Provincial Assemblies were completed by April 1946. The Congress contested the elections on the issue of the Quit India resolution and the Muslim League on the issue of Pakistan. The result showed that the Congress obtained absolute majority in eight Provinces (Assam, Bihar, Bombay, Central Provinces, Madras, N.W.F.P., Orissa and U.P.). In the remaining three Provinces, the Congress was the second largest party. The Congress also secured majority of the elected seats (56 out of 102) in the Central Assembly. However, while the record of Congress successes was most impressive in the general constituencies and the party in fact improved its position over the 1937 results, it fared badly in the reserved Muslim constituencies.

When the elections to the Provincial Assemblies were in progress in India, on 19 February, 1945, Lord Pethick Lawrence announced in Parliament that a special Mission of Cabinet Ministers consisting of the Secretary of State, the President of the Board of Trade (Stafford Cripps) and the First Lord of Admiralty (A.V. Alexander) would go to India to act in association with the Viceroy in this matter. The Mission was in India from March 1946 to May 1946.

The Mission rejected the League demand for a separate

sovereign State of Pakistan as "impracticable" inasmuch as it would contain a large proportion of non-Muslim population and a sizeable Muslim population would be left outside Pakistan, in India.

The Cabinet Mission also rejected the Congress scheme of a loose federation as involving constitutional disadvantages and anomalies. It recommended a three-tier structure consisting of the Union of India at the top, groups of Provinces in the middle and provinces and princely states at the bottom.

The Cabinet Mission recommended that the constitution should take the following basic form:

1. There should be a Union of India, embracing both British India and the States which should deal with the following subjects: Foreign Affairs, Defence and Communications; and should have the powers necessary to raise the finances required for the above subjects.
2. The Union should have an Executive and a Legislature constituted from British Indian and States' representatives. Any question raising a major communal issue in the Legislature should require for its decision a majority of the representatives present and voting of each of the two major communities as well as a majority of all the members present and voting.
3. All subjects other than the Union subjects and all residuary powers should vest in the Provinces.
4. The States will retain all subjects and powers other than those ceded to the Union.
5. Provinces should be free to form groups with Executives and Legislatures, and each group could determine the Provincial subjects to be taken in common.
6. The constitutions of the Union and of the groups should contain a provision whereby any Province could by a majority vote of its Legislative Assembly call for a reconsideration of the terms of the Constitution after an initial period of ten years and at ten yearly intervals thereafter.

In making these suggestions, the Cabinet Mission made it clear that its object was not to lay down the details of a constitution but to set in motion a machinery whereby a constitution could be settled by Indians for Indians. It had become necessary to make this recommendation because the Cabinet Mission was satisfied that not until that was done was there "any hope of getting the two major communities to join in the setting up of the constitution-making machinery".

Interim Government: The first Interim National Government was announced on August 24, 1946. It included Pandit Jawaharlal Nehru, Sardar Vallabhbhai Patel, Dr. Rajendra Prasad, Asaf Ali, Sarat Chandra Bose, Dr. John Mathai, Sir Shafat Ahmed Khan, Jagjivan Ram, Sardar Baldev Singh, Syed Ali Zaheer, C. Rajagopalachari and Dr. C.H. Bhabha. Technically, they were all members of the Viceroy's Executive Council and the Viceroy continued to be the head of the Council. However, Pandit Nehru was designated as the Vice-President of the Council and he and eleven of his colleagues took the oath of office on September 2, 1946. The group included three Muslims. The door was kept open for the entry of the Muslim League even at a later date.

By the end of October, the Viceroy somehow succeeded in bringing in the League. The Government was reconstituted on October 26. Three of the original members—Syed Ali Zaheer, Sarat Chandra Bose and Sir Shafat Ahmed—were dropped and five representatives of the Muslim League included. Thus the League became a partner in the Government.

Mountbatten Plan: In March 1947, Lord Louis Mountbatten was sent as the new Viceroy to arrange for a smooth transfer of power. He reached India on 22 March 1947. Very soon he came to the firm conclusion that it would not be possible for the Congress and the Muslim League to work together either in the Interim Government or in the Constituent Assembly and the only way, therefore, to prevent the orgy of communal violence from assuming still more fierce dimensions was to transfer power to Indian hands with the greatest expedition. It was already becoming quite obvious and the Congress had also come to realise that partition of the country was inevitable and was left as the only alternative to utter chaos, anarchy and civil war. Accordingly, he fixed the date of 15 August 1947 for transfer of power. The Congress too was gradually veering round to the inevitability of partition of the country.

Mountbatten prepared a plan for partition and after consultations with the leaders of the opposition parties in Britain, a fresh policy statement embodying the Mountbatten Plan was issued on 3 June 1947. The scheme underlying this statement recognised the inevitability of the partition of the country. According to the statement, the constitution framed by the existing Constituent Assembly could not be forced on unwilling parts. As such, it laid down a procedure for ascertaining the wishes of such areas on whether they wanted a separate constituent assembly. The net result and effect of the whole scheme, it was obvious, was to be the partition of India into India and Pakistan.

Indian Independence Act, 1947

Based on the Mountbatten Plan, the British Parliament passed the Indian Independence Bill, 1947.

i. It fixed the date of 15 August 1947 for setting up the two Dominions.
ii. It indicated the territorial divisions of India into India and Pakistan and the constitution of the two provinces each in Bengal and Punjab. India would comprise all the British India Provinces excepting the areas which were to go to Pakistan.
iii. Pakistan was to comprise East Bengal, West Punjab, Sind and the Sylhet district of Assam.
iv. The responsibility of His Majesty's Government in India and the suzerainty of His Majesty over the Indian States would lapse on 15 August 1947.

v. The Indian States could accede to either of the two Dominions.

vi. There would be a separate Governor-General for each Dominion who would be appointed by His Majesty and would represent His Majesty for the purposes of the government of the Dominion.

vii. There would be a separate Legislature for each Dominion with full authority for making laws unhindered by the British Parliament.

viii. The Act also laid down temporary provision for the government of the Dominions by giving to the two Constituent Assemblies the status of Parliament with the full powers of Dominion Legislature.

ix. It authorised the Governor-General to issue temporary orders for making provisions as appeared to him to be necessary or expedient in order to bring the Act into effective operation.

x. Lastly, it prescribed the conditions and terms of the Secretary of State's Services and the Indian Armed Forces, the continuance of the jurisdiction or authority of His Majesty's Government over the British army, navy and air force.

On the midnight of 14-15 August, in terms of the Indian Independence Act, two Dominions of India and Pakistan were constituted.

3

MAKING OF THE CONSTITUTION

The Constituent Assembly

Generally, the task of framing the constitution of a sovereign democratic nation is performed by a representative body of its people. Such a body elected by the people for the purpose of considering and adopting a constitution may be known as the constituent assembly.

The concept of a constituent assembly had always been linked with the growth of the national movement in India. The idea of a constituent assembly, whereby Indians themselves might frame a constitution for their country, was implicit in the opposition to the 1919 Act. But, the first definite reference to a constituent assembly for India, though not in those words or under that particular name, was made by Mahatma Gandhi in 1922, soon after the inauguration of the Government of India Act, 1919.

In 1922 itself, a joint meeting of members of the two Houses of the Central Legislature was held at Simla at the initiative of Mrs. Annie Besant, which decided to call a convention for the framing of a constitution. Yet another conference attended by members of the Central and Provincial Legislatures was held in Delhi in February 1923. This conference outlined essential elements of a constitution placing India on equal footing with the self-governing Dominions of the British Empire. A "National Convention" was called which met on 24 April, under the presidentship of Sir Tej Bahadur Sapru. This convention drafted the "Commonwealth of India Bill". The draft Bill was submitted in slightly amended form to a committee of the All Parties Conference held at Delhi in January 1925, which was presided over by Mahatma Gandhi. Finally, the draft was submitted to a Drafting Committee which published the Bill. The Bill was sent to an influential member of the Labour Party in Britain accompanied by a memorandum signed by 43 leaders of various political parties. It found wide support in the Labour Party and was accepted with slight modifications. The Bill had the first reading after it was introduced in the House of Commons. Though with the defeat of the Labour Government the fate of the Bill was sealed, it was a major effort by the Indians to outline a constitutional system for India with the help of peaceful and constitutional means.

The adoption of the famous Motilal Nehru resolution in 1924 and 1925 on the National Demand was a historic event inasmuch as the Central Legislature had, for the first time, lent its support to the growing demand that the future constitution of India should be framed by Indians themselves.

In November 1927, when the Simon Commission was appointed without any Indians represented on it, an all-party meeting held at Allahabad said that apart from being virtual negation of the "National Demand", it amounted to a "deliberate insult to the people of India" for, not only did it "definitely assign to them a position of inferiority" but also denied to them "the right to participate in the determination of the constitution of their own country".

Earlier on 17 May 1927, at the Bombay Session of the Congress, Motilal Nehru had moved a resolution calling upon the Congress Working Committee to frame a constitution for India in consultation with the elected members of the Central and Provincial Legislatures and leaders of political parties. Adopted by an overwhelming majority with amendments, it was this resolution on the Swaraj constitution which was later amplified and reiterated by Jawaharlal Nehru in a resolution passed by the Madras Session of the Congress on 28 December 1927. An All-Parties Conference organised at Bombay on 19 May 1928 appointed a committee, under the chairmanship of Motilal Nehru "to determine the principles of the constitution of India". The report of the Committee (submitted on 10 August 1928) was later to become famous as the Nehru Report. It was the first attempt by Indians to frame a full-fledged constitution for their country and has been described by Coupland as "not only an answer to the challenge that Indian nationalism was unconstructive" but "frankest attempt yet made by Indians to face squarely the difficulties of communalism". The Report embodied not only the perspective of the contemporary nationalist opinion but also an outline of a draft constitution for India. The latter was based on the principle of Dominion Status with full responsible government on the parliamentary pattern. It asserted the principle that sovereignty belongs to the Indian people, laid down a set of fundamental rights and provided for a federal system with maximum autonomy granted to the units but residuary powers vesting in the Central Government and joint electorates for elections to the Federal Lower House and the Provincial Legislatures with reservation of seats for minorities in certain cases for a limited period.

It would be seen that the broad parliamentary system with a government responsible to Parliament, a chapter of justiciable fundamental rights and rights of minorities envisaged in the Nehru Report in 1928 were very largely embodied in the constitution of independent India that was adopted 21 years later, on 26 November 1949.

The White Paper issued after the third Round Table Conference outlined the British government's proposal for constitutional reforms in India. The Joint Parliamentary Committee which examined these proposals observed that "a specific grant of constituent power to authorities in India is not at the moment a practicable proposition".

In June 1934, the Congress Working Committee declared that the only satisfactory alternative to the White Paper was a constitution drawn up by a constituent assembly elected on the basis of adult suffrage. This was the first time that a definite demand for a constituent assembly was formally put forward. The Working Committee of the All India Congress Committee at its meeting held at Patna on 5-7 December 1934 adopted a resolution rejecting the scheme of Indian constitutional Reforms as recommended in the Report of the Joint Parliamentary Committee (1933-34) and reiterated the view that the only satisfactory alternative to the scheme was a constitution drawn up by a constituent assembly.

The failure of the Simon Commission and the Round Table Conference which led to the enactment of the Government of India Act, 1935 to satisfy Indian aspirations accentuated the demand for a constituent assembly of the people of India. The Congress adopted a resolution at its Lucknow Session in April 1936 in which it declared that no constitution imposed by an outside authority shall be acceptable to India; it has to be one framed by an Indian constituent assembly elected by the people of India on adult franchise.

Since the Congress had contested elections to the Provincial Legislatures on the issues of total rejection of the Act of 1935 and the demand for a constituent assembly, following a decisive victory it adopted at Delhi on 18 March 1937 a resolution asserting the electorate's approval of the demand for a constituent assembly. It desired to frame "a constitution based on national independence, through the medium of a constituent assembly elected by adult franchise". This demand was firmly reiterated by the All India National Convention of Congress Legislators held in Delhi in March, 1937. During August-October 1937, the

Central Legislative assembly and the Provincial Assemblies of each of the Provinces where the Congress held office, adopted resolutions reiterating the Congress demand to convene a constituent assembly to frame a new constitution for a free India.

After the outbreak of the War in 1939, the demand for a constituent assembly was reiterated in a long statement issued by the Congress Working Committee on 14 September, 1939.

Gandhiji wrote an article entitled "The Only Way" in the *Harijan* of 19 November 1939 in which he expressed the view that "constituent assembly alone can produce a constitution indigenous to the country and truly and fully representing the will of the people". He declared that the only way out to arrive at a just solution of communal and other problems was a constituent assembly.

The demand for a constituent assembly was for the first time authoritatively conceded by the British Government, though in an indirect way and with important reservations, in what is known as the "August Offer" of 1940.

The Cripps proposals marked an advance over the "August Offer" in that the making of the new constitution was now to rest solely and not merely "primarily" in Indian hands and a clear undertaking to accept the constitution framed by the proposed constitution-making body was given by the British Government. After the failure of the Cripps Mission, no steps were taken for the solution of the Indian constitutional problem until the War in Europe came to an end in May, 1945.

In July, with the new Labour Government coming into power in England, its Indian policy was announced on 19 September 1945 by Lord Wavell who had succeeded Lord Linlithgow as Viceroy in 1943. The Viceroy affirmed His Majesty's Government's intention to convene a constitution-making body "as soon as possible".

The Cabinet Mission realised that the most satisfactory

method to constitute a constitution-making body would have been by election based on adult franchise, but that would have caused "a wholly unacceptable delay" in the formulation of the new constitution. "The only practicable course" according to them was, therefore, "to utilise the recently elected Provincial Legislative Assemblies as electing bodies". As what they called the "fairest and as most practicable plan" in the circumstances, the Mission recommended that the representation of the Provinces in the constitution-making body be on the basis of population, roughly in the ratio of one Member to a million and the seats allocated to the Provinces be divided among the principal communities, classified for this purpose as Sikhs, Muslims and General (all except Sikhs and Muslims), on the basis of their numerical strength. The representatives of each community were to be chosen by members of that community in the Provincial assembly and voting was to be by the method of proportional representation with single transferable vote. The number of Members allotted to the Indian States was also to be fixed on the same basis of population as adopted for British India, but the method of their selection was to be settled later by consultation. The strength of the constitution-making body was to be 389. Of these 296 representatives were to be from British India, (292 representatives drawn from the eleven Governors' Provinces of British India and a representative each from the four Chief Commissioners' Provinces of Delhi, Ajmer-Merwara, Coorg and British Baluchistan) and 93 representatives from the Indian States.

The Cabinet Mission recommended a basic framework for the constitution and laid down in some detail the procedure to be followed by the constitution-making body.

Elections for the 296 seats assigned to the British Indian Provinces were completed by July-August 1946. The Congress won 208 seats including all the General seats except nine and the Muslim League 73 seats, that is, all but five of the seats allotted to Muslims.

The party-wise break-up of the assembly's British Indian membership was as follows:

Congress	208
Muslim League	73
Unionist	1
Unionist Muslim	1
Unionist Scheduled Castes	1
Krishak Praja	1
Scheduled Castes Federation	1
Sikh (Non-Congress)	1
Communist	1
Independents	8
	296

With the partition and independence of the country, on 14-15 August 1947, the Constituent Assembly of India could be said to have become free from the fetters of the Cabinet Mission Plan. It became a fully sovereign body and the successor to the British Parliament's plenary authority and power in the country. Moreover, following the acceptance of the Plan of 3 June, the members of the Muslim League Party from the Indian Dominion also took their seats in the assembly. The representatives of some of the Indian States had already entered the Assembly on 28 April 1947. By 15 August 1947 most of the States were represented in the Assembly and the remaining States also sent their representatives in due course.

The Constituent Assembly thus became a body, it was believed, fully representative of the states and provinces in India and fully sovereign of all external authority. It could abrogate or alter any law made by the British Parliament applying to India, including the Indian Independence Act itself.

The Constituent Assembly duly opened on the appointed day Monday, the ninth day of December, 1946 at eleven in the morning.

The historic Objectives Resolution was moved in the Constituent Assembly by Nehru, on 13 December 1946, after it had been in session for some days. The beautifully worded draft of the Objectives Resolution cast the horoscope, so to say, of the Sovereign Democratic Republic that India was to be. The resolution envisaged a federal polity with the residuary powers vesting in the autonomous units and sovereignty belonging to the people. "Justice, social, economic and political; Equality of status, of opportunity and before the law; Freedom of thought, expression, belief, faith, worship, vocation, association and action" were to be guaranteed to all the people along with "adequate safeguards" to "minorities, backward and tribal areas and depressed and other backward classes". Thus, the Resolution gave to the Assembly its guiding principles and the philosophy that was to permeate its tasks of constitution-making. It was finally adopted by the Assembly on 22 January 1947 and later took the form of the Preamble to the Constitution.

Framing the Constitution

The assembly appointed a number of committees to deal with different aspects of the problem of framing the constitution. These included the Union Constitution Committee, Union Powers Commmittee, Committees on Fundamental Rights, Minorities, etc. Some of these Committees were headed by either Nehru or Patel to whom the President of the assembly gave the credit for working out the fundamentals of the constitution. The Committees worked hard and in a business-like manner and produced valuable reports. Between the third and the sixth sessions, the Assembly considered the reports of committees on Fundamental Rights, on Union Constitution, on Union Powers, on Provincial Constitution, on Minorities and on Scheduled Areas and Scheduled Tribes. Recommendations of the other Committees were later considered by the Drafting Committee.

The first draft of the constitution of India was prepared in October, 1947 by the Advisory Branch of the Office of the Constituent Assembly under Sir B.N. Rau. Before the preparation of this draft, voluminous background material had been collected and supplied to the members of the assembly in the shape of three series of 'Constitutional Precedents' which gave salient texts from the constitutions of about 60 countries. The Constituent Assembly on 29 August 1947 appointed the Drafting Committee with Dr. B.R. Ambedkar as the Chairman to scrutinise the draft of the text of the constitution of India prepared by the Constitutional Adviser (B.N. Rau) giving effect to the decisions taken in the assembly.

The Draft Constitution of India prepared by the Drafting Committee was submitted to the President of the assembly on 21 February 1948. A large number of comments, criticisms and suggestions for the amendment of the Draft Constitution were received. The Drafting Committee considered all these. A special committee was constituted to go through them along with the recommendations of the Drafting Committee thereon. The suggestions made by the Special Committee were again considered by the Drafting Committee and certain amendments were picked up for incorporation. To facilitate reference to such amendments the Drafting Committee decided to issue a reprint of the Draft Constitution which was submitted to the President of the assembly on 26 October 1948.

While introducing the Draft Constitution in the assembly for consideration on 4 November 1948, Dr. Ambedkar replied to some common criticisms of the Draft, particularly the criticism in regard to there being very little in it that could claim originality. He observed:

> One likes to ask whether there can be anything new in a constitution framed at this hour in the history of the world. More than hundred years have rolled over when the first written constitution was drafted. It has been followed by

> many countries reducing their constitutions to writing. What the scope of a constitution should be has long been settled. Similarly what are the fundamentals of a constitution are recognised all over the world. Given these facts, all constitutions in their main provisions must look similar. The only new things, if there can be any, in a constitution framed so late in the day are the variations made to remove the faults and to accommodate it to the needs of the country. The charge of producing a blind copy of the constitutions of other countries is based, I am sure, on an inadequate study of the constitution. As to the accusation that the Draft Constitution has produced a good part of the provisions of the Government of India Act, 1935, I make no apologies. There is nothing to be ashamed of in borrowing. It involves no plagiarism. Nobody holds any patent rights in the fundamental ideas of a constitution.

The clause by clause consideration of the Draft Constitution was completed during 15 November 1948–17 October 1949. The Preamble was the last to be adopted. The Drafting Committee, thereafter, carried the consequential or necessary amendments, prepared the final draft and placed it before the assembly.

The second Second Reading of the constitution was completed on 16 November 1949 and on the next day the Assembly took up the Third Reading of the constitution, with a motion by Dr. Ambedkar "that the constitution as settled by the assembly be passed". The motion was adopted on 26 November 1949 and thus on that day, the people of India in the Constituent Assembly adopted, enacted and gave to themselves the Constitution of the Sovereign Democratic Republic of India.

Adoption of the Constitution was, however, not the journey's end. The Chairman of the Drafting Committee, Dr. Ambedkar, and the President of the Assembly, Dr. Rajendra Prasad, speaking on 25 and 26 November 1949 sounded words of warning and wisdom. Dr. Ambedkar said:

I feel, however good a constitution may be, it is sure to turn out bad because those who are called to work it, happen to be a bad lot. However bad a constitution may be, it may turn out to be good if those who are called to work it, happen to be a good lot. The working of a constitution does not depend wholly upon the nature of the constitution. The constitution can provide only the organs of State such as the legislature, the executive and the judiciary. The factors on which the working of those organs of State depends are the people and the political parties they will set up as their instruments to carry out their wishes and their politics. Who can say how the people of India and their parties will behave?

...In addition to our old enemies in the form of castes and creeds we are going to have many political parties with diverse and opposing political creeds. Will Indians place the country above their creed or will they place creed above country? I do not know. But this much is certain that if the parties place creed above country, our independence will be put in jeopardy a second time and probably be lost for ever. This eventuality we must all resolutely guard against. We must be determined to defend our independence with the last drop of our blood.

Dr. Rajendra Prasad in his concluding speech observed that they had been able, on the whole, to draft a good constitution which he trusted would serve the country well. But, he added:

If the people who are elected are capable and men of character and integrity, they would be able to make the best even of a defective constitution. If they are lacking in these, the constitution cannot help the country. After all, a constitution like a machine is a lifeless thing. It acquires life because of men who control it and operate it, and India needs today nothing more than a set of honest men who will have the interest of the country before them. There is a fissiparous tendency arising out of various elements in our life. We have communal differences, caste differences,

> language differences, provincial differences and so forth. It requires men of strong character, men of vision, men who will not sacrifice the interests of the country at large for the sake of smaller groups and areas and who will rise over the prejudices which are born of these differences. We can only hope that the country will throw up such men in abundance.

The Constitution was finally signed by members of the Constituent Assembly on 24 January 1950—the last day of the assembly.

Besides framing the Constitution, the Constituent Assembly performed several other important functions like passing certain statutes of a constituent nature, adopting the national flag, declaring the national anthem, ratifying the decision in regard to the membership of the Commonwealth and election of the first President of the Republic.[1]

It was no mean achievement that within a period of less than three years, the founding fathers succeeded in evolving a Constitution acceptable throughout the length and breadth of this vast and populous country and one capable of salvaging and strengthening the threads of national unity in the midst of the multiplicity of religions, races, languages and all the variants of diversity. Our founding fathers were some of the most distinguished and the wisest of men and women—great jurists, patriots and freedom fighters. It is difficult to imagine any better or more representative results at that time even if the Constituent Assembly was directly elected by the people on the basis of universal adult franchise.

The Constitution of India evolved an integrated method of resolving conflicts by incorporating provisions catering to the needs of the different identities and ideologies and

---

1. See Subhash C. Kashyap, *The Framing of India's Constitution: A Study*, 2nd Ed., Universal Law Pub., New Delhi, 2004.

balancing the proportion and priority of rights. By adopting a democratic form of government, the polity created choices and accommodated various pluralities. The fundamental right to speech and conscience became the platform to air grievances and maintain their identity without demolishing the structure of the polity. The constitutional format in respect of human rights is remarkable as a significant and unique attempt at conflict resolution for the delicate balance it sought to achieve between political and civil rights on the one hand and social and economic rights on the other or between the individual rights and the social needs. The philosophy behind this is the dialogue between individualism and social control and the belief that civil, political, economic and social rights are equally important and not contradictory.

The Constitution was the result of a great deal of mutual accommodation, compromise and wide ranging consensus. The makers of the Constitution realilzed that it was necessary to grapple with multiple pulls and pressures of various ethnic diversities, to transcend conflicts or to subsume them under the overall Indian national identity. Where they failed to arrive at an acceptable consensus, they agreed to postpone the problem as in the case of the language issue where English was allowed to continue.

The institutions continued by us after Independence and/or embodied in the Constitution were those which had grown and developed on the Indian soil itself. The Founding Fathers chose to build further on the foundations of the old, on the institutions which they had already known, become familiar with and worked, despite all the limitations and fetters. The Constitution rejected British rule, but not the institutions that had developed during the period of British rule. Thus the Constitution did not represent a complete break with the colonial past.

Also, constitution-making and institution-building being a living, growing, dynamic process, it did not come to a stop on 26 November 1949 when the people of India in their Constituent Assembly, were said to have "adopted, enacted and given to themselves" the Constitution. Even after its commencement on 26 January 1950, the Constitution of India was being further made through its actual working, judicial interpretations and constitutional amendments. The Constitution kept growing for better or worse and acquired newer and newer by the manner in which and the men by whom it was worked from time to time. The story continues. For the Constitution, there is no journey's end. We have to keep abreast of the times and remain prepared for necessary reforms from time to time while retaining the fundamentals of our polity.[1]

1. See Subhash C. Kashyap, *Constitution Making Since 1950 - An Overview*, Universal Law. Pub., New Delhi, 2004]

4

SALIENT FEATURES OF THE CONSTITUTION

The Constitution of India is unique in many ways. It has several special features that distinguish it from other Constitutions of the world.

Size of the Constitution

In sheer physical terms, it is the lengthiest Constitution ever given to any nation. It is a very comprehensive document and includes many matters which could legitimately be the subject matters of ordinary legislation or administrative action. This happened because the Government of India Act, 1935, which was after all basically a statute, was used as a model and an initial working draft and large portions of it got reproduced in the Constitution. Also, the Constitution-makers did not want to leave certain matters subject to doubts, difficulties and controversies to be handled by future legislation. Unlike the United States where in addition to the federal Constitution, each State had its own separate Constitution, the Constitution of India included not only the Constitution of the Union but also of the States. The size, complexities and the diversities of the Indian situation also necessitated several special, temporary, transitional and miscellaneous provisions for certain regions of the country or classes of people. Not only does the Constitution contain a very comprehensive charter of justiciable fundamental rights, it also delineates the limitations under which these must necessarily operate unlike the United States, where limitations had to be read into the rights by Court decisions. Besides, our Constitution contains a description of several Directive Principles of State Policy and Fundamental Duties of citizens which though not enforceable in courts of law are expected to guide the State and the citizens respectively. In recent years, in fact, Courts have given to them considerable meaning and importance.

Types of Constitution

***Written or unwritten*:** Constitutions may be written like the U.S. Constitution or unwritten and based on conventions like the British. Our Constitution is written even though conventions also play a part insofar as they are in keeping with the provisions of the Constitution.

***Rigid or Flexible*:** Constitutions may be called rigid or flexible on the ground of the amending procedure being difficult or easy. Federal Constitutions are usually classified as rigid because of their difficult amending processes. Our Constitution may be said to be a combination of rigid and flexible inasmuch as certain provisions of the Constitution—*e.g.* articles 2, 3 and 4, and 169—can be amended like ordinary legislation by simple majority in the Houses of Parliament, other provisions can be amended under article 368 by the Houses of Parliament by a special majority of 2/3rd of the members present and voting and a majority of the total membership in each House. Only in the case of a few of the provisions, in addition to a special majority in the two Houses of Parliament, an amendment would require the ratification of not less than one half of the States. The fact that during 60 years, there were as many as 94 amendments disproves the charge of the rigidity of our Constitution.

***Federal or Unitary*:** Constitutions are also divided between federal and unitary. The classic example of the first category again is the U.S. Constitution and of the second the U.K. Constitution. In a unitary constitution, all powers are vested in the Central Government to which the authorities in the units are subordinate and function as the agents of the Government at the Centre and exercise authority by delegation from the Centre. In a federal polity, usually, there must be a rigid, written constitution, it must be supreme and it must specifically divide powers between the federal government and the governments of the units—both exercising powers in their respective spheres in their own right and independently. In fact, in a classic federation, the federal government enjoys only those powers that are by agreement surrendered to it by the units. Also, there must be an independent supreme court as the arbiter of any disputes between the Union and the States.

India's Constitution has been variously described as quasi-federal, federal with a strong unitary or pro-centre bias, federal in structure but unitary in spirit, federal in normal times but with possibilities of being converted into a purely unitary one during Emergency, etc. The fact is that it is difficult to put our Constitution in any strict mould of a federal or unitary type; it has features of both. It cannot be considered unitary because it provides, for example, for distribution of executive and legislative powers between the Union and the States and provisions affecting the powers of the States or Union-State relations cannot be amended without ratification by the States. It cannot be considered strictly federal either because the residuary powers vest in the Union. As Dr. Ambedkar said, rigidity and legalism were the two serious weaknesses of federalism. The Indian system was unique in that it created a dual polity with a single Indian citizenship. It could be both unitary and federal according to requirements of time and circumstances. Under article 249, the Union Parliament can invade the State List. Under articles 356 and 357, on the ground of failure of constitutional machinery in any State, all its executive and legislative powers may be taken over by the Union and under articles 352 to 354, the Constitution can be converted into an entirely unitary one inasmuch as during Proclamation of Emergency, the executive and legislative powers of the Union extend to matters even in the State List. Finally, under articles 2, 3 and 4, new States may be formed and areas, boundaries or names of existing States altered by the Union Parliament by ordinary law passed by simple majority votes.

Reasons for this unique unitary-federal mix are to be found in the constitutional history of India, the sheer size of the country and in the nature of her complex diversities based on religion, language, region, culture etc. Moving the Draft Constitution for adoption by the Constituent Assembly, the Chairman of the Drafting Committee, Dr. B.R. Ambedkar tried to explain the significance of using the term "Union of States" instead of "Federation of States" in the following words:

> The Drafting Committee wanted to make it clear that though India was to be a federation, the federation was not the result of an agreement by the States to join in a federation and that the federation not being the result of an agreement, no state has the right to secede from it. The federation is a Union because it is indestructible. Though the country and the people may be divided into different States for convenience of administration, the country is one integral whole, its people a single people living under a single imperium derived from a single source.

The text of the Constitution does not use the term 'federal' or 'federation'. The Supreme Court has spoken of the Indian Union as 'federal', 'quasi-federal' or 'ambhibian' meaning sometimes 'federal' and sometimes 'unitary'.[1]

Parliamentary or Presidential System

India is a Republic and the head is the President in whom all the executive power vests and in whose name it is to be exercised. He is also the Supreme Commander of the armed

---

1. *State of Rajasthan v. Union of India*, AIR 1977 SC 1361. Also see under Chapter 6, 'The Union and its Territory'.

forces. It has been held, however, that unlike the U.S. President, our President is only a nominal or constitutional head of the executive; he acts only with the aid and advice of the real political executive which is the Council of Ministers. The Ministers are collectively responsible to the popular House of Parliament *i.e.* the Lok Sabha. Thus, following the British pattern, the Constitution of India has basically adopted, both at the Union and State levels, the parliamentary system of government with ministerial responsibility to the popular House as against the U.S. system of Presidential Government with separation of powers and a nearly irremovable President as the Chief Executive for a fixed term. In the U.S. system, the President chooses his team of ministers from among the citizens at large and the ministers are not members of the legislature while in the Parliamentary System, the Ministers are from Parliament and remain part of it and responsible to its House of the People. The Parliamentary System may be said to be laying greater stress on the concept of the responsibility of the executive while the Presidential system obviously promotes more the stability of the executive.

It would, however, be wrong to assert that we have adopted the British parliamentary system *in toto.* There are several fundamental differences and departures. To name a few; the U.K. Constitution is still largely unitary, while ours is largely federal. They are a monarchy with a hereditary King/ Queen while we are a republic with an elected President, unlike the British we have a written constitution and our Parliament, therefore, is not sovereign even in theory and legislation passed by it is subject to judicial review. Our Constitution includes a charter of justiciable fundamental rights which are enforceable by the Courts not only against the executive but also against the legislature unlike the position in U.K. Of course, in U.K. also such rights have now become enforceable after the Bill passed in 1998 came into operation in 2000.

There has been some debate in our country on the desirability or otherwise of moving over to the Presidential model. The founding fathers, however, preferred the parliamentary form because they had some experience of operating it and there were advantages in continuing established institutions. After a long struggle for responsible government and against arbitrary executive authority, they were naturally allergic to a fixed term irremovable executive. In a highly pluralistic society with India's size and diversity and with many pulls of various kinds, they believed that the parliamentary form was the most suited for accommodating a variety of interests and building a united India.

Discussing the problem of making a choice between the U.S. Presidential model and the British parliamentary model, both of which were democratic, Dr. Ambedkar had said in the Constituent Assembly:

> A democratic executive must satisfy two conditions—1) It must be a stable executive and 2) it must be a responsible executive. Unfortunately it has not been possible so far to devise a system which can ensure both in equal degree. You can have a system which can give you more stability but less responsibility or you can have a system which gives you more responsibiligy but less stability. The American and the Swiss systems give more stability but less responsibility. The British System on the other hand gives you more responsibility but less stability….The Draft Constitution in recommending the Parliamentary system of Executive has preferred more responsibility to more stability.

K.M. Munshi put the argument more candidly when he said:

> We must not forget a very important fact that during the last hundred years, Indian public life has largely drawn upon the traditions of British Constitutional Law. Most of

us have looked up to the British model as the best. For the last thirty or forty years, some kind of responsibility has been introduced in the governance of this country. Our constitutional traditions have become parliamentary. After this experience, why should we go back upon the tradition that has been built for over a hundred years and buy a novel experience?

Parliamentary Sovereignty Vs. Judicial Supremacy

In the British parliamentary system, Parliament was supposed to be supreme and sovereign. There were no limitations on its powers, at least in theory, inasmuch as there was no written constitution and the Judiciary had no powers of judicial review of legislation even if a law violated fundamental human rights.

In the U.S. system, the Supreme Court with its power of judicial review and of interpreting the Constitution has assumed supremacy.

In India, the Constitution has arrived at a middle course and a compromise between the British sovereignty of Parliament and American judicial supremacy. We are governed by the rule of law and judicial review of administrative action is an essential part of rule of law. Thus, courts can determine not only the constitutionality of the law but also the procedural part of administrative action (*State of Bihar v. Subhash Singh,* AIR 1997 SC 1390). But, since we have a written constitution and the powers and functions of every organ are defined and delimited by the Constitution, there is no question of any organ—not even Parliament—being sovereign. Both Parliament and the Supreme Court are supreme in their respective spheres. While the Supreme Court may declare a law passed by Parliament *ultra vires* as being violative of the Constitution, Parliament may within certain restrictions amend most parts of the Constitution.

Adult Franchise

Dr. Ambedkar said in the Constituent Assembly that "by parliamentary democracy we mean 'one man, one vote'. Almost as an act of faith, the founding fathers decided to opt for universal adult suffrage with every adult Indian without any distinction at once having equal voting rights. This was particularly remarkable in the context of the vast poverty and illiteracy of the Indian populace. Even in the advanced democracies of the West, the franchise was extended only gradually.

Charter of Fundamental Rights

One of the most fundamental demands of the leaders of our national struggle for independence was that of the people having some basic human rights of freedom, equality etc. The problems of minorities accentuated the need of having a formal declaration of certain justiciable fundamental rights in the text of the Constitution itself. By and large, the fundamental rights incorporated in Part III of the Constitution are the inviolable rights of the individual against the State. Any law or executive action depriving an individual citizen of his freedom, for example, can be challenged in the Supreme Court or High Courts. It would be held unconstitutional and invalid unless it is covered by any of the restrictions spelled out again in the Constitution itself. Thus, the Constitution also lays down the machinery and mechanism for the enforcement of fundamental rights. In the U.S. Constitution, the fundamental rights were expressed in absolute terms. But there can be no absolute individual rights. For, the rights of each individual are limited at least by similar rights of other individuals. The Supreme Court of the United States had to find out and identify the legitimate restrictions on fundamental rights. Our founding fathers, however, decided to incorporate the restrictions within the relevant provisions themselves. Thus, our Constitution presents a balance between the rights of the individual on the one hand and the interests of society and the needs of the security of the State on the other.

Directive Principles

The Directive Principles of State Policy inspired by the Irish precedent, are a unique feature of our Constitution. Most of the socio-economic rights of the people have been included under this head. Even though said to be not enforceable in courts of law, these principles are expected to guide the governance of the country. They are in the nature of ideals set by the founding fathers before the State and all the organs of the State must strive to achieve them. In recent years, the Directive Principles have increasingly assumed greater relevance and importance not only for the legislatures but also in the eyes of the courts.

Citizenship

In keeping with their aim of building an integrated Indian fraternity and a united nation, the founding fathers provided for one single citizenship despite the federal structure. Unlike the U.S., there was to be no separate citizenship of the Union and of the States and all citizens were entitled to same rights all over the country without any discrimination subject to a few special protections in case of the State of Jammu and Kashmir, tribal areas etc.

Fundamental Duties

The 42nd Amendment to the Constitution *inter alia* added a new Part to the Constitution under the head Fundamental Duties. It lays down a code of eleven duties for all the citizens of India. Inasmuch as there can be no rights without corresponding duties and rights of citizens have no meaning without respect for political obligations of the citizens towards the State, it is unfortunate that the code of fundamental duties of the citizens has not so far been accorded by us the importance it deserves.

Independent Judiciary

The Constitution of India establishes an independent judiciary with powers of judicial review. The High Courts and the Supreme Court form a single integrated judicial structure with jurisdiction over all laws—Union, State, Civil, Criminal or Constitutional. Unlike the U.S., we do not have separate federal and State court systems. The entire judiciary is one hierarchy of courts. It not only adjudicates disputes and acts as the custodian of individual rights and freedoms but may from time to time need to interpret the Constitution and review legislation to determine its *vires* vis a vis the Constitution. The word of the Supreme Court is the final law of the land. The Supreme Court also functions as the arbiter of any disputes in regard to jurisdiction and distribution of powers between the States or between the Union and the States.

Conclusion

The Constitution of India is a most comprehensive document. It is unique in many ways. It cannot be fitted in any particular mould or model. It is a blend of the rigid and the flexible, federal and unitary and presidential and parliamentary. It attempts a balance between the fundamental rights of the individual on the one hand and the socio-economic interests of the people and security of the State on the other. Also, it presents a *via media* between the principles of parliamentary sovereignty and judicial supremacy.

While many Constitutions of nations framed after the Second World War have floundered and gone into oblivion, our Constitution has successfully faced many crises and survived. This itself is evidence of its resilience, dynamism and growth potential.

5

THE PREAMBLE

THE FUNDAMENTALS AND THE PHILOSOPHY OF THE CONSTITUTION

The Preamble to a Constitution is expected to embody the fundamental values and the philosophy on which the Constitution is based and the aims and objectives which the founding fathers enjoined the polity to strive to achieve.

The Preamble to our Constitution, as adopted by the Constituent Assembly, spoke of "We, the People of India", making a solemn resolve to constitute India into a "Sovereign Democratic Republic" securing for all its citizens Justice, Liberty and Equality, and promoting among them all Fraternity. Justice is further defined as social, economic and political. Liberty includes liberty of thought, expression, belief, faith and worship, and Equality means equality of status and of opportunity.

In fact, justice, liberty, equality and fraternity are the most essential concomitants of a truly democratic order and therefore only elucidate the concept of a democratic republic. The ultimate goal is that of "securing the dignity of the individual and unity of the nation." Thus, the Preamble serves the purpose of declaring that 'The People of India' are the source of the Constitution, that sovereignty in Indian polity vests in the people and that Indian polity is democratic with fundamental rights and freedoms guaranteed to all the people and amity among the people and dignity of the individual and integrity and unity of the nation assured.

The words used in the Preamble of our Constitution are some of the noblest. They embody the highest values that human ingenuity and experience have been able to devise thus far. The Oxford University Political Science professor Sir Ernest Barker was so moved by the text that he quoted it as a preface to his treatise and thought that it represented the quintessence of his work. He said:

> It seemed to me, when I read it, to state in a brief and pithy form the argument of much of the book; and it may accordingly serve as a keynote.

In the *Berubari case,* the Supreme Court agreed that the Preamble was the key to the minds of the framers of the Constitution. Where the words were found to be vague or their meaning was unclear, help of the Preamble could be taken to understand the intention of the framers and find out whether a particular word was used in a wide or narrow context. Nevertheless, Justice Gajendragadkar said, the Preamble was not a part of the Constitution. Also, it did not confer any substantial powers upon the legislatures or other organs of State. These must have their source in express or implied grant by the provisions of the Constitution.[1]

In *Sajjan Singh V. State of Rajasthan,* Justice Madholkar said that the Preamble had the stamp of "deep deliberation", was "marked by precision" and the "framers of the Constitution attached special significance to it." The Preamble was "an epitome" of the broad features of the Constitution which were an amplification or concretization of the concepts set out in the Preamble. The earlier Supreme Court opinion regarding the Preamble not being a part of the Constitution, perhaps needed reconsideration. Justice Hidyatullah also invoked the Preamble as an aid to

1. Also see *Synthetics and Chemicals Ltd. v. State of U.P.,* (1990) SCC 109.

construction. It was felt that attention should be paid to the intention of the framers of the Constitution as expressed through the Preamble. In *Golak Nath V. State of Punjab,* Justice Hidyatullah observed that the Preamble to the Constitution epitomized principles on which the Government was to function. The Preamble was the very "soul of the Constitution—eternal and unalterable." Our Preamble, he said, was a declaration of our faith and belief in certain fundamentals of national life, a standard from which we must not depart and a resolve we must not shake.

As held by the Supreme Court later in *Bharti Chandra Bhavan V. State of Mysore* (AIR 1970SC 2042), the scope of the Directive Principles and the Fundamental Rights also could be better understood in the light of the objectives enshrined in the Preamble.

In the *Berubari case,* it seems, the Supreme Court did not realise that as contradistinguished from a Preamble to an Act which is not discussed or voted in the Houses of the Legislature, the Preamble to our Constitution was fully discussed, duly enacted and adopted by the Constituent Assembly just like any other part of the Constitution. While putting the Preamble to the final vote, the President of the Assembly had said: "The question is that the Preamble stand part of the Constitution". Appropriately, therefore, the Supreme Court later revised its stand.

In *Kesavananda Bharti V. State of Kerala,* (1973) 4SCC 225, AIR 1973 SC 1461, the majority of the judges referred to the Constituent Assembly Debates and held that the Preamble was "part of the Constitution and observations to the contrary in *Berubari Case* were not correct". The Preamble, in fact, contained the basic structure of the Constitution. Justice Sikri said that the legislative history of the Preamble to the Constitution justified its importance. The Preamble was not only very much a part of the Constitution, but was of "extreme importance and the Constitution should be read and interpreted in the light of the grand and noble vision expressed in the Preamble". Any provisions of the Constitution could be amended under article 368 only "within the broad contours of the Preamble and of the Constitution". In fact, the inalienable basic elements of the Constitution were sought to be traced from the words of the Preamble and it was held that the provisions of the Constitution could not be amended so as to alter the basic elements. Although the basic elements were not precisely defined, those mentioned in the Preamble were specifically included.

In the words of the learned Supreme Court,

> The edifice of our Constitution is based upon the basic elements mentioned in the Preamble. If any of these elements are removed, the structure will not survive and it will not be the same Constitution or it cannot maintain its identity.

Thus, it was established that the basic elements or features of the Constitution as contained in the Preamble could not be altered by any amendment under article 368.

But, even though the Preamble is now taken to be an inviolable part of the Constitution and assumes special position as an aid to interpreting the Constitution, it also remains a fact that it is neither a source of any power nor a limitation thereon. First asserted in the *Berubari case,* this point was reiterated by Justice Mathew in *Indira Nehru Gandhi v. Raj Narain* (AIR 1975 SC 2291).

During the Emergency, the Forty-Second Constitution Amendment Act of 1976 added to the Preamble the words 'socialist' and 'secular'. Also, 'unity of the Nation' was amended to read 'unity and integrity of the Nation'. These qualifying terms, it was felt, were generally clarificatory in nature and did not make any substantial difference to the nature of the polity or the State inasmuch as socialism, secularism and national integrity were, according to the lawmakers, already implicit in the Preamble and in the rest of the Constitution as originally framed.

In *Bommai v. Union of India* (AIR 1994 SC 1918, JT (1994) SC 215) regarding the dismissal of BJP governments in Madhya Pradesh, Rajasthan and Himachal Pradesh, Justice Ramaswamy said:

> The Preamble of the Constitution, is an integral part of the Constitution. Democratic form of government, federal structure, unity and integrity of the nation, secularism, social justice and judicial review are basic features of the Constitution.

According to the text of the Preamble as it stands today after the forty-second amendment, the supreme or fundamental constitutional values in which the founding fathers believed, which they wanted to foster among the people of the Republic and which, they hoped, would guide all those who, from generation to generation, were called upon to work the Constitution were :

- Sovereignty
- Socialism
- Secularism
- Democracy
- Republican Character
- Justice
- Liberty
- Equality
- Fraternity
- Dignity of the Individual, and
- Unity and Integrity of the Nation

Sovereignty

In Political Science and Jurisprudential terms, sovereignty is considered to be one of the essential attributes of a State and connotes absolute and supreme power not subject to control by any internal or external authority. Cooley defines a sovereign State as one "where there resides within itself a supreme and absolute power acknowledging no superior".

In the *Keshvananda Bharti case*, Justice Mathew said that the Republic of India was "sovereign" because it could make or unmake any decision with respect to itself without any interference from outside (AIR 1973 SC 1461).

In these traditional terms of sovereignty, no State today can be said to be fully sovereign. Membership of international organisations like the United Nations, European Union etc. and international treaties, accords, conventions etc. cast obligations, put restraints and erode sovereignty.

The Constitution of India does not contain any specific provision in regard to the vesting of sovereign powers. The only place from where the residence of sovereignty and the source of the Constitution itself can be ascertained is the Preamble. The words 'We the People of India' remind us of the opening words of the Preamble of the U.S. Constitution. But, the Preamble in the U.S. Constitution speaks in the name of "We, the People of the United States". Its earlier drafts and history make it amply clear that the framers of the American Constitution were referring to the people of the several (13) independent States seeking 'a more perfect union' and not to one people of a nation. The Preamble to the Constitution of India, on the other hand, did not talk of the people of the States of the Indian Union. Unlike the U.S. Constitution, our Constitution did not even require any ratification by the States. By saying that "We, the People of India" "adopt, enact and give to ourselves this Constitution", the founding fathers solemnly affirmed that we were one people, people of India, and not people of different States etc., that sovereignty belonged to the whole people of India and not to those of separate States and that the Constitution was framed and adopted not by the people of States but by the whole people of India in their collective capacity as one indivisible sovereign unit. It was sought to be stressed that we were one nation and had one Constitution and one polity.

Unlike the United States and Australia, where

sovereignty is divided between the Union or the Commonwealth and the States, each being sovereign in the sphere assigned to it by the Constitution, in India, despite the division of powers between the Union and the States, there is no division of sovereignty. The Union can override the States in national interest during emergencies. Even during normal times it can invade the States' sphere by legislating on subjects in the State list under article 249.

Because our national sovereignty was one and indivisible, no State or group of States could annul the Constitution or move out of the Union established by the Constitution. In the United States, a civil war had to be waged and won in order to establish the indestructibility of the Union. But, our founding fathers at the very outset provided for the indestructibility of the Union and for States having no right to secede from the Union.

Article 1(3)(C) of the Constitution made it clear that the Union of India could acquire foreign territory. Also "one of the attributes of sovereignty is the power to cede parts of national territory if necessary."[1] The Union could also cede its territory subject to necessary constitutional amendment.[1]

Under Articles 2, 3 and 4 of the Constitution, the Union Parliament can by ordinary legislation admit or establish new States in the Union, alter the name, area and boundaries of the existing States. Under the citizenship provisions, there is only one citizenship for all the people of India and no double citizenship of the Union and of the States as in the United States.

Thus, the Preamble provisions of our Constitution put an end to concepts of traditional federalism, divided sovereignty, autonomy of States etc. Also, the founding fathers sought to clarify for all times that Sovereignty in our scheme of things vests in the people themselves and that all

---

1. *In re the Berubari Union* AIR 1960 SC 845.
2. *Maganbhai Ishwarbhai Patel v. Union of India* (1970) 3 SCC 100.

the organs and functionaries of the Union and the States draw their powers only from the people of India.

Socialism

The founding fathers did not want the Constitution to be wedded to any particular political ideology or ism or to be limited by any economic doctrine. They did not, therefore, agree to include any reference *inter alia* to socialism. But, the Preamble did mention the resolve to secure to all citizens economic justice and equality of status and opportunity. It was the Constitution (Forty-Second Amendment) Act, 1976 that introduced the word "Socialist" to qualify our "Republic". The text of the Preamble as amended gives almost the highest place of honour to the objective of 'Socialism'. It is mentioned next only to 'Sovereign'. However, the term 'Socialist' has not been defined by the Constitution.

The Constitution (Forty-fifth Amendment) Bill, attempted to define 'Socialist' to mean "free from all forms of exploitation—social, economic and political." The Bill was, however, finally adopted as the 44th Amendment without the definition. "Socialism" is difficult to define. It has meant different things to different people and is hardly left with any one definite connotation. Dictionary meaning of the word would imply, in full or in part, placing means of production and distribution in public hands, *i.e.* under public (meaning 'State') ownership and/or control as against private ownership and free enterprize.

Socialism meant elimination of inequality in income and status and standards of living. Also, after addition of the word 'socialist' in the Preamble, the Courts in their interpretation[1] of the Constitution could expectedly lean more in favour of nationalisation and state ownership of

---

1. *Minerva Mills V. Union of India*, AIR 1980 SC 1789; *Dharwad Employees V. State of Karnataka*, (1990) 2SCC 396; *Atam Prakash V. State of Haryana*, AIR 1986 SC 859.

private property, industry, etc. and the right to equal pay for equal work. But, the new economic policy of liberalization, free market competition, entry of foreign companies, disinvestment in public sector undertakings, privatization etc. hardly qualified to be considered socialistic by any definition.

Secularism

Dictionaries define 'secularism' as pertaining to this world or to things 'not spiritual', 'not concerned with religion', 'a system of belief which rejects all forms of religious faith and worship', 'irreligious' etc. *Encyclopaedia Britannica* defines secularism as "utilitarian ethic" designed for the physical, spiritual and moral improvement of mankind which neither affirms nor denies the theistic premise of religion. *Encyclopaedia of Social Sciences* defines it as an attempt to establish an autonomous sphere of knowledge purged of supernatural presuppositions.

A.R. Blackshield who tried to fix the perception and parameters of secularism in the West, was unable to arrive at any fully viable and acceptable definition of the term. It was, he concluded, not exactly opposite of religion, but then it was not easy to define religion either. According to him, secularism could be understood to imply religious freedom and tolerance and respect for ideas of rationalism, materialism, humanism etc.

An academic definition of the concept of secularism in the Indian context has been attempted by Donald Eugene Smith in the following words:

> The secular state is a state which gives individual and corporate freedom of religion, is not constitutionally connected to a particular religion, nor does it seek either to promote or interfere with religion.

As Justice Desai put it, a secular state deals with the individual as a citizen irrespective of his religion, is not connected to a particular religion nor does it seek to promote or interfere with religion. Secular State must have nothing to do with religious affairs except when their management involves crime, fraud or becomes a threat to unity and integrity of the State.

Delivering his judgement in *Ziyauddin Burhammudin Bukhari Vs. Brijmohan Ramdass Mehra and Bros.* (1975 Suppl. S.C.R. 281) Justice M.H Beg said :

> The secular state, rising above all differences of religion, attempts to secure the good of all its citizens irrespective of their religious beliefs and practices. It is neutral or impartial in extending its benefits to citizens of all castes and creeds. Maitland has pointed out that such a state has to ensure, through its laws that the existence or exercise of political or civil right or the right or capacity to occupy any office or position under it or to perform any public duty connected with it does not depend upon the profession or practice of any particular religion.
>
> Our Constitution and the laws framed thereunder leave citizens free to work out happy and harmonious relationships between their religious and the quite separable secular fields of law and politics. But they do not permit an unjustifiable invasion of what belongs to one sphere by what appertains really to another. It is for courts to determine, in a case of dispute, whether any sphere was or was not properly interfered with, in accordance with the Constitution, even by a purported law.

Anything that is pernicious and exploitative cannot be allowed to remain outside the control of law simply because it is paraded under the garb of religion.

Justices Gajendragadkar, Dhawan and Beg found secularism practised by ancient Hindu society and equally traceable to Islamic jurisprudence. Justice Beg suggested that "a happy harmony and synthesis of the best in secularism and religion" was possible. A theory of secularism could be built on ancient jurisprudence. In the *Kesavananda Bharti* case

(AIR 1973 SC 1461), secularism was held to be part of the basic structure. Quoting from Manu and Parashara, Justice Beg, however said :

> Even our ancient jurists recognized the principles that one generation has no right to tie down future generations to its own views or laws even on fundamentals. They not only differ between one society and another but also as between one generation and another of the same society or nation.

In *S.R. Bommai V. Union of India* (AIR 1994 SC 1918) the Supreme Court dwelt at length on the basic feature of secularism in the Constitution and justified the proclamations under article 356 imposing President's rule in the BJP ruled States in the aftermath of Babri Masjid demolition on the ground of threat to 'secularism' which it held to be a basic feature of the Constitution and one that was there even before the word 'secular' was inserted in the Preamble by the 42nd Amendment.

In the *Ayodhya case* (AIR 1995 SC 605), the Supreme Court explained secularism thus:

> It is clear from the constitutional scheme that it guarantees equality in the matter of religion to all individuals and groups irrespective of their faith emphasizing that there is no religion of the State itself. The Preamble of the Constitution read in particular with articles 25 to 28 emphasises this aspect and indicates that it is in this manner the concept of secularism embodied in the constitutional scheme as a creed adopted by the Indian people has to be understood while examining the constitutional validity of any legislation on the touchstone of the Constitution. The concept of secularism is one facet of the right to equality woven as the central golden thread in the fabric depicting the pattern of the scheme in our Constitution.

In the absence of any precise or formal definition of 'secularism' in the Indian context, several different interpretations were possible. The perceptions of the apex court also have varied from case to case depending upon the constitution of each Bench. Unlike the West, in India, secularism was never born out of the conflict between the Church and the State. It was perhaps rooted in India's own past history and culture, a very likely response to her pluralism or the desire of the founding fathers to be just and fair to all communities irrespective of their numbers. Very often, in our common parlance, the term secularism therefore is used merely as an opposite of 'communalism'.

The original text of the preamble as adopted by the Constituent Assembly did not contain the word 'secular'. Like the word 'socialist', it was also inserted as an additional adjective before 'republic' by the Forty-second Constitutional Amendment Act during the Emergency. The meaning sought to be given to the term has been that of *Sarva Dharm Sambhava* i.e. treating all religions alike or giving equal respect to all religions, instead of *Dharm Nirpeksh* or *Panth Nirpeksh* i.e. State neutrality in matters of religion. This, however does not mean that the State has no say whatsoever in matters of religion. Laws can be made for regulating the secular affairs of temples, mosques and other places of worship and maths.[1] Even acquisition by the state of a place of worship—temple, mosque or church—cannot be said to be against secularism.[2]

This was the natural and the only possible interpretation because the hard facts of the Indian situation made the Western concept of secularism entirely inapplicable. Secularism in our context only means that ours was a nontheocratic state, that the state as such does not have its own religion, that in its eyes all religions are equal and that it would make no distinction between citizens on grounds of religion.

1. *S.P. Mittal v. Union of India* (AIR 1983 SC1, (1983) 1 SCR 729.
2. *Ismail Faruqui v. Union of India* [(1994) 6 SCC 360, AIR 1995 SC 605.

Justice Gajendragadkar defined secularism of the Indian Constitution to mean equality of rights to all citizens as citizens with their religion being entirely irrelevant in the matter. "The State" he said "does not owe loyalty to any particular religion as such; it is not irreligious or anti-religious; it gives equal freedom to all religions". Indian secularism sought to establish a rational synthesis between the "legitimate functions of religion and the legitimate and expanding functions of the State". M.C. Setalvad also believed that under a secular State all citizens are to be treated alike and not discriminated against on account of their religion.

Before the Forty-second Amendment, the only mention of the word 'secular' in the Constitution was in article 25(2) wherein State had been empowered to regulate or restrict any 'secular activity' associated with religious practice. Obviously, here the connotation of 'secular' was 'non-religious' or pertaining to matters other than purely religious. The Forty-second Constitutional Amendment Act which added the word 'secular' to the Preamble did not attempt to define it. It was, however, felt that the addition had the effect only of affirming and clarifying what was believed to be already present as a basic feature of the Constitution. In the *Kesavananda Bharti* and *Minerva Mills cases,* secularism came to be mentioned as a basic feature. Also, it was inherent in the guarantee of freedom of religion as a fundamental right. In *St. Xavier College Society Vs. State of Gujarat,* it was held by the Supreme Court in 1974 that even though the Constitution did not speak of a secular state there could be no doubt that the Constitution-makers wanted to establish such a state.[1]

The Constitution (45th Amendment) Bill sought to lay down that secular and democratic character of the Constitution would be regarded as being among the basic features of the Constitution. However, before the Bill was

1. AIR 1973 SC 1461; AIR 1980 SC 1787; AIR 1974 SC 1389.

enacted as the 44th Amendment, the list of basic features was dropped. This abortive Bill had also tried to define secular republic to mean a republic in which there is equal respect for all religions. Also, apart from using the word secular in the preamble, our Constitution does not anywhere categorically say that religion and politics would not be allowed to be mixed or that religious issues, funds and places of worship would not be allowed to be exploited for political ends.

In the *Shah Banu case,* the law-makers yielded to the pressure of fundamentalist Muslim opinion and much against the letter and spirit of the constitutional precepts of secularism or equal justice for all, Muslim Women (Protection of Right on Divorce) Act, 1986 was brought in to nullify the Supreme Court judgement.[1]

Notwithstanding anything, the only operative interpretation of the term 'secular' in Indian Constitutional Law now would be what can be gathered from the different provisions of the Constitution *e.g.* articles 14, 15, 16, 19, 25 to 28, 44 etc. The preamble itself even in its original unamended form contained the concept of liberty *inter alia* that of belief, faith and worship. In other words, it stood for a solemn commitment to religious freedom for all. This was reinforced by the principles of equality of status and opportunity and of fraternity among all the people of India.

The vision of the founding fathers was that of a nation transcending all diversities of religion, caste and creed. They were not hostile to religion but they hoped that it would be possible to forge political unity and that religious differences would not hamper nation building. The Constitution envisaged a new social order free from communal conflicts and based on Justice, social, economic and political. It visualized a polity under which laws would not discriminate between citizens on grounds of religion, caste or the like.

1. *Ahmad Khan v. Shah Banu*, AIR 1985 SC 945.

The Constitution sought to establish a 'secular' order under which the majority of the population did not enjoy any special privileges or preferential treatment at the hands of the State and the 'religious' rights of the minorities were protected in different ways.

It seems necessary that the term secularism be clearly defined in the Constitution itself, firmer legislation passed and already existing legislation firmly implemented for preventing misuse of religion for political purposes by any party or person.[1]

Democracy

Like 'socialism' or 'secularism', democracy also meant different things to different people. Literally, the Greek word 'demos' meant 'the people' and 'Kratos' meant 'government' or 'rule'. Democracy, therefore, meant government by the people as against monarchy or dictatorship which were autocratic rule of one person, oligarchy or aristocracy being rule by the few. Its basic postulates are that the sovereign power resides in the people, that irrespective of religion, caste, creed, colour or sex and irrespective of the level of economic, educational or professional background, all are equal in the eyes of law and that each individual is capable of governing oneself and of managing ones own affairs the way one deems fit. In a democracy the people are supposed to be their own masters. They have an inalienable right to rule themselves, or to be ruled in the way they like and by the people they choose.

Democracy also recognises the fact that from time immemorial human beings have been fighting with each other for power or for supremacy. Democracy tries to substitute a more civilised manner of fighting. It is

1. For the abortive attempt to amend the Constitution by the Constitution (80th Amendment) Bill, 1993 and for a fuller discussion of the topic see Subhash C. Kashyap, *Delinking Religion and Politics*, New Delhi, 1993.)

substitution of the methods of discussion and persuasion for methods of armed conflict. The ballot substitutes the bullet; we sit together, we talk and we discuss. We try to persuade each other and win each other by force of our conviction, ideas and arguments.

In the ancient Indian Village Republics and the Greek City States, all the citizens assembled together and decided issues of governance. People, thus, exercised their power directly in deciding matters of State and this kind of polity could be called direct popular democracy. In this case, both legal and political sovereignty could be said to vest in the people. But with the gradual increase in the size and population of the political units and ultimately with the advent of the modern nation states, it became impossible to arrange for all the people to assemble at a place to discuss matters of State and arrive at decisions smoothly. Also, matters of legislation and State administration grew more and more complex. All forms of direct democracy, therefore, soon became practically extinct from all over the world except for a few Swiss cantons where even issues whether schools should remain closed on a particular day or the price of bread should be increased and the like are still decided by a popular vote. There may be a few referenda on very major international issues in some places. Also, there have been provisions in constitutions of some countries (*e.g.* France, Ireland, Japan and Switzerland) whereunder referendum is provided for constitutional amendments. But, by and large, the only issue on which the people at large in different countries vote these days at periodic intervals is selection of their representatives. Modern democracy thus has of necessity to be indirect representative democracy whereunder government is carried on and laws are made by the elected representatives of the people.

Thus, while democratic polity becomes one of the basic features of our Constitution which cannot be altered by any constitutional amendment, there are many variants of democracy which can be considered equally representative and legitimate.

We have adopted what is called representative parliamentary democracy. The founding fathers tried to provide for the fullest representation by enfranchising all the vast adult population of the country without any literacy, property, income tax, or sex criteria. This is borne out by the provisions for universal adult franchise with all adults—men and women—of 18 years and above having the right to vote (article 326) and the executive being responsible to the popular house of the legislature [articles 75(3) and 164(2)].

Republican Character

The concept of 'republic' is that of a State in which the people are supreme, there is no privileged class and all public offices are open to every citizen without any discrimination. There is no hereditary ruler and the head of the State is elected by the people for a fixed term. He is usually called the President of the Republic. For Cooley, a republican form of government is "a government by representatives chosen by the people." In the words of Justice Hidayatullah: "A Republic is a State in which the supreme power rests in the final analysis with the people and not with a single individual like a king or the like." Democratic republic may, therefore, broadly mean a State with an elected head and a government by the representatives of the people. According to Madison in *The Federalist* :

> Republic is a government which derives its powers directly or indirectly from the great body of the people, and is administered by persons holding their offices during pleasure, for a limited period, or during good behaviour.

It is in the widest sense that the Preamble speaks of India being a Republic. With the commencement of the Constitution on 26 January 1950, India ceased to be a dominion and no more owed any allegiance to the Crown.

The head of the Union is a President who is elected for a fixed term by an electoral college of the representatives of the people. All citizens are equal in the eyes of law, there is no privileged class and all public offices are open to every citizen without any distinction of race, caste, sex or creed.

***Membership of the Commonwealth*:** Even though after Independence, India decided to remain a member of the Commonwealth of Nations, it did not in any way compromise her position or imply any diminution of her status as a sovereign nation or as a Republic. In fact, it was the Commonwealth which was transformed. From the British Commonwealth, it became the Commonwealth of Nations which was to be a free association of equal and fully sovereign States with the Crown being accepted only as a symbol of the free association. The Commonwealth specifically recognised India's status as a sovereign independent Republic. The new Commonwealth in the words of Nehru was "an agreement by free will" which could be "terminated by free will" at any time. It did not therefore, affect the sovereign, democratic or republican nature of the State.

***Social and Economic Democracy*:** Democracy conceived in merely political terms meant the right of every citizen to freely vote at periodic elections. The 'one man, one vote' principle applied in all democratic elections emanated from the recognition of equal rights of all men—whether highly educated or illiterate, experts, technocrats, industrialists or labourers. For our founding fathers, however, democracy did not mean merely political democracy or the people's right to periodically vote to elect their representatives. Without social and economic democracy, political democracy had no meaning in a poor country like India. For Dr. Ambedkar, social and economic democracy was the real aim and ultimate goal. He said that parliamentary democracy was meaningless unless it was geared to achieving the real goal of economic democracy. Jawaharlal Nehru had observed later that Democracy of his conception was only a means to an end. The end was the good life for the individual which must include a certain satisfaction of the essential economic needs. Only in the measure that democracy succeeds in solving the economic problems, does it succeed even in the political field. If the economic problems are not solved then the political structure tends to weaken and crack up. Therefore, from political democracy, we must progress to economic democracy which means "working for a certain measure of well being for all". It could be called a Welfare State. But, it also "means working for a certain measure of equality of opportunity in the economic sphere". This is made clear by the words of the Preamble which speak of securing to all citizens of the Republic 'Justice, Social, Economic and Political'.

Justice

The Preamble promises justice to all citizens. Justice means harmonization of interests between the individuals, between groups and between the individuals and groups on the one hand and interests of the community on the other. Most significantly, the Preamble places Justice higher than the other principles of Liberty, Equality and Fraternity. The concept of Justice in the Preamble is indeed very wide. It is not confined to the narrow legal justice as administered by the courts. Our courts are, after all, only courts of law. Justice is defined or elaborated as social, economic and political, again giving precedence to social and economic over political justice.

The Preamble is designed to realise socio-economic justice to all people including workmen.[1]

Social justice implies that all citizens are treated equally irrespective of their status in society as a result of the accident

---

1. *All India Statutory Corporation v. United Labour Union*, AIR 1997 SC 645.

of birth, race, caste, religion, sex, title etc. Article 15 prohibits discrimination or disability in the matter of access to public places. Article 38 enjoins the State to strive to promote the welfare of the people "by securing and protecting as effectively as it may a social order in which justice social, economic and political shall inform all the institutions of the national life". In the words of Jawaharlal Nehru:

> Social justice has always exercised an appeal to sensitive persons. The basic attraction of Marxigm for millions of people was not, I think, its attempt at scientific theory but its passion for social justice.

Provisions for humane conditions of work, maternity relief, leisure, reduction of wide disparities, promoting of economic interests and a decent standard of living for the workers, weaker sections and backward classes, minimum wage, banning of forced labour (articles 23 and 43) were all directed towards social justice.[1]

Economic Justice would require that the rich and the poor are treated alike and that efforts are made to bridge the gap between them. In pursuance of the objective of economic justice, article 39 directs the State to try to secure that the citizens have an adequate means of livelihood, that ownership and control of the material resources of the community are so distributed as best to subserve the common good, that operation of the economic system does not result in the concentration of wealth and means of production to the common detriment, that there is equal pay for equal work for both men and women, that women and children are not abused and citizens are not forced by economic necessity into vocations unsuited to their age or strength, and that the children are given opportunities and facilities to develop in a healthy manner and in freedom and

---

1. *Sadhuram V. Polin*, AIR 1984 SC 1471; *Lingappa V. State of Maharashtra*, AIR 1985 SC 389.

dignity and childhood and youth are protected against exploitation etc.

In fact, various other articles in Part IV of the Constitution (articles 36 to 51) are also directed towards securing a new social and economic order imbued with justice. Thus, there are provisions for right to work, to education and to public assistance in certain cases, for just and humane conditions of work and maternity relief, for living wage etc. for workers, for free and compulsory education of children, for promotion of educational and economic interests of weaker sections, for separation of judiciary from executive etc.

Political justice means equal share to all citizens in the rights to participation in the political process without any distinction of race, caste, creed, religion or place of birth. Article 16 guarantees equality of opportunity in matters of public employment and articles 325 and 326 provide for equal rights to all adults to participate in elections.

Founding fathers like Nehru and Ambedkar were quite clear in their minds that political justice was meaningless without economic justice. In our society ridden with religious, caste and creed discriminations, even economic justice was not enough unless it was coupled with social justice. Dr. Ambedkar had said:

> On 26th January, 1950 we are going to enter into a life of contradictions. In politics, we will have equality and in social and economic life we will have inequality. In politics, we will be recognising the principle of one man one vote and one vote one value. In our social and economic life, we shall, by reason of our social and economic structure, continue to deny the principle of one man one value.

Liberty

Derived from the Latin word 'liber', liberty taken literally would mean freedom from captivity, imprisonment, slavery, serfdom or despotism. As conceived in the liberal western traditions and in the context of doctrines of *laissez-faire*, liberty was largely a negative concept. It meant absence of restraint on freedom of trade and enterprize, equality of opportunity in trade and business, freedom of contract and competition. Liberty was conceived as absence of interference in individual freedom of action by the Government. But 'liberty' in the Preamble to our Constitution does not mean mere absence of restraint or domination. It is a positive concept of the right to "liberty of thought, expression, belief, faith and worship". It comprehends various freedoms later concretized in the Fundamental Rights part of the Constitution and considered essential for the development of the individual and the nation. Thus, for example, article 19 guarantees protection of rights of freedom of speech, expression etc. while articles 25–28 embody rights to freedom of religion including that of belief, faith, and worship. In this positive connotation, liberty would mean freedom of the individual to do what one likes. But, again 'liberty' has to be distinguished from license. The liberty of thought, expression, belief, faith and worship as elaborated in the fundamental rights part of the Constitution has to be so regulated as not to endanger the security of the State, public interest etc.

Equality

Leaders of the French Revolution believed that all men were equal in the eyes of law. Whether it protected or punished, it must do so without any regard to distinction of birth etc. Also, all citizens were equally eligible to all public offices, honours and positions strictly according to their capacities, virtues and talents only.

'Equality' in political science terms does not mean that all men (and women) are equal in all circumstances. There are bound to be physical, mental and economic differences. The concept embodied in our Preamble is only that of equality of status and opportunity. This has legal, social, political and economic aspects. All citizens are equal before law and enjoy equal protection of the laws of the land. There can be no discrimination between one person and another on grounds of religion, race, caste, sex or place of birth in the matter of access to public places and public employment. All citizens are equally entitled to enjoy the political rights to vote and participate in the process of governance without any distinction. In the economic field, equality means that for the same ability and same labour, the salary would also be the same. Also, one man or one class would not exploit other men or classes. The concept of equality of status and opportunity has been given concrete substance and shape in articles 14 to 18.

Fraternity

The ideals of justice, liberty and equality are relevant and meaningful only inasmuch as these promote a common feeling of brotherhood, of Indian fraternity, of being sons of same Mother India despite all the racial, linguistic, religious and other diversities of many sorts. Provisions relating to common citizenship are directed towards strengthening Indian fraternal feelings and building a strong Indian fellowship. The fundamental rights guaranteed to all citizens without any discrimination and the Directive Principles directed at achieving social and economic equality are also designed to promote fraternity. The concept has been more specifically elaborated in the new Part IV A of the Constitution laying down the Fundamental Duties of the citizens. It casts a duty on every citizen *inter alia* to promote among all the people of India harmony and the spirit of common brotherhood and of belonging to one Indian family transcending all religious, linguistic and regional or sectional diversities. In fact, the concept of fraternity is far wider than the concept of secularism. It goes beyond separation of religion and politics, freedom of religion, equal respect for all religions etc. Unfortunately, not enough importance has been attached by the jurists and judges to this concept.

Speaking on the need for the recognition of the principle of fraternity, Dr. Ambedkar remarked in the Constituent Assembly:

> What does fraternity mean? Fraternity means a sense of common brotherhood of all Indians—of Indians being one people. It is the principle which gives unity and solidarity to social life. It is a difficult thing to achieve.

There is also an international aspect of fraternity which takes us to the concept of universal brotherhood, the ancient Indian ideal of *Vasudhaiv Kutumbakam*—of the entire world being a family. This has been elaborated in article 51 of the Constitution under the Directive Principles.

Dignity of the Individual

Fraternity was expected to preserve and promote the dignity of the individual. In the minds of the founding fathers, dignity of the individual was of supreme importance. The objective was to improve the quality of life for the individual by guaranteeing the fundamental rights of freedom, equality etc. and by issuing guidelines to the State in the form of Directive Principles to so orient its policies as to provide to all citizens, *inter alia* adequate means of livelihood, just and humane conditions of work and a decent standard of life. Article 17 as a fundamental right is directed at abolishing the practice of untouchability which was an affront to human dignity. To enforce any of his fundamental rights and his individual dignity a person could approach even the Supreme Court directly.

Unity and Integrity of the Nation

In order to safeguard the dignity of the individual, we need to build the nation and protect its unity and integrity. It was only through a spirit of common brotherhood and fraternity that we could hope to build national unity in a highly pluralistic and heterogenous society. Also, without unity and integrity of the nation, we could not succeed in our efforts at economic development and could not hope to preserve either democracy or the independence of the country and the honour of the countrymen. Article 51A, therefore, appropriately makes it the duty of every citizen to uphold and protect the sovereignty, unity and integrity of India and promote harmony and brotherhood. At least in matters which involve threat to the unity and integrity of the nation, it is expected of every citizen to forget all differences and rise above all considerations of self-interest. If this does not happen, nation building becomes an impossibility.

Conclusion

Thus, an analysis of the various concepts and terms in the Preamble shows that the noble words of our Preamble represent the quintessence, the philosophy, the ideals or the soul of the entire Constitution of India. Other parts and provisions of the Constitution are only an elaboration and an attempt to give concrete shape, content and meaning to the words of the Preamble. No wonder that the Supreme Court found that the Preamble contained some of the basic features of the Constitution which could not be altered even by an amendment of the Constitution under article 368. It is, however, felt that words like 'socialist', 'secular' etc. used in the Preamble are very ambiguous and our polity has suffered greatly due to their having not been precisely defined in the Constitution. It may, therefore be most advisable to define them through a constitutional amendment.[1]

---

1. For an analysis of how far the principles and values embodied in the Preamble have been fulfilled in practice see Subhash C. Kashyap (ed), *Constitutional Reforms*, New Delhi, 2nd ed., 2004; *Basic Constitutional Values*, New Delhi 1994; *Nation and Polity Under Strain* New Delhi 1996; and The case for a Divorce between religion and politics in *Hinduism and Secularism* ed. By Arvind Sharma, Palgrave, N.Y., 2001.

6

THE UNION AND ITS TERRITORY

PART I, ARTICLES 1–4

Article 1 lays down that India, that is Bharat, shall be a Union of States. The territory of India shall consist of (i) the territories of the States, (ii) the Union Territories, and (iii) any territories that may be acquired *e.g.* the French and Portuguese possessions in India like Pondicherry, Karikal, Mahe and Yanam (French), and Goa, Daman and Diu and Dadra and Nagar Haveli (Portugese), which were added to the Union by the 14th, 12th and 10th Constitutional Amendments following their *de jure* transfer to India.[1]

The names of the States and Union Territories and the territories covered by each of them have been described in the First Schedule. It has been held by the Supreme Court that the 'territory of India' at any point of time is the territory specified in the First Schedule under article 1 of the Constitution.[2]

The First Schedule as adopted by the Constituent Assembly and incorporated in the Constitution mentioned four categories of States and Territories—Part A, Part B and

---

1. See *Amar Singh v. State of Rajasthan,* AIR 1955 SC 504; *Masthan Sahib v. Chief Commissioner,* AIR 1962 SC 797; and *Harivansh v. State of Maharashtra,* (1971) 2 SCC 54.
2. *Amar Singh v. State of Rajasthan,* AIR 1955 S.C. 504; *Masthan Sahib v. Chief Commissioner*, AIR 1962 S.C. 797.

Part C States and Part D territories. Part A included the nine erstwhile provinces of British India. The princely States with legislatures were put in Part B which listed five States. Part C included five centrally administered States. The territory of Andaman and Nicobar Islands was mentioned in Part D. During the years following the commencement of the Constitution, the map underwent considerable changes. Andhra was created as a separate State on linguistic basis by the Andhra Act, 1953. Finally, the reorganization of States largely on linguistic basis under the States Reorganisation Commission Report and the Constitution (Seventh Amendment) Act, 1956 abolished the distinction between Part A and Part B States. Subsequently, several new States were formed, *e.g.* Haryana, Himachal Pradesh, Nagaland, Manipur, Mizoram, Arunachal Pradesh, Goa, Chhattisgarh, Jharkhand and Uttarakhand. As at present, the Schedule lists the following 28 States and seven Union Territories:

The States: (1) Andhra Pradesh, (2) Arunachal Pradesh, (3) Assam, (4) Uttarakhand, (5) Bihar, (6) Goa, (7) Gujarat, (8) Chhattisgarh, (9) Jharkhand, (10) Haryana, (11) Himachal Pradesh, (12) Jammu & Kashmir, (13) Karnataka, (14) Kerala, (15) Maharashtra, (16) Madhya Pradesh, (17) Manipur, (18) Meghalaya, (19) Mizoram, (20) Nagaland, (21) Orissa, (22) Punjab, (23) Rajasthan, (24) Sikkim, (25) Tamil Nadu, (26) Tripura, (27) Uttar Pradesh, (28) West Bengal.

Union Territories: (1) Andaman and Nicobar Islands, (2) Chandigarh, (3) Dadra and Nagar Haveli, (4) Daman and Diu, (5) Delhi (now named the National Capital Territory), (6) Lakshadweep, (7) Puducherry.

The question of the name of the country was discussed in the Constituent Assembly at some length. While 'Bharat' was the ancient name and represented the first expression of the consciousness of the unity and identity of the country, India was the modern name by which the country had since become known all over the world. As a member of the United Nations also the name was India and all international agreements were entered in that name. Both the names, therefore, had strong votaries. Finally, the name 'India, that is Bharat' was adopted as a happy compromise.

The emphasis on India being a 'Union' was to convey the fact that it was not the result of a compact or agreement between the constituent units but a forthright declaration by the Constituent Assembly which derived its power and authority from the sovereign people of India. No State could, therefore secede from the Union nor could it *suo motu* vary its territory as laid down in the First Schedule to the Constitution. Dr. Ambedkar said in the Constituent Assembly:

> The Americans had to wage a civil war to establish that the States have no right of secession and that their Federation was indestructible. The Drafting Committee thought that it was better to make it clear at the outset rather than to leave it to speculation or to dispute.

There has been a great deal of discussion on whether or not we are a federation.[1]

Article 2 provides that Parliament may by law admit new States into the Union of India or establish new States on such terms and conditions as it deems fit. The latest addition was that of the State of Sikkim by the 35th and 36th Constitutional Amendments in 1974 and 1975. This was done at the request of the Sikkim Assembly and on approval of the people of Sikkim through a referendum.

The Parliament is empowered under article 3 to form a new State by separating a part of the territory of a State or by uniting two or more States or parts of States or by uniting any territory to a part of any State. It can increase or decrease the area of any State and can also alter the boundaries or even the name of any State. There is thus no guarantee of the territorial integrity or continued existence of any State. But, at the same time, it has been held that the Parliament's

---

1. See under Chapter 4 'Salient Features of the Constitution'.

power to diminish the area of any State does not cover cession of Indian territory to a foreign State.[1] It has, therefore, been aptly said that India is an indestructible Union of destructible States.

There is, of course, a saving clause in the Constitution to protect the right of the States to have a say in regard to the changes in their territories envisaged under article 3. The first condition is that no Bill for the purpose can be introduced in either House of Parliament except on the recommendation of the President. Secondly, where the proposal contained in the Bill affects the area, boundaries or name of any of the States, the Bill must be referred by the President to the Legislatures of the concerned States for expressing opinion thereon. Such an opinion has to be expressed within a period specified by the President. In any case, the views expressed by the State Legislature/s are not binding on the President or Parliament.[2]

Article 4 makes it clear that laws for admission or establishment of new States and alteration of names, areas, boundaries etc. of the existing States under articles 2 and 3 are not to be considered amendments of the Constitution under article 368, *i.e.* these can be passed without resorting to any special procedure and by simple majority, like any other piece of ordinary legislation.

While the Constitution has provided for acquisition of fresh territory, admission and formation of new States etc., there is no provision for cession or transfer of Indian territory.

In re Berubari Union (AIR 1960 S.C. 845) on a Presidential reference, the Supreme Court expressed the opinion that no cession of territory could be made without a constitutional amendment. To give effect to an agreement with Pakistan for transfer of part of the Berubari territory, therefore, the Constitution (Ninth Amendment) Act was passed.

---

1. *In re Berubari Union and Exchange of Enclaves,* AIR 1960 SC 845, 857.
2. *Babulal v. State of Bombay,* AIR 1960 SC 51.

The ease with which the map of India has been redrawn and reorganisation of States effected during the last sixty years bears eloquent testimony to the unique resilience and flexibility of the Constitution and vindicates the need and the justification for articles 2, 3 and 4. On the other hand, there have been strong views expressed on the wisdom or otherwise of the reorganisation of States on linguistic lines. Also, demands for further reorganisation have become an unending phenomenon and there is a body of opinion in favour of a much larger number of small States.

7

CITIZENSHIP

PART II, ARTICLES 5–11

Citizenship constitutes the indispensable foundational principle of democratic polity. It involves the individual's full political membership in the State, his permanent allegiance to the State and the official recognition by the State of his integration into the political system. Citizenship brings certain rights, duties, privileges and obligations that do not belong to aliens. All public offices are open to a citizen, he is eligible for recruitment to all public services. The right to vote and certain fundamental rights are available only to citizens and citizens have obligations like paying taxes, defending the nation etc. Citizenship may also be viewed as the legal relationship between the individual and the State under which the individual pledges his loyalty to the State and the State offers its protection to the individual. This relationship is regulated by national law and recognized by international law.

There existed no concept of Indian citizenship before 26 November 1949 when the Constituent Assembly adopted the Constitution and at once brought into force articles 5 to 9 relating to citizenship. Until then, those of us who lived in British India were under the Crown and as such British subjects governed by the British Nationality Acts and those who came from any of the princely States had the status of British protected persons.

The partition of India and massive migrations created stupendous problems for citizenship determination. Citizenship provisions in the Constitution—articles 5 to 11—gave the Constitution Drafting Committee the maximum headache and took a large number of drafts and more than two years to be finalized. Even then, the Constitution only laid down the law in regard to who would be citizens of India at the time of the commencement of the Constitution. It did not provide for the mode of acquisition and termination of citizenship. Article 11 said that Parliament could regulate the right of citizenship by law. The Indian Citizenship Act passed in 1955 laid down the law for acquisition and termination of Citizenship.

Articles 5–8 conferred citizenship on 'every person' who was covered under one of the following categories at the time of the commencement of the Constitution:

1. domiciled in India and born in India—these formed the bulk of the population of the Union of India;
2. domiciled, not born in India but either of whose parents was born in India;
3. domiciled, not born in India but ordinarily resident for more than five years;
4. resident in India but migrated to Pakistan after 1 March 1947 and later returned to India on resettlement permit;
5. resident in Pakistan but who migrated to India before 19 July 1948 or who came after that date but had resided in India for more than six months and got registered in the prescribed manner;
6. resident outside India but who or either of whose parents or grand parents were born in India.

Thus, Citizenship at the commencement of the Constitution included provisions for Citizenship (i) by domicile (ii) of migrants from and to Pakistan, and (iii) of Indians residing in foreign countries.

***Domicile*:** Domicile is an important criterion for citizenship of any country. Though the term is not defined in the Indian Constitution, domicile ordinarily connotes a person's residence where he intends to live on a permanent basis. Thus, a permanent residence and the intention to reside there indefinitely are two important ingredients constituting 'domicile'.[1] Article 5 provides that a person becomes entitled to the Citizenship of India if, at the commencement of the Constitution, he has his domicile in the territory of India, he or either of his parents were born in India, or he has been ordinarily resident in the territory of India for not less than five years immediately before the commencement of the Constitution.

Domicile by birth or residence as aforesaid can be changed by a person by exercising his choice declaring his intention to reside in some other country for an indefinite period. In fact, citizenship is denoted by domicile and not *vice-versa.* The latter is distinguishable from citizenship inasmuch as it is vitally connected with territory and not membership of the community which is at the root of the notion of citizenship.[2] The Constitution avoids dual citizenship; there is one citizenship related to the domicile in the territory of whole of India and not in a part of it. There is no separate State citizenship as in the U.S.A. Thus, it is not correct to say that a citizen of India is domiciled in one State or another forming part of the Union of India. The domicile which he has is only one domicile, namely, domicile in the territory of India.[3]

***Migrants from Pakistan*:** Article 6 provides for citizenship rights of migrants from Pakistan before the commencement of the Constitution. It makes two types of distinctions among such migrants, *i.e.* those migrating to India before July 19, 1948 when the permit system for migration was introduced

1. *Md. Raza v. State of Bombay,* AIR 1966 SC 1436.
2. *Abdul Rehman v. State,* AIR 1964 Pat. 384.
3. *Pradeep Jain v. Union of India,* AIR 1984 SC 1420, 1984 3 SCC 654.

and those who came after that date. A person who migrated from Pakistan to India before July 19, 1948, shall be deemed to be a citizen of India on the commencement of the Constitution provided he or either of his parents or any of his grandparents was born in India as defined in the Government of India Act, 1935 and he had been ordinarily residing in India since the date of his migration.

The Government of India Act 1935 *vide* its section 311 (1) defined India to mean "British India together with all territories of any Indian ruler under the suzerainty of His Majesty, all territories under the suzerainty of such an Indian ruler, the tribal areas, and any other territories which His Majesty-in-Council may, from time to time, after ascertaining the views of the Federal Government and the Federal Legislature, declare to be part of India."

In *Shanoo Devi V. Mangal Sain* (AIR 1961 SC 58), the Supreme Court had held that the word 'migrated' in article 6 was used in the narrow sense to mean "coming from one place to another with the intention of residing permanently in the latter place". In *Kulathil v. Kerala* (AIR 1966 SC 1614), the Supreme Court overruled its earlier judgement and held that 'migrated' was used in the wider sense to mean "coming from one place to another".

In the case of one migrating after July 19, 1948, he should have been registered as citizen of India by an officer appointed for the purpose by the Government of India. But, in the latter case, no person shall be so registered unless he has been residing in India for at least six months immediately preceding the date of his application.

***Migrants to Pakistan*:** Article 7 makes special provisions regarding the citizenship rights of persons who migrated to Pakistan after March 1, 1947 but returned to India subsequently. While it has been made clear that any person migrating to Pakistan after March 1, 1947 ceased to be a citizen of India, an exception has been made in the case of those returning to India on the basis of permits for resettlement in India. Such persons became entitled to be citizens of India if they fulfilled the conditions stipulated for migrants from Pakistan provided under article 6. It is necessary that in such cases too the visits of the migrants must not be for short or limited periods or be of a temporary nature for purposes of business or otherwise.[1] It is well to remember that the "migration" referred to in this article connotes migration before the commencement of the Constitution. Cases pertaining to the period thereafter are to be governed by the Citizenship Act, 1955. Also, "migrated" has been defined to mean voluntarily going over to Pakistan from India permanently or temporarily.[2]

Persons of Indian origin residing outside India: Several persons of Indian origin have been residing in foreign countries or have been migrating there for purposes of employment or otherwise. The founding fathers were far sighted enough to have made provisions in the Constitution to protect the citizenship rights of such persons in India. Article 8 thus provides that any person who or either of whose parents or grandparents was born in India as defined in the Government of India Act, 1935 and who is ordinarily residing in any country outside India shall be deemed to be a citizen of India if he has been registered as an Indian citizen by the diplomatic or consular representative of India in that country on an application made by him in the prescribed form to such diplomatic or consular representative, whether before or after the commencement of the Constitution. Thus article 8 takes care of the future citizenship needs of all Indians residing abroad.

Voluntary acquisition of citizenship of another country: Article 9 provides that if a person has voluntarily acquired the citizenship of a foreign State he shall forfeit the right of

---

1. *State v. Amar Singh*, AIR 1955 SC 282; *Ataur Rahman v. State of Madhya Pradesh*, AIR 1951 Nag. 44.
2. *Kultahil Mammu v. State of Kerala*, AIR 1966 SC 1974.

citizenship of India. While this was applicable to cases arising before the commencement of the Constitution, the cases arising after such commencement were to be dealt with in accordance with the provisions of the Citizenship Act, 1955. It has been held by the Supreme Court that the question whether a person has lost the citizenship of India on acquiring the citizenship of another country has to be determined by the Government of India and only after it has decided the matter can a State Government deal with him as an alien. If the question arises during the proceedings before a court of law, the court also has to await determination of the issue by the Government of India. The mere fact that a person has obtained a passport from a foreign country is not enough for deportation or prosecution.[1]

***Continuance of Citizenship rights*:** Article 10 provides that every person who is or is deemed to be a citizen of India under any of the provisions in articles 5 to 10 shall continue to be a citizen of India, subject to the provisions of any law that may be made by Parliament. In other words, it means that the right of citizenship cannot be taken away from a citizen except through express parliamentary legislation.[2]

The term 'every person' used in articles 5 and 10 has been interpreted to cover persons who may be in jail under trial or who may be undergoing imprisonment.[3] Subject to Parliament's powers under article 33, members of the armed

1. *Kulathil Mammu v. State of Kerala,* AIR 1966 SC 1614, 1617; *State of U.P. v. Rehmatullah* (1971) 2 SCC 113, 118, AIR 1971 SC 1382; *Government of Andhra Pradesh v. Syed Mohammad,* AIR 1962 SC 1778; *State of U.P. v. Roshan,* (1969) 2 SCWR 232; *State of Gujarat v. Ibrahim,* AIR 1974 SC 645; *Ayub Khan v. Commissioner of Police,* (1965) 2 SCR 884; *Moinuddin v. Government of India* (1967) 2 SCR 401; *Akbar v. Union of India,* AIR 1962 SC 70; *State of M.P. v. Peer Mohammad,* AIR 1963 SC 645; *Izhar Ahmed v. Union of India,* AIR 1962 SC 1052; *Anwar v. State of J&K* (1971) 3 SCC 104.
2. *Ebrahim Wazir v. State of Bombay,* AIR 1954 SC 229.
3. *State of Maharashtra v. Prabhakar,* AIR 1966 SC 424; *Sunil Batra v. Delhi Administration,* AIR 1978 SC 1675.

forces are also included.[1] For some time, there were sharp differences on whether corporations were also covered as legal persons. The Citizenship Act, however made it clear that corporations were not citizens. The Supreme Court also said that the corporations could not claim rights under article 19 which were for citizens only.[2]

Parliament's power to regulate right of Citizenship by law and the Citizenship Act, 1955: Article 11 endows Parliament with unfettered powers for enacting legislation pertaining to the acquisition and termination of the citizenship of India and all matters connected therewith. Parliament accordingly passed the Citizenship Act, 1955 providing for the acquisition and termination of citizenship. Thus, all matters relating to the citizenship rights, after the commencement of the Constitution are to be dealt with in accordance with its provisions. This Act was amended in 1986 to tackle the situation created by the large-scale unlawful immigration into India of persons from Bangladesh, Sri Lanka and some African countries. The amendment made the acquisition of Indian citizenship more stringent. Broadly, the amended section 3 of the principal Act provided that citizenship by birth could be acquired by a person only if either of his parents was a citizen of India at the time of birth. Besides, the Act made detailed provisions for acquisition of Indian citizenship by birth, descent, registration, naturalisation or through incorporation of territory. Likewise, it provided for termination of citizenship by way of renunciation, voluntary acquisition of citizenship of another country, or through compulsory deprivation by the Government of India on certain grounds. The Act also made specific provisions regarding Commonwealth Citizenship.

Briefly, the Citizenship Act 1955 provided that

1. *Prithi v. Union of India*, AIR 1982 SC 1413.
2. *State Trading Corporation v. Commercial Tax Officer*, (1964) 4 SCR 99; *Tata Engineering and Locomotive Co. Ltd. v. Bihar* (1964) 6 SCR 885.

a. a person born in India after 26 January 1950 would, subject to certain exceptions—like those of children of diplomats and of enemy aliens—be a citizen of India by birth;
b. anyone born outside India after 26 January 1950, subject to certain requirements, would be a citizen of India if his father was an Indian citizen, at the time of his birth;
c. under certain conditions, certain category of persons could acquire Indian citizenship by registration in the prescribed manner;
d. foreigners could acquire Indian citizenship on application for naturalization on certain conditions;
e. if any territory became part of India, the Government of India could by order specify the persons who would become citizens of India as a result thereof;
f. citizenship could be lost by termination, renunciation or deprivation on certain grounds;
g. a citizen of a Commonwealth country would have the status of a Commonwealth citizen in India. Government could make suitable provisions on the basis of reciprocity.

While the Act has been amended from time to time in important respects, the most fundamental changes came in 2003 and 2005. Under Amendment Acts of 2003 and 2005 provisions have been made *inter alia* for maintenance of a national register of Indian citizens and for 'Overseas Citizenship of India' for certain categories of persons of Indian origin settled in other countries and enjoying their citizenship. A person of Indian origin, subject to certain conditions, may be registered as an overseas citizen of India by the Government of India and extended some of the citizenship rights like owning property, traveling to India without visa, making investment in business etc. However, overseas citizens shall not be entitled to vote at elections or be candidates for high elective offices of the State nor can they be appointed as judges or to public services or claim equality of opportunity in matters of public employment.

The provision of double citizenship to "overseas citizens of India" applies only to those in some specified countries. These are Australia, Canada, Finland, France, Greece, Ireland, Israel, Italy, Netherlands, New Zealand, Portugal, Republic of Cyprus, Sweden, Switzerland, United Kingdom and United States of America.[1]

It is important to remember in regard to the citizenship provisions in the Constitution and the law that it was in keeping with the aim of building an integrated Indian nation and a united fraternity that the constitution-makers decided to provide for a single Indian Citizenship. All citizens irrespective of the State in which they were born have the same rights and duties all over the country without any discrimination subject only to a few special protections in case of Jammu & Kashmir, tribal areas etc. and the power of Parliament under article 16 to prescribe residence within a State or Union Territory as a necessary qualification for certain classes of employment under that State or Union Territory.[2]

---

1. For details see Subhash C. Kashyap, *Constitutional Law of India*, Universal, New Delhi, 2008, Vol. I, pp. 394-400 and ——, *Concise Encyclopedia of Indian Constitution*, Vision, New Delhi, 2009, pp. 328-29.
2. For a study of citizenship values under the Constitution, see Subhash C. Kashyap, *Citizen and the Constitution*, Pub. Div, Min. I&B, G.O.I., New Delhi, 2nd ed. 2002.

8

FUNDAMENTAL RIGHTS

PART III, ARTICLES 12–35

Representing the crystallization of the values and concepts held dear in India's varied and rich cultural heritage and having its roots deep in the motivational forces of the national struggle for independence, the formulation of a bill of rights was among the first tasks to which the Constituent Assembly addressed itself. A comprehensive charter of rights was soon evolved through various stages in the Assembly and its Committees. Described by Dr. Ambedkar as "the most criticized part" of the Constitution, Part III dealing with the fundamental rights was discussed for as many as 38 days—11 in the Sub-Committee, 2 in the Advisory Committee and 25 in the Constituent Assembly. Coming closely on the heels of the Universal Declaration of Human Rights, inclusion of a bill of rights in the Constitution of India accorded with the contemporary democratic and humanitarian temper and constitutional practice in other nations of the world. It reflected in no small measure the anxiety of the founding fathers to incorporate and implement the basic principles enunciated in the Universal Declaration. Also, incorporation of a Charter of Fundamental Rights in our Constitution became necessary in view of the special problem of minorities and the need to assure them of the fullest protection of their rights.

The Fundamental Rights incorporated in Part III, the Directive Principles in Part IV and the Fundamental Duties in Part IVA added later actually constitute one organic whole which follows from the Preamble. Taken together, they really proclaim the fundamental values and constitute the foundational principles of the Constitution. Thus, the preambular assurance of the dignity of the individual, which in fact happens to be the basic principle underlying the Universal Declaration of Human Rights, is sought to be implemented through various provisions of Parts III and IV. The values of freedom and equality befitting the dignity of the human individual, made more complete and substantive by ideals of economic and social justice, so eloquently proclaimed by the Preamble, are elaborated in the Fundamental Rights and the Directive Principles.

Part III of the Constitution which contains perhaps one of the most elaborate charters of human rights yet framed by any State, consistent with the aim of the unity of the nation and the interests of the public at large, has been described by Justice Gajendragadkar as the "very foundation and cornerstone of the democratic way of life ushered in this country by the Constitution".[1] These fundamental rights substantially cover all the traditional civil and political rights enumerated in articles 2 to 21 of the Universal Declaration. According to Justice Bhagwati:

> These fundamental rights represent the basic values cherished by the people of this country since the Vedic times and they are calculated to protect the dignity of the individual and create conditions in which every human being can develop his personality to the fullest extent. They weave a 'pattern of guarantee' on the basic structure of human rights and impose negative obligations on the State not to encroach on individual liberty in its various dimensions.[2]

1. *Sajjan Singh v. State of Rajasthan,* AIR 1965 SC 845.
2. *Maneka Gandhi v. Union of India,* AIR 1978 SC 597.

The fundamental rights have been guaranteed under six broad categories, namely,

i. the right to equality including equality before law and the equal protection of laws (article 14), prohibition of discrimination on grounds of religion, race, caste, sex, or place of birth (article 15), equality of opportunity in matters of public employment (article 16); and abolition of untouchability and the system of titles (articles 17 and 18);
ii. the right to freedom including the right to protection of life and personal liberty (article 21), and the right to freedom of speech and expression, assembly, association or union, movement and to reside and settle in any part of India, and the right to practise any profession or occupation (article 19).
iii. the right against exploitation, prohibiting all forms of forced labour, child labour and traffic in human beings (articles 23 and 24);
iv. the right to freedom of conscience and free profession, practice and propagation of religion (articles 25 to 28);
v. the right of minorities to conserve their culture, language and script and to establish and administer educational institutions of their choice (articles 29 and 30);
vi. the right to constitutional remedies for the enforcement of all these Fundamental Rights (article 32).

Some of the fundamental rights like 'equality before law and equal protection of all laws' (article 14), protection in respect of conviction for offences (article 20), protection of life and personal liberty (article 21), free and compulsory education for all children of 6-14 years (article 21A) protection against arrest and detention in certain cases (article 22), freedom of religion (articles 25 28) etc. are available to all 'persons'. There are, however, some rights which can be claimed only by the citizens *e.g.* not to be discriminated on grounds of religion, race, caste, sex or place of birth (article 15), equality of opportunity in the matter of public employment (article 16) and freedom of speech and expression, assembly, association, movement, residence and profession (article 19).

Originally, article 19(1)(f) and article 31 contained the right to property *i.e.* to acquire, hold and dispose of property subject to the right of the State to compulsory acquisition for public purpose by authority of law. However, right to property ceased to be a fundamental right when the Constitution (Forty-fourth Amendment) Act, 1978 omitted sub-clause(f) of clause (1) of article 19 and the whole of article 31 from the Constitution.

Articles 31A and 31B inserted by the First Constitutional Amendment and article 31C inserted by the Twenty-fifth Amendment sought to protect laws providing for acquisition of estates, Acts and regulations specified in the Ninth Schedule and laws giving effect to Directive Principles.

Articles 33 35 deal with the power of Parliament to modify the rights conferred by Part III of the Constitution in their application to forces.

It is true that the fundamental human rights enshrined in the Constitution of India are hedged in by many limitations and restrictions. Replying to the criticism that the Fundamental Rights were riddled with so many restrictions that no value could be attached to them and referring in particular to critics who had relied on the U.S. Constitution in support of their contention that Fundamental Rights were not 'fundamental' unless they were also 'absolute', Dr. Ambedkar had observed in the Constituent Assembly on November 4, 1948 as follows:

> The whole of the criticism about fundamental rights is based upon a misconception. In the first place, the criticism in so far as it seeks to distinguish fundamental rights from non-fundamental rights is not sound. It is incorrect to say that fundamental rights are absolute while non-fundamental rights are not absolute. The real distinction between the two is that non-fundamental rights are created by agreement between parties while fundamental rights

> are the gift of the law. Because fundamental rights are the gift of the State it does not follow that the State cannot qualify them. In the second place, it is wrong to say that fundamental rights in America are absolute... The Supreme Court invented the doctrine of police power and refuted the advocates of absolute fundamental rights by the argument that every State has inherent in it police power which is not required to be conferred on it expressly by the Constitution...There is really no difference in the result. What one does directly, the other does indirectly. In both cases, the fundamental rights are not absolute.

The fundamental rights secured to the individual are in the nature of limitations or restrictions on the actions of the State. As Patanjali Sastry, Chief Justice, said:

> The whole object of Part III of the Constitution is to provide protection for the freedoms and rights mentioned therein against arbitrary invasion by the State. *(State of West Bengal v. Subodh Gopal Bose,* AIR 1954 SC 92).

The Supreme Court has, however come to believe that fundamental rights are not only 'negative' or 'against the state' but also have a positive content inasmuch as they cast certain responsibilities on the state. This, in a way, has heralded the beginning of what has come to be regarded as 'judicial activism' with its by-product of public interest litigation.[1]

Described by Dr. S. Radhakrishnan "as a pledge to our people and a pact with the civilized world", the fundamental rights are made binding on the State, *i.e.* the executive as well as the legislature.

Article 13(2) declares all laws and executive orders in force immediately before the commencement of the

---

1. *Sunil Batra v. Delhi Administration,* AIR 1978 SC 1675; AIR 1980 SC 1579; *Maneka Gandhi v. Union of India,* AIR 1978 SC 597; *Hussainara v. State of Bihar,* AIR 1979 SC 1369; *Sher Singh v. State of Punjab,* AIR 1983 SC 465. Also see under the chapter on 'Judiciary'.

Constitution, inconsistent with the fundamental rights to be *ultra vires* and void to the extent of such inconsistency. It also says:

> The state shall not make any law which takes away or abridges the rights conferred by this part and any law made in contravention of this clause shall to the extent of contravention be void.

The article thus provides for judicial review of all legislation in India whether past or present through acts done before the commencement of the Constitution in contravention of the provisions of any law which becomes void by virtue of Part III, are not affected retrospectively.[1] In *R.C. Cooper v. Union of India* (AIR 1973 SC 106), the Supreme Court expressed the view that the State action must be adjudged in the light of its operation upon the rights of the individual and group of individuals in all its dimensions.

Clause (4) of article 13 makes it clear that the term "law" in that article does not cover constitutional amendments made under article 368 and therefore validity of a constitutional amendment cannot be questioned on the ground of its being violative of fundamental rights unless a fundamental right is held to be part of the basic feature, of the Constitution.[2]

Under article 12, "the State" includes (i) the Government and Parliament of India, (ii) the Government and the Legislature of each of the States, (iii) all local authorities like municipalities, district boards, Panchayats, Improvement Trusts etc. and (iv) other authorities within the territory of India or under the control of the Government of India. The last category "other authorities" naturally posed some difficulties. However, it has been held to include many authorities created by the Constitution or statute on whom

---

1. *Habeeb Mohd. v. State of Hyderabad,* AIR 1953 SC 287.
2. See chapter 21 'Amendment of the Constitution'.

powers are conferred by law, *e.g.* Rajasthan Electricity Board, Cochin Devasom Board, Children Aid Scoeity, *etc.* The Life Insurance Corporation, the Oil and Natural Gas Commission, the Delhi Transport Corporation, the Airports Authority and the Finance Commission have similarly been held to be 'State' under article 12.[1] Even a private body, it has been held, may be "State" covered by the term "other authorities" if it is entrusted with some public service responsibility as an agency or instrumentality of the State.[2]

On the other hand, the Supreme Court in *Sabhajit Tewary v. India* (AIR 1975 SC 1329) held that a body like the Council of Scientific and Industrial Research, registered under the Societies Registration Act, was not a 'state'. In another case, a registered society (Regional Engineering College) was held to be an 'authority' for purposes of article 12. Justice P.N. Bhagwati said:

> The mandate of a corporation may be adopted in order to free the Government from the inevitable constraints of red tapism and slow motion but by doing so, the Government cannot be allowed to play truant with the basic human rights. Otherwise, it would be the easiest thing for the Government to assign to a plurality of corporations almost every State business such as Post and Telegraph, TV and Radio, Rail Road and Telephone—in short every economic activity—and thereby cheat the people of India out of the Fundamental Rights guaranteed to them.[3]

Earlier in *Raman D. Shetty v. International Airports Authority* (AIR 1979 SC 1628), the Supreme Court holding the Airports Authority in the category of "other authorities"

---

1. *Electricity Board, Rajasthan v. Mohan Lal,* AIR 1967 SC 1857; *P.B.M. Namboodiripad v. Cochin Devasom Board,* AIR 1956 SC 19; *D.T.C. v. Mazdoor Congress,* AIR 1991 SC 101; *Sukhdev v. Bhagat Ram,* AIR 1975 SC 1331.
2. *Star Enterprises v. City & Industrial Dev. Corp. Maharashtra* (1990) 3SCC 280.
3. *Ajay Hasia v. Khalid Mujib,* AIR 1981 SC 481.

propounded the proposition that an 'instrumentality' or 'agency' of the Government would be regarded as an 'authority' or 'state' and also laid down some tests to examine the question. For example, the Courts may examine whether the body in question is wholly controlled by the Government in carrying out its functions. Is the entire share capital owned by the Government? Is the administration of the body controlled by the directors appointed by the Government and whether they are subject to Government control? Does the state exercise deep and pervasive control over the body? Or, does it enjoy monopoly status conferred or protected by the state? And so on. The list is not exhaustive but each case has to be decided by the Courts on whether the body in question falls within the purview of article 12. In regard to 'judiciary', the Supreme Court has held that even if a court is treated as 'state' a writ under article 12 cannot be issued to a High Court of competent jurisdiction against its judicial orders, because such orders cannot be said to violate the fundamental rights.[1]

The National Commission to Review the Working of the Constitution (2002), among others, recommended that:

(i) freedom of the press should be specifically mentioned as a fundamental right,
(ii) truth should be made admissible as a defence in contempt of court cases,
(iii) those deprived of life or liberty should have an enforceable right to compensation,
(iv) law must ensure the right to rural wage employment for a minimum of 80 days in a year,
(v) right of access to Courts and Tribunals should be guaranteed to everyone and should include the right to reasonably speedy and effective justice,

---

1. *Naresh v. State of Maharashtra*, AIR 1967 SC 1; *Tejinder Singh v. Petroleum Corp.* (1986) 4 SCC 237; *State of Punjab v. Raja Ram*, (1981) 2 SCC 66; *Som Prakash v. Union of India*, AIR 1981 SC 212. See also Subhash C. Kashyap, *Constitutional Law of India*, Universal, New Delhi, 2008, Vol. I, pp. 401-425.

(vi) right to equal justice and free legal aid should become fundamental rights,
(vii) every child should have the right to care and assistance and the right of free education upto 14 years of age,
(viii) every one should be guaranteed safe drinking water, protection of environment, prevention of pollution and ecological degradation, promotion of conservation, use of natural resources etc.

RIGHT TO EQUALITY

Equality before the law or Equal protection of the laws: Article 14 of the Constitution enunciates the fundamental right of every person not to be denied "equality before the law" or the "equal protection of the laws" within the territory of India. Here the protection provided by the article is not limited to citizens only but is applicable to all persons. It embodies the principle contained in the Universal Declaration of Human Rights that "All are equal before the law and are entitled without discrimination to equal protection of the law". The two expressions "equality before the law" and "equal protection of the laws" used in our Constitution, in fact, embody the concepts of the rule of law and of equal justice. 'Law' in singular in the term 'equality before the law' means what Dicey meant by rule of law or the concept of law or of justice including the principle that no one is above law, that there is absolute supremacy of law as opposed to arbitrary power of Government and that there is one system of law and Courts for all. The word 'laws' in plural in the term 'equal protection of the laws', on the other hand, clearly refers to statute law and the provision thereby enjoins the State to ensure that the laws that are made should provide equal protection to all without any distinction *i.e.* the laws passed by the legislature and their implementation by the executive should lead to non-discriminatory and equal protection to all. However, there has been no occasion for

Dr. Rajendra Prasad, President of the Constituent Assembly, signs the Constitution.

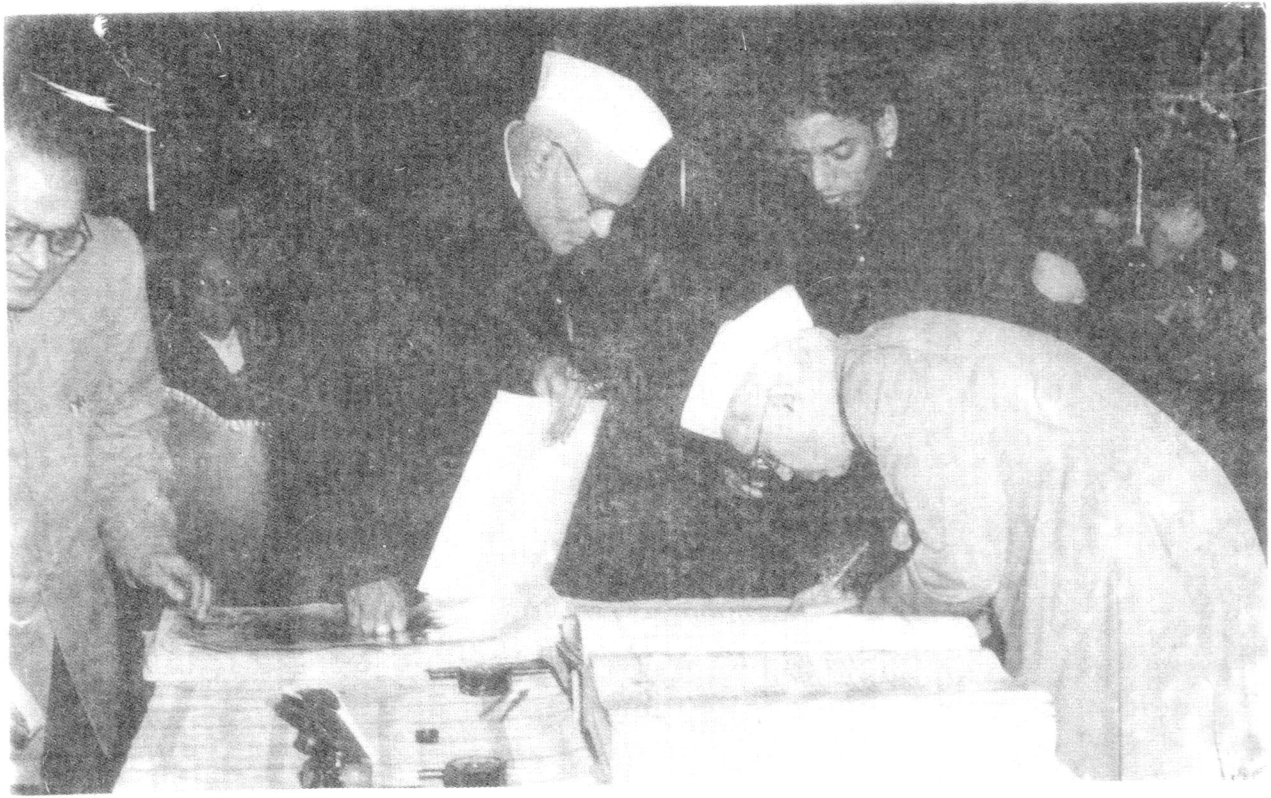

Pandit Jawaharlal Nehru signs the Constitution as Shri K.M. Munshi (left) looks on.

Maulana Abul Kalam Azad and Pandit Jawaharlal Nehru at a session of the Constituent Assembly.

Sardar Baldev Singh, Pandit Jawaharlal Nehru and others at the midnight session of the Constituent Assembly, 14/15 August, 1947.

the Supreme Court to enunciate or appreciate any such distinction. In fact, it has been observed by Patanjali Sastri, Chief Justice, that the second expression is really a corollary of the first and it is difficult to imagine a situation in which the violation of the equal protection of the laws will not be the violation of the equality before the law. It is quite conceivable that there are laws which violate the 'rule of law' or 'equality before law' principles. The founding fathers had not obviously forgotten what Gandhi meant by 'lawless laws'.[1]

The guiding principle underlying article 14 is that all persons and things similarly circumstanced shall be treated alike both in privileges conferred and liabilities imposed. Laws should be applied to all in the same condition.[2]

Not only should the laws be non-discriminatory for persons in the same condition but the processes of implementation by the administrative agencies should also not discriminate between them.[3]

The Supreme Court has held that the varying needs of different classes of persons often require separate treatment. Those who are not equal are not only allowed to be treated unequally but they have got to be so treated.[4] The maxim of equality before the law therefore leads to the inevitability of classification. For, article 14 applies where equals are treated differently without any reasonable basis. Where equals and unequals are treated differently, it does not apply. It thus forbids only class legislation but not reasonable classification. But it is necessary that the classification must not be "arbitrary, artificial or evasive" and should be based on some

1. *State of West Bengal v. Anwar Ali Sarkar,* AIR 1952 SC 75.
2. *B.C. & Co. v. Union of India,* AIR 1973 SC 106.
3. *Indian Express Newspapers v. Union of India,* AIR 1986 SC 319; *Iron and Metal Traders v. Jaskiel,* AIR 1984 SC 629; *G.J. Fernandez v. State of Karnataka,* AIR 1990 SC 958.
4. *St. Stephens' v. University of Delhi,* (1992) 1 SCC 558; *Chiranji Lal v. Union of India,* AIR 1951 SC 41, as per Das J).

real and substantive distinction bearing a just and reasonable relation to the object sought to be achieved by the legislation.[1] It can be based on the basis of geography or other objects or occupation.[2] Permissible classification, to be valid, must in fact fulfil two conditions, namely, (i) the classification must be founded on an intelligent differentia which distinguishes persons or things that are grouped together from others left out of the group, and (ii) the differentia must have a rational relation to the object sought to be achieved by the statute in question.[2] The test was followed in several cases since then, *e.g. Chiranji Lal v. Union of India,* AIR 1951 SC 41; *Budhan Choudhary v. State,* AIR 1955 SC 191; *Ramkrishna Dalmia v. Justice Tendulkar,* AIR 1958 SC 538; *Prabodh Verma v. State of U.P.* (1984) 4 SCC 251; *Atam Prakash v. State of Haryana,* AIR 1986 SC 859; *Rajpal Sharma v. State of Haryana* (1985) Supp. SCC 72, 75.

In *E.P. Royappa v. State of Tamil Nadu (*AIR 1974 SC 555) the traditional concept of equality was challenged and a new approach to the right of equality under article 14 was propounded when Justice Chandrachud, and Justice Krishna Iyer observed:

> Equality is a dynamic concept with many aspects and dimensions and it cannot be 'cribbed, cabined and confined' within traditional and doctrinaire limits. From a positivistic point of view, equality is antithetic to arbitrariness. In fact, equality and arbitrariness are sworn enemies; one belongs to the rule of law in a republic while the other, to the whim and caprice of an absolute monarch. Wheere an act is arbitrary, it is implicit that it is unequal both according to political logic and constitutional law and is therefore violation of article 14.

---

1. *R.K. Garg v. Union of India,* AIR 1981 SC 2138; *Prabhakar Rao v. State of Andhra Pradesh,* AIR 1986 SC 210.
2. *Shashi Mohan v. State of West Bengal,* AIR 1958 SC 194.
3. Das, J. in *State of West Bengal v. Anwar Ali Sarkar,* AIR 1952 SC 75.

Justice P.N. Bhagwati, concurring with this approach, speaking for himself and Justice Krishna Iyer observed:

> Article 14 enunciates a vital principle which lies at the core of our republicanism and shines like a beacon light towards the goal of classless egalitarian socio-economic order which we promised to build for ourselves when we made a tryst with destiny on that fateful day when we adopted our Constitution. If we have to choose between fanatical devotion to this great principle of equality and feeble allegiance to it, we would unhesitatingly prefer to err on the side of the former as against the latter.

He went on to say:

> What the equality clause is intended to strike at are real and substantial disparities and arbitrary and capricious actions of the executive and it would be contrary to the object and intendment of the equality clause to exalt delicate distinctions, shades of harshness and theoretical possibilities of prejudice into legislative inequality or executive discrimination. (*M. Chhaganlal v. Greater Bombay Municipality*, AIR 1974 SC 2009, 2029 and 2039).

In later judgements[1] Justice Bhagwati became more forthright in his approach to article 14 which received unanimous approval of a Constitution Bench of the Court in the following words:

> It must...now be taken to be well settled that what article 14 strikes at is arbitrariness because an action that is arbitrary, must necessarily involve negation of equality. The doctrine of classification which is evolved by the courts is not paraphrase of article 14 nor is it the objective and end of that article. It is merely a judicial formula for determining whether the legislative or executive action in question is arbitrary and therefore constituting denial of

1. *Maneka Gandhi v. Union of India*, AIR 1978 SC 597; *Ramana Dayaram Shetty v. International Airports Authority*, AIR 1979 SC 1628; and *Ajay Hasia v. Khalid Mujib*, AIR 1981 SC 487.

> equality. If the classification is not reasonable and does not satisfy the two conditions referred to above, (of (i) intelligible differentia and (ii) rational relationship between the differentia and the object sought) the impugned legislation or executive action would plainly be arbitrary and the guarantee of equality under article 14 would be breached. Wherever, therefore, there is arbitrariness in state action whether it be of the legislative or of the executive or of an 'authority' under article 12, article 14 immediately springs into action and strikes down such State action." (AIR 1981 SC 487).

Thus, the approach propounded by the Supreme Court has widened the scope of application of article 14.[1] It is clear that an arbitrary or unreasonable action—any act which is so arbitrary or unreasonable that no fair minded authority could ever have made it—would be *per se* discriminatory and violative of article 14.[2]

Non-discrimination on grounds of religion, race, caste, sex or place of birth

While article 14 covers all persons and proclaims the general principle of equality before the law and equal protection of the laws, the subsequent articles 15 to 18 specify some areas for application of the general principle mostly in regard to the citizens of India.[3]

Article 15 is available only to citizens and enjoins the state not to discriminate against any citizen on grounds only of religion, caste, race, sex, place of birth or any of them. The use of the word "only" is significant. A discrimination based on one or more of these grounds and also on other ground or grounds would not be affected by the article[4], nor would

1. *A.L. Kalra v. Project and Equipment Corporation,* (1984) 3 SCC 316, 328.
2. *Shri Sita Ram Sugar Co. Ltd. v. Union of India,* AIR 1990 SC 1277.
3. *State of Sikkim v. S.P. Sharma,* JT (1994) 3SC 372.
4. *Dattatraya v. State of Bombay,* AIR 1953 BOM 311.

discrimination based on residence be invalidated[1]

Clause (2) of the article provides for special application of the injunction which declares that no citizen shall, on grounds only of religion, race, caste, sex, place of birth or any of them, be subjected to any disability, liability, restriction or condition with regard to (a) access to shops, public restaurants, hotels and places of public entertainment, or (b) the use of wells, tanks, bathing ghats, roads and places of public resort maintained wholly or partly out of State funds or dedicated to the use of the general public. The prohibition obviously covers actions both on the part of the State as well as the citizens at large.

Clauses (3), (4) and (5) of article 15 embody exceptions to the general principles of non-discrimination. They respectively empower the State to make special provisions for women and children and for the advancement of any socially and educationally backward classes of citizens or for the Scheduled Castes and Scheduled Tribes. The 93rd constitutional amendment assented to by the President on 20 January 2006 – added the new clause (5) which empowers Parliament to make special provisions by law for socially and educationally backward classes and for Scheduled Castes and Scheduled Tribes in regard to admission to educational institutions including private aided or unaided institutions other than minority institutions. The pronouncements of the Supreme Court on the validity of certain measures for protection of these sections of the society amply bear out the need and justification for these exceptions.[2] However, inspite of these special provisions, it has been held that the general prohibition under article 14 would nevertheless apply to such cases also; the special

1. See *D.P. Joshi v. State of Madhya Bharat*, AIR 1955 SC 334.
2. See *Yusuf Abdul Aziz v. State of Bombay*, AIR 1954 SC 321; *Girdhar v. State*, AIR 1953 MB 147; *State of Madras v. Champakam Dorairajan*, AIR 1951 SC 226.

provisions which the State makes should not be arbitrary or unreasonable.[1]

The biggest problem raised by article 15(4) and (5) is regarding determination of who constitute the "socially and educationally backward classes". The Constitution does not define the term. Various factors would naturally come into play in evolving proper criteria for such determination. As held by the Supreme Court, the caste of a person cannot be the sole test for ascertaining whether a particular class is a backward class or not. In *Chitralekha v. Mysore* (AIR 1964 SC 1823) it ruled that though caste may be a relevant circumstance in ascertaining the backwardness of a class, there is nothing to preclude the authority concerned from determining the special backwardness of a group of citizens if it can do so without reference to caste. In another case the Supreme Court held that "caste and poverty may be both relevant for determining the backwardness. But neither caste alone nor poverty alone could be the determining test".[2]

Reservations for OBCs

The question of reservations on grounds of social and educational backwardness has assumed great significance and received considerable political attention in recent years. Intense pressure has been exerted for providing reservations for various classes and groups besides the Scheduled Castes and Scheduled Tribes. It is important to remember that while in the cases of the Scheduled Castes and the Scheduled Tribes, reservation is provided in legislative seats also, the reservations for OBCs as at present are intended to be confined to Government jobs and admission to educational institutions.

---

1. See *N. Vasundara v. State of Mysore,* AIR 1971 SC 1439; *State of Sikkim v. S.P. Sharma,* JT (1994) 3SC 372; *V.A. Sawant v. Municipal Corp. Bombay,* JT (1994) 3 SC 573; *State of A.P. v, Balram,* AIR 1972 SC 1375; *Jayashree v. State of Kerala,* AIR 1976 SC 2381.
2. *K.S. Jaysree v. Kerala,* AIR 1976 SC 2381; Also see *Chhotey Lal v. Uttar Pradesh,* AIR 1979 All. 135.

It must be acknowledged that basically any reservation would be discriminatory for it would violate the principle of equality and give a lower priority to merit, thus causing frustration to many a deserving candidate. The validity of any reservation could therefore be tested on whether it was based on any rational and relevant criteria.

From time to time, the Supreme Court has indicated the types of classification which would be discriminatory. The Uttar Pradesh Government had made reservation of seats for admission to Medical Colleges in the State in favour of candidates hailing from the rural areas, Hill and Uttarakhand areas. The Supreme Court in *State of U.P. v. Pradeep Tandon* (AIR 1975 SC 563) held that while reservation for candidates coming from rural areas was unconstitutional, for those coming from the Hill and Uttarakhand areas was valid. It observed that these areas were instances of socially and educationally backward-class citizens. It held that reservation for 80 per cent of the State's population which was in 'rural areas' could not be a homogenous class by itself. Likewise, the Supreme Court declared the fixation of district-wise quota on the ratio of district population to the total population of the State as discriminatory.[1] In the *Chandhala case,* however, university-wise allocation of seats for admission to Medical Colleges in the State of Kerala was held to be valid.[2] Since then it has been decided to cover certain castes under the expression "socially and educationally backward classes" and provide reservations to them subject to total reservations not exceeding 50 per cent. In fact, in some states this quota is allowed to exceed 50 per cent by legislation *e.g.* in Tamilnadu and Karnataka.

From time to time, the Supreme Court has indicated the types of classification which would be discriminatory.

1. *P. Rajendran v. Madras,* AIR 1971 SC 2303.
2. *D.N. Chandhala v. Mysore,* AIR 1971 SC 1762; Also see *Ajay Kumar v. State of Bihar,* JT (1994) 3SC 662 holding reservation in medical colleges valid.

In *P.A.Inamdar and others v. State of Maharashtra* the Supreme Court in its judgement of August 2005 abolished state quotas in private unaided professional colleges. This was followed by the government bringing forth before Parliament a Bill to amend the Constitution and the Constitution was amended for the 93rd time. Taking advantage of the constitutional amendment, the Union Government brought forth a legislation for reservation of seats not exceeding 50% in all for the socially and educationally backward classes and Scheduled Castes and Scheduled Tribes in institutions of higher learning and professional institutes like IIMs, IITs and Medical colleges including private ones whether aided or unaided. However, provision of reservation was not to apply to minority institutions.

The legislation[1] generated a great deal of controversy, tension and protests particularly from the medical colleges, IITs, Management Institutes and other professional institutions. It is to be noted that the 93rd Amendment – article 15(5) – does not specifically provide for 'reservation' as such. It is only an enabling provision which empowers the legislature to lay down by law 'special provisions' in the matter of admission to 'educational institutions'. There is no particular mention of institutions of higher learning, universities or professional institutions as such. Educational institutions could also mean primary and secondary schools. Also, the 'special measures' could mean several measures other than reservation. In fact, article 15(4) already provided for 'any special provision for the advancement of any socially and educationally backward classes of citizens or for the Scheduled Castes and the Scheduled Tribes'. Article 15(5) practically reproduces this provision with the addition of a specific reference to admission to educational institutions – aided or unaided – and to pointedly exclude minority institutions from the effect of the special provision.

---

1. Central Educational Institutions (Reservation in Admission) Act 2006.

On 10 April 2008, the Supreme Court delivering its judgement in *Ashok Thakur v. Union of India*, put its stamp of approval on 27% reservations for OBCs in educational institutions subject to exclusion of creamy layer and a review of the quota every five years.

Equality of Opportunity in Public Employment

Under clauses (1) and (2) of article 16, all citizens of India are guaranteed equality of opportunity in matters relating to employment or appointment to any office under the State and no citizen can be discriminated against or be ineligible for any employment or office under the State on grounds only of religion, race, caste, sex, descent, place of birth or residence. The subsequent clauses (3), (4), (4A), (4B) and (5) however provide for situations when departures can be made from the general rule of equality of opportunity for, in effect, implementing the essence of the principle of equality of opportunity. Thus, under clause (3), Parliament has been empowered to regulate the extent to which it would be permissible for a State or Union Territory to depart from or expand or supplement the general principles enunciated in clauses (1) and (2). By virtue of this power, Parliament passed the Public Employment (Requirement as to residence) Act, 1957 which while repealing all the laws in force prescribing any requirement as to residence within a State or Union Territory for any public employment, provided that no one will be disqualified on the ground that one is not the resident of a particular State. The Act, however, made an exception in the case of Himachal Pradesh, Manipur, Tripura and the Telengana Area of Andhra Pradesh where residential qualifications were prescribed for a limited period not exceeding five years on grounds of the backwardness of the areas. In *Narasimha Rao v. Andhra Pradesh* (AIR 1970 SC 422), however, the Supreme Court declared part of the Act unconstitutional expressing the view that Parliament could impose a residential qualification in the whole State and not a part of it.

The basic principle in article 16 is that of equality of opportunity and non-discrimination in public employment. Clauses (1) and (2) state this principle. But, clauses that follow contain provisions allowing special advantages to certain sections of the people. The question is how to reconcile these opposites. In several cases upto the *Devadasan v. U.O.I.*, the Supreme Court treated Clause (4), for example, as an exception to the general principle in Clauses (1) and (2) but subsequently in *State of Kerala v. Thomas* and *Indra Sawhney v. U.O.I.* (Mandal) Cases, the Supreme Court found that article 16 (4) was actually supportive of article 16 (1) and (2) or that it was only an extension or expansion of the general principle of equality and non-discrimination. It has however to be borne in mind that there are limits to the extent to which historical wrongs can be righted or compensated by the present generation. The need is to look forward and not backwards. Any policy that seeks to ameliorate the conditions of the backward classes in our society and make them, as early as a possible, worthy of competing with the others on terms of equality and non-discrimination, is unexceptionable and deserves to be appreciated as forward looking. On the other hand, any effort at compensating for past wrongs in perpetuity is bound to generate a vested interest in backwardness and smacks of an approach of looking backward and not forward. It seems governed not so much by any constitutional principles as by demands of vote bank politics.

Clause 4 as the second exception in article 16 empowers the State to make special provision for the reservation of appointments or posts in favour of any "backward class of citizens" which in the opinion of the State are not adequately represented in the services under the State. The clause however is only an enabling provision and no right or duty can be read into it.[1] But as held in the *N.M. Thomas* case (AIR

1. *Rajasthan v. Union of India*, AIR 1968 SC 507.

1976 SC 490), it is not an exception to the general principle in article 16(1) but an emphatic statement of equality of opportunity guaranteed under clause (1) which means equality between members of the same class of employees and not equality between members of separate and independent classes. Thus, in the case of the Scheduled Castes and Scheduled Tribes who suffer from socio-economic backwardness, the fundamental right to equality of opportunity justifies separate categorisation for the purpose of "adequate representation in State services".[1] The courts, however held that article 16 (4) has to be read with article 335 inasmuch as the latter stated that while considering SC & ST claims maintenance of efficiency of administration must be kept in view.[2] Since then a proviso has been added to article 335 by the 82nd Amendment to clarify that it would be in order to provide for reducing the standards of evaluation and requirement of minimum marks for filling by promotion vacancies reserved for SC & ST in the services of the Union and the States.

The only condition for the exercise of the powers conferred by article 16(4) is that the State must be satisfied that any backward class of citizens is not adequately represented in the services. And, this condition may refer not only to the numerical inadequacy of representation in the services but also the qualitative one. In other words, the powers could be exercised not only to provide for reservation of appointments but also to provide for representation in selection posts as well as posts filled by promotion.[3] However, reservation should not be excessive and could not be taken to the extent of effacing the guarantee contained in

1. *A.B.S.K. Sangh (Rly) v. Union of India,* AIR 1981 SC 298.
2. *C&A G v. Jagannathan,* AIR 1987 SC 537; *Devadasan v. Union of India,* AIR 1985 SC 983; *K.C. Vasant Kumar v. State of Karnataka* AIR 1985 SC 1495
3. *General Manager S. Rly. v. Rangachari,* AIR 1962 SC 36; *Comptroller and Auditor-General of India v. K.S. Jagannath,* (1986) 2 SCC 679.

article 16(1). In *Devadasan v. Union of India* (AIR 1964 SC 179) the Supreme Court when called upon to pronounce on the constitutionality of the "carry forward rule", held the rule *ultra vires* by a majority of four to one on the ground that the power vested in the State Government under article 16(4) could not be so exercised as to deny reasonable equality of opportunity in matters of public employment to members of classes other than backward. It declared that more than 50 per cent reservation of posts in a single year would be unconstitutional as it *per se* destroyed article 16(1).

The Mandal Commission had in its report recommended 27 per cent reservation for backward classes in view of the limit of 50 per cent imposed by the Supreme Court. In its judgement in what has come to be known as the *Mandal* case, the Supreme Court decided on 16 November, 1992 by a 6 to 3 majority that 27 per cent reservation of posts for the socially and educationally backward classes were in order provided that the advanced amongst them—"the creamy layer"—were excluded from the list of beneficiaries, reservations were restricted to initial employment alone as article 16(4) did not permit any reservation in promotions, and the total reserved quota did not exceed 50 per cent except in some extraordinary situations. The court held that any reservation in promotions was invalid as "this would be a serious and unacceptable inroad into the rule of equality of opportunity" and would not be in the interest of efficiency of administration.

To meet the situation, article 16(4)(A) added by the seventy-seventh Constitution Amendment Act provided that in matters of promotion in services under the State in any category or categories, the State can make reservations for the Scheduled Castes and Scheduled Tribes. By adding a new clause (4B) to article 16, the Eighty-first Constitution Amendment Act (2000) however clarified that the unfilled reserved vacancies are to be treated as a separate class and are not to be included under the prescribed ceiling of fifty percent reservation of vacancies of the year. The Eighty-fifth Constitution Amendment (2001) further clarified that the employees so promoted shall also be entitled to consequential seniority. The Eighty-fifth Amendment came into operation *w.e.f.* 17 June 1995.

The term "backward class of citizens" has not been defined by the Constitution. But, since the emphasis in article 16(4) is on social and not economic backwardness, backward class cannot be identified only and exclusively with reference to economic criteria. The Court, therefore, struck down the notification which sought to reserve another 10 per cent posts for the economically backward sections not covered by any existing schemes of reservation. On the other hand, the Court held that a caste could quite often be a social class. "If it is socially backward, it would be a backward class for the purpose of article 16(4)". Also, several socially backward occupational groups, sects and denominations among the non-Hindus would also be covered by article 16(4). It would be incorrect therefore to say that the backward classes under article 16(4) were the same as the socially and educationally backward classes under article 15(4). Even though caste is mentioned in articles 15(2) and 16(2) as a prohibited ground of discrimination and the word used in articles 15(4) and 16(4) is "class", the majority judgement held that "identification of the backward classes can certainly be done with reference to castes among, and along with, other occupation groups, classes and sections of people". It, however, said that it may not be advisable to provide for reservations in certain areas, *e.g.* in technical posts, research and development organisations, in specialities and super specialities in medicine, engineering and other such courses in physical sciences and mathematics, in defence services and connected establishments. Reservations may also not be advisable in higher posts like those of professors in education, pilots in airlines, scientists and technicians in nuclear and space application etc.[1] In *Kartar Singh v. the State of M.P.* (1999) the Supreme Court disallowed lowering of qualifications for admission to super speciality medical course in favour of the reserved category candidates.

In Tamil Nadu, the total number of positions in the reservation quota far exceeded 50 percent. It was as much as 69 per cent. On the insistence of the Tamil Nadu government the Union Parliament had to pass the 76th Constitution Amendment to place the relevant Tamil Nadu law in the Ninth Schedule of the Constitution so that it became an entrenched law beyond judicial purview. Other States like Bihar, Orissa, U.P. and Karnataka were also proposing higher reservation quotas.

Another exception to the general rule of equality of opportunity in public employment is contained in clause 5 of article 16 which provides that a law may prescribe that the incumbent of an office in connection with the affairs of a religious or denominational institution, or a member of the governing body thereof shall belong to the particular religion or denomination.

Abolition of Untouchability

Article 17 abolishes "untouchability" and forbids its practice in any form. If practised, it shall be treated as an offence punishable in accordance with law. The objective of the article was to end the inhuman practice of treating certain fellow human beings as dirty and untouchable by reason of their birth in certain castes.[2] The Supreme Court has held that the fundamental right against untouchability guaranteed in this article is available against private individuals and it is the constitutional duty of the State to take necessary steps to see that this right is not violated.[3]

---

1. *Indra Sawhney v. Union of India*, AIR 1993 SC 477.
2. *Devarajiah c. Padmanna*, AIR 1961 Mad 35.
3. *People's Union for Democratic Rights v. Union of India*, AIR 1982 SC 1473.

Most importantly, it is the bounden duty of every citizen to ensure that untouchability is not practised in any form. The Untouchability (Offences) Act, 1955 later modified to read as the Protection of Civil Rights Act, 1976 provided for punishment of offenders.

Abolition of Titles

Article 18 prohibits the State to confer titles on anybody, whether an Indian citizen or a foreign national. An exemption has however been made in the case of Military and academic distinctions. Under clause (2) of the article, a citizen of India has also been prohibited from accepting any title from a foreign State. Clause (3) provides that a foreigner holding any office of profit or trust under the State cannot accept any title from a foreign State without the permission of the President. And under clause (4) no person holding any office of profit or trust under the State shall, without the consent of the President, accept any present, employment, or office of any kind from or under any foreign State.

A question had arisen whether the Bharat Ratna, Padma Vibhushan, Padma Bhushan and Padma Shri civilian Awards conferred by the President on Republic Day for outstanding meritorious service were violative of article 18 of the Constitution. Under stay orders from the Supreme Court, no awards were announced for several years. Awards have since been resumed. The Supreme Court has held that these awards are not titles within the meaning of article 18 and that if any awardee uses the award as a title by suffixing or prefixing it with his or her name, he should forfeit the award.[1]

1. *Balaji Raghavan v. Union of India*, AIR 1996 SC 770.

RIGHT TO FREEDOM

Article 19 of the Constitution specifically guarantees to the citizens of India six basic freedoms, *viz.* of speech and expression, of 'peaceable assembly, without arms', 'to form associations', of 'movement throughout the territory of India', of 'residing and settling in any part of India', and of 'practising any profession and carrying on any occupation, trade or business'. These freedoms are recognised as the 'natural rights inherent in the status of a citizen'.[1] This enumeration of the freedoms has however been held to be not exhaustive by the courts for the full enjoyment of the democratic values of a free citizen. In their decisions, the courts have held several other freedoms also as necessary concomitants for a democratic polity even though they are not specifically mentioned in article 19[2], as for example, the freedom to live[3], to vote and contest election[4], freedom of the Press,[5] the Government servants' right to continue in employment[6], the right to strike[7], the right to know[8].

The right to the protection of the six freedoms against State action is available to all citizens. Not being citizens, corporations cannot invoke the article.[9] But the shareholders who are citizens have rights.[10] Article 19 does not confer an absolute or unlimited right. As observed by J. Das, "social interest in individual liberty may well have to be subordinated to other greater social interests".[11] Thus, clauses

1. *State of W. Bengal v. Subodh Gopal Bose,* AIR 1954 SC 92, 95.
2. *Maneka Gandhi v. Union of India,* AIR 1978 SC 597.
3. *Jagmohan Singh v. State of U.P.,* AIR 1973 SC 947.
4. *N.P. Punnuswami v. Returning Officer,* AIR 1952 SC 64, 71.
5. *Brij Bhushan v. State of Delhi,* AIR 1950 SC 129.
6. *P. Balkotiah v. Union of India,* AIR 1958 SC 232, 238.
7. *Radhey Shyam Sharma v. P.M.G., Nagpur,* AIR 1965 SC 311, 313.
8. *L.K. Koolwal v. State of Rajasthan,* AIR 1988 Raj 2.
9. *Khoday Industries v. State of Tamilnadu,* AIR 1990 Mad 124.
10. *D.C.M. v. Union of India,* AIR 1974 SC 937.
11. *A.K. Gopalan v. State of Madras,* AIR 1950 SC 27.

2 to 6 of article 19 empower the State to impose "reasonable" restrictions on the exercise of this right by enacting proper legislation "in the interests of the sovereignty and integrity of India, the security of the State, friendly relations with foreign states, public order, decency or morality or in relation to contempt of court, defamation or incitement to an offence". It is necessary that the restrictions imposed by law must be reasonable and not arbitrary or of excessive nature and the onus of proving it to the satisfaction of the court lies with the State.[1] The harsher the restriction, the heavier the onus to prove the reasonableness.[2]

Since the Constitution does not define the expression "reasonable restrictions", each case has to be judged on its own merits. The test could be the underlying purpose of the restrictions imposed, the extent, urgency and proportion of the evils sought to be remedied thereby, the prevailing conditions at the time and the duration of the restrictions.[3] The standard is really an elastic one and varies with time, space and condition from case to case.[4]

The reasonableness of restrictions has to be determined not on abstract considerations but in an objective manner and from the point of view of persons upon whom the restrictions are imposed.[5] It is the effect of a law which really constitutes the test of its reasonableness; its object, whether good or bad is immaterial for this purpose. And, not only substantive but the "procedural provisions of a statute also enter the verdict of its reasonableness".[6] The restrictions must strike a proper balance between the freedoms guaranteed under article 19(1) and the social control permitted by clauses

1. *Khyerbari Tea Co. v. State of Assam*, AIR 1964 SC 925.
2. *Saghir Ahmed v. State of U.P.*, AIR 1954 SC 728, 738.
3. *State of Madras v. V.G. Rao*, AIR 1952 SC 196.
4. *Golak Nath v. State of Punjab*, AIR 1967 SC 1643, 1655.
5. *Hanif Quareshi v. State of Bihar*, AIR 1958 SC 751.
6. *N.B. Khare v. State of Delhi*, AIR 1950 SC 211; Also see *Kishan Chand Arora v. Commissioner of Police*, AIR 1961 SC 705.

(2) to (6) of article 19.[1] The restrictions imposed in carrying out the Directive Principles of State Policy have been held to be in favour of their reasonableness.[2]

Freedom of Speech and Expression

Freedom of speech and expression is a *sine qua non* of the functioning of a democratic polity. Democracy means a government by persuasion and unless there is freedom for discussion of political as well as other matters, the polity could not be termed democracy. And, as a natural corollary, the term includes freedom of the press as well. Its import has been succintly brought out by Justice Patanjali Sastri in the following words:

> Freedom of speech and of the press lay at the foundation of all democratic organisations, for without free political discussion no public education, so essential for the proper functioning of the process of popular government, is possible. A freedom of such amplitude might involve risks of abuse. But the framers of the Constitution may well have reflected with Madison, who was the leading spirit in the preparation of the First Amendment of the Federal Constitution, that it is better to leave a few of its noxious branches to their luxuriant growth than by pruning them away, to injure the vigour of those yielding the proper fruits.[3]

Article 19(1)(a) guarantees to every Indian citizen the right to freedom of speech and expression.Though it does not specifically refer to the freedom of the press, this right has been held to be included in the right to freedom of speech and expression.

> Freedom of the Press is the heart of social and political intercourse. It is the primary duty of the courts to uphold

1. *Dwarka Prasad Lakshmi Narain v. State of U.P.,* AIR 1954 SC 224, 227.
2. *State of Bombay v. F.N. Balsara,* AIR 1951 SC 318, 328.
3. *Romesh Thapar v. State of Madras,* AIR 1950 SC 124, 128.

the freedom of the press and invalidate all laws or administrative actions which interfere with it contrary to the constitutional mandate".[1]

This means that every citizen is free to express his views, beliefs and convictions freely and without inhibitions by word of mouth, through writing, printing, picturising or in any other manner.

Thus, imposition of free censorship on a newspaper[2] or prohibiting it from publishing its own views or those of its correspondents on a burning topic of the day would constitute a violation of the right to freedom of speech and expression.[3] The right is enjoyed by the citizens not only within the territory of India but also beyond its borders.[4] Freedom of the Press is regarded as the "mother of all liberties" in a democratic society but it is not absolute and unfettered. An unrestricted freedom of speech and expression would amount to an uncontrolled license and could lead to disorder and anarchy. The freedom is not to be misunderstood by the press so as to disregard its duty to be responsible. If a newspaper publishes what is improper, mischievously false or illegal and abuses its liberty it must be punished by Court of Law. Some restrictions are, therefore essential even for preservation of the freedom of the Press itself.[5] The National Commission to Review the working of the Constitution (2002) recommended that freedom of the press be specifically included under article 19(1)(a).

Telephone tapping unless it comes within the grounds of restrictions under article 19(2) would infringe article 19 (1) (a) of the Constitution.[6] A government employee cannot

1. *Express Newspapers (P) Ltd. v. Union of India,* AIR 1958 SC 578; *Indian Express Newspapers v. Union of India,* (1985) 1 SCC 641.
2. *Brij Bhushan v. State of Delhi,* AIR 1950 SC 129.
3. *Virendra v. Punjab,* AIR 1957 SC 896.
4. Bhagwati, J. in *Maneka Gandhi v. Union of India,* AIR 1978 SC 597.
5. *In re. Harijai Singh, In re. Vijay Kumar,* AIR 1997 SC 73.
6. *People's Union for Civil Liberties v. Union of India,* AIR 1997 SC 568.

seek the protection of article 19(1) against his dismissal on account of misconduct in publicly making allegations against head of his organisation.[1]

Reasonable limits or restrictions can be imposed on the exercise of the right to freedom of speech under article 19(2) in the interests or on the grounds of: (i) Security of the State, (ii) Friendly relations with foreign countries, (iii) Public Order, (iv) Decency or morality, (v) Contempt of court, (vi) Defamation, (vii) Incitement to offence, and (viii) Sovereignty and integrity of India.

Right to Information: Article 19(1)(a) has been construed to include the right to know or to seek information. The Right to Information Act 2005 specifically confers on all citizens the right to access information and makes it obligatory for all public authorities to disclose official information only subject to certain essential restrictions. The Act aims at promoting openness, transparency and accountability in administration.

Security of the State: Security of the State refers only to "serious and aggravated forms of public disorder". In other words, rebellion, waging war against the State, insurrection etc. are most likely to threaten the security of the State. Thus, expression of views or making of speeches which tend to incite or encourage the people to commit violent crimes like murder, would constitute reasonable grounds for imposition of restrictions under article 19(2).[2] Making a speech which tends to overthrow the State can be made punishable.[3] Though 'public order' was added as a ground for imposing restrictions through the 1951 Constitution Amendment, ordinary breaches thereof like unlawful assembly, riot etc. would remain outside the purview of clause (2).

---

1. *M.H. Devendrappa v. Karnataka State Small Industries Development Corporation*, AIR 1998 SC 1064.
2. *State of Bihar v. Shailbala Devi*, AIR 1952 SC 329.
3. *Santosh Singh v. Delhi Administration*, AIR 1973 SC 1091.

***Friendly relations with foreign countries*:** This ground for imposing restrictions on freedom of speech and expression was brought in by the Constitution (First Amendment) Act, 1951 with a view to avoiding embarrassment to India through persistent and malicious propaganda. The ground, however has been criticized for being susceptible of supporting regulation curbing even criticism of the Government's foreign policy.

Public Order: This ground too was added by the 1951 Amendment to overcome the situation arising out of the Supreme Court judgment in *Romesh Thapar v. State of Madras* (AIR 1950 SC 124) wherein it was held that ordinary or local breaches of public order were no grounds for imposing restrictions on the freedom of speech and expression, observing that "public order" was an expression of wide connotation and signified "that state of tranquility which prevails among the members of political society as a result of internal regulations enforced by the Government which they have established".

Decency or Morality: With no clear meanings and the perceptions changing in regard thereto from time to time, these terms have obviously been included as grounds for imposing restrictions on the freedom of speech and expression mainly to safeguard the society from depraved and corrupt actions or behaviour. Sections 292–294 of the Indian Penal Code which indicate the scope of indecency or obscenity were upheld because "the law against obscenity seeks no more than to promote public decency and morality."[1] The Supreme Court in the instant case had followed the test laid down in the English case of *R. v. Hicklin*, (LR 3 QB 360) holding *Lady Chatterley's Lover* as an obscene book, as it had the tendency to corrupt the mind of those who read it. The term 'morality' in clause (2) has to be given a wider meaning to include not only 'public morality' but

---

1. *Ranjit Udeshi v. Maharashtra*, AIR 1965 SC 881.

'morality as understood by the people as a whole'.[1]

***Contempt of Court*:** The underlying idea for this ground for imposing restrictions is to preserve the authority of courts in punishing for their contempt. In *Parashuram v. King* (1945 AC 264), it was observed that contempt power is a power which the court must, of necessity, possess but its usefulness depends upon the wisdom and restraint with which it is used. The power of courts to punish for their own contempt has been considerably modified in U.K., U.S.A. and other countries. The Phillimore Committee in U.K. recommended that truth in public benefit should be admissible as a defence in a charge of contempt. In U.S.A. contempt plea is admissible only in cases of 'clear and present danger to administration of justice.'

Articles 129 and 215 of our Constitution empower the Supreme Court and the High Courts respectively to punish for their respective contempt. The Contempt of Courts Act 1971 seeks to codify the Indian Law of Contempt of Court. The Supreme Court has upheld the law of contempt under article 129 as reasonable under article 19(2).[2] Since contempt jurisdiction is exercised in certain cases contrary to the dictum that no one should be a judge in his own case, judges have to be careful. Public criticism of a judgement cannot be stifled so long as it is fair, reasonable and legitimate. The conduct of a judge in his judicial capacity can also be subject of a fair and proper comment.[4] Path of justice is not strewn with roses and Justice is not a cloistered virtue and she must be allowed to suffer the scrutiny and be respectful, even though outspoken, comments of ordinary men.[3] In *E.M.S. Namboodiripad v. T.N. Nambiar* (AIR 1970 SC 2015) the Court observed that freedom of speech shall always prevail except where contempt of court is manifest, mischievous or

---

1. *Manohar v. Maharashtra*, AIR 1984 BOM 47.
2. *C.K. Daphtary v. O.P. Gupta*, AIR 1971 SC 1132.
3. *Rama Dayal Markarha v. State of M.P.*, AIR 1978 SC 922.
4. *Perspective Publications v. State of Maharashtra*, AIR 1971 SC 221.

substantial. Justice Krishna Iyer laid down the principle in *Barada Kant v. Registrar Orissa High Court* (AIR 1974 SC 710) thus:

> The cornerstone of the contempt law is the accommodation of two constitutional values – the right to free speech and the right to independent justice. The ignition of contempt action should be substantial and *mala fide* interference with fearless judicial action, not fair comment or trivial reflections on the judicial process and personnel.

In *re Mulgaonkar* (AIR 1978 SC 72) Justice Iyer asserted that the keynote was to be 'justice' and not 'judge' and that activist efforts at judicial reforms should not be stalled under contempt action. The Supreme Court also suggested some guidelines for action under the contempt of court law. The Court took a liberal view of the law of contempt in *M.R. Parashar v. Farooq Abdullah* (AIR 1984 SC 615) also and said:

> *Bona fide* criticism of any system or institution is aimed at inducing the administration of that system or institution to look inwards and improve its public image. Courts do not like to assume the posture that they are above criticism and that their functioning needs no improvement.[1]

The National Commission to Review the Working of the Constitution (2002) found that under the law of contempt as it stood and as it was interpreted (*e.g.* in *Dr. Saxena case*) even truth could not be pleaded as a defence to a charge of contempt of court. The Commission recommended that a proviso be added to article 19(2) to say that

> in matters of contempt it shall be open to the court to permit a defence of justification by truth on satisfaction as to the *bona fides* of the plea and it being in public interest.

---

1. Also see *Conscientious Group v. Md. Yunus* (AIR 1987 SC 145); *P.N. Duda v. Shiv Shankar* (AIR 1988 SC 1208); and In *re. Dr. D.C. Saxena Contemnor v. Hon'ble Chief Justice of India*, AIR 1996 SC 2481.

Since then the contempt of Courts Act, 1971 has been amended (2006) to allow truth as a defence against contempt charges. It is, however doubtful whether, in the absence of a constitutional amendment as recommended by the Constitution Commission, the law would be deemed binding on the Supreme Court and the High Courts.

Defamation: The right to free speech and expression does not entitle a citizen to defame a person. The constitutional validity of Section 499 of the Indian Penal Code which defines the law of defamation as exposing a man to hatred, ridicule or contempt has been upheld by the courts. The press is also subject to the defamation law.[1]

***Incitement to an offence*:** This ground for restricting freedom of speech and expression was also added in 1951. The Supreme Court has taken the view that incitement to murder or other violent crimes would generally endanger the security of the State. Hence a restriction imposed on this ground would be valid under article 19(2).[2]

Sovereignty and integrity of India: This ground for imposing restrictions on the right to freedom of speech and expression was added by the Sixteenth Amendment in 1963 so as not to permit anyone to challenge the integrity or sovereignty of India or to preach cession of any part of the territory of India.

Freedom to Assemble

Meetings, processions and demonstrations are inevitable corollaries of a democratic system. The people can be informed, educated or persuaded only through such exercises. Article 19(1)(b) secures to all citizens of India the right "to assemble peaceably and without arms". This consequentially leads to the conferment of the right to hold public meetings and demonstrations and take out processions peacefully.[3] The two inherent restrictions for any

1. *Printers Mysore v. Asstt. Comm. Law Officer,* JT (1994) ISC 692.
2. *State of Bihar v. Shailabala Devi,* AIR 1952 SC 329.
3. *Babulal v. State of Maharashtra,* AIR 1961 SC 884.

assembly are of remaining peaceful and to be unarmed. In addition, under clause (3), reasonable restrictions can be imposed on the right by the State by law "in the interests of the sovereignty and integrity of India or public order" as may be deemed necessary from time to time. Thus, an assembly declared unlawful can be validly banned and the people thereof ordered to be dispersed.

Freedom of Association

Article 19(1)(c) guarantees to all citizens the right to form associations and unions for pursuing lawful purposes. Under clause 4 of the article, however, reasonable restrictions can be imposed by the State "in the interests of the sovereignty and integrity of India or public order or morality". The associations so formed would include political parties, societies, clubs, companies, organisations, partnership firms, trade unions and indeed any body of persons. There is complete liberty to form associations for lawful purposes subject to reasonable restrictions. The Supreme Court has held that even a liberal interpretation of article 19(1)(c) cannot mean that the trade unions have a guaranteed right to strike. The right to strike can be controlled by appropriate industrial legislation.[1] Similarly, nobody can be compelled to become a member of a Government sponsored union.[2]

Freedom of Movement and Residence

The right of every citizen of India "to move freely throughout the territory of India" and his right "to reside and settle in any part of the territory of India" guaranteed under clauses (d) and (e) respectively of article 19(1) are really interlinked. Both the rights lay stress on the oneness of the territory of India. Any citizen can travel to or reside in any part of India.

1. *All India Bank Employees Association v. The National Industrial Tribunal,* AIR 1962 SC 171; *Delhi Police Sangh v. Union of India,* AIR 1987 SC 379.
2. *Raghubar Dayal v. Union of India,* AIR 1962 SC 263.

Clause 5 of article 19 however, provides for imposition of reasonable restrictions on the exercise of either of them by law "in the interests of the general public or for the protection of the interests of any Scheduled Tribe". Both the rights get affected whenever restrictions are placed on the movement or residence of a citizen. Generally, the protection afforded by these rights is invoked to challenge the validity of externment or deportation orders which go to curtail the two freedoms. In *N.B. Khare v. State of Delhi* (AIR 1950 SC 211), the Supreme Court held that the mere fact that the externment order depended on the subjective satisfaction of the Executive, and there was no provision for judicial review in the impugned Act, did not render it invalid. In another case the court ruled that a law which subjected a citizen to the extreme penalty of a virtual forfeiture of his citizenship upon conviction for a mere breach of the permit regulations (under the Influx from Pakistan (Control) Act, 1949) or upon a reasonable suspicion of having committed such breach could hardly be justified upon the ground that it imposed a reasonable restriction in the interests of the general public.[1] Restrictions to protect the interests of the Scheduled Tribes have been provided keeping in view mostly the aboriginal tribes which have their own distinct culture, language and customs. Unrestricted entry of outsiders in the areas inhabited by the tribal people might jeopardize their interests.[2]

Resstrictions imposed on prostitutes to carry on their trade within a specified area and to reside in or move from particular areas have been held to be valid.[3] Likewise, restrictions on residence imposed on habitual offenders have been upheld by the courts as being reasonable.[4] Restrictions

---

1. *Ebrahim Wazer Mavat v. State of Bombay*, AIR 1954 SC 229.
2. *Dhan Bahadur Ghorti v. State*, AIR 1953 ASS. 61.
3. *State of U.P. v. Kaushalya*, AIR 1964 SC 416.
4. *Arumugham v. State of Madras*, AIR 1953 Mad. 664.

on the movements of persons afflicted by AIDS have been held by the Bombay High Court to be valid.[1]

Freedom of Profession and Trade

Under article 19(1)(g) every citizen of India has the right to practice any profession or to carry on any occupation, trade or business. The right to carry on a business includes the right to close it any time the owner likes.[2] Thus no citizen can be compelled to carry on business against his will. In *Excel Wear v. Union of India* (AIR 1979 SC 25) the court held that refusal or approval for closure of a business was invalid when the owner could not pay even the minimum wages to his employees.

As in the case of the various rights to freedom, right to trade and profession is also not absolute and the State can impose reasonable restrictions on the exercise of this right too "in the interests of the general public". For example, there could be no fundamental right to carry on trade or business in noxious, hazardous or dangerous goods like intoxicating drugs or liquors, adulterated foods etc. or to indulge in trafficking in women or children.

Under clause 6 of article 19, the State has also been empowered to prescribe professional or technical qualifications necessary for practising any profession or carrying on any occupation, trade or business, as well as for enabling the State to carry on any trade or business to the exclusion of citizens wholly or partially. In fact, the State is competent to nationalise any trade or business wholly or partially to the exclusion of all citizens. In the *Excel Wear* case the court held that while there may be greater emphasis on nationalisation and State ownership of industries, private ownership of industries is recognised and private enterprise forms an overwhelmingly large proportion of India's

1. *Lucy v. State of Goa,* AIR 1990 Bom. 355.
2. *Hathisingh Mfg. Co. v. Union of India,* AIR 1960 SC 923.

economic structure. Limited companies having shareholders own a large number of industries. There are creditors and depositors and various other persons having dealings with the undertakings. Socialism cannot go to the extent of ignoring the interests of all such persons.[1] Nevertheless, the State is not required to justify its trade monopoly as a 'reasonable' restriction or as being in the interests of the general public.[2] In fact, no objection can be taken under article 19(1)(g) if the State carries on a business either as a monopoly, complete or partial, to the exclusion of all or some citizens only, or in competition with any citizen.

Protection in Respect of Conviction for Offences

Under article 20, the Constitution has taken care to safeguard the rights of persons accused of crimes. This article has been considered so important that the Forty-fourth Amendment provides that it cannot be suspended even during an Emergency by an order under article 359.

***Ex-post facto law*:** According to clause 1 of article 20, "no person shall be convicted of any offence except for violation of law in force at the time of the commission of the act charged as an offence, nor be subjected to a penalty greater than that which might have been inflicted under the law in force at the time of the commission of the offence". Thus the Legislature is prohibited to make criminal laws having retrospective effect. This protection against *ex post facto* law provides immunity to the person liable for being convicted under it[3] though the immunity cannot be claimed against preventive detention[4] or against demanding security from a person.[5] It has also to be borne in mind that the protection

1. AIR 1979 SC 36; *New Bihar Biri Leaves Co. v. Bihar,* AIR 1981 SC 679.
2. *Saghir Ahmed v. State of U.P.,* AIR 1954 SC 728; *P T Society v. R.T.A.,* AIR 1960 SC 801.
3. *Maharashtra v. K.K. Subramanian Ramaswamy,* AIR 1977 SC 2091.
4. *Prahlad v. Bombay,* AIR 1952 Bom. 1.
5. *State of Bihar v. Shailbala,* AIR 1952 SC 329.

granted under article 20(1) will apply only in cases of conviction for criminal offences but would not cover trial[1] nor is a person protected for civil liability.[2] The word 'penalty' is in fact used in a narrow sense in clause (1) as meaning a payment

> which has to be made or a deprivation of liberty which has to be suffered as a consequence of finding that the person accused of a crime is guilty of the charge.[3]

Double jeopardy: Clause (2) of article 20 incorporates the doctrine of "double jeopardy" inasmuch as it is emphatic that "no person shall be prosecuted and punished for the same offence more than once". The words "prosecuted" and "punished" have to be read together to invoke the protection. The principle has of course been already recognised in the existing law, *i.e.* vide Sec. 26 of the General Clauses Act and Section 300 of the Criminal Procedure Code. The protection afforded by clause (2) is, however, attracted only in respect of the punishment inflicted by a court of law or judicial tribunal. It does not immunize a person from proceedings which are not before a court of law. Thus, a Government servant prosecuted and convicted by a court of law can nonetheless be punished under departmental proceedings for the same offence.[4] Similarly, a person punished departmentally may be prosecuted in a court of law.[5] Also, since the operation of article 20(2) is limited to indictment before a criminal court, it does not ban proceedings before a civil court for disobedience of an injunction along with

---

1. *Shiv Bahadur Singh v. State of Vindhya Pradesh,* AIR 1963 SC 394; *Union of India v. Sukuman Pyre,* AIR 1966 SC 1206; *G.P. Nayyar v. State, AIR 1979 SC 602.*
2. *Jawala Ram v. State* of *PEPSU,* AIR 1962 SC 1246; see also *State of W.B. v. S.K. Ghosh,* AIR 1963 SC 255.
3. See *Shiv Dutt Rai Fateh Chand v. India,* AIR 1984 SC 1194; *R.S. Joshi v. Ajit Mills Ltd.* (1977) 4 SCC 98.
4. *Motising Chhagansing Voghela v. S.D. Mehta,* AIR 1966 Guj 233.
5. *Venkataraman v. Union of India,* 1954 SC 375.

criminal proceedings, as the former are not in the nature of criminal proceedings.[1]

***Prohibition against self-incrimination*:** Under the canons of common law criminal jurisprudence, a person is presumed to be innocent; the prosecution must establish his guilt. Secondly, a person accused of an offence need not make any statement against his will. These principles are embodied in clause (3) of article 20 which lays down that

> No person accused of any offence shall be compelled to be a witness against himself.

This privilege to an accused person contains three components, *viz.*, that he has a right of protection against "compulsion to be a witness", and against such compulsion resulting in his giving evidence "against himself". In other words, the accused person is protected against incriminating himself under compulsion, *e.g.* making "a statement which makes the case against the accused person at least probable considered by itself". Compulsion in this context would mean "duress".[2] In the *Nandini Sathpathy case* (AIR 1978 SC 1025) the court held that "relevant replies which furnish a real and clear link in the chain of evidence indeed to bind down the accused with the crime become incriminatory and offend article 20(3) if elicited by pressure from the mouth of the accused". It widened the scope of compulsion and held that "compelled testimony" is evidently procured not merely by physical threats or violence but also by psychic torture, atmospheric pressure, environmental coercion, tiring interrogative proximity, overbearing and intimidating methods and the like. The court also laid down some guidelines for the police authorities for due observance, *e.g.* the accused must be informed that he has a right to call a lawyer before answering to any of their questions.[3]

---

1. *Bachcha Lal v. Lalji*, AIR 1976 All. 393.
2. *State of Bombay v. Kathi Kolu Oghad*, AIR 1961 SC 1808, 1816.
3. *Nandini Sathpathy v. P.L. Dani*, AIR 1978 SC 1025.

Clause (3) of article 20, however only gives a privilege to the accused person which may be waived by him if he so likes. The article is not violated when he volunteers evidence against himself.[1]

The immunity granted to the accused does not extend to compulsory production of material objects or compulsion to give specimen writing, specimen signature, finger impression or compulsory exhibition of the body or giving of blood specimens.[2] Also, compulsion for production of documents is prohibited only if the documents convey the personal knowledge of the accused relating to the charge.[3]

Search of the premises of a person accused of an offence under a search warrant and seizure of documents are not violative of article 20(3) as a search warrant is issued to a police officer and so the search and seizure cannot be regarded as the acts of the occupier of the premises in question but of another to which the occupier is obliged to submit and are not therefore his testimonial acts in any case.[4] If any document is recovered as a result of the search and seizure, it can be produced in the courts as an evidence against the accused as he is not compelled to give evidence against himself.[5]

Protection of Life and Personal Liberty

Article 21 of the Constitution guarantees that no person shall be deprived of his life or personal liberty "except according to procedure established by law". This right is available to the citizens as well as non-citizens. In the famous *Gopalan case*, 'personal liberty' was held to mean only liberty relating to or concerning the person or body of the individual. Also, it covered protection only against arbitrary executive action.[6]

1. *Laxmipat Chorasia v. Maharashtra*, AIR 1968 SC 938.
2. See *Destogir v. State of Madras*, AIR 1960 SC 756.
3. *State of Bombay v. Kathi Kolu*, AIR 1961 SC 1808, 1816.
4. *M.P. Sharma v. Satish*, 1954 SC 300, 306.
5. *V.S. Kuttan Pillai v. Ram Krishan*, AIR 1980 SC 185.
6. *A.K. Gopalan v. State of Madras*, AIR 1950 SC 27.

But, later on, its ambit was widened to say that the 'procedure established by law' had to be just fair and reasonable. It must include protection against legislative action also and to cover within itself all the varieties of rights which go to make up the personal liberty of man, other than those provided in article 19(1). In *Maneka Gandhi v. Union of India* (AIR 1978 SC 597), the Supreme Court in fact over ruled the Gopalan's case expressing the view that

> the attempt of the Court should be to expand the reach and ambit of the Fundamental Rights rather than to attenuate their meaning and context by a process of judicial construction.

It held that the right to 'live' is not merely confined to physical existence but it includes within its ambit the right to live with human dignity (AIR 1978 SC 597). Elaborating this view in *Francis Coralie v. Union Territory of Delhi* (AIR 1981 SC 746) the Court said that the right to live is not restricted to mere animal existence. The Court further held that non-payment of minimum wages to the workers amounted to denial of their right to live with basic human dignity and violated article 21.[1] In the case popularly known as the *Pavement Dwellers' case*, the Supreme Court observed that the word 'life' in article 21 included the 'right to livelihood'. It said that if the right to livelihood was not treated as a part of the constitutional right to life, the easiest way of depriving a person of his right to life would be to deprive him of his means of livelihood There-fore, right to livelihood is an integral facet of the right to life.[2]

In the various cases which came up before the Supreme Court, this liberal outlook and thinking has been all along sustained. Thus, it has been held:

---

1. *People's Union for Democratic Rights v. Union of India*, AIR 1982 SC 1473.
2. *Olga Tellis v. Bombay Municipal Corporation*, AIR 1986 SC 180; *Narendra Kumar v. State of Haryana*, JT (1994) 2 SC 94.

- that imprisonment of a poor person for non-payment of debts amounted to deprivation of his personal liberty (*Jolly George Verghese v. Bank of Cochin,* AIR 1980 SC 470);
- that under the Bonded Labour System (Abolition) Act, 1976 it is not enough merely to identify and release bonded labourers but it is more important that they should be suitably rehabilitated to meet the plainest requirement of article 21 (*Neerja Choudhari v. State of M.P.,* AIR 1984 SC 1099);
- that section 309 I P C is *ultra vires* the Constitution as a person cannot be forced to enjoy the right to life to his detriment (*P. Rathinam N. Patnaik v. Union of India,* JT (1994) 3SC 392);
- that the expression 'life' is not limited to bodily restraint or confinement to prison but something more than mere animal existence (*Kharak Singh v. State of U.P.,* AIR 1963 SC 1295);
- that the 'right to privacy'—by itself—has not been identified under the Constitution but the right to converse on telephone without interference can certainly be claimed as "right to privacy". Telephone tapping would infract article 21 unless permitted by law (*People's Union of Civil Liberties v. Union of India,* AIR 1997 SC 568); right to privacy would have to go through a process of case by case development (*Govind v. State of M.P.,* AIR 1975 SC 1379); this right is available even to a woman of easy virtue, and no one can invade her privacy (*State of Maharashtra v. Madhulkar Narain,* AIR 1991 SC 207);
- that handcuffing is permissible only in extraordinary circumstances (*Sunil v. State of M.P.,* (1990) 2 SC 409; the police and the jail authorities on their own shall have no authority to direct the handcuffing of any inmate of a jail in the country or during transport and in case of extraordinary circumstances necessitating handcuffing special orders of the Magistrate must be obtained (*Citizens for Democracy v. State of Assam,* AIR 1996 SC 2193);
- that public hanging of a convict is violative of article 21 (*Attorney-General v. Lachma Devi,* AIR 1986 SC 467);
- that so long as surveillance by police officers is for the purposes of preventing crimes and confined to the limits prescribed by law, a person cannot complain against the inclusion of his name in the surveillance register but if it is excessive and goes beyond the prescribed limits, its validity may be challenged as infringing the right of privacy of a citizen as his fundamental

right to personal liberty under article 21 and freedom of movement under article 19(1)(d) (*Malak Singh v. State of Punjab*, AIR 1981 SC 760);

- that persons kept in jail without being charged or tried must be released (*Mathews v. State of Bihar* AIR 1984 SC 1854; *Kamladevi v. State of Punjab*, AIR 1984 SC 1895);
- that an undertrial prisoner already in jail for a period more than the maximum awardable for the offence he is charged of must be released (*Hussainara v. State of Bihar*, AIR 1979 SC 1369, 1377, 1819; *R.D. Ram v. State of Bihar*, AIR 1987 SC 1333);
- that refusal to grant bail in a murder case without reasonable ground would amount to deprivation of personal liberty under article 21 (*Babu Singh v. State of U.P.*, AIR 1978 SC 527);
- that protection of article 21 is available even to convicts in jails and the prisoners cannot be subjected to torture etc. (*D.B.M. Patnaik v. State of A.P.*, AIR 1974 SC 2092; *Javed v. State of Maharashtra*, AIR 1985 SC 231; *Sher Singh v. State of Punjab*, AIR 1983 SC 465;
- that arrestee subjected to inhuman treatment during police custody should be paid compensation by the State, the quantum of compensation depending upon the facts in each case (*D.K. Basu v. STate of W.B.*, AIR 1997 SC 610);
- that if by imposing solitary confinement there is total deprivation of camaraderie amongst co-prisoners, coming and talking and being talked to, it would offend article 21 (*Sunil Batra v. Delhi Administration*, AIR 1978 SC 1675; AIR 1980 SC 1579);
- that speedy trial is a component of personal liberty (*Kartar Singh v. State of Punjab*, JT (1994) 2 SC 423);
- that a detenu can be subjected only to such restrictions on his personal liberty as are authorised by or under the law of preventive detention; imposition of any unauthorised restriction will violate article 21 (*State of Maharashtra v. Prabhakar Pandurang*, AIR 1986 SC 424);
- that the 'right to travel abroad' is part of a person's 'personal liberty' which is a comprehensive term and a citizen's passport cannot be impounded for an indefinite period of time. (*Satwant Singh v. Assistant Passport Officer*, AIR 1967 SC 1836; *Maneka Gandhi v. Union of India*, AIR 1978 SC 597);
- that it is the professional obligation of all doctors, whether

government or private, to extend medical aid to the injured immediately to preserve life without waiting for legal formalities to be complied with by the police under Cr. P.C. (*Parmanand Katara v. Union of India,* AIR 1989 SC 2039); failure to give timely medical treatment to a seriously injured person is violation of his right to life (*Paschim Banga Khet Mazdoor Samity v. State of West Bengal,* AIR, 1996, SC 2426);

- that when one seeks relief for breach of Article 21, one must confine oneself to some direct, overt and tangible act which threatens the fullness of life or the lives of others in the community (*Ramsharan Autrynuprasi v. Union of India,* AIR 1989 SC 549 and 552);
- that right to pollution free air falls within article 21 (*Subhash v. State of Bihar,* AIR 1991 SC 420);
- that compelling a person to live in sub-human conditions also amounts to the taking away of his life, not by execution of a death sentence but by a slow and gradual process by robbing him of all his human qualities and graces, a process which is much more cruel than sending a man to the gallows (*Sankar Banerji v. Durgapur Project Ltd.,* AIR 1988 Cal. 136);
- that the requirement of a public hearing in a court of law for a fair trial is subject to the need of proceeding being held in camera to the extent necessary in public interest and to avoid prejudice to the accused (*Vineet Narain v. Union of India,* AIR 1998 SC 889).

In its judgement in *Mohini Jain v. State of Karnataka* (AIR 1992 SC 1858), the Supreme Court extended the scope of article 21 further to include under the right to life, 'right to education' also. In fact, the Court declared even higher education in professional fields like medicine as a fundamental right. Later, however the Court overruled its decision in the Mohini Jain case and decided that under article 21, there is no fundamental right to education for a professional degree. Three of the five judges, however thought that early education up to the age of 14 could be a fundamental right of the citizens.[1]

1. *J.P. Unnikrishnan and others v. State of Andhra Pradesh and others,* etc. JT 1993(1) SC 474.

In several judgements, the Supreme Court reiterated that right to life under article 21 included the right to livelihood because no person can live without the means of living. If the right to livelihood is not treated as a part of the right to life, the easiest way of depriving a person of his right to life would be to deprive him of his means of livelihood.[1]

Right to Education

Article 21A added as a new article by the Constitution (86th Amendment) Act 2002 provides for free and compulsory education for all children between the age of 6 to 14 years.

Protection Against Arrest and Detention

Detention of persons without trial was a common feature of the colonial rule and a major issue during the struggle for freedom. Article 22 in clauses 1 and 2 lays down that no person who is arrested shall be detained without being informed of the grounds of arrest, he shall not be denied the right to consult and be defended by a lawyer and he shall be produced before the nearest magistrate within 24 hours.

The Supreme Court has held that the communication of the grounds of arrest to the detenu, allowing consultation with and defence by a counsel and production before the nearest magistrate are mandatory requirements under the article.[2]

The Supreme Court has also clarified that arrest under the orders of the Court, deportation of an alien and arrest on a civil cause are not covered under article 22(1) and (2).[3] Also,

---

1. *Olga Tellis v. Bombay Municipal Corp.*, AIR 1986 SC 180; *D.T.C. v. ITC Mazdoor Congress*, AIR 1991 SC 101; *Unni Krishnan v. State of A.P.*, AIR 1993 SC 2178; *Madhu Kishwar v. State of Bihar*, AIR 1996 SC 1964.
2. *Gopalan v. State of Madras* (1950) SCR 88; *Hansmukh v. State of Gujarat*, AIR 1981 SC 28; *State of M.P. v. Shobaram*, AIR 1968 SC 1910; *State of U.P. v. Abdul Samad*, AIR 1962 SC 1506.
3. *State of U.P. v. Abdul Samad*, AIR 1962 SC 1506; *In re Madhu Limaye*, AIR 1969 SC 1014; *State of Punjab v. Ajaib Singh*, (1953), SCR 254.

clauses 1 and 2 do not apply to an alien or to cases of preventive detention.

Clauses (3) to (7) of article 22 cover cases of preventive detention under a law. Preventive detention is, by definition, for preventing an illegal act and not for punishing a person for any illegal act. Article 22 authorises Parliament to make a law providing for preventive detention, laying down the circumstances, the classes of cases, the maximum period of detention, establishing an Advisory Board and its procedure. It has been held that

> the State Government may, if satisfied with respect to any bootlegger or drug offender (or forest offender) or *goonda* or immoral traffic offender or slum grabber that with a view to prevent him from acting in any manner prejudicial to the maintenance of public order it is necessary to do so to make an order directing that such person be detained.[1]

As a protection against possible misuse of power of preventive detention, certain safeguards have been provided. Thus, preventive detention cannot be authorised by law to exceed 3 months unless an advisory board finds sufficient cause. In every case of preventive detention the grounds thereof shall be conveyed to the detenu who would also be afforded an opportunity to make a representation.

Courts have taken a very serious view of detention without trial except in the *bona fide* cases of preventive detention under a law. If the law is found to be unreasonable or unjust, it may be struck down or if any order of arrest and detention under the law suffers from an infirmity, the detenu may be ordered forthwith to be set free by the Court.[2]

Representation made in case of preventive detention

---

1. *T. Devaki v. Government of Tamil Nadu,* AIR 1990 SC 1086.
2. *Gopalan v. State of Madras,* (1950) SCR 88; *A.D.M. v. Shukla,* AIR 1976 SC 1207; *Dharmandir Suganchand Chetawal v. Union of India,* AIR 1990 SC 1196; *Sanjeev v. Union of India,* AIR 1990 SC 204; *Vijay Kumar v. Union of India,* AIR 1990 SC 1184.

must be considered by the Union Government even if it is in addition to the Advisory Board or when representation under COFEPOSA is received after the confirmation of the order by the Government.[1]

RIGHT AGAINST EXPLOITATION

Articles 23 and 24 seek to provide protection against (i) exploitation through traffic in human beings,(ii) *begar* and other forced labour, and (iii) employment of children in factories etc. Traffic in human beings—women, children etc.—and forced labour militate against human dignity which is a fundamental constitutional value enshrined in the Preamble. Under the old zamindari system, the tenants were sometimes forced to render free service to their landlords. This was called *begar*. Courts have held that even if some remuneration is paid, the labour may be a forced one.[2]

Children of the prostitutes may be made to live away from them and *Devadasis* are also covered under the term "traffic in human beings".[3]

The whole idea is not to allow the State or anyone to compel a person to work against his will or to misuse the human person in any way. The only exception allows the State to impose compulsory service for public purposes as, for example, military service or social service which should be imposed equally on all without any discrimination of religion, race, caste or class.

Article 24 specifically prohibits the employment of

1. *Gracy v. State of Kerala*, AIR 1991 SC 1090; *Abdulla v. Union of India*, AIR 1991 SC 574.
2. *People's Union v. Union of India*, AIR 1982 SC 1473; *Sanjit v. Rajasthan*, AIR 1983 SC 328.
3. *Gaurav Jain v. Union of India*, AIR 1990 SC 292; *Vishal Jeet v. Union of India*, AIR 1990 SC 1412.

children below the age of 14 in factories or mines or in any other hazardous jobs. This is in keeping with the human rights concepts and United Nations norms.

Some laws have since been enacted by Parliament to implement the provisions of articles 23 and 24.

RIGHT TO FREEDOM OF RELIGION

The Preamble describes our Republic *inter alia* as secular. The concept of secularism in the Constitution is not that of irreligion or anti-religion. It only means that there is no State religion, there is equal respect for and protection of all religions, no one is to be discriminated against on grounds of religion and everyone is guaranteed full and equal freedom of religion.[1] Articles 25 to 28 provide to all persons guarantees of the right to freedom of religion in all its aspects.

Freedom of Conscience and Religion

Article 25 lays down that all persons—not only citizens—are equally entitled to freedom of conscience and the right to freely profess, practice and propagate religion. This right to religious freedom is, however subject to (i) public order, (ii) morality (iii) health and (iv) other fundamental rights. The State would be free to regulate by law any secular activity associated with religious practice and to provide for social welfare and reform or the throwing open of Hindu temples etc. to all classes of Hindus. The wearing of *Kirpans* was to be deemed to be included in the profession of the Sikh religion and the Hindus for purposes of the article were to include Sikhs, Jains and Buddhists.

The Supreme Court has held that the right to propagate religion does not include any right to forcible conversions as these may disturb public order.[2] In the Anand Marg case

1. See under the chapter on 'The Preamble'.
2. *Stainslaus v. State of M.P.*, AIR 1977 SC 908.

the right to perform *tandav* dance with lethal weapons and human skulls in a public procession was held not to be an essential religious practice and banning of the procession in the interest of 'public order and morality' was considered a reasonable restriction.[1] Similarly, cow slaughter on bakrid was held not to be an essential practice of Islam and could therefore be prohibited by law in the interest of public order.[2] Laws regarding public order, morality and health cannot be violated in the name of freedom of conscience or religion.[3] Secular activities associated with religious practice which can be regulated by the State have been interpreted to mean non-essential aspects of religion or, for example, matters of secular administration of religions properties which must be handled in accordance with law.[4]

Freedom to Manage Religious Affairs

Article 26 which flows from article 25 bestows a fundamental right on all religious denominations and sections thereof to establish and maintain institutions for religious and charitable purposes, to manage their own affairs in matters of religion, to own and acquire and administer property. But, the administration of property has to be according to law. As in the case of rights under article 25, those under article 26 are also subject to public order, morality and health but not subject to other fundamental rights. As under article 25, Courts have made a distinction between the essentials and non-essentials of religion. It has been held that administration of the property of religious institutions can be regulated by law but the right of administration cannot

1. *Jagdishwaranand v. Police Commissioner,* AIR 1984 SC 51.
2. *Mohd. Hanif Quareshi v. State of Bihar,* AIR 1958 SC 731.
3. *TMA Pai case,* AIR 2003 SC 355.
4. *Ratilal v. State of Bombay,* (1954) SCR 1055; *Ramanuja v. State of Tamilnadu,* AIR 1972 SC 1586; *Commissioner, HRE v. Lakshmindra* (1954) SCR 1005; *Digyadarshan v. State of Andhra Pradesh,* AIR 1970 SC 181.

be taken away altogether.[1]

Articles 25 and 26 together seem to define the separate spheres and roles of the State and religion with both being free to carry on their secular and religious activities without interference from each other.

Freedom Not to Pay Taxes for Religious Promotion

Article 27 says that no person shall be compelled to pay any taxes for expenses on promotion or maintenance of any particular religion *i.e.* there could be no objection if the taxes were used for promotion of all religions. This is in keeping with the concept of secularism which means equal respect for all religions.

Freedom Not to Attend Religious Instruction

Article 28 forbids totally any religious instruction being imparted in educational institutions wholly maintained by State funds. In case of other institutions recognized and aided by the State, there will be freedom for every person not to participate in religious instruction or worship.

CULTURAL AND EDUCATIONAL RIGHTS

Protection of Interests of Minorities

Article 29 guarantees to "every section of the citizens" residing anywhere in India and "having a distinct language, script or culture" the right to conserve the same. No citizen can be denied admission to any educational institution maintained or aided by the State on grounds only of religion, race, caste or language.

Although the marginal heading of the article uses the

---

1. *Ratilal v. State of Bombay,* (1954) SCR 1055; *Ramanuja v. State of Tamilnadu,* AIR 1961 SC 1402; *Sarup v. State of Punjab,* AIR 1959 SC 850; *Narendra v. State of Gujarat,* AIR 1974 SC 2092; *Ram v. State of Punjab,* AIR 1981 SC 1576.

term 'minorities', it has not been mentioned in the text of the article and it has been held that it is equally available to any section of citizens—whether in minority or majority.[1]

Right of Minorities to Establish and Administer Educational Institutions

The Constitution does not anywhere define the term 'minorities'. Article 30(1) says that all minorities, whether religious or linguistic, shall have the right to establish and administer educational institutions of their choice. Clause 1(A) added by the 44th Amendment, in effect provides that if the property of any such institution is acquired, the compensation paid would be proper and adequate so that the right given by the article remains meaningful. Clause 2 provides that in the matter of giving aid, the State shall not discriminate against minority-managed institutions.

Article 30 is strictly in the nature of a minority right, *i.e.* one intended to protect the rights of minorities. Autonomy of a minority institution cannot be taken away completely. It is quite wide inasmuch as it is not confined like article 29 only to conservation of language, script and culture.[2] Also, the right of minorities under this article to 'establish and administer' educational institutions 'of their choice' includes the right to choose the medium of instruction, curricula, subjects to be taught etc.[3]

The right to administer, however does not mean right to maladministration. The right is subject to regulatory power of the State. Legislation in the interests of social welfare, industrial relations, academic standards, efficiency, discipline, health, sanitation, public order, morality,

1. *Ahmedabad St. Xaviers College Society v. State of Gujarat,* AIR 1974 SC 1389; *DAV College Bhatinda v. State of Punjab,* AIR 1971 SC 1731.
2. *Rev. Father Proost v. State of Bihar,* AIR 1969 SC 465; *Ahmedabad St. Xaviers College Society v. State of Gujarat,* AIR 1974 SC 1389; *St. Stephens' College v. University of Delhi,* (1992) SCC 558.
3. *D.A.V. College Bhatinda v. State of Punjab,* AIR 1971 SC 1731; *In re Kerala Education Bill,* AIR 1958 SC 956.

reasonable regulation to prescribe syllabus etc. does no violence to article 30 so long as it does not deprive the minority of its right to manage the institution. A law made to safeguard the service interests of teachers and regulate their conditions of service in the matter of dismissal, removal or reduction in rank did not violate article 30.[1]

Also, educational institution must be genuinely an educational institution of the minorities to be entitled to the right given by article 30(1). The Government, the University and the Court could go behind the claim of a minority institution. Where the claim was a mere cloak or pretension and the real motive was business adventure, the protection of article 30(1) would not be available.[2]

In *T.M.A. Pai v. State of Karnataka*, (AIR 2003 SC 355, (2004) 1 SCC 86) and *Islamic Academy v. State of Karnataka*, (AIR 2003 SC 3724, (2003) 6 SCC 697) the Supreme Court in their judgements of 31 October 2002 and 14 August 2003 held:

(i) Private educational institutions have a right to determine their own fee structure but education cannot be made a means of personal profit or help in other profession or business. Every State shall constitute a committee which will settle the appropriate fee structure for every private educational institution. It will be impermissible to ask for additional amounts in the name of donation or capitation fee.

(ii) It will not be correct to say that under article 30 minority educational institutions do not have any special rights which are not available to educational institutions of the majority community. The protection of article 30 is not for members of the majority community.

---

1. *In re Kerala Education Bill*, AIR 1958 SC 956; *Ahmedabad St. Xaviers College Society v. State of Gujarat*, AIR 1974 SC 1389; *St. Stephens' v. University of Delhi* (1992) 1 SCC 558; *State of T.N. v. Joseph*, (1991) 3 SCC 87; *Frank Anthony Public School Employees' Association v. Union of India*, (1986) 4 SCC 707; *Virendra Nath v. Delhi, (1990)* 2 SCC 307; *All Saints High School v. Government of Andhra Pradesh*, AIR 1980 SC 1042.
2. *A.P. Christians Medical Education Society v. Government of A.P.*, AIR 1986 SC 1490.

(iii) National interest must stand above the fundamental rights of individuals. Therefore, it is necessary that in professional (medical, engineering etc.) colleges—whether of the majority or minorities—the basis for admission should be merit alone.

In non-minority professional institutions, with the exception of seats reserved for the management, all admissions should be on the basis of merit determined through common entrance tests conducted by official agencies. Even in professional institutions established and administered by minority communities, admissions should be on the basis of merit but this merit has to be determined among the candidates of the concerned minority community only. The number of seats that should be reserved for minority candidates would depend upon the particular requirements of the minority community in each state. Such colleges can select meritorious candidates on the basis of private common admission tests.

(iv) Every state shall set up a standing committee to see that the admission procedure and tests etc. are transparent and just.

Article 30 has been criticized *inter alia* on the ground that the right to establish and administer educational institutions of their choice available to the minorities is denied to the majority community. Also, since the term 'minority' has not been defined in the Constitution anywhere and there are advantages in belonging to the minority, groups within the majority Hindu fold have started claiming minority status *e.g.* Arya Samaj in Punjab. The Ramakrishna Mission in Bengal had to declare that it is not Hindu at all but represented an independent minority religion. All this became necessary to claim the protection and benefits of article 30 for the DAV and Ramakrishna Mission institutions.[1]

---

1. *vide* affidavit filed by Ramakrishna Mission in Calcutta High Court, Constitutional Writ Jurisdiction, C.O. No.1283, W. of 1980; *DAV College v. State of Punjab*, AIR 1971 SC 1731, 1737; *Arya Samaj Education Trust v. Director of Education*, AIR 1976 Del. 207.
Also see under the Chapter on 'Language Provisions'.

RIGHT TO PROPERTY AND SAVING OF CERTAIN LAWS

The right to property has proved to be the most complicated and controversial. It had a very chequered history in our Constitution. During the various stages of the framing of the Constitution of India in the Constituent Assembly, the property provisions had proved to be the most controversial and had taxed the framers' imagination, sagacity, drafting skill and the spirit of accomodation and compromise to the maximum. At last a consensus was found which each of the contenders interpreted in his own way.

At one stage, speaking on a compromise formula proposed by Nehru, the eminent jurist and Drafting Committee member, Alladi Krishnaswami Ayyar said that although he had not always seen eye to eye with Nehru in regard to the property clause, he accepted Nehru's view on compensation without any reservation.[1] Nehru himself had said that the judiciary could not stand in judgement over the sovereign will of Parliament or function as a kind of third house of correction.[2]

The consensus was embodied in articles 31 and 19(1)(f) of the Constitution. But, even after the commencement of the Constitution, the property clauses remained the most contentious. They caused sharp confrontations between the legislature and the judiciary and necessitated several constitutional amendments. Finally, the Constitution (44th Amendment) Act, 1978 repealed articles 19(1)(f) and 31 from the category of fundamental rights completely with effect from 20 June, 1979. Instead, in Part XII of the Constitution, a new Chapter—Chapter IV—and a new article—300A was added to provide that no person shall be deprived of his property save by authority of law. Thus, the right to property ceased to be a fundamental right. It still remains a legal and constitutional right. Article 300A gives protection against

1. C.A. Deb., Vol. IX, pp. 1272-74
2. Ibid., pp. 1191-3.

executive action but not against legislative decision.

Notwithstanding the repeal of article 31, articles 31A (added by the 1st Amendment in 1951 and amended by the 4th, 17th, 42nd and 44th Amendments), 31B (added by the 1st Amendment in 1951) and 31C (added by the 25th Amendment in 1971 and amended by 42nd & 44th Amendments) remain part of the Fundamental Rights. These are intended to save certain laws providing for acquisition of estates etc. from being questioned and invalidated on grounds of inconsistency with articles 14 and 19, certain Acts and Regulations listed in the 9th Schedule being specifically validated and saved against challenge on the ground of inconsistency with any of the fundamental rights and certain laws giving effect to Directive Principles being saved from being questioned and invalidated on grounds of inconsistency with articles 14 and 19.

In *Kesavananda Bharti v. State of Kerala* (AIR 1973 SC 146), the Supreme Court held that the words "and no law containing a declaration that it is for giving effect to such policy shall be called in question in any court on the graound that it does not give effect to such policy" were invalid, that despite inclusion in the 9th Schedule, a law could be challenged on the ground of being violative of the basic features of the Constitution and the power of judicial review to question whether a law was in pursuance of directive principles could not be taken away. In the *Minerva Mills v. Union of India* (AIR 1980 SC 1789) the Court said that omnibus withdrawal of legislation from judicial review by the 42nd Amendment to article 31C undermined the basic structure of the Constitution.[1]

---

1. Also see *Srinivasa v. State of Karnataka*, AIR 1987 SC 1518; *Minerva Mills v. Union of India*, AIR 1986 SC 2030; *Sanjeev Coke v. Bharat Coking*, AIR 1983 SC 239; *State of Maharashtra v. Basantibai* (1986) 2 SCC 516; *Waman Rao v. Union of India*, AIR 1980 SC 273; *Niyami v. Union of India*, AIR 1990 SC 2128; *Assam Sillimanite v. Union of India*, (1992) Supp (I) SCC 692.

RIGHT TO CONSTITUTIONAL REMEDIES

Rights in order to be meaningful must be enforceable and backed by remedies in case of violation. Our Constitution not only guarantees certain fundamental rights but under article 32 it also guarantees the right to move the highest court in the land directly by appropriate proceedings for the enforcement of the fundamental rights. The Supreme Court may issue writs in the nature of *habeas corpus, mandamus, prohibition, quo warranto* and *certiorari*. Parliament may empower any other courts also to exercise these powers. The right guaranteed by article 32 cannot be suspended except as provided by the Constitution. For example, during a proclamation of Emergency (a) the right to move court for enforcement of any of the fundamental rights except articles 20 and 21 can be suspended under article 359 and (b) executive and legislative power of the State shall not stand restricted under article 358 by the rights to freedom enshrined in article 19. Where the suspension of fundamental right is protected by the Constitution, article 32 will not apply.[1] It has been held by the Supreme Court that this right cannot be taken away even by amending the Constitution as it is a basic feature of the Constitution.[2] Even at the time of framing the Constitution, Dr. Ambedkar had described this provision as the very soul and heart of the Constitution. Only the fundamental rights guaranteed by the Constitution can be enforced under article 32. Article 32 is not exactly concerned with an erroneous order or even with the unconstitutionality of a legislation unless it directly affects or invades any of the fundamental rights.[3] Since right to constitutional remedy

---

1. *Somavanti v. State of Punjab*, AIR 1964 SC 131.
2. *Fertilizer Corporation of India v. Union of India*, AIR 1981 SC 344; *Kihoto v. Zachilhu*, AIR 1993 SC 412.
3. *Chiranjee Lal v. Union of India*, 1950 SC 109; *Sadhu Singh v. Delhi Administration*, AIR 1965 SC 9; *Gopal Das v. Union of India*, AIR 1955 SC 1; *Haji Esmail v. Competent Officer*, AIR 1967 SC 1244; *Kuriakose v. State of Kerala*, AIR 1977 SC 1509.

under article 32 is itself a fundamental right, the Supreme Court may not refuse relief for violation of a substantive fundamental right. Article 226 grants powers to the High Courts also to issue various writs. In case of violation of fundamental rights, the Supreme Court and the High Courts both have concurrent jurisdiction and an affected person can approach either.[1] However, the Supreme Court has since held that where relief through High Court under article 226 is available, the High Court should be approached first.[2]

Under the new concept of public interest litigation[3] propounded by the Supreme Court in the Transfer of Judges case, it is no more necessary to be the affected party to approach the Court for violation of fundamental rights. Any member of the public can do so even through a letter on behalf of a person or group of persons who for any reason may not be in a position to approach the Court.[4]

Article 33 empowers Parliament to modify the application of fundamental rights to the armed forces or forces charged with maintenance of public order, intelligence personnel, etc. in the interest of discharge of duties and maintenance of discipline.[5] However, even when the appellate jurisdiction of courts is excluded in cases of court martial, the writ jurisdiction remains (unless taken away by law under article 33) and there have been several resorts to the remedy.[6]

---

1. *Kochuni v. State of Madras,* AIR 1959 SC 725; *M.K. Gopalan v. State of Madhya Pradesh,* (1955) ISCR 168; *Basappa v. Nagappa,* (1955) ISCR 250.
2. *Kanubhai Brahmbhatt v. State of Gujarat,* AIR 1987 SC 1159; *P.N. Kumar v. Municipal Corporation of Delhi* (1987) 4 SCC 609.
3. For meaning and description of the writs and for Public Interest Litigation, see under the Chapter on 'The Judiciary'.
4. *S.P. Gupta v. President of India,* AIR 1982 SC 149.
5. *Gopal v. Union of India,* AIR 1987 SC 413; *Ram Sarup v. Union of India,* AIR 1965 SC 247; *Delhi Police Sangh v. Union of India,* AIR 1987 SC 379; *Achudan v. Union of India* (1976) ISCWR 80.
6. *Ranjit v. Union of India,* AIR 1987 SC 2386; *Mukherjee v. Union of India* (1990) 3 SC J 93; *Laxmi v. Union of India* (1991) 2 SCJ 86.

Under article 34, Parliament may by law indemnify any person for anything done in contravention of fundamental rights for maintenance of order during the operation of martial law.

Article 35 lays down that the power to make laws to give effect to certain specified fundamental rights shall vest only in the Union Parliament and not in State Legislatures.

9

DIRECTIVE PRINCIPLES

PART IV, ARTICLES 36-51

The Directive Principles of State Policy embodied in Part IV are a unique feature of our Constitution. Besides the precedent of the Irish Constitution, the basic inspiration for the Directive Principles chapter came from the concept of a welfare state.[1] While seeking to protect the basic rights of the individual, the framers of the Constitution also wanted it to become an effective instrument for social revolution. The possible conflict between the rights of the individual and the needs of the community was sought to be resolved on the one hand by hedging the fundamental rights themselves by necessary restrictions in 'public interest' etc. and, on the other, by incorporating a chapter on the more positive 'Directive Principles of State Policy'. Article 37 declares that the Directive Principles are "fundamental in the governance of the country" and that "it shall be the duty of the State to apply these principles in making laws". Thus, it is clear that these constitutional directives were not intended to be merely moral precepts but were to be treated as positive mandates and part and parcel of the human rights provisions of the Constitution. The Directive Principles, however, did not give rise to any legal rights for the violation

---

1. *Kesavananda Bharti v. State of Kerala,* AIR 1973 SC 146.

of which any individual could seek a remedy nor did these bestow any power on the legislature. Also, no law could be declared *ultra vires* on the ground of inconsistency with these principles.[1]

These mandates were made "not enforceable by the courts" and were deliberately couched in terms that left to the Legislature a measure of latitude in deciding the order, the time and mode of fulfilling them as their implementation depended on several imponderable factors, such as the availability of requisite resources, the readiness of society to accept the socio-economic changes envisaged, etc.

Speaking in the Constituent Assembly, Dr. Ambedkar had categorically said that the Directive Principles were not intended to be mere pious declarations. They were instead in the nature of an instrument of instructions and whoever captured power "will have to respect these". He had said:

> It is the intention of the Assembly that in future both the legislature and the executive should not merely pay lip service to these principles enacted in this part, but that they should be made the basis of all executive and legislative action that may be taken hereafter in the matter of the governance of the country.

The non-justiciability clause in article 37 sought only to make it clear that the judiciary could not compel the State to perform a 'duty' under the 'Directives' because as Dr. Ambedkar said:

> A State just awakened from freedom with its many preoccupations might be crushed under the burden unless it was free to decide the order, the time, the place and the mode of fulfilling them.

1. *State of Madras v. Champakam Dorairajan,* (1951) SCR 525; *In re Kerala Education Bill,* AIR 1958 SC 956; *Deep Chand v. State of U.P.*; AIR 1959 SC 648; *UPSE Bd. v. Hari,* AIR 1979 SC 65.

The Directive Principles constitute an operative part of the Constitution and an important part at that, for through them the Constitution seeks to achieve the ideal of a democratic welfare state set out in the Preamble and to bring about the social and economic revolution of which the founding fathers of our republic dreamt. In the words of Justice K.S. Hegde:

> The purpose of the fundamental rights is to create an egalitarian society, to free all citizens from coercion or restriction by society and to make liberty available for all. The purpose of the Directive Principles is to fix certain social and economic goals for immediate attainment by bringing about a non-violent social revolution. Through such a social revolution the Constitution seeks to fulfil the basic needs of the common man and to change the structure of our society. It aims at making the Indian masses free in the positive sense.

The decisions of the Supreme Court from the 1970s onwards have emphasized the positive aspects of the Directive Principles. These have been held to supplement fundamental rights for achieving the objective of a welfare state. Even the fundamental rights may be amended by Parliament to implement the Directives and such legislation may be held to be valid unless it offends any of the basic features of the Constitution. It has been held by the apex court that under articles 38, 39 and 46, it is the duty of local bodies—Panchayats, Zila Parishads and Municipalities—to implement the Directive Principles in a planned manner by annual budgets providing right to residence to the poor.[1]

---

1. *State of Kerala v.Thomas*, AIR 1976 SC 496; *Mehta v. Union of India*, (1992) Supp (2) SCC 85; *Chief Justice v. Dikshitulu* (1979) 2 SCC 34; *Mukesh v. State of M.P.*, AIR 1985 SC 537; *Laxmi Kant v. Union of India*, AIR 1987 SC 232; *V.A. Sawant v. Municipal Corp.*, Bombay, JT (1994) 3 SC 573; *Ahmedabad Municipal Corp. v. N.K.G. Khan*, AIR 1997 SC 152; *State of Haryana v. Ram Chander*, AIR 1997 SC 2468.

The Directive Principles are directed towards the ideals of building a true welfare state and *inter alia* envisage an end to economic exploitation and staggering inequalities and inequities and cast upon the State the duty to secure a just social order. Thus, article 38 which is the keystone or the core of the Directive Principles lays down that

> the State shall strive to promote the welfare of the people by securing and protecting as effectively as it may a social order in which justice, social, economic and political, shall inform all the institutions of national life.

Article 39 says that the State shall direct its policy in such a manner as to secure that all men and women have the right to an adequate means of livelihood, that the ownership and control of the material resources of the community are so distributed as best to subserve the common good; that the economic system is not allowed to result in the concentration of wealth and means of production to the detriment of the common good, that there is equal pay for equal work for both men and women[1], that the health and strength of workers, men and women, and the tender age of children are not abused, that citizens are not forced by economic necessity to enter avocations unsuited to their age or strength, and that the children are given opportunities and facilities to develop in a healthy manner in freedom and dignity and that childhood and youth are protected against exploitation. This article has been referred to for interpreting the fundamental rights.[2] Article 41 seeks, within the limits of the State's economic capacity and development, to make effective provision for securing the right to work, education and public assistance in the event of unemployment, old age,

1. "not a fundamental right but a constitutional goal"—*Randhir v. Union of India,* AIR 1982 SC 879; *Ramchandra v. Union of India,* AIR 1984 SC 541.
2. *Kesavananda Bharti v. State of Kerala,* AIR 1973 SC 146; *Srinivasa v. State of Karnataka,* AIR 1987 SC 1518.

sickness and disablement or other cases of undeserved want. Articles 42 and 43 provide for endeavouring to secure for workers a living wage, humane conditions of work, maternity relief, a decent standard of life and full enjoyment of leisure and social and cultural opportunities.

Invoking the provisions of articles 39, 41 and 47 and the Child Labour (Prohibition and Regulation) Act, 1986, the Supreme Court held in *M.C. Mehta v. State of Tamil Nadu* (AIR 1997 SC 699) that the offending employer should be asked to deposit in a Child Welfare Fund Rs.20,000 for each child employed and the State should put Rs.5,000.

Some of the important Directives relate to promotion of educational and economic interests of Scheduled Castes, Scheduled Tribes and other weaker sections (article 46); duty of the State to raise the level of nutrition and the standard of living and to improve public health (article 47); organization of agriculture and animal husbandry and prohibition of cow slaughter (article 48); organisation of village Panchayats (article 40); separation of judiciary from the executive (article 50); promulgation of a uniform civil code for the whole country (article 44); protection of national monuments (article 49); and the promotion of international peace and security, just and honourable relations between nations, respect for international law and treaty obligations and settlement of international disputes by arbitration (article 51). It has to be remembered that international treaties do not automatically become part of the national law. These have to be adopted/incorporated by legislation. This comes under the jurisdiction of the Union under article 253. While interpreting national law, courts try to maintain harmony with principles of international law but in case of conflict national law has to be respected.[1]

There has been considerable and continuing

---

1. *In re Berubari Union*, AIR 1960 SC 845; *Gramophone Co. v. Birendra*, AIR 1984 SC 667.

controversy in regard to the directive regarding a Uniform Civil Code enshrined in article 44. In the Constituent Assembly, Dr. Ambedkar was strongy in favour of a uniform code. In *S.R. Bommai v. Union of India* (AIR 1994 SC 1918), the Court upheld the legislative power of Parliament to reform personal laws and urged the government to enact a uniform civil code to promote national integration. The Court regretted that article 44 had remained a dead letter. In a case where a marriage solemnized under one personal law was sought to be dissolved under another personal law after conversion of one partner, the Court dissolved the dissolution and again urged the need for a Uniform Civil Code.[1] In *Pannalal Bansilal Pitti v. State of A.P.,* (1996 (2) SCC 498) the court favoured a gradual reform towards bringing about uniformity, preferably from within. In the famous *Ahmad Khan v. Shah Banu* (AIR 1985 SC 945) when the Court granted maintenance, under the Cr. P.C., Parliament enacted the Muslim Women (Protection of Rights on Divorce) Act 1986 to annul the Court's decision. In the (July 2003) *Christian Bequests Case,* the Court held Section 118 of the Indian Succession Act 1925 unconstitutional because it imposed restrictions only on Christians. The Court said that marriage and succession laws could not be saved under the right to profess and propagate religion. Again, it stressed the need for a uniform civil code.

Even though made non-justiciable, the Directive Principles have thus far guided the Union and State Legislatures in enacting social reform legislation, the courts have cited them in support of their interpretation of constitutional provisions and the Planning Commissions have accepted them as useful guidelines for determining their approach to national reconstruction and rejuvenation.

The Constitution (Forty-second Amendment) Act, 1976 added certain new directives to the effect :

---

1. *Sarla Mudgal v. Union of India,* AIR 1995 SC 1531.

i. that children are given opportunities and facilities to develop in a healthy manner and in conditions of freedom and dignity (article 39(f);
ii. that the operation of the legal system promotes justice, on a basis of equal opportunity, and in particular the State provides free legal aid in cases of economic or other disability (article 39A). This right was inherent in article 21 also;[1]
iii. that the participation of workers in management of industries is secured (article 43A); and
iv. that the environment is protected and improved and the forests and wild life are safeguarded (article 48A).

The Forty-fourth Amendment added a clause to article 38 to say that the State shall, in particular, try to reduce inequalities of income and eliminate inequalities in status, facilities and opportunities among individuals and among groups of people living in different areas or engaged in different vocations. (Also see the chapter on 'Fundamental Rights' under 'Right to Property and Saving of certain Laws', article 31 C).

Besides, (i) by amending article 31 C, it was laid down that no law giving effect to any or all of the Directive Principles shall be void on ground of contravening any of the fundamental rights under articles 14, 19 or 31, and (ii) a new article 31 D provided specifically that no law authorising prevention or prohibition of anti-national activities or associations would be void on ground of inconsistency with any of the fundamental rights under articles 14, 19 and 31.

Article 45 originally provided for free and compulsory education for all children upto the age of 14. But the Eighty-sixth Amendment (2002) made education a fundamental right for children of 6 to 14 years by inserting a new article 21A. As a corollary, article 45 was substituted by a new article providing for early child care and education to children below 6 years.

---

1. *State of Haryana v. Darshana*, AIR 1979 SC 855; *Khatri v. State of Bihar*, AIR 1981 SC 928; *Suk Das v. Union Territory*, AIR 1986 SC 991.

The Relationship between the Preamble, the Fundamental Rights and the Directive Principles

It should be remembered that the Preamble, the Fundamental Rights and the Directive Principles are all integral parts of the same constitutional edifice. They are all equally important and have to be read with each other.

The emphasis in the entire scheme of the Constitution under the headings of the Preamble, the Fundamental Rights and the Directive Principles is on building an egalitarian society and on the concept of socio-economic justice. Inasmuch as the Directive Principles though declared to be fundamental as guiding principles for making and administering laws were not made enforceable in courts of law, they represented a subtle compromise between what the framers, as the leaders of the freedom struggle, looked upon as the ideal or the goal and what, as realists, they found to be immediately feasible. The Fundamental Rights and the Directive Principles together constituted the soul of the Constitution.

It is now clearly understood that there is no essential dichotomy between Rights and Duties or between the Fundamental Rights and the Directive Principles. They complement and supplement each other.[1] If the Fundamental Rights represent the don'ts for the Government and the legislature, the Directive Principles represent the do's. There is no conflict. While moving for the reference of the Constitution (First) Amendment Bill, 1951 to a Select Committee, Jawaharlal Nehru referred to the possibility of a conflict between the Fundamental Rights and the Directive Principles and explained the difficulty thus :

> The real difficulty which has come before us is this : The Constitution lays down certain Directive Principles of State Policy and after long discussion we agreed to them and they point out the way we have got to travel. The

1. *Kesavananda Bharti v. State of Kerala,* AIR 1973 SC 146.

Constitution also lays down certain Fundamental Rights. Both are important. The Directive Principles of State Policy represent a dynamic move towards a certain objective. The Fundamental Rights represent something static, to preserve certain rights which exist. Both again are right. But somehow and sometime it might so happen that that dynamic movement and that static standstill do not quite fit into each other.

A dynamic movement towards a certain objective necessarily means certain changes taking place: that is the essence of movement. Now, it may be that in the process of dynamic movement certain existing relationships are altered, varied or affected. In fact, they are meant to affect those settled relationships and yet if you come back to the Fundamental Rights they are meant to preserve, not indirectly, certain settled relationships. There is a certain conflict in the two approaches, not inherently, because that was not meant, I am quite sure. But there is that slight difficulty and naturally when the courts of the land have to consider these matters they have to lay stress more on the Fundamental Rights than on the Directive Principles of State Policy. The result is that the whole purpose behind the Constitution, which was meant to be a dynamic Constitution leading to a certain goal step by step, is somewhat hampered and hindered by the static element being emphasised a little more than the dynamic element and we have to find out some way of solving it.

...If in the protection of individual liberty you protect also individual or group inequality, then you come into conflict with that Directive Principle which wants, according to your own Constitution, a gradual advance, or let us put it in another way, not so gradual but more rapid advance, wherever possible to a state where there is less and less inequality and more and more equality. If any kind of an appeal to individual liberty and freedom is construed to mean as an appeal to the continuation of the existing inequality, then you get into difficulties. Then you become static, unprogressive and cannot change and you

> cannot realise that ideal of an egalitarian society which I hope most of us aim at.

While speaking on the Constitution Fourth Amendment in the Lok Sabha, Nehru declared that the responsibility for the economic and social welfare policies of the nation should lie with Parliament and not with the courts. In so far as the decisions of courts had shown that there was some inherent contradiction between the Fundamental Rights and the Directive Principles, it was for Parliament to remove the contradiction and "make Fundamental Rights subserve the Directive Principles of State Policy."

As the Supreme Court said later in 1971 :

> Freedom of trade does not mean freedom to exploit. The provisions of the Constitution are not erected as barriers to progress. They provide a plan for orderly progress towards the social order contemplated by the preamble to the Constitution. They do not permit any kind of slavery, social, economic or political. It is a fallacy to think that under our Constitution there are only rights and no duties. While rights conferred under Part III are fundamental in the governance of the country, we see no conflict on the whole between the provisions contained in Part III and Part IV. They are complementary and supplementary to each other. The provisions of Part IV enable the Legislature and the Government to impose various duties on the citizens. The provisions therein are deliberately made elastic because the duties to be imposed on the citizens depend on the extent to which the directive principles are implemented. The mandate of the Constitution is to build a welfare society in which justice, social, economic and political, shall inform all institutions of our national life. The hopes and aspirations aroused by the Constitution will be belied if the minimum needs of the lowest of our citizens are not met.[1]

---

1. *Chandra Bhavan Boarding and Lodging Bangalore Vs. The State of Mysore and others*, 1970, 2 S.C.R. 600.

Again, in Keshavanand Bharti's case, Justice Mathew made the following significant observations:

> The Fundamental Rights themselves have no fixed content; most of them are mere empty vessels into which each generation must pour its content in the light of its experience. Restrictions, abridgment, curtailment, and even abrogation of these rights in circumstances not visualized by the Constitution-makers might become necessary; their claim to supremacy or priority is liable to be overborne at particular stages in the history of the nation by the moral claims embodied in Part IV. Whether at a particular moment in the history of the nation, a particular fundamental right should have priority over the moral claim embodied in Part IV or must yield to them is a matter which must be left to be decided by each generation in the light of its experience and its values. And, if Parliament in its capacity as the amending body, decides to amend the Constitution in such a way as to take away or abridge a Fundamental Right to give priority value to the moral claims embodied in Part IV of the Constitution, the Court cannot adjudge the constitutional amendment as bad for the reason that what was intended to be subsidiary by the Constitution-makers has been made dominant. Judicial review of a constitutional amendment for the reason that it gives priority value to the moral claims embodied in Part IV over the Fundamental Rights embodied in Part III is impermissible. [1973 (4) S.C.C. 225].

A distinction is sometimes sought to be made between what may be called 'positive rights' and 'negative rights'. Broadly speaking, while Part III deals with areas of individual freedom and the extent to which the State can restrain it, Part IV deals with positive duties cast upon the State to attain the ideal of social and economic justice. Even among the fundamental rights, however, there are some positive injunctions which seek to protect the interests of the society and the rights of the poor citizens from encroachment by entrenched sections. Thus, article 17 abolishes untouchability and makes its practice in any form an offence punishable by law. Article 15 *inter alia* provides that no citizen shall be discriminated against in the use of public places like shops, wells, roads, eating houses etc. on account of his religion, race, caste, sex or place of birth. Article 23 prohibits another great social evil, that of forced labour. The whole effort has been to ensure that the fundamental rights of the citizens do not degenerate into the liberties of the few against the interests of the many.

The National Commission to Review the Working of the Constitution (2002) *inter alia* recommended:

(i) A strategic plan of action to create a large number of employment opportunities,

(ii) Setting up a National Education Commission every five years to report on compulsory education etc.,

(iii) Promoting through civil society initiatives interfaith and inter-religious harmony and social solidarity, and

(iv) Establishing a high status body to review the implementation of Directive Principles.

10

FUNDAMENTAL DUTIES

PART IVA, ARTICLE 51A

Even though brought in by the Constitution (Forty-Second Amendment) Act, 1976 during the operation of the proclamation of Emergency, Part IV A, laying down certain duties of the citizens, is one of the most valuable parts of the Constitution. It is also the most neglected.

The fundamental duties enshrined in article 51A now are in consonance with article 29(1) of the Universal Declaration of Human Rights which says:

> Everyone has duties to the community in which alone the free and full development of his personality is possible.

While the Fundamental Rights provisions covered the rights of the individual and the Directive Principles the duties of the State, there were until 1976 no provisions in our Constitution laying down the duties of the individual even though the traditions and temper of Indian thought through the ages laid greater emphasis on duties. As the Verma Committee (HRD Min. GOI, 1999) on Fundamental Duties said:

> Essentially all that is contained in the Fundamental Duties is just a codification of tasks integral to the Indian way of life. A close scrutiny of the clauses of article 51A indicate that a number of these clauses basically refer to such values

as have been a part of the Indian tradition, mythology, religions and practices. At this juncture of history, the nation realises an urgent need to re-emphasise these in a manner that would be acceptable to and be imbibed by all generations. To achieve these objectives, *it would be essential to create public awareness of the need to appreciate and internalise the concept and practice of Fundamental Duties with particular emphasis on the necessity of creating a harmonious society with a scientific outlook, free from tensions and turmoils.*

The Supreme Court of India has in several cases relied on Fundamental Duties contained in article 51A to determine the duty of the State, and when necessary, give directions or frame guidelines to achieve the purpose. This has been done in several cases relating to preservation and conservation of environment, ecology, and prevention of degeneration of forests, wild life, flora and fauna, etc. The court has observed that preservation of environment and maintenance of the ecological balance are the responsibility not only of the Government but also the Fundamental Duty of every citizen.

Even though belatedly, it was thought appropriate that citizenship must carry with it certain fundamental obligations and that these should be specifically and explicitly incorporated in the Constitution. It does not mean that before the Forty-second Amendment the citizens had no duty. There was a specific provision in article 33 regarding the need "to ensure the proper discharge of the duties and the maintenance of discipline" among the armed forces etc. Also, each of the Fundamental Rights of individual citizens and others embodied in Part III of the Constitution implied a corresponding duty and obligation. In fact, there can be no rights in a society where there are no duties. Rights and duties are not only reconcilable but inseparable. For every right, there is a corresponding duty. Duty is an inalienable part of right; the two represent the two sides of the same coin. What is duty for one is another's right and *vice versa.* If all men have a right to life, a duty is also cast upon all men to respect human life and not to injure another person. The right to freedom implies that the citizens must create conditions and so fashion society that freedom for every individual is assured. Freedom by its very nature requires self-discipline and promotion of social and political harmony. For the freedom of one individual is limited by the similar freedom of other individuals. And each individual comes to have a duty to accord the same rights to others which he wants for himself. Freedom for each individual can endure when one respects the freedom of all other individuals. Discharge of duties by them strengthens their own rights.

When Gandhiji was requested to give his thoughts on the Universal Declaration of Human Rights, he said:

> The source of right is duty. If we all discharge our duties, rights will not be far to seek. If leaving duties unperformed we run after rights, they will escape us like will o' the wisp, the more we pursue them, the further they will fly.
>
> I learned from my illiterate but wise mother that all rightsto be deserved and preserved come from duty well done. Thus the very right to live accrues to us only when we do the duty of citizenship of the world. From this one fundamental statement, perhaps it is easy enough to define duties of man and woman and correlate every right to some corresponding duty to be first performed. Every other right can be shown to be a usurpation hardly worth fighting for.

Gandhiji sought to emphasise the economic and social responsibilities of all citizens. It was in keeping with his ideas that the Constitution (Forty-Second Amendment) Act, 1976 added to the Constitution a new Part IVA titled 'Fundamental Duties' after the original Parts III and IV of Fundamental Rights and Directive Principles respectively.

The new Part IVA, article 51A (a) to (j) laid down 10 duties for every citizen of India. Later, the Constitution (Eighty-sixth Amendment) Act, 2002 added a new Clause

(k) as the eleventh duty.

(1) *To abide by the Constitution and respect its ideals and institutions, the National Flag and the National Anthem:* The first and the foremost duty assigned to every citizen of India is to abide by the Constitution and respect its ideals and institutions, the National Flag and the National Anthem. These are the very physical foundations of our citizenship. All of us are supposed to maintain the dignity of the Constitution by not indulging in any activities in violation of the letter or spirit of the Constitution. Ours is a vast country with many languages, sub-cultures and religious and ethnic diversities, but the essential unity of the country is epitomised in the one Constitution, one flag, one people and one citizenship. We are all governed and guided by this Constitution irrespective of caste, religion, race, sex etc. The Constitution was the result of the many commitments, promises and pledges made by nationalist leaders to the people of India. Also, it embodied efforts at reconciliation, accommodation and compromise. All of us and the Fundamental Rights of each of us are protected by it. Similarly the National Flag and the National Anthem are symbols of our history, sovereignty, unity and pride. If a citizen of India by any overt or covert act shows disrespect to the Constitution, the National Anthem or the National Flag, it would be not only an anti-social and anti-national activity but it would also spell doom to all our rights and our very existence as citizens of a sovereign nation. Each citizen must therefore not only refrain from any such activity but also do his best to prevent any miscreant trying to show disrespect to our national symbols. Every nation is proud of its citizens because of their dedication, sincerity and patriotism. We, the citizens of India, have to be equally proud of our nation, our Constitution, our Flag and our Anthem. We must put the nation above our narrow personal interests and then only we will be able to protect our hard-earned freedom and sovereignty.

(2) *To cherish and follow the noble ideals which inspired our national struggle for freedom:* The citizens of India must cherish and follow the noble ideals which inspired the national struggle for freedom. The battle of freedom was a long one where thousands sacrificed their lives for our freedom. It becomes our duty to remember the sacrifices made by our forefathers for the cause of the country. But, what is much more important is to remember, imbibe and follow the ideals which pervaded our unique struggle. It was not a struggle merely for political freedom of India. It was for the social and economic emancipation of the people all over the world. Its ideals were those of building a just society and a united nation, of freedom, equality, non-violence, brotherhood and world peace. If we, the citizens of India remain conscious of and committed to these ideals, we will be able to rise above the various fissiparous tendencies raising their ugly heads now and then here and there.

Parties and politicians who use religion, casteism, separatism etc. for political ends and for capturing power are clearly violating their Fundamental Duties under the Constitution.

(3) *To uphold and protect the sovereignty, unity and integrity of India:* To protect the sovereignty, unity and integrity of India is a pre-eminent national obligation of all citizens of India. In a democratic system of governance, sovereignty lies with the people. To defend our sovereignty is our own responsibility. If the freedom and unity of the country are jeopardized, the nation ceases to exist and if there is no nation, who lives?

(4) *To defend the country and render national service when called upon to do so:* The primordial origins of the State are said to be in the need to defend ourselves against external enemies. In modern nation-States, it is considered axiomatic that every citizen is bound to be ready to defend the country against war or external aggression. Present-day wars are not fought on the battlefield only nor are they won only by the

armed forces; the citizens at large play a most vital role in a variety of ways. Sometimes, civilians may be required also to take up arms in defence of the country, if the situation warrants it. By fighting to defend the country, the citizens are fighting only to defend their own liberty and that of their posterity.

Here, mention may be made of article 23(2) whereunder State is allowed to impose "compulsory service for public purposes" subject to the condition that no discrimination is made on grounds of religion, race, caste or class or any of them.

(5) *To promote harmony and the spirit of common brotherhood amongst all the people of India transcending religious, linguistic and regional or sectional diversities; to renounce practices derogatory to the dignity of women:* To promote harmony and the spirit of common brotherhood amongst all the people of India essentially flows from the basic value of fraternity enshrined in the Preamble to the Constitution. India is a country of different castes, languages, religions and many cultural streams but we are one people with one Constitution, one flag and one citizenship. Spirit of brotherhood should come very normally among the citizens of a country like India where the norm has been to consider the entire world as one family. The Constitution also casts upon us the Fundamental Duty of ensuring that all practices derogatory to the dignity of women are renounced. This again should come normally to a country where the ideals said that gods reside where women are worshipped. (*yatra naryastu pujyante ramante tatra devata)*. It is for us to rise above the later day degenerations and aberrations which tarnished the image of our society. Incidentally, it may be noted that under Article 23(1) of the Fundamental Rights, traffic in human beings is prohibited.

(6) *To value and preserve the rich heritage of our composite culture*: To preserve the rich heritage of our composite culture is another Fundamental Duty of every

citizen. Our cultural heritage is one of the noblest and the richest. Also, it is part of the heritage of the earth. What we have inherited from the past, we must preserve and pass on to the future generations in tact. Each generation leaves its footprints on the sands of time. We must hold precious and dear what our fore-fathers have created and their successive generations bequeathed to us as symbols of their artistic excellence and achievements. Generations to come always draw inspiration from past history which stimulates them to aim at ever greater heights of achievement and excellence. It becomes the ardent duty of every citizen to ensure that these monuments and pieces of art are not in anyway damaged, disfigured, scratched or subjected to vandalism or greed of unscrupulous traders and smugglers.

One of the most ancient civilizations of the world, India can take legitimate pride in having been a civilizational unity without a break for more than five thousand years. We all are part of this great civilization and culture. Our contributions in the fields of art, sculpture, architecture, mathematics, science, medicine etc. are well-known. Some of the oldest, deepest and most sublime philosophical thought and literature was born in India. We have several historical monuments of great archaeological value spread over the entire country. These include forts, palaces, temples, etc. Also, this territory had had the honour of being the birth place of several great religions like Hinduism, Buddhism, Jainism and Sikhism. Our past has shown us the path of peace, love, non-violence and truth. As citizens of this country, it is the responsibility of all of us to work for the preservation of this rich heritage and its cultural values and live in love and harmony.

The Directive Principle under article 49 similarly enjoins the State to protect monuments and places and objects of national, artistic or historic importance.

(7) *To protect and improve the natural environment including forests, lakes, rivers and wild life, and to have compassion*

for living creatures: In the face of menace of the increasing pollution and environmental degradation, it is the duty of every citizen to protect and improve natural environment including forests, lakes, rivers and wild life and to have compassion for living creatures. The rising air, water and noise pollution and large-scale denudation of forests is causing immense harm to all human life on earth. The mindless and wanton deforestation in the name of the needs of development is causing havoc in the form of natural calamities and imbalances. By protecting our forest cover, planting new trees, cleaning rivers, conserving water resources, reforesting wastelands, hills and mountains and controlling pollution in cities, villages and industrial units, we can help save the future of our fellow citizens and of planet earth itself. What is needed is a concerted effort at an awareness campaign and a planned strategy to move forward through voluntary citizen initiatives. Governmental steps alone cannot help bring about a pollution-free atmosphere to live now and in the future.

The mention of protection of environment etc. as a duty of citizens is intended to reinforce the other constitutional provision—Article 48A—under the Directive Principles which enjoins the State to protect and improve environment and safeguard the forests and wild life.

Earth is the common heritage of man and animals. We have no right to annihilate or drive away from their territory or natural habitat the wild denizens. Ancient Indian thought talks of *Sarvesham Shantir bhavatu* (peace unto all living beings and entire environment) or *Ahimsa paramodharma, Ahimsa paramo tapah* (non-violence is the greatest duty and the greatest penance).

(8) *To develop the scientific temper, humanism and the spirit of inquiry and reform:* One of our great Founding Fathers, Jawaharlal Nehru always laid great emphasis on the need for Indian citizens developing a scientific temper and a spirit of inquiry—an inquisitiveness for learning from

developments around the world. This was particularly necessary because of the most revolutionary scientific advances during this century and in the context of our background of superstitions and obscurantism. Nehru laid the foundations of the the modern industrialised India by building the necessary scientific and technological infrastructures. Now, it is the bounden duty of every citizen to preserve and promote a scientific temper and a spirit of inquiry to keep pace with the fast changing world. Also, the Constitution ordains that science and technology must be tempered with a sense of humanism because ultimately the end of all progress is the human being and the quality of life and relationships that is developed.

(9) *To safeguard public property and to abjure violence:* It is most unfortunate that in a country which preaches non-violence to the rest of the world, we see from time to time spectacles of senseless violence and destruction of public property indulged in by a few of its citizens. This is why it became necessary to prescribe the responsibility "to safeguard public property and abjure violence" as a fundamental citizenship duty.

(10) *To strive towards excellence in all spheres of individual and collective activity, so that the nation constantly rises to higher levels of endeavour and achievement:* The drive for excellence in all spheres of individual and collective activity is the demand of times and a basic requirement in a highly competitive world. Nothing but the best would have survival potential in tomorrow's world. This would include respect for professional obligations and excellence. Whatever work we take up either as individual citizens or as groups, our effort should be directed to achieving the goal of excellence. Also, special emphasis is called for in the area of collective activity. It is often said that the performance of individual Indians is excellent but we lack team spirit. If this drawback can be remedied we can put India on the map as a fast developing country.

(11) *Every parent or guardian to provide opportunities for education to his child or ward between the age of 6 and 14 years:* The National Commission to Review the Working of the Constitution had recommended making education a fundamental right for all children upto the age of 14. The Constitution (Eighty-sixth Amendment) Act 2002, however provided for free and compulsory education as a legally enforceable fundamental right for all children between the age of 6 and 14 years. To meet the criticism of not covering the children below 6 years, the Act amended Directive Principles to say that the State shall endeavour to provide early childhood care and education for all children below the age of six years. Also, it added a new clause (k) to chapter IVA, Article 51A to cast on parents and guardians a duty to provide opportunities for education to children between the age of 6 and 14 years.

There is no provision in the Constitution for direct enforcement of the Fundamental Duties enshrined in article 51A nor is there any provision to prevent or punish their violation. But, as Justice Venkataramiah has pointed out, there is no provision declaring them non-justiciable either and in the context of the use of the terms 'fundamental' and 'duties', these should *prima facie* be enforceable. It may be expected that in determining the constitutionality of any law, if Supreme Court finds that it seeks to give effect to any of these Duties, it may consider such law to be "reasonable" in relation to article 14 or 19 and thus save such law from unconstitutionality.[1] The purpose of incorporating the Fundamental Duties in the Constitution is to make the citizens aware of their social and economic obligations and to warn them to do and not to do certain things in the interest of their country, their fellow citizens and themselves.

For the implementation of atleast some of the fundamental duties of citizens as the Verma Committee

1. *Mohan v. Union of India,* (1992) 1 SCC 594.

(1999) has stated, legal provisions exist:

A. The Emblems and Names (Prevention of Improper Use) Act 1950 was enacted soon after independence, *inter alia,* to prevent improper use of the National Flag and the National Anthem.

B. In order to ensure that no disrespect is shown to the National Flag, Constitution of India and the National Anthem, the Prevention of Insults to National Honour Act 1971 was enacted.

C. In order to ensure that correct usage regarding display of the National Flag is well understood, the instructions issued from time to time on the subject have been embodied in *Flag Code India* which has been made available to all the State Governments and Union Territory Administrations (UTs).

D. There are a number of provisions in the existing criminal laws to ensure that the activities which encourage enmity between different groups of people on grounds of religion, race, place of birth, residence, language, etc. are adequately punished. Writings, speeches, gestures, activities, exercises, drills, etc. aimed at creating a feeling of insecurity or ill will among the members of other communities, etc. have been prohibited under Section 153A of the Indian Penal Code (IPC).

E. Imputations and assertions prejudicial to national integration constitute a punishable offence under section 153B of the IPC.

F. A communal organization can be declared unlawful association under the provisions of unlawful Activities (Prevention) Act 1967.

G. Offences related to religion and caste are covered in Sections 295 298 of the IPC (Chapter XV) and provisions of the Protection of Civil Rights Act, 1955 (earlier the Untouchability (Offences) Act 1955).

H. Sections 123(3) and (3A) of the Representation of People Act, 1951 declare that soliciting of votes on the ground of religion and the promotion or attempt to promote feelings of enmity or hatred between different classes of citizens of India on grounds of religion, race, caste, community or language is a corrupt practice. A person indulging in a corrupt practice can be disqualified for being a Member of Parliament or a State Legislature under Section 8A of the Representation of People Act, 1951.

The courts can certainly take fundamental duties of citizens into consideration while construing a law amenable to more than one interpretation. Article 51A(g) regarding protection of environment has particularly come up before the courts. Oral orders were issued by the Supreme Court for stopping quarrying operations in some areas in the State of U.P. Also, orders were issued in respect of declaring certain disputed areas as reserved forests under the Indian Forests Act 1927 [Section 20].[1]

The Verma Committee on Fundamental Duties has listed and documented as many as 138 Supreme Court cases in the area of environmental protection which are mainly as follows: *Buffalo Traders Welfare Asso. v. Maneka Gandhi,* 1994 Supp (3) SCC 448 (Slaughter House Idgah, Delhi); *M.C. Mehta v. Union of India,* 1994 Supp (3) SCC 717 (Air Polution by industries); *Vellore Citizens Welfare Forum v. Union of India,* 1996 AIR (SC) 2715 (Right to clean environment); *M.C. Mehta v. Union of India,* (1999) SCC 413 (Traffic Management and pollution, Delhi); *T.N.G. Thirumulkpad v. Union of India,* (1998) 9 SCC 632 (Protection of forests); *M.C. Mehta v. Union of India,* (1998) 9 SCC 93 (Protection of Taj Mahal); *M.C. Mehta v. Union of India,* (1998) 8 SCC 648 (Lead free petrol for pollution control); *M.C. Mehta v. Union of India,* (1998) 1 SCC 363 (Removal of hoardings); *S. Jagannath v. Union of India,* 1997 (1) JT 160 (Coastal pollution due to shrimp farming); *Indian Council for Enviro-Legal Action v. Union of India,* AIR (SC) 1446 (Industrial Pollution).

The High Court of Allahabad in *Ram Prasad v. State of U.P.*(AIR 1988 All. 309) held that addition of Part IV A in the Constitution has brought performance of citizenship duties within the sphere of constitutional law and the purview of courts. Discussing the significance of article 51A (g), the court

---

1. *Mumbai Kamgar Sabha v. Abdulbhai,* AIR 1976 SC 1455; *Rural Litigation Kendra v. State of U.P.,* AIR 1987 SC 2426; *Sachidanand v. State of West Bengal,* AIR 1987 SC 1109; *Banvasi Seva Ashram v. State of U.P.,* AIR 1987 SC 374.

said that it was intended to regulate behavior and to inspire citizens to strive towards excellence. Excellence meant surpassing merit, virtue, honest performance.

The Constitution expects the citizens to perform their duties in an excellent way rather than half-heartedly.

The rulers and the legislators—the Ministers, the lawmakers and the administrators—have to be conscious not only of the fundamental duties of citizens at large but also of their own fundamental duties as citizens. It is one of their most fundamental constitutional obligations to be all the time aware of the Fundamental Rights of the citizens under the Constitution. For, wherever an obligation is cast on the 'State' it is for the citizens in positions of authority to implement it.

Inasmuch as we are dependent on the Constitution of India and on the unity and integrity of the Indian nation for our continued status as citizens of India, it is our bounden duty not only to observe every one of the citizenship duties enumerated in Part IVA of the Constitution but also to meticulously respect and try to implement through every means at our disposal and through all our conduct and actions all the citizenship values—explicit or implied—under the Constitution.

Justice Venkataramiah very aptly quotes a former U.S. Senator, Elihu Root on this point. The Senator says:

> Of course, voting is fundamental and essential part of the qualified citizen's duty to the Government of his country. A man who does not think it worthwhile to exercise this right to vote for public offices and on such public questions as are submitted to the voters, is strangely ignorant of the real basis of all prosperity that he has or hopes for and the real duty which rests upon him as a man of elementary morals. A man who will not take the trouble to vote is a poor spirited fellow willing to live on the labours of others and to shirk an honourable obligation, to do his share in return.

> The experiment of popular government cannot be successful unless citizens of a country generally take part in the government. There is no man free from responsibility which is exactly proportional to each man's capacity, to his education, to his experience in life, to his disinterestedness, to his capacity for leadership—in brief to his equipment for effective action in the great struggle that is continually going on to determine the preponderance of good and bad forces in government and upon the issue of which depend results so momentous to himself and his family, his children, his country and mankind. The selfish men who have special interests to subserve are going to take part, the corrupt men who want to take something out of government are going to take part, the demagogues who wish to attain places of power through passion and prejudice of their fellows are going to take part. The forces of unselfishness, of self-control, of justice, of love of country, of honesty are set off against them and these forces should have every possible attraction and personality and power among men, or they will go down in the irrepressible conflict. The scheme of popular government upon which so much depends cannot be worked successfully unless a great body of such men do their share and no one of us can fail to do his share without forfeiting something of his title to self-respect.

Public spirited citizens have to come forward to take interest in the local community problems and decision making processes. It will give them an understanding of what government is all about and thus feel involved in the life of the community and the country. Proper functioning of democracy is dependent on the quality of citizenship and this requires dedicated, dynamic, disciplined and intelligent citizens. The very right to live accrues to us only when we do our duties as good citizens. The Fundamental Duties that the Constitution enjoins on us, represent the minimum of our obligations as citizens.

A good citizen is law abiding. Enlightened citizenship requires placing public interest above personal interest. Individual citizens should observe certain standards of self-discipline, control baser instincts, respect the rights of others, perform their duties to society, pursue national goals, and train themselves in the art of peaceful living and democratic governance through implementation of their Fundamental Rights and citizenship duties. Only with such a responsible citizenry can both the individual citizen and the society develop to their full potential and democratic polity attain its full stature.

The eleven fundamental constitutional duties for citizens are like the commandments—morally and ethically binding on all of us. In addition, every article of the Constitution casts a duty on citizens to see it fulfilled in letter and spirit.

There are some articles under Fundamental Rights like articles 17, 18 to 23 which seek to abolish untouchability and titles and prohibit traffic in human beings and forced labour or begar. These specifically obligate the citizens not to practise untouchability, not to accept or use titles and not to indulge in traffic in human beings or in taking begar. Somewhat similarly, article 15(a) demands of citizens not to discriminate between fellow citizens on grounds of religion, race, caste, sex or place of birth.

In a democracy it is most important for citizens to exercise their right to vote with a great sense of responsibility to elect the right people. But, it is not enough to discharge the responsibility of casting a vote once in five years. It is even more important to exercise a constant vigil over the conduct and actions of our representatives and ensure that they keep to the right track, that power does not go to their head or corrupt them and that they do not indulge in anti-national or anti-people activities. For, the ultimate responsibility is of the people (read citizens) themselves. Freedom and democracy cannot be sustained and citizenship itself cannot survive if we, the citizens of India do not respect the rights of others and do not fulfil our basic obligations towards our fellow citizens. For, the most fundamental citizenship value and constitutional obligation is that of caring for our fellow citizens as our equal brothers and sisters and respecting their liberty, freedom and rights.

In the ultimate analysis, the only way to bring about adherence to fundamental duties is through public opinion and education in citizenship values and duties, and building adequate awareness and a congenial climate wherein every citizen feels proud and bound to perform his constitutional duties to the nation and pay his debt to society.[1]

The National Commission to Review the Working of the Constitution has recommended that for effectuating Fundamental Duties, the following steps should be taken:

(i) The first and foremost step required by the Union and State Governments is to sensitise the people and to create a general awareness of the provisions of fundamental duties amongst the citizens on the lines recommended by the Justice Verma Committee on the Subject. Consideration should be given to the ways and means by which Fundamental Duties could be popularized and made effective;

(ii) Right to freedom of religion and other freedoms must be jealously guarded and rights of minorities and fellow citizens respected;

(iii) Reform of the whole process of education is an immediate but immense need, as is the need to free it from governmental or political control; it is only through education that will power to adhere to our Fundamental Durties as citizens can be inculcated;

(iv) Duty to vote at elections, actively participate in the democratic process of governance and to pay taxes should be included in article 51A; and

---

1. For a detailsed study of the theme, see Subhash C. Kashyap, *Citizen and the Constitution,* Pub. Div., Min. I & B, G O I, New Delhi, 2nd ed., 2002.

(v) The other recommendations of the Justice Verma Committee on operationalisation of Fundamental Duties of Citizens shoud be implemented at the earliest.

The following should also be incorporated as fundamental duties in article 51A of the Constitution:

(i) To foster a spirit of family values and responsible parenthood in the matter of education, physical and moral well-being of children.

(ii) Duty of industrial organizations to provide education to children of their employees.

11

THE UNION EXECUTIVE

PART V, CHAPTER 1, ARTICLES 52-78

Our Constitution-makers chose for us the system of parliamentary democracy with ministerial responsibility to the representatives of the people in the Lok Sabha. Under the British system, the head of the State is the hereditary monarch. But, as the relationship between the King and the Parliament has evolved over the centuries, real political and executive power has come to be vested in the Cabinet while the King has become a constitutional, nominal or ceremonial head only. We, in India, do not have a monarchy. Also, we are not a small unitary State like the United Kingdom (U.K.). We are a large republic and a Union of States like the United States with an elected President at the head of the Republic. We are thus in the unique position of being at once a parliamentary polity and a Republic with a President.

Under article 73 of the Constitution, the executive power of the Union extends to all matters with respect to which Parliament may make laws and to the exercise of all powers that accrue to the Government of India from any international treaty or agreement. It is important to remember that all executive power has to be exercised in accordance with the Constitution.

THE PRESIDENT

Position and Powers of the President

Article 52 of the Constitution says that there shall be a President of India. The position of the President in the scheme of our Constitution is one of the highest honour, dignity and prestige. He is the Head of the State and it would be very wrong to say that he is only a nominal or titular head. As Nehru said in the Constituent Assembly, it was not intended to make the President of India a mere figurehead. All executive power of the Union is vested in him and is to be exercised by him either directly or through officers subordinate to him in accordance with the Constitution, 'Officers subordinate' are supposed to include Ministers (*Emperor V. Srinath,* AIR 1945 PC 163). All executive action of the Government of India is taken in his name. The Supreme Command of the Defence Forces is vested in him and is to be exercised in accordance with law (articles 53 and 77).

The President appoints the Prime Minister and on his advice other Ministers. All the Ministers hold office during the pleasure of the President (article 75).

Along with the two Houses of Parliament, the President is an integral part of Parliament. He summons the two Houses to meet, prorogues their sittings, and may dissolve the Lok Sabha (article 85). He addresses the members of the two Houses assembled together at the beginning of the first session each year and after each General Election. The President may also, otherwise, send messages to Houses of Parliament or address either or both of them. All Bills after being passed by the two Houses of Parliament must receive the assent of the President in order to become laws. Bills belonging to certain categories (*e.g.* money bills) can be introduced and proceeded with only with the President's recommendation (articles 79, 85–87, 111 and 117). When during the Ninth Lok Sabha an amendment proposing pension to members of Parliament after only a year's service was allowed to be introduced and passed without President's recommendation, President Venkataraman did not give his assent to the Bill.

When both Houses of Parliament are not in session and the President is satisfied about the need for immediate action, he can promulgate ordinances which have the same force and effect as laws passed by Parliament (article 123). These are in the nature of interim or temporary legislation. For, their continuance is subject to parliamentary approval and enactment of laws to replace the ordinances. The President's power to issue ordinances extends to only those matters in which Parliament can make laws. The Supreme Court has upheld the legitimacy and validity of the President's power to issue ordinances.[1]

There are certain other functions which the President is required to perform under the Constitution in relation to Parliament. He appoints the Speaker *pro tem* of Lok Sabha and an acting Chairman of Rajya Sabha as and when the need arises. He summons the joint sitting of both Houses in case of final disagreement between them on a Bill. The President causes to be laid, every year, before Parliament, the Budget of the government, referred to in the Constitution as the "annual financial statement" and certain other reports of constitutional functionaries like the Comptroller and Auditor-General of India, Finance Commission, Union Public Service Commission, National Commission for Scheduled Castes, National Commission for Scheduled Tribes and Backward Classes Commission. He may nominate not more than two members of the Anglo-Indian Community to Lok Sabha, if he is of the opinion that the community is not adequately represented in the House. The President also nominates 12 members to the Rajya Sabha from amongst persons having special knowledge or practical experience

1. *A.K. Roy v. Union of India,* AIR 1982 SC 710; *R.K. Garg v. Union of India,* AIR 1981 SC 2139.

in respect of such matters as literature, science, art and social service. Besides, he is empowered to decide, after obtaining the opinion of the Election Commission, whether any member duly elected attracts the disqualifications laid down in article 102 of the Constitution. His decision in the matter is final.

All the high functionaries of the State including the judges of the Supreme Court and of the High Courts, the Attorney-General of India, the Comptroller and Auditor-General of India, the Governors etc. are appointed by the President (articles 76, 124, 148, 155 and 217).

Under article 72, the President has the power to grant pardons, reprieves, respites or remissions of punishment or to suspend, remit or commute the sentence of any person in all cases where the punishment has been awarded by a Court Martial, is for an offence against a Union law, or is a sentence of death. The power of the President under article 72 is independent of the judiciary. He does not function as a court of appeal. The idea is to enable correction of any judicial error. Also, the President may decide to give relief from what may appear to him to be too harsh a punishment. Justifying the vesting of this power in the President, the Law Commission in its 1967 Report on capital punishment said :

> There are many matters which may not have been considered by the courts. The hands of the court are tied down by the evidence placed before it. A sentence of death passed by a Court after consideration of all the materials placed before it may yet require reconsideration because of: (i) facts not placed before the court, (ii) facts placed before the court but not in the proper manner, (iii) acts discovered after the passing of the sentence, (iv) events which have developed after the passing of the sentence, and (v) other special features.

The President cannot be compelled to give a hearing to a petitioner. The courts cannot interfere with the decisions of the President on merits, but they can look into whether the President has considered all relevant materials.[1]

Since in the exercise of all his functions, the President has to act in accordance with the advice of the Council of Ministers (article 74), in the exercise of function of granting pardons etc. also, the President is taken to be acting only on the advice of the Council of Ministers.

Under article 352, the President may proclaim a state of emergency in the whole or part of India if he is satisfied that a grave situation exists whereby the security of India or part of its territory is threatened by war or external aggression or armed rebellion. Under article 354, the President may restrict or prohibit the distribution of revenues. When a proclamation of emergency is in operation, the President may suspend the enforcement of fundamental rights (article 359). Under article 356, in case of failure of constitutional machinery in any State, the President may impose by proclamation President's rule in that State. Article 360 empowers the President to declare financial emergency. Thus, the emergency powers of the President are drastic and far-reaching.

To sum up, the President has (1) executive powers to be exercised by him directly or through officers; (2) powers to appoint high functionaries of the State including judges of the Supreme Court and High Courts; (3) military powers as the Supreme Commander of the armed forces with the authority to declare war and peace; (4) power to grant pardon, reprieve etc.; (5) diplomatic powers including appointment of ambassadors and receiving the credentials of foreign diplomatic representatives; (6) legislative powers including powers to summon and prorogue Houses and

1. *Hukam Singh v. State of Punjab*, AIR 1975 P&H 902; *Harbans v. State of U.P.*, AIR 1982 S.C. 849; *Kuljit v. Lt. Governor*, AIR 1982 S.C. 774; *Maru v. Union of India*, AIR 1980 S.C. 2147; *Godse v. State of Maharastra*, AIR 1961 SC 600; *Nanavati v. State of Bombay*, AIR 1961 S.C. 122; *State of Punjab v. Joginder Singh*, (1990) GLJ 1464 (SC).

dissolve Lok Sabha, assent to Bills etc. and issue ordinances having the force of law; (7) Emergency powers.

Despite all this array of impressive powers, our President's position is conceived as that of a constitutional head of State. It has to be remembered that article 53 makes it clear that the executive power of the Union has to be exercised by the President "in accordance with the Constitution" and the exercise of the powers of the President as the Supreme Commander of the armed forces has to be "regulated by law".[1] Also, under article 60, the President takes an oath "to preserve, protect and defend the Constitution and the law". Article 74(1) requires the President to act only with the aid and advice of the Council of Ministers in the discharge of all his functions. This follows also from our adoption of the parliamentary form of Government with ministerial responsibility. The Supreme Court through various decisions has upheld the position that the President is a constitutional head who must act on the advice of the Council of Ministers and that the real executive power in our system vests in the Council of Ministers.[2] Also, the Constitution does not make any distinction between normal times and Emergency in the matter of the exercise of President's powers. There is no special provision for any discretionary exercise of powers during the Emergency. Article 74 governs exercise of all powers by the President and as such the President is as much bound by the advice of Council of Ministers during Emergency as during normal times. By the 44th constitutional amendment, the position was finally put beyond all doubt and it was made clear that Emergency can be declared by the President only after

1. *U.N. Rao v. Indira Gandhi,* AIR 1971 S.C. 1002; *Sanjeev v. State of Madras,* AIR 1970 S.C. 1102.
2. *Samsher Singh v. State of Punjab,* AIR 1974 SC 2192; *U.N. Rao v. Indira Gandhi,* AIR 1971 SC 1002; *M/s Bishamber Dayal Chandra Mohan v. State of U.P.* AIR 1982 S.C. 33; *Ram Jawaya v. State of Punjab,* AIR 1955 S.C. 544.

receiving in writing a communication regarding the Union Cabinet deciding to advise him to do so.

Even though the Constitution makes it obligatory for the President to act on advice of the Council of Ministers, there are some grey areas where the President may still have to use his own judgement and wisdom. These are:

1 Appointment of the Prime Minister (article 75(1)) in a situation where no single party or coalition commands the clear support of the majority of the Lok Sabha members. Obviously, the President cannot appoint the new Prime Minister on the advice of the outgoing Prime Minister who may have lost the election or the support of the House.
2. Appointment of a Prime Minister in case of sudden death (for example, by assasination as in the case of Indira Gandhi) of the incumbent, where the ruling legislature party is unable to meet immediately to elect a leader, there is no settled seniority among Cabinet ministers and a name from outside the Cabinet is suggested.
3. Dissolution of Lok Sabha (article 85(2)(b)) on the advice of a Council of Ministers that may have lost the majority support in Lok Sabha or against whom a vote of no-confidence may have been passed.
4. Dismissal of Ministers (article 75(2)) in case the Council of Ministers loses the confidence of the House but refuses to resign.

In some such situations, the role of the President may become most crucial and decisive. This happened, for instance, when Charan Singh, Rajiv Gandhi and Chandra Sekhar came to be appointed to the office of Prime Minister.

A question was raised whether a person who was not a member of either house of Parliament could be appointed Prime Minister. It was held that under article 75(5), such a person could be a Minister for six months and since the Prime Minister was also a Minister he could be appointed from among non-members if he had the confidence of the House.[1]

---

1. *S.P. Anand v. H.D. Deve Gowda*, AIR 1997 SC 272.

Besides, article 78(a) casts on the Prime Minister the responsibility to keep the President informed of all decisions relating to the administration of the affairs of the Union and proposals for legislation and to furnish the information asked for by the President in that regard. If a decision has been taken by a Minister, the President may require that it be referred to the Council of Ministers for consideration. Also, under the Proviso to article 74 inserted in 1978 by the 44th Amendment, the President may require the Council of Ministers to reconsider their advice. He shall, of course, act on the reconsidered advice. But according to article 74 (2), the question whether any, and if so what advice was tendered by the Ministers to the President is confidential between them and cannot be inquired into in any court of law. Of course, the Government itself is not barred from producing on its own any papers relating to the cabinet decisions and advice to the President and the Court can then look into them.[1] It is true that in *Kartar Singh's case*, the Supreme Court had held that the Court was within its rights to look into the basis of the advice tendered by the Council of Ministers to the President. But, in view of the very clear words of article 74(2), the view in *Kartar Singh v. State of Punjab* (JT (1994) 2 SC 423) may not be fully correct and may need review.

When a Bill is presented to the President for his assent under article 111, he may declare that he assents to the Bill or withholds assent. There is no time limit prescribed for the President giving his assent or declaring his decision to withhold it. But the President may, as soon as possible, also return the Bill, if it is not a money Bill, for reconsideration to the Houses of Parliament. When after reconsideration, the Bill is passed, with or without amendments, and is presented to the President again, he shall not withhold his assent.

---

1. *State of M.P. v. Nandlal*, AIR 1987 SC 251; *S.P. Gupta v. Union of India*, AIR 1982 S.C. 149; *State of Rajasthan v. Union of India*, AIR 1977 S.C. 1361.

Inasmuch as giving assent to Bills is one of the functions of the President to be discharged on the advice of the Council of Ministers, it is open to him to seek clarificatory information from the Prime Minister under article 78(b) or to send a Bill back to the Government for reconsideration under Proviso to article 74(1). Presumably this is what was done by the President in the case of the controversial Postal Bill and the Bill seeking *inter alia* to provide to Members of Parliament pension after merely one year's service.

Twice during his tenure, President Narayanan was reported to have returned for reconsideration to his Council of Ministers its advice regarding imposition of President's rule in U.P. and Bihar. The 'satisfaction' stipulated under article 356 is of one single authority, that of the President acting on the advice of the Council of Ministers or, in other words, that of the Union Government. It may be debatable whether in view of article 74(2), what transpires between the President and his Ministers should become matters of public debate and controversy in the media.

Election of the President

When the question of the method of the election of the President came up for consideration before the Constituent Assembly, one of the suggestions made was that he should be elected directly by the people under universal adult franchise. On the other extreme was a suggestion that members of the two houses of Parliament alone may elect the President. The Constituent Assembly devised a unique mechanism which represented a middle course.

Since the membership in the two houses of Parliament was likely to be dominated by one party, election of the President merely by a majority of members of the Union Parliament could make him a nominee of the ruling party like the Prime Minister and such a President could not represent the constituent States of the Union. On the other hand, if the President was elected directly by the people, he could become a rival centre of power to the Council of Ministers which would have been against the parliamentary system with ministerial responsibility. As Nehru said in the Constituent Assembly, we could not have a directly elected President and not give him "real powers".

Like the President of the United States, our President is also elected by an electoral college. But, here the electoral college consists of the elected members of the two Houses of Parliament and Legislative Assemblies of the States (article 54). The thinking in the Constituent Assembly was that such an electoral college would make the President the elected representative of the whole nation with a clear voice given to the States as well.

Article 58 of the Constitution lays down that no person shall be eligible for election as President unless he (a) is a citizen of India; (b) has completed the age of thirty five years; and (c) is qualified for election as a member of the House of the People. A person shall not be eligible for election as President if he holds any office of profit under the Government of India or the Government of any State or under any local or other authority subject to the control of any of the said Governments. But a person shall not be deemed to hold any office of profit by reason only that he is President or Vice-President of the Union or the Governor of any State. Dr. S. Radhakrishnan and Dr. Zakir Husain contested the election to the office of the President of India in 1962 and 1967, respectively, without resigning from the office of Vice-President of India. However, notwithstanding the constitutional provisions, Shri V.V. Giri, who was then the Vice-President and Dr. N. Sanjiva Reddy, who was the Speaker of Lok Sabha, resigned their respective offices before filing their nomination papers for election to the office of President in 1969. Dr. N. Sanjiva Reddy again resigned from the office of Speaker in 1977 before a nomination proposing him as a candidate for the office of President was filed. Vice-President, Shri R. Venkataraman and Vice-President, Dr. S.D. Sharma, who contested and won the Presidential Election in 1987 and 1992 respectively did not resign from the office of Vice-President till they assumed the office of President of India.

The Election Statute: The Presidential and Vice-Presidential Elections Act, 1952 and the Rules framed thereunder regulate all matters relating to or connected with the election to the offices of the President and the Vice-President of India. The Act of 1952 was amended in 1974 and 1997 to make certain changes therein in the light of the experience gained during the elections held earlier. Similarly, the Presidential and Vice-Presidential Election Rules 1952, were also revised. The main requirements of the Act are:

i. A nomination paper for election to the office of President of India should be completed in the prescribed form, subscribed by the candidate as assenting to the nomination and also by at least fifty electors as proposers and at least fifty electors as seconders. Before 1997, the number of proposers and seconders required was only ten each. The requirement was held to be in order because article 58 provided only the qualifications for eligibility and not the requirements for a valid nomination *(Charan Lal Sahu v. Neelam Sanjeeva Reddy,* AIR 1978 SC 499);

ii. Each nomination paper should be accompanied by a certified copy of the entry relating to the candidate in the electoral roll for the Parliamentary constituency in which the candidate is registered as an elector.

Article 55 provides that, as far as practicable, there shall be uniformity in the scale of representation of the different States at the election of the President; the election shall be held in accordance with the system of proportional representation by means of the single transferable vote and the voting shall be by secret ballot. The article also provides that for the purpose of securing uniformity among the States *inter se* as well as parity between the States as a whole and the Union, the number of votes which each elected member of Parliament and of the Legislative Assembly of each State is entitled to cast at such election shall be determined in the following manner:

a. Every elected member of the Legislative Assembly of a State shall have as many votes as there are multiples of one thousand in the quotient obtained by dividing the population of the State by the total number of elected members of the Assembly;

b. If, after taking the said multiples of one thousand, the remainder is not less than five hundred, then the vote of each member referred to in (a) above shall be further increased by one.

Illustration

Total population of a State	:	43,502,708
Total No. of elected Members in the Assembly	:	294
No. of votes for each [Value of each vote]	:	43,502,708 divided by 1000 x 294
	=	147.96 or 148

c. Each elected member of either House of Parliament shall have such number of votes as may be obtained by dividing the total number of votes assigned to the members of the Legislative Assemblies of the States under (a) and (b) above by the total number of elected members of both Houses of Parliament, fractions exceeding one half being counted as one and other fractions being disregarded.

The total number of members in the electoral college for a Presidential election, for example, was 4,848 as detailed below:

a.	Rajya Sabha	...	233
b.	Lok Sabha	...	543
c.	State Assemblies	...	4,072
	Total	...	4,848

The value of the vote of each Member of Parliament (both Rajya Sabha and Lok Sabha) is arrived at by dividing the total value of all the votes assigned to elected members of Legislative Assemblies (5,49,511) by the total number of the elected members of the two houses of Pafrliament (776). The value of the vote of each member of Parliament thus came to 708. The value of the vote of each member of the State Legislative Assembly differed from State to State depending on the strength of the Assembly and the population of the State as per the 1971 census. The lowest value for a State was 7 and the highest 208.

The method of providing parity between the States as a whole on the one hand and the Union on the other meant that the whole process was weighted in favour of the representatives of the States. They got double representation—first as members of the Council of States and secondly as members of the State Assemblies. This was done deliberately to make the office of President command unquestioning support from the entire country and the constituent States. The idea of providing uniformity in the scale of representation of different States *inter se* was broadly to provide representation on the basis of population and to respect the one man one vote principle and the concepts of one Indian Citizenship and equality among all citizens.

Explanation to article 55 clarifies that the reference to population in that article means the population ascertained at the last preceding census but that until the figures of a census after the year 2026 become available, the reference to last preceding census would mean the 1971 census. The 84th Constitution Amendment substituted the year 2026 for the year 2000 so that population continues to mean the population as in 1971.

The system of proportional representation by single transferable vote for the Presidential election was adopted presumably and simply because it was believed to give representation to minorities. There was hardly any discussion on the point in the Constituent Assembly. The proposal was just accepted. The system is hardly very relevant in a single-member constituency situation. The system is useful only when there are more than one seat to be filled by the same electorate at the same poll. In fact to call the present system proportional representation by single transferable vote is a misnomer. It could better be called a system of alternate vote because it does in practice operate as such.

There have been 13 Presidential Elections so far. The only person to be elected without a contest was Dr. Sanjiva Reddy in 1977. The most hotly contested election was that of Shri V.V. Giri when second preference votes had to be counted. The only person to be elected to the office of President for two terms was Dr. Rajendra Prasad.

The election which was politically most interesting and caused the greatest anxiety in political circles was that of 1987 when besides Shri R. Venkataraman and Justice Krishna Iyer, there was a third valid candidate.

One of the most noteworthy things during Presidential Elections till recently was that most often many nominations were filed. Although most of these were non-serious candidates and their nominations on scrutiny were found to be invalid, this did make the point very loudly that in our democracy any citizen without any distinction could aspire to occupy the highest office. Before the 1997 Presidential election, an effort was made to curb the number of non-serious candidates by increasing the required number of proposers and seconders from ten each to fifty each and the amount of security deposit from Rs.2500 to Rs.15,000.

Election Disputes: Article 71 of the Constitution lays down that all doubts and disputes relating to or connected with the Presidential and Vice-Presidential elections shall be enquired into and decided by the Supreme Court whose decision shall be final.

The election of the President or the Vice-President cannot be called in question simply on the ground of there being any vacancy among the members of the electoral college.

A person who is neither a candidate nor an elector cannot file a suit challenging the validity of the election of the President.[1]

In the Presidential Election case, on a reference made by the President under article 143(1) (A.I.R. 1974 SC 1682) the Supreme Court held that election to the office of the President cannot be postponed or invalidated on the ground that the electoral college was incomplete or not fully constituted because of some State Assembly having been dissolved. It must be held before the expiry of the term of the incumbent President.

Conditions of President's office

Article 59 of the Constitution lays down the conditions of the President's office. The President shall not be a member of any house of Union or State Legislature. He shall not hold any office of Profit. He shall be entitled to the free use of his official residences and such emoluments, allowances and privileges as may be determined by Parliament by law.

Ex-Presidents draw a pension, get a staff car, secretarial staff, free travel by highest class by air, free telephone, water and electricity, rent free furnished accommodation etc. provision has also been made for family pension, free residence and medicare for the President's spouse.

President's Term of Office

Article 62(1) provides that an election to fill a vacancy caused by the expiration of the term of office of President shall be completed before the expiration of that term.

Article 56(1) provides that the President shall hold office for a term of five years from the date on which he enters upon his office. He can resign his office by writing under his

---

1 *N.B. Khare v. Election Commissioner of India,* AIR 1958 SC 139.

hand addressed to the Vice-President. The President shall, notwithstanding the expiration of his term, continue to hold office until his successor enters upon his office.

Procedure for Impeachment

Article 61 lays down that the President may be removed from his office by impeachment on grounds of violation of the Constitution. The charge for impeachment may be preferred in either House of Parliament by a resolution signed by at least one-fourth of the total number of members of the House and passed by a majority of not less than two-thirds of the total membership of the House. When a charge is so preferred by one House, it shall be investigated or got investigated by the other House and if a resolution is passed by this other House by a majority of 2/3rd of its total membership, the President shall stand removed from his office from the date of the passing of the resolution.

VICE-PRESIDENT

Next to the President of India, the highest position in the Official Warrant of Precedence is accorded to the Vice-President. His office, therefore, is highly prestigious. Article 63 of the Constitution says that there shall be a Vice-President of India. The Vice-President shall be the *ex-officio* Chairman of Rajya Sabha (article 64). This follows the U.S. practice. As the Chairman of Rajya Sabha, he presides over the proceedings of the House and functions with reference to all its matters as the counterpart of the Speaker in Lok Sabha. But, as the Vice-President as such, no functions have been assigned to him in the Constitution. By practice, he has come to have several ceremonial functions like meeting ambassadors, visiting foreign dignitaries etc. Article 65 lays down that he shall act as the President in the event of a vacancy in the office of President by reason of his death, resignation or removal or otherwise. In case the President is unable to discharge his functions owing to absence, illness or any other cause, the Vice-President shall discharge his functions. While acting as President or discharging the functions of President, the Vice-President shall not perform the duties of the office of the Chairman of Rajya Sabha (article 64).

It has been proved on many occasions, *e.g.* when two of our Presidents—Dr. Zakir Husain and Fakhruddin Ali Ahmed—died in office and Vice-Presidents V.V. Giri and B.D. Jatti acted as President, that the contingency functions of the Vice-President are of crucial importance to the nation.

The Vice-President is elected by an electoral college consisting of the members of the two houses of Parliament in accordance with the system of proportional representation with single transferable vote (article 66). This is intended to ensure that he enjoys the confidence of both the houses of Parliament.

The term of the office of the Vice-President is five years and election to the office has to be completed before the expiration of the term. All doubts and disputes regarding this election shall be enquired into and decided by the Supreme Court. The Vice-President may resign from his office by writing under his hand to the President. He may also be removed from his office by a resolution passed by a majority of all then members of Rajya Sabha and agreed to by Lok Sabha (articles 67, 68 and 71). The Vice-President shall not be a member of either house of Parliament or of a State Legislature (article 66).

The eligibility conditions for election of a person as Vice-President are the same as those for election as President except that for the former, the candidate must be qualified for election as a member of the Rajya Sabha (article 66).

The Vice-President draws a salary as Chairman Rajya Sabha. In addition, he is entitled to a daily tax free allowance, free furnished residence, travel, water, electricity, telephone medical and other facilities.

On retirement, the Vice-President gets facilities like free furnished residence, travel, water, electricity, telephone, secretarial and other facilities besides a monthly pension. Provision has also been made for family pension, free residence and medicare for the spouse of the Vice-President.

The emoluments *etc.* are determined by Parliament by law from time to time *vide* article 97 of the Constitution.[1]

COUNCIL OF MINISTERS

Article 74 of the Constitution lays down that there shall be a Council of Ministers with the Prime Minister at the head to aid and advise the President who shall, in the exercise of his functions, act in accordance with such advice. The President may, however, require the Council of Ministers to reconsider such advice. The President shall act on the advice tendered after such reconsideration.

That there shall be a Council of Ministers has to be understood to mean that it shall always be there. The Constitution does not envisage a situation where there will be no Prime Minister or no Council of Ministers. There is no provision for failure of constitutional machinery (as under article 356) and direct President's rule at the Union level.

Acceptance by the President of the advice tendered by the Council of Ministers has become obligatory particularly after the 42nd and 44th Constitutional Amendments. Before the amendments also the Supreme Court had taken the view that the advice was binding in all cases.[2]

Even after the dissolution of Lok Sabha, the President, in the exercise of his powers, was bound by the aid and advice of the Council of Ministers. It was held by the Supreme Court in *U.N. Rao v. Indira Gandhi* (A.I.R. 1971 SC

1. See Vice-Presidential Pension Act, 1997 (as amended) and officers of Parliament (Salary and Allowances) Act, 1997 (as amended).
2. *Samsher v. State of Punjab*, AIR 1974 S.C. 2192.

1002) that any exercise of powers by the President without the advice of the Council of Ministers shall be unconstitutional as being violative of article 74(1).

However, the acceptance of the advice of the Council of Ministers by the President is not automatic or mechanical. The President is entitled to consider it by applying his mind. The 44th Amendment allows to the President an opportunity to advise and caution the Council of Ministers and seek reconsideration of any matter before the President puts his seal of approval and accepts the proposed course of action.

The decisions of the Cabinet are taken confidentially and the advice tendered to the President is also protected by confidentiality between the President and the Council of Ministers. As such, these cannot be questioned in a court of law. Of course, there is no bar to the court looking at them if these are produced by the Government.[1]

Under article 75, the Prime Minister is appointed by the President and other Ministers are appointed by him on the advice of the Prime Minister. The Ministers hold office during the pleasure of the President but the Council of Ministers is collectively responsible to Lok Sabha.

While the President is to be fully guided in the discharge of all his functions by the advice of the Council of Ministers with the Prime Minister at its head, it is not clear as to on whose advice he performs the most crucial function of appointing the Prime Minister. So far as the letter of the Constitution goes, the President can appoint almost anyone as the Prime Minister but he has to remember that under the Constitution the Council of Ministers headed by the Prime Minister has to be responsible to the House and would have to go if it loses the confidence of the Lok Sabha. The President, therefore would appoint only a person who, in his best

---

1. *S.P. Gupta v. Union of India,* AIR 1982 S.C. 149; *State of Rajasthan v. Union of India,* AIR 1977 S.C. 1361; *State of M.P. v. Nandlal,* AIR 1987, S.C. 251; *Choudhary v. Government of Bihar,* AIR 1980 S.C. 383.

judgement would be acceptable to the House. If a party or a pre-election alliance commands absolute majority support in the Lok Sabha, there is no difficulty. For, the President in such cases, following well established parliamentary practices and conventions, has to invite the Leader of the majority party, front or alliance to take over as the Prime Minister and form a Government. But, where no single party or coalition is in a position to form a Government on its own, the role of the President in choosing the Prime Minister becomes most delicate and difficult. He may have to use all his abilities to decide on the leader most likely to command the confidence of Lok Sabha. The golden rule in such an eventuality is to call the leader of the single largest party or alliance first or seek to be satisfied in advance about a leader having the support of more than half of the members of the Lok Sabha. Since in any case, ultimately it is necessary for the Prime Minister to have the confidence of the Lok Sabha and it is his responsibility to find out who can command such confidence, the most logical and above board solution would be that instead of getting involved in political controversies, appointing someone and then asking him to seek a confidence vote in the House, the President can ask the House to elect its leader who can then be appointed by the President as the Prime Minister. This has been recommended by the Constitution Commission (2002) also.

While the Ministers are also appointed by the President and said to hold office during the pleasure of the President, in actual effect, it means they are selected by the Prime Minister—the President cannot appoint anyone not recommended by the Prime Minister—and hold office at his pleasure. If the Prime Minister is unhappy or dissatisfied with any Minister, he can advise him to resign, advise the President to dismiss him or tender the resignation of his Council of Ministers and then reconstitute it after deleting the name of the Minister in question.

In the U.K. the concept is that of individual and

collective responsibility of Ministers. Our Constitution, however, provides only for collective responsibility which means that there can be no no-confidence in a single Minister. The entire Council of Ministers is jointly responsible to Lok Sabha for all acts of Government. Therefore, it stands or falls together. If it loses the confidence of the House, the entire Council of Ministers must resign. Also, collective responsibility would mean that the Ministers must not speak in public in different voices. If any Minister disagrees with a decision taken or a policy adopted by the Cabinet, he must either resign or own equal and joint responsibility.

Again, in the U.K., historically the concept of ministerial responsibility was a by-product or corollary of the doctrine that the King can do no wrong. Since the King could not be held responsible for any wrong acts of the State, ministers came handy as a peg to hang responsibility on. For every act of the State, there was a Minister responsible. Every order of the Crown for any public act had, therefore, to be countersigned by a Minister. In India, on the other hand, ministerial responsibility was conceived and evolved on the basis of the highest principles of representative democracy, as the responsiblity of the Government to the directly elected representatives of the people in the Lok Sabha. Actually, in India the Ministers have no legal accountability for acts of the State which are done in the name of the President and required to be countersigned by way of authentication not by a Minister but by a Secretary (or other authorised officer) to the Government in accordance with the rules made by the President (article 77).

The Constitution speaks only of Ministers. It does not indicate any classification or categories of Ministers into Cabinet Ministers, Ministers of State, Deputy Ministers etc. While Prime Minister is mentioned as one heading the Council of Ministers (article 74), there is no reference made to any Deputy Prime Minister. In *K.M. Sharma v. Devilal*, (AIR 1990 SC 528), oath by Devi Lal as Deputy Prime Minister was questioned as being *ultra vires* the Constitution as the Constitution provided only for the 'Prime Minister' and 'Ministers'. The Court upheld the oath as valid but said that 'Deputy Prime Minister' was only a descriptive term and did not confer on him any powers of the Prime Minister. Also, the Constitution mentions only the Council of Ministers and makes no reference to the Cabinet except in article 352 (as amended in 1979) where Cabinet is defined as the Council consisting of Ministers of Cabinet rank. For all practical purposes, it is the Cabinet which takes policy decisions and advises the President. The whole Council of Ministers including all categories of Ministers almost never meets to transact any business.

Coalition Government

For the major part of the last six decades single party governments have been in power at the Union level. Several of the States, however had coalition governments from as far back as 1967.

The Constitution has no provision in regard to single party or coalition governments. It only speaks of the Prime Minister/Chief Minister being appointed by the President/Governor and the Council of Ministers being responsible to Lok Sabha/State Assembly.

Coalition is the *ad hoc* coming together or entering into an alliance of two or more separate parties, persons or interests, for a temporary period and with a specific objective of taking combined action like formation of government and carrying on the activities of the State. Coalition arrangements presume that the parties coming together retain their distinct identities but they usually agree on a common minimum programme or a national agenda to be followed by their government.

The National Democratic Alliance (NDA) government in power at the Union level during 1999-2004 was a coalition of several parties functioning on the basis of an agreed national agenda of governance. The United Progressive Alliance (UPA) government in power since 2004 is also a coalition government.

Caretaker Government

At the level of States, if the government cannot be carried on in accordance with the Constitution, there is provision for President's rule. But, at the Union level, the Constitution envisages that there shall always be a Council of Ministers to aid and advise the President who shall act in accordance with the advice tendered. There is no provision in the Constitution for anything like a caretaker government. The term has come to be used in common parlance to describe the status of a Council of Ministers that has resigned on having lost the confidence of the Lok Sabha or otherwise but is asked by the President to continue till alternative arrangements are made. If an alternative government cannot be formed immediately and general elections have to be held, the outgoing Council of Ministers may have to hold charge till the conclusion of elections and formation of new government. In any case, the presumption is that such an arrangement is for as short a period as absolutely necessary, that elections, if necessary, are held at the earliest possible and that during the interregnum no new schemes are launched or major policy decisions taken by the Government unless dictated by demands of national security and the like.

Governmental Instability

In the words of the Constitution Commission (NCRWC) Report, the administrative and economic costs of political instability and short-lived governments were 'simply collossal'. During 1989-1999, there were five general elections for Lok Sabha—3 in 4 years (1996-1999). In all these elections, no single party emerged with a majority of seats in the House. This aroused considerable concern about political stability, especially in the context of the needs of national development efforts and the far-reaching changes in international economic and security paradigms. During ten years, there were seven governments. In the situation of a hung house where no single party commanded majority support, India got either minority governments or governments formed by a workable multi-party alliance. On the question of stability *versus* accountability in parliamentary polity, the Commission said:

> Need for political stability has to be seen in two emerging contexts: that in administering any economy in the global context, a reasonable degree of stability of Government and strong governance is important. Secondly, the economic and administrative costs of political instability might reach unaffordable levels.

In a situation where no single political party or pre-poll alliance of parties succeeds in securing a clear majority in the Lok Sabha after elections, instead of involving the highest office of the President in the controversies of finding out who could command the confidence of the House, the Commission recommended it would be best to leave it to the House itself to determine majority support to a leader. It would remove uncertainty and also obviate the need for the President asking his appointee as Prime Minister to seek a vote of confidence within certain number of days.

The Rules of Procedure and Conduct of Business in Lok Sabha could provide for the election of the Leader of the House by the Lok Sabha along with the election of the Speaker and in like manner. The Leader could then be appointed as the Prime Minister. The same procedure could be followed for the office of the Chief Minister in the State concerned.

Anti-defection Law

The Commission further recommended an amendment in the Rules of Procedure of the Legislatures for adoption of a system of constructive vote of no-confidence. For a motion of no-confidence to be brought out against a government at least 20% of the total number of members of the House should give notice. Also, the motion should be accompanied by a proposal of alternative Leader to be voted simultaneously.

The Commission felt that instability of elected governments was in part attributable to unprincipled, opportunistic political realignments from time to time and defections and re-defections.

The Anti-Defection Law in the Tenth Schedule of the Constitution which was supposed to prevent defections, in effect, had become an enabling law for larger defections. The Commission recommended that all defectors—whether individual or in groups—must resign and contest fresh election. They should be debarred from holding any public office of a minister or any other remunerative political post without winning at a fresh election. Also, votes cast by them to topple a government should be treated as invalid.

The Commission further recommended that the practice of having oversized Councils of Ministers must be prohibited by law. A ceiling on the number of Ministers in any State or the Union government be fixed at the maximum of 10% of the total strength of the popular house of the legislature as provided in article 239AA applicable to Delhi. The practice of creating a number of political offices with the position, perks and privileges of a minister should be discouraged and their number should be limited to 2 per cent of the total strength of the lower house.

The Commission added:

> A law or parliamentary convention to limit the size of the Cabinet is all the more desirable at the present juncture in view of a manifest sense of abandonment with which large size of Cabinets are resorted to. There are also other political rewards for the party members and supporters in the form of chairmenship of statutory corporations,

usually attached with status of a Minister of Cabinet rank. The magnitude of the harm caused to public-interest, to the efficiency of administration and to the exchequer is, indeed, incalculable. This has increasingly become the pervasive political culture of the day.

The Constitution (Ninety-first Amendment) Act, 2003 partly accepting the recommendations of the Commission, amended the tenth Schedule of the Constitution to take away the protection from defectors on grounds of split in the party and added a new article 361B to make them ineligible for Ministership or other remunerative public office till re-election. Also, by amending articles 75 and 164 the size of Council of Ministers was limited to 15% of the number of Members in the lower House.[1]

PRIME MINISTER

Duty has been specifically cast on the Prime Minister to keep the President informed of all decisions relating to administration and legislation, to furnish such information in these matters as the President may call for and to place before the Council of Ministers, if so desired by the President, any matter on which a decision might have been taken by a Minister (article 78).

In a parliamentary system of Government, the Prime Minister occupies a unique position as the most powerful functionary who controls both the Parliament and the Executive. Increasingly parliamentary Government has come to be regarded as Prime ministerial Government. As the head of the Council of Ministers, the Prime Minister is the head of the Government. Also, he is the leader of his party or/and of a coalition of parties in Parliament and usually the Leader of the popular House. In the ultimate analysis, however,

1. Also see under Chapter 12.

much depends on the personality of the Prime Minister and the level of acceptance and support he commands from the nation, his party or alliance and Parliament. The Prime Minister enjoys large powers of patronage. All the Ministers are appointed at his recommendation and stand dismissed at his demand. The Prime Minister allots work among the Ministers. Also, he can change their portfolios at will. The Prime Minister is the channel of communication between the Council of Ministers and the President.

Questions relating to the relationship between the Prime Minister and the President and between the Prime Minister and other Ministers have been subject matters of controversy right from the commencement of the Constitution. The perceptions of Sardar Patel as Home Minister and Nehru as the Prime Minister varied widely. Similarly, there were fundamental differences between the first President Dr. Rajendra Prasad and the first Prime Minister Jawaharlal Nehru. Later, despite all the amendments and judicial clarifications about the President being only a constitutional head, President Zail Singh had come very close to taking up cudgels against Prime Minister Rajiv Gandhi and as much as threatening to dismiss him. More recently, relations between the holders of the two highest offices have been cordial.[1]

ATTORNEY-GENERAL OF INDIA

Under the chapter on 'The Executive', the Constitution includes a provision (article 76) for the President appointing a person qualified to be a Supreme Court judge as the Attorney-General of India to advise the Government on legal

---

1. For an analysis of relationship between the first President and the first Prime Minister *see* Subhash C. Kashyap, 'President-Prime Minister relationship: Dr. Rajendra Prasad's Presidential Years', *South Asia Politics*, September 2008 Vol.7, No.5.

matters and perform other duties of a legal nature as may be assigned.

The Attorney-General holds office during the pleasure of the President. However, inasmuch as he is appointed on the advice of the Government, a convention has grown that with a change of Government, he submits his resignation.

The Attorney-General is the Chief Law Officer of the Government. He has the first right of audience in all courts in India. Also, he has the right to speak and take part in the proceedings of either House of Parliament without a right to vote. He is not a full-time officer of the House nor is he a member of the Cabinet as in U.K. Also, he is not barred from private practice except that he cannot advise or hold briefs against the Government of India.

12

THE UNION LEGISLATURE

PART V, CHAPTERS II AND III, ARTICLES 79–123

THE PARLIAMENT

The supreme legislature of the Union of India is called the Parliament. As is natural in a system of parliamentary democracy, the Parliament of India occupies a place of primacy in the governance of the country.

Composition of Parliament

The Parliament consists of the President and the two Houses—the Rajya Sabha (Council of States) and the Lok Sabha (House of the People). Article 79 begins by saying that there shall be a Parliament for the Union which means that there must always be a Parliament for the Union. Of the three constituents of Parliament, only the Lok Sabha is subject to dissolution. The Rajya Sabha is a permanent or continuing House and there must always be a President or a person performing the functions of the President.

The President: Though the President of India is a constituent part of Parliament, he does not sit or participate in the discussions in either of the two Houses. The two Houses are, however, summoned by the President to meet from time to time. He can prorogue the two Houses and dissolve the Lok Sabha. Prorogation terminates the session while dissolution puts an end to the life of the House. The President's assent is essential for a Bill passed by both Houses to become law. Not only that, when both the Houses of Parliament are not in session and he is satisfied that circumstances exist which render it necessary for him to take immediate action, the President can promulgate Ordinances having the same force and effect as a law passed by Parliament (arts. 85, 111 and 123).

At the commencement of the first session after each general election to Lok Sabha and at the commencement of the first session of each year, the President addresses both Houses of Parliament assembled together and informs Parliament of the causes of its summons. Besides, he may address either House of Parliament or both Houses assembled together and for that purpose require the attendance of members. He is also empowered to send messages to either House whether with respect to a Bill then pending in Parliament or otherwise, and a House to which any message is so sent has to, with all convenient despatch, consider any matter required to be considered by the message (articles 86 and 87). Bills belonging to certain categories can be introduced and proceeded with only after the recommendation of the President has been obtained (articles 117 and 274(1)).[1]

***Rajya Sabha*:** The Rajya Sabha is, as its name indicates, the Council of States. It represents the people in an indirect way inasmuch as they are grouped into several components of the Union—the States and the Union territories—and members of Rajya Sabha are elected by the elected members of the State Legislative Assemblies in accordance with the system of proportional representation by means of single transferable vote (article 80(4)). The different States of the Union have not been given equal representation in the Rajya Sabha. The number of representatives from each State in

1. Also see under chapter 11.

India depends largely on its population. Thus, while Uttar Pradesh has 31 members in Rajya Sabha, smaller States like Manipur, Mizoram, Sikkim, Tripura, etc. have only one member each. The populations in some of the Union territories such as Andaman and Nicobar Islands, Chandigarh, Dadra and Nagar Haveli, Daman and Diu, and Lakshadweep are too small to have any representative in Rajya Sabha. Under the Constitution, Rajya Sabha consists of not more than 250 members. It includes twelve members nominated by the President and 238 members elected by the States and the Union territories (art.80(1)).

The Rajya Sabha at present consists of 245 members as follows:

Andhra	- 18	Meghalaya	- 1
Arunachal	- 1	Mizoram	- 1
Assam	- 7	Nagaland	- 1
Bihar	- 16	Orissa	- 10
Goa	- 1	Punjab	- 7
Gujarat	- 11	Rajasthan	- 10
Chhattisgarh	- 5	Sikkim	- 1
Jharkhand	- 6	Tamil Nadu	- 18
Haryana	- 5	Tripura	- 1
Himachal	- 3	Uttar Pradesh	- 31
Jammu & Kashmir	- 4	Uttarakhand	- 3
Karnataka	- 12	West Bengal	- 16
Kerala	- 9	Delhi	- 3
Madhya Pradesh	- 11	Puducherry	- 1
Maharashtra	- 19	Nominated	- 12
Manipur	- 1		

Unlike the Lok Sabha, which has a fixed term but can be dissolved by the President at any time, the Rajya Sabha is a permanent body and is not subject to dissolution. While the term of an individual member of Rajya Sabha is six years, as nearly as possible, one-third of its members retire at the expiration of every second year in accordance with the provisions made in that behalf by Parliament by law (article

83(1)). The Vice-President, who is elected by the members of both Houses of Parliament, is the *ex-officio* Chairman of Rajya Sabha, whereas the Deputy Chairman is elected by the members of the Rajya Sabha from amongst themselves (articles 64, 66 and 89).

Lok Sabha: The other House—the Lok Sabha—is the House of the People. It is directly elected by the people. Every citizen of India who is not less than 18 years of age is entitled to vote in elections to Lok Sabha unless he is otherwise disqualified under law (article 326). The Constitution provides that the Lok Sabha shall consist of not more than 530 members chosen by direct election from territorial constituencies in the States, and not more than 20 members to represent the Union territories, chosen in such manner as Parliament by law provides (article 81(1)). In addition, the President may nominate not more than two members to represent the Anglo-Indian community (article 331). The maximum strength of the House envisaged in the Constitution is thus 552. At present, the Lok Sabha consists of 545 members as follows:

STATES

Andhra Pradesh	42	Madhya Pradesh	29
Arunachal Pradesh	2	Maharashtra	48
Assam	14	Manipur	2
Uttarakhand	5	Meghalaya	2
Bihar	40	Mizoram	1
Goa	2	Nagaland	1
Gujarat	26	Orissa	21
Chhattisgarh	11	Punjab	13
Jharkhand	14	Rajasthan	25
Haryana	10	Sikkim	1
Himachal Pradesh	4	Tamil Nadu	39
Jammu & Kashmir	6	Tripura	2
Karnataka	28	Uttar Pradesh	80
Kerala	20	West Bengal	42

UNION TERRITORIES

Andaman & Nicobar	1	Delhi	7
Chandigarh	1	Lakshdweep	1
Dadra & Nagar Haveli	1	Puducherry	1
Daman & Diu	1	Nominated (Anglo-Indian)	2

The total elective membership is distributed among the States in such a manner that the ratio between the number of seats allotted to each State and the population of the State is, so far as possible, the same for all States (article 81(2)(a)). Population for this purpose means the population as ascertained at the 1971 census. There was to be no change in the number of seats in Lok Sabha until the year 2000 (article 81(3)). The position is now frozen for another 25 years by substituting the figure "2026" for the figure "2000" in articles 55, 81, 82, 330 and 332 by the Constitution (Eighty-fourth Amendment) Act 2001 and the Constitution (Eighty-seventh Amendment) Act, 2003.

Seats are reserved for the Scheduled Castes and Scheduled Tribes in Lok Sabha Statewise on the basis of population ratios. Originally, the reservation was for ten years but it is being extended every time for the next ten years (articles 330 and 334). The Seventy-ninth Amendment has extended it to 2010.

The Lok Sabha has been provided with a fixed term as in the case of the popularly elected House of Representatives in the United States of America and the House of Commons in the United Kingdom. The *raison d'etre* of representative democracy is that the government should obtain the mandate of the people periodically in order to continue in office legitimately. The term of the House in India is five years from the date appointed for its first meeting. The expiration of the period of five years operates as its dissolution. The House may be dissolved before the expiration of its full term under certain circumstances. When a Proclamation of Emergency is in force, the term of Lok Sabha can be extended by Parliament for a period not exceeding one year at a time and not exceeding in any case a period of six months after the Proclamation has ceased to operate (art.83). In fact, right from the First Lok Sabha, strictly viewed, every House has been dissolved before completing its full term. Once, when during the Emergency, its life was extended, the House was dissolved before the completion of the extended term.

Members of Parliament

Qualification for Membership: Article 84 lays down the qualifications for membership of the two Houses of Parliament. In order to be eligible to be chosen as a member, a person must be a citizen of India and not less than 30 years of age in case of Rajya Sabha membership and not less than 25 years of age in case of Lok Sabha membership. Additional qualifications may be prescribed by law.

Disqualifications for Membership: Under article 102, a person shall be disqualified for being chosen as and for being a member of either House (i) if he is not a citizen of India or otherwise owes allegiance to a foreign State, (ii) if he is an undischarged insolvent or one declared by a competent court to be of unsound mind, (iii) if he holds any office of profit under the Union or a State Government other than the office of Minister or any office exempted by Parliament by law, and (iv) if he is otherwise disqualified under any law made by Parliament.

Also, a person may be disqualified on grounds of defection under the Tenth Schedule which was added to the Constitution by the 52nd Amendment.

If any question arises whether a member of either House has become subject to any disqualification, it shall be decided by the President after obtaining the opinion of the Election Commission and in accordance with that opinion. In case of disqualification on grounds of defection, the matter will be decided by the Speaker Lok Sabha or Chairman Rajya Sabha as the case may be.

The job of Parliament and its Members is to represent the people, to lay down policies, to make laws and to exercise surveillance over executive action. With the exception of Members who become Ministers, other Members are not expected to exercise any executive powers by accepting any office of profit under the Government. If those charged with the responsibility of overseeing the executive, themselves become part of the executive establishment or become beholden to the executive for an office of profit under the Government, obviously they cannot be expected to faithfully perform any worthwhile oversight functions. That is why, article 102 of the Constitution provides that apart from certain other things, holding an office of profit under the Government would constitute a disqualification for membership of Parliament. Giving a somewhat arbitrary power to the Parliament/State Legislatures, it is provided that any offices can be exempted from disqualification.

A Member was divested of her Rajya Sabha Membership in March 2006 by the President on the advice of the Election Commission as per article 103 of the Constitution. Several other cases were also reported to be pending when the two Houses of Parliament passed a Bill to retrospectively prevent the disqualification of a large number of Members who were alleged to be occupying high offices of profit under the Government. These included the Speaker Lok Sabha, Shri Som Nath Chatterjee and Leader of the United Progressive Alliance, Smt. Sonia Gandhi. The President, however returned the Bill to the Houses of Parliament for reconsideration. When the Bill, after reconsideration was again presented to the President under article 111, he gave his assent after a few days and not before the Government announced the appointment of a Committee to consider the issues raised by the President.

Constitutional provisions for State Legislatures corresponding to articles 102 and 103 are articles 191 and 192.

***Vacation of Seats*:** Article 101 lays down that a member shall be required to vacate his seat in a House if he is elected to both Houses of Parliament or to a House of State Legislature. In the latter case, if the member does not resign his seat in the State Legislature within a period of 14 days from the date of publication of the election result, his seat in the House of Parliament may be declared vacant. A seat may also stand vacated if a member becomes subject to any disqualification or voluntarily resigns his seat. The House may declare a seat vacant if the concerned member fails to attend the House for more than 60 days without permission.

***Oath by Members*:** The first sitting of the first session of the Lok Sabha after a general election is devoted to members making and subscribing the prescribed oath or affirmation to "bear true faith and allegiance to the Constitution of India" and to "uphold the sovereignty and integrity of India" and to faithfully discharge the duty of a Member of Parliament. The oath/affirmation is a prerequisite for every member taking his seat in either House (article 99 and 3rd Schedule).

***Salary and Allowances*:** Members of both the Houses are entitled to salaries and allowances as may be determined by Parliament by law from time to time (article 106). It would be seen that there is no separate mention of pensions in the provision. Parliament has, however sanctioned to Members a pension under the Members of Parliament (Salaries, Allowances and Pension) Act. A Bill passed by the two Houses during the ninth Lok Sabha period *inter alia* provided for a pension after only a year's service as a member. This, however, was not assented to by the President.[1]

---

1. For details of salaries, allowances etc. of Members see Subhash C. Kashyap, *Our Parliament*, N.B.T., New Delhi, and –, *Parliamentary Procedure*, Universal, New Delhi, 2nd ed., 2006.

Officers of the Houses

The Constitution provides for a Speaker and a Deputy Speaker for the Lok Sabha and a Chairman and a Deputy Chairman for the Rajya Sabha. The Vice-President of India is the *ex-officio* Chairman of Rajya Sabha. A Deputy Chairman is chosen by the House from among its own members. The Speaker and the Deputy Speaker are chosen by the Lok Sabha from among its members. In the absence of the Speaker in the House, the Deputy Speaker discharges the functions of the Speaker. Similarly, in the absence of the Chairman, the Deputy Chairman presides over the Rajya Sabha. While so presiding, the Deputy Presiding Officer in either case exercises all the powers of the Presiding Officer in the House. (articles 64, 89, 91 and 93 95).

Generally speaking, the position of the Speaker in India more or less corresponds to that of the Speaker of the House of Commons. His office is one of prestige, splendour and authority. He is the head of Lok Sabha. The smooth and orderly conduct of the business of the House is primarily his responsibility. Within the House and in all matters connected with the House, his word is final. His salary and allowances are charged on the Consolidated Fund of India—that is, they do not have to be voted by Parliament. His conduct cannot be discussed except on a substantive motion. He does not vote in the House except when there is an equality of votes (articles 94, 96, 100(1) and 112(3)(b)).

The Constitution gives the Speaker a special position in so far as relations between the two Houses in certain matters are concerned. He determines what matters are financial matters which fall within the exclusive jurisdiction of Lok Sabha. If he certifies a Bill to be a 'Money Bill', his decision is final (article 110). Whenever, in the event of final disagreement between the Houses on a legislative measure a joint sitting is called, he presides over such a joint sitting and all the Rules of Procedure in such a sitting operate under his directions and orders (articles 108 and 118(4)).

The Speaker or Deputy Speaker of Lok Sabha vacates his office if he ceases to be a member of the House, he can resign by writing to the Deputy Speaker/Speaker and he can be removed by a resolution of the House, with 14 days' notice, passed by a majority of all the then members of the House (article 94). A similar provision exists for the Deputy Chairman Rajya Sabha in article 90. Irrespective of the dissolution of the House, the Speaker, however, continues in office until immediately before the first sitting of the new House (article 94, proviso 2).[1]

Sessions of Parliament

It is for the President to summon each House of Parliament from time to time. But article 85(1) provides that six months must not intervene between two sessions of the House. Normally there are three sessions of Parliament each year *viz*. the Budget Session (Feb. May), the Monsoon Session (July Sept.) and Winter Session (Nov. Dec.). In the case of the Rajya Sabha, however, the Budget Session is split up into two sessions with a three to four week break in between so that it has four sessions in a year. The schedule of sessions may vary during an election year or under other special circumstances.

Conduct of Business and Legislative Procedure

Each House is the master of its procedure and may make rules for regulating its procedure and conduct of business subject to the provisions of the Constitution (article 118). The validity of any proceedings in Parliament cannot be questioned in a court of law on grounds of any alleged irregularity of procedure and no officer or member of Parliament is subject to jurisdiction of courts in respect of

1. For further study see Subhash C. Kashyap, *The Speaker's Office*, Shipra, Delhi, 2nd ed., 2001 and _____, *Parliamentary Procedure*, Universal, New Delhi, 2nd ed., 2006).

exercise of any powers in the matter of regulating procedure or conduct of business in Parliament (article 122).

Some of the basic rules of procedure and conduct of business have been laid down in the Constitution itself. Thus, article 100 provides (1) that except where otherwise provided in the Constitution (*e.g.* in the case of Constitutional Amendments, impeachment of the President, removal of the Presiding Officers, judges etc.), all questions at any sitting of either House or joint sitting of the Houses shall be determined by a majority of votes of the members present and voting other than the presiding officer who shall exercise a casting vote only in case of an equality of votes; (2) that all proceedings of either House shall be valid irrespective of any vacancies in membership or any unauthorised participation in debate or voting; and (3) that the quorum to constitute a meeting of either House shall be one-tenth of the total number of members.

Except Money Bills and other Financial Bills, a Bill may originate in either House. Such a Bill, before being presented to the President for his assent, must be passed by both the Houses either without any amendment or with such amendments as may be agreed to by both Houses. In case of final disagreement between the two Houses on any Bill other than a Money Bill, the President may summon a joint sitting of the two Houses to resolve the differences (articles 107 108).

***Financial Bills*:** The Constitution makes a distinction between Money Bills and Financial Bills. Generally speaking, a Financial Bill may be any Bill which relates to revenue or expenditure. Besides providing for any of the matters specified in the Constitution for a Money Bill, a Financial Bill may also provide for other matters. For the sake of convenience, the Financial Bills may be divided into two categories: Category A: those Bills which make provisions for any of the matters specified in article 110 for the Money Bill but do not contain solely those matters, *e.g.* a Bill which contains a taxation clause, but does not deal solely with taxation. Category B: those Bills containing provisions involving expenditure from the Consolidated Fund (articles 110 and 117).

Special Procedure for Money Bills

Article 110 defines a Money Bill as a Bill which contains only provisions regarding taxes, borrowings, custody of the Consolidated and Contingency Funds, appropriations, declaring of any expenditure as charged on the Consolidated Fund, receipt and custody of money in the Consolidated Fund, audit of the accounts of the Union (or of a State) or any other incidental matters. A Bill shall not become a Money Bill simply because it provides for imposition of fines or other pecuniary penalties, or for payment of fees for licenses, or for fees for services rendered or by reason that it provides for imposition, regulation etc. of any tax by any local authority or body for local purposes. In case of any question arising whether a Bill is a Money Bill, the decision of the Speaker shall be final. While being presented to the President for his assent, every Money Bill has to be certified by the Speaker as such a Bill (article 110). A Money Bill can be introduced only in the Lok Sabha and only on the recommendation of the President. After it is passed by the Lok Sabha and transmitted to Rajya Sabha, the latter may make its recommendations, if any, within a period of 14 days and the Lok Sabha may accept or reject all or any of the recommendations. The Bill is deemed to be passed by both the Houses with the amendments accepted by Lok Sabha. If no amendment recommended by Rajya Sabha is acceptable to Lok Sabha or if the Bill is not returned by Rajya Sabha within 14 days, it is deemed to have been passed by both the Houses in the form in which it was passed by Lok Sabha (article 109).

Assent to Bills

Article 111 says that when a Bill passed by the two Houses

of Parliament is presented to the President, the President shall either assent to the Bill or withhold assent therefrom. He may return a Bill, if it is not a Money Bill, to the Houses for reconsideration. If the Bill is passed again with or without any amendments and presented to President for assent, he shall not withhold assent (article 111). Another option available to the President is to seek some information or clarifications or to return the Bill to the Government *i.e.*, the Council of Ministers, for reconsidering their advice for according assent to the Bill (articles 74(1) and 78(b)). President Zail Singh did not give his assent to the Postal Bill and President Venkataraman returned to the Government the Bill seeking to give pension to Members of Parliament after just one year's service.

Procedure in Financial Matters

The Budget: The President is required to cause to be laid before both Houses of Parliament in respect of each financial year a statement of the estimated receipts and expenditure of the Government. This is termed the annual financial statement or the budget.

The estimates of expenditure embodied in the annual financial statement shall show separately

(a) the sums required to meet expenditure described by the Constitution as expenditure charged upon the Consolidated Fund of India; and

(b) the sums required to meet other expenditure proposed to be made from the Consolidated Fund of India and shall distinguish expenditure on revenue account from other expenditure.

The expenditure charged on the Consolidated Fund of India shall include:

(a) the emoluments and allowances of the President and other expenditure relating to his office;

(b) the salaries and allowances of the Chairman and the Deputy Chairman of the Council of States and the Speaker and the Deputy Speaker of the House of the People;

(c) debt charges for which the Government of India is liable including interest, sinking fund charges and redemption charges, and other expenditure relating to the raising of loans and the service and redemption of debt;

(d) (i) the salaries, allowances and pensions payable to or in respect of judges of the Supreme Court; (ii) the pensions payable to or in respect of judges of the Federal Court; (iii) the pensions payable to or in respect of judges of any High Court which exercises jurisdiction in relation to any area included in the territory of India or which at any time before the commencement of this Constitution exercised jurisdiction in relation to any area included in a Governor's Province of the Dominion of India;

(e) the salary, allowances and pension payable to or in respect of the Comptroller and Auditor-General of India;

(f) any sums required to satisfy any judgment, decree or award of any court or arbitral tribunal;

(g) any other expenditure declared by the Constitution or by Parliament by law to be so charged (article 112).

Estimates and Demands for Grants: Estimates relating to expenditure charged on the Consolidated Fund are not submitted to the vote of Parliament but discussion thereon is not barred. Other estimates are presented to Lok Sabha in the form of demands for grants and the Lok Sabha may either assent to or refuse any demand. It may also assent to a demand subject to a reduction in the amount asked for. Every demand for grant must receive the prior recommendation of the President (article 113).

Appropriation Bills: After the Demands for grants are voted by the Lok Sabha, a Bill is introduced for appropriation out of the Consolidated Fund of India, moneys required to meet the grants are voted by the House and the expenditure is charged on the Consolidated Fund. No amendment is permitted which seeks to vary the amount or alter the allocation of any grant head or vary the amount of any charged expenditure. Appropriation Bill is necessary because no money can be drawn from the Consolidated Fund without parliamentary sanction through an Appropriation Act. Additional, supplementary or excess grants may be voted separately but the same procedure shall apply to them as well (articles 114–115).

Article 116 provides for (i) a vote on account, *i.e.* grants being made in advance of the budget approval and completion of the whole procedure, (ii) an exceptional grant which does not form part of the current service of any financial year, and (iii) a grant to meet an unexpected demand of large magnitude or of an indefinite character (article 116). Parliament may by law regulate the procedure for the purpose of timely completion of the financial business. (article 119).

Language in Parliament

Hindi and English have been declared by the Constitution to be the languages for conducting business in Parliament. The Presiding Officers may, however, allow any member not proficient in either to address the House in his mother tongue (article 120).

Parliamentary Privileges

Article 105 of the Constitution provides for the powers, privileges etc. of the Houses of Parliament and of the members and committees thereof.

'Privilege' means a special or exceptional right or freedom or an immunity enjoyed by a particular class of persons or some individuals. In its legal sense it means an exemption from some duty, burden, attendance or liability to which others are subject. Privilege can also be defined as a right which others do not have. Parliamentary privileges are those special rights belonging to each House of Parliament, its members and committees, without which they cannot perform their functions in the manner they are expected to. The privileges are granted with a view to maintaining the independence of action and the dignity of the Houses of Parliament, their committees and members and to enable them to function without any let or hindrance. The privileges, in practice, give rise to certain powers, immunities and exemptions. It does not, however, imply that the privileges belonging to members place them on a footing different from that of an ordinary citizen in the eyes of law unless there are good reasons in the interest of Parliament itself to do so. The basic law is that all citizens including members of Parliament should be treated equally before the law. They have the same rights and liberties as ordinary citizens except when they perform their duties in Parliament. The privileges are available to the members only when and to the extent that they are functioning as representatives of the people in Parliament and discharging their parliamentary responsibilities. The privileges do not, in any way, exempt the members from their normal obligations to society which apply to them as much and perhaps more closely in that capacity, as they apply to others.

The more important of the privileges, namely freedom of speech in Parliament and immunity of members from any proceedings in courts in respect of anything said or any vote given by them in Parliament, are specified in article 105 of the Constitution.

1. There shall be freedom of speech in Parliament but subject to the provisions of the Constitution and to the rules and standing orders regulating the procedure of Parliament.
2. Clauses(2) and (3) of the article provide that no member of Parliament shall be liable to any proceedings in any court in respect of anything said or any vote given by him in Parliament or any committee thereof, and no person shall be so liable in respect of the publication by or under the authority of either House of Parliament of any report, paper, votes or proceedings.[1]

---

1. *Tej Kiran v. Sanjiva,* AIR 1970 SC 1573; *Gatish v. Harisadhan* (1956) 60 CWN 971, A.I.R. 1961 SC 613.

3. In other respects, the powers, privileges and immunities of each House of Parliament, and of the members and the committees of each House, shall be such as may from time to time be defined by Parliament by law, and, until, so defined, shall be those of that House and of its members and committees immediately before the coming into force of section 15 of the Constitution (Forty-Fourth Amendment) Act, 1978.
4. The provisions of clauses (1), (2) and (3) shall apply in relation to persons who by virtue of this Constitution have the right to speak in, and otherwise to take part in the proceedings of a House of Parliament or any committee thereof as they apply in relation to members of Parliament.

In other words, each House, its Committees and members in actual practice, shall enjoy the powers and privileges (other than those specified in the Constitution) that were available to the British House of Commons as on 26 January 1950.

The most important of parliamentary privileges is that of freedom of speech while performing parliamentary duties. Article 19 also gives a citizen the right of free speech but articles 105 and 194 lay special emphasis on the right of free speech of members of the legislatures. Under article 19, the right of free speech is subject to reasonable restrictions, for instance, the law of libel. An ordinary person who speaks something libellous is liable to be proceeded against but a member of Parliament speaking in the House or in one of its committees is immune from any attack on the ground that his speech was libellous or defamatory.

Members have to give expression to public grievances and raise various matters of public importance. In doing this, members should not suffer any inhibition and they should be able to speak out their mind and express their views freely. Inside the House or Committees of Parliament, a member is absolutely free to say whatever he likes subject only to the Constitution and internal discipline of the House or the

Committee concerned; no outside authority has any right to interfere. Freedom of speech is absolutely necessary for a member to function freely without any fear or favour in the Committees and in the Houses of Parliament. Unless whatever a member says enjoys immunity from legal action, he cannot be expected to speak freely and frankly. The Constitution provides, therefore, that no action can be taken against a member of Parliament in any court or before any authority other than Parliament in respect of anything said or a vote given by him in Houses of Parliament or any Committee thereof. It has been held by the Supreme Court that provisions of the tenth schedule in regard to disqualification on ground of defection are not violative of article 105(1)[1]

It is a breach of privilege to molest a member or to take any action against him on account of anything said by him in Parliament or a Committee thereof. Likewise, it would be a breach of privilege to institute any legal proceedings against a member in respect of anything said by him in Parliament or in a Committee thereof. It has been held by the Supreme Court in the *Searchlight case* that the freedom of speech conferred on members under article 105 is subject only to those provisions of the Constitution which regulate the procedure of Parliament and to the rules and standing orders of the House, but is free from any restrictions which may be imposed by any law made under article 19(2) upon the freedom of speech of an ordinary citizen. Any investigation outside Parliament in respect of anything said or done by members in the discharge of their parliamentary duties would amount to a serious interference with the members' rights. Even though a speech delivered by a member in the House may amount to contempt of court, no action can be taken against him in any court. A court, being an outside authority, does not have the power to investigate the matter.

1. *Kihoto v. Zachillhu*, AIR 1993 SC 412 (CB).

Article 122 specifically forbids any inquiry by courts into proceedings of Parliament.

The courts of law in India have thus recognised that a House of Parliament or a State Legislature is the sole authority to judge as to whether or not there has been a breach of privilege in a particular case. It has also been held that the power of the House to commit for contempt is identical with that of the House of Commons and that a court of law would be incompetent to scrutinise the exercise of that power.

The immunity from external influence or interference, however, does not mean an unrestricted licence of speech within the walls of Parliament. It is important to remember that the privileges of the Houses and members and committees thereof are subject to other provisions of the Constitution being construed harmoniously. Thus, for example, the privilege of freedom of speech in Parliament will be subject to rules of procedure framed by Houses of Parliament under article 118 and article 121 forbids discussion in Parliament on the conduct of judges except on a motion for their removal.[1]

In 1965, the Supreme Court in its advisory opinion in Special Reference Case of 1964, (*Keshav Singh's case*), observed as follows:

> It would not be correct to read the majority decision in the Searchlight case as laying down a general proposition that whenever there is a conflict between the provisions of the latter part of article 194(3) and any of the provisions of the fundamental rights guaranteed by Part III, the latter must yield to the former. The majority decision, therefore, must be taken to have settled that article 19(1)(a) would not apply, and article 21 would.
>
> In dealing with the effect of the provisions contained in clause (3) of article 194, whenever it appears that there is a conflict between the said provisions and the provisions

1. *M.S. Sharma v. Sri Krishna Sinha*, AIR 1959 SC 395.

pertaining to fundamental rights, an attempt will have to be made to resolve the said conflict by the adoption of the rule of harmonious construction.

The Allahabad High Court, in their judgement in *Keshav Singh's case* dated 10 March 1965 (*i.e.* delivered after the advisory opinion of the Supreme Court), observed as follows:

i. In our opinion, both upon authority and upon a consideration of the relevant provisions of the Constitution, it must be held that the Legislative Assembly has, by virtue of article 194(3), the same power to commit for its contempt as the House of Commons has.

ii. In our opinion, the provisions of article 22(2) of the Constitution cannot apply to a detention in pursuance of a conviction and imposition of a sentence of imprisonment by competent authority.

iii. Since we have already held that the Legislative Assembly has the power to commit the petitioner for its contempt and since the Legislative Assembly has framed rules for the procedure and conduct of its business under article 208(1), the commitment and deprivation of the personal liberty of the petitioner cannot but be held to be according to the procedure laid down by law within the meaning of article 21 of the Constitution.

iv. Once we come to the conclusion that the Legislative Assembly has the power and jurisdiction to commit for its contempt and to impose the sentence passed on the petitioner, we cannot go into the question of the correctness, propriety or legality of the commitment. This Court cannot, in a petition under article 226 of the Constitution, sit in appeal over the decision of the Legislative Assembly committing the petitioner for its contempt. The Legislative Assembly is the master of its own procedure and is the sole judge of the question whether its contempt has been committed or not.

The Government, therefore, decided that an amendment of the Constitution was not necessary. It was of the opinion that the Legislatures and the Judiciary would develop their own conventions in the light of the opinion given by the Supreme Court and the judgement pronounced by the Allahabad High Court.

More recently, when 11 Members were expelled from their respective Houses—10 from Lok Sabha and 1 from Rajya Sabha—and the matter reached the Supreme Court, upholding the power of the Houses of legislatures to expel their members, the Court held:

> Parliament would always be presumed to perform its functions and to exercise its powers in a reasonable manner subject to exception of there being no scope for a general rule that the exercise of powers by the legislature is not amenable to judicial review. Scope for judicial review in matters concerning Parliamentary proceedings despite being limited and restricted is subject to scrutiny on breach of other constitutional provisions. Sheer irregularity of the procedure is no ground of challenge to the proceedings in Parliament or effect thereof but in case of gross illegality or violation of constitutional provisions the Court has the jurisdiction to examine the procedure adopted. Power to punish for contempt is a broad power encompassing a variety of other powers. Only limitation the Court recognizes in the power of the legislatures to punish for contempt is that such powers cannot be used to divest the ordinary Courts of their jurisdiction. Duty of Supreme Court is to ensure that there is no abuse or misuse of power by the Legislature. Court, therefore, should exercise its power of judicial review with utmost care, caution and circumspection.[1]

Thus, the latest position is that exercise of power under the privilege law has also been brought under judicial review.

Codification of Privileges: Article 105(3) of the Constitution stipulates that, apart from the privileges mentioned in the

---

1. *Raja Ram Pal v. Speaker Lok Sabha*, (2007) 3 SCC 184.

Constitution itself, Parliament may, from time to time, define its privileges by law. No law, however, has so far been enacted by Parliament in pursuance of this provision to define the powers, privileges and immunities of each House and its members and the Committees thereof.

As far as the constitutional stipulation "until defined by Parliament by law" and the question of defining or codifying the parliamentary privileges are concerned, opinions are divided.

Legislative Powers of the President

Article 123 empowers the President to promulgate ordinances when both Houses of Parliament are not in session and he is satisfied that a situation has arisen that requires immediate action. Ordinances issued by the President have the same force and effect as laws made by Parliament except that all such ordinances become inoperative on the expiry of six weeks from the reassembly of Parliament or earlier if disapproved by the two Houses.

It has been held that the satisfaction of the President is beyond judicial review but it means satisfaction on the aid and advice of the Council of Ministers.[1]

Repromulgation of an ordinance without any attempt to get the corresponding Bill passed by the legislature and the practice of proroguing the House merely to promulgate an ordinance has been held to be a fraud on the Constitution in case of the Governor of Bihar[2] but the same should apply equally to Presidential Ordinances.

The President's ordinance making power has been challenged in courts in a number of cases. It is clear that

1. *A.K. Roy v. Union of India*, AIR 1982 SC 710; *Cooper v. Union of India*, AIR 1970 SC 564; *Satpal v. Lt. Governor*, AIR 1979 SC 1550; *Venkata v. State of A.P.*, AIR 1985 SC 725; *Nagaraj v. State of A.P.*, AIR 1985 SC 55; *State of Rajasthan v. Union of India*, AIR 1977 SC 136.
2. *D.C. Wadhwa v. State of Bihar*, AIR 1987 SC 579.

while the constitutional validity of the ordinances has been upheld, the ordinance making power of the President is subject to the same limitations as the legislative power of Parliament *e.g.* in the matter of being subject to judicial review, fundamental rights, and distribution of legislative powers under the Seventh Schedule.[1]

Relative Role of the Two Houses

The two Houses of Parliament enjoy co-equal power and status in all spheres except in financial matters and in regard to the responsibility of the Council of Ministers, which are exclusively in the domain of Lok Sabha. Accordingly, the following limitations have been placed on the powers of Rajya Sabha:

i. A Money Bill cannot be introduced in Rajya Sabha.
ii. Rajya Sabha has no power either to reject or amend a Money Bill. It can only make recommendations on the Money Bill. If such a Bill is not returned to Lok Sabha within a period of 14 days, the Bill is deemed to have been passed by both the Houses at the expiration of the said period in the form in which it was passed by Lok Sabha (article 109).
iii. Whether a particular Bill is a Money Bill or not is to be decided by the Speaker of Lok Sabha (article 110(3)).
iv. Rajya Sabha may discuss the Annual Financial Statement (article 113). It has no power to vote on the Demands for Grants.
v. Rajya Sabha has no power to pass a vote of no-confidence in the Council of Ministers (article 75(3)).

Every non-financial measure must be passed by both the Houses individually before it can become an Act. Rajya

---

1. *State of Punjab v. Mohar Singh*, AIR 1955 SC 84; *State of Orissa v. Bhupendra*, AIR 1962 SC 945; *Nagaraj v. State of A.P.*, AIR 1985 SC 551; *Venkata v. State of A.P.*, 1985 SC 724; *R.K. Garg v. Union of India*, 1981 SC 2139; *A.K. Roy v. Union of India*, AIR 1982 SC 710.

Sabha has equal powers with Lok Sabha in important matters like the impeachment of the President, removal of the Vice-President, constitutional amendments, and removal of the Judges of the Supreme Court and the High Courts (articles 56, 61, 67, 124(1) and 217(1)(b)). Every Presidential Ordinance, Proclamation of Emergency and Proclamation of the failure of constitutional machinery in a State must be placed before both Houses of Parliament (articles 123, 352(4) and 356(4)). Disagreement between the two Houses on a Bill, other than a Money Bill and a Constitution Amendment Bill, is resolved by both the Houses in a joint sitting where matters are decided by majority vote. Such joint sitting of the two Houses is presided over by the Speaker of Lok Sabha (articles 108 and 118(4)).

The Constitution has assigned some special powers to the Rajya Sabha. It alone has the power to declare that it would be in national interest for the Parliament to legislate in respect of a matter in the State List. If by a two-thirds majority, Rajya Sabha passes a resolution to this effect, the Union Parliament can make laws for the whole or any part of the country even with respect to a matter enumerated in the State List (article 249). Also, Parliament is empowered to make laws providing for the creation of one or more All India Services common to the Union and the States, if the Rajya Sabha declares by a resolution supported by not less than two-thirds of the members present and voting that it is necessary or expedient in the national interest to do so (article 312).

Parliament and the Executive

After a new Lok Sabha is duly elected and constituted, the President invites the leader of the party or parties commanding the support of more than half of the members of the Lok Sabha, to form the government.

While the Prime Minister usually is a member of the Lok Sabha, the Ministers are drawn from both Houses of

Parliament. A person other than a Member of Parliament may also be appointed as Minister, but he has to vacate the office after six months unless, in the meanwhile, he manages to get himself elected to either of the two Houses. Since the Council of Ministers is collectively responsible to Lok Sabha (article 75), Ministers are under a constitutional obligation to resign collectively as soon as they lose the confidence of Lok Sabha.

The scheme of the Constitution represents a real fusion of the highest executive and legislative authorities. The relationship between the Executive and Legislature thereunder is one that is most intimate and ideally does not admit of any antagonism or dichotomy. The two are not visualized as competing centres of power but as inseparable partners or co-partners in the business of government. Strictly speaking, Parliamentary system of government should mean Government by Parliament. But, the Parliament is a large body. It does not and cannot itself govern. The Council of Ministers may in a sense be described as the grand executive committee of Parliament charged with the responsibility of governance on behalf of the parent body. In other words, the Executive is not a separate or outside body. Inasmuch as the Council of Ministers is drawn from and remains part of Parliament and responsible to Lok Sabha, the relationship may be said to be that of a part to the whole and one of interdependence. There is, however, a clear distinction between the functions of the Executive and the functions of Parliament (article 75). The Parliament is to deliberate, discuss, legislate, advise, criticize and ventilate public grievances. Also, it has a legitimatizational role.The Executive is to govern, albeit on behalf of Parliament and the People.

While the Executive has almost unlimited right to initiate and formulate legislative and financial proposals before Parliament and to give effect to approved policies unfettered and unhindered by Parliament, the latter has the unlimited power to call for information, to discuss, to scrutinize and to put the seal of popular approval on proposals made by the Executive. The Executive remains responsible and the administration accountable to Parliament. The function of Parliament is to exercise political and financial control over the Executive and to ensure parliamentary surveillance of administration. This control is exercised through various procedural devices like Question Hour, Motions, Resolutions, various kinds of discussions and scrutiny by parliamentary committees.

Parliament and the Judiciary

Parliament has the power to make laws regulating the constitution, organisation, jurisdiction and powers of the Courts. It was laid down in the Constitution that the number of Judges other than the Chief Justice would not be more than seven. The number now (2009) *vide* Supreme Court (Number of Judges) Amendment Act, 2008 is thirty. The Parliament was, however, empowered to prescribe a larger number of Judges by law (article 124). Under our Constitution, the Parliament may by law:

i. extend the jurisdiction of a High Court to, or exclude the jurisdiction of a High Court from, any Union territory;
ii. establish a common High Court for two or more States or for two or more States and a Union territory; and
iii. constitute a High Court for a Union territory or declare any Court in any such territory to be a High Court for all or any of the purposes of the Constitution (Art.241).

A judge of the Supreme Court or any High Court may by writing under his hand, addressed to the President, resign his office. He can be removed from his Office by the President, only if a joint address passed by both Houses of Parliament with a special majority (*i.e.*, by a majority of the total membership of the House and by a majority of not less than two-thirds of the members of each House present and voting) is presented to him (article 124(4) and 218).

Parliament is not empowered to discuss the conduct of any Judge of the Supreme Court or of a High Court in the discharge of his duties except in the case of a motion for presenting an address to the President praying for the removal of a Judge (article 121).

Parliament may by law provide for the establishment of an administrative tribunal for the Union and a separate administrative tribunal for each State or for two or more States. The law made under the provision may specify the jurisdiction and powers of the tribunals. Such law may exclude the jurisdiction of all Courts, except the jurisdiction of the Supreme Court under article 136, with respect to certain specified matters (articles 323A and 323B). Further, the Constitution empowers Parliament to create an all India judicial service which shall not include any post inferior to that of a district judge (articles 312(1) and (3)).

The validity of any proceedings in either House of Parliament cannot be questioned before a court of law on the ground of any alleged irregularity of procedure (articles 122(1) and 212(1)) (*Kihoto v. Zachilhu,* AIR 1993 SC 412). The presiding officer of each House or any other officer or Member of Parliament who is for the time being vested with the powers to regulate procedure, or to enforce or carry out the decision of either House of Parliament, is not subject to the jurisdiction of the courts in exercise of those powers (articles 122(2) and 105(3)).

The constitutional validity of a law can be challenged in India on the ground that the subject matter of the legislation:

i. is not within the competence of the Legislature which has passed it;
ii. is repugnant to the provisions of the Constitution; or
iii. it infringes one of the Fundamental Rights.

There is no appeal against the judgement of the Supreme Court. It remains the law of the land unless its interpretation is reviewed or reversed by the Supreme Court itself or the law or the Constitution is suitably amended by Parliament. If an Act of Parliament is set aside by the judiciary, Parliament can re-enact it after removing the defects for which it was set aside. Also, Parliament may, within the limits of its constituent powers, amend the Constitution in such a manner that the law no longer remains unconstitutional.

Thus the Parliament in India is not as supreme as the British Parliament where traditionally no judicial review of legislation is permitted. At the same time the judiciary in India is not as supreme as in the United States of America which recognises virtually no limit on the scope of judicial review.

On the issue of the sovereignty of Parliament, different views have been expressed even by the Supreme Court.[1] It has, however, been held in the *Gopalan case* that within the specified limits of its powers, the Parliament is supreme.

Functions of Parliament

***Legislation*:** Traditionally the main function of a legislature is to legislate. Under articles 245–246 Parliament can make laws for the whole or any part of India within its area of competence as defined and delimited under the distribution of legislative powers between the Union and the States *vide* the Seventh Schedule. In regard to the Union List, the Parliament's jurisdiction is exclusive. Both the Union and the States have concurrent power to legislate in respect of entries in the Concurrent List. In case of conflict between the Union and the State laws, the former prevails (article 254). Also, the residuary powers vest in the Union Parliament (article 248 and entry 97 of the Union List). A large number of articles empower the Parliament to make laws in various matters by saying things like 'save as otherwise provided

---

1. See *A.K. Gopalan v. State of Madras*, (1950) SCR 88; *In re Delhi Laws case* (1951) SCR 747; *Shankari Prasad v. Union of India*, AIR 1951 SC 458.

by Parliament by law', 'Parliament may by law.....' or 'until Parliament by law prescribes' etc. Parliament may by law change the name, the boundaries, area etc. of the States or establish new States (articles 2,3 and 4), increase the number of judges of the Supreme Court or establish additional courts (articles 124, 247). Under article 249, Parliament may legislate even on matters in the State List. Under article 253, it may legislate for implementing a treaty or agreement with a foreign country even though the matter falls in the State List. Also, in circumstances of President's rule (article 356) or proclamation of Emergency (article 352), Parliament can legislate in the State field.

Constituent Powers: Under article 368, Parliament exercises constituent powers in accordance with the procedure laid down for different categories of amendments. While a large number of articles can be amended by Parliament itself by a special majority, in certain cases concurrence of the States is required (See under 'Amendment of the Constitution').

Parliamentary control over Government: In a parliamentary system of Government and under the scheme of our Constitution, Parliament has to ensure Executive or Ministerial responsibility, financial control and administrative accountability. Executive or Ministerial responsibility to Parliament or what is often termed parliamentary control over the Executive or the Government is based on: (i) the constitutional provision of collective responsibility of the Council of Ministers to the popular House of Parliament; and (ii) the Parliament's control over the Budget (Articles 75, 114–116 and 265).

Parliamentary control over the Executive is political in nature. The answerability of the Executive is direct, continuous, concurrent and day-to-day. When Parliament is sitting, the continuance of the Government in office depends from moment to moment on its not losing the confidence of the House of the People. The House may at any time decide to throw out the Government by a majority vote, *i.e.* if the ruling party loses the confidence of the majority of the members of the House, its Government goes. No grounds, arguments, proofs or justification are necessary. When the House clearly and conclusively pronounces that the Government of the day has lost its confidence, the Government must resign. Want of parliamentary confidence in the Government may be expressed by the House of the People by: (a) passing a substantive motion of no-confidence in the Council of Ministers; (b) defeating the Government on a major issue of policy; (c) passing an adjournment motion; or (d) refusing to vote supplies or defeating the Government on a financial measure.

***Parliamentary control over public finance*:** The power to levy or modify taxes and the voting of supplies and grants is one of the most important checks against the Executive assuming arbitrary powers. No taxes can be legally levied and no expenditure incurred from the public exchequer without specific parliamentary authorization by law (articles 114 116 and 265).

In fact, except in the theoretical sense of the budgetary control or the ultimate sanction of a vote of no-confidence, parliamentary control over the Government is no more valid even in the 'Mother of Parliaments'. In actual practice, it is the Government which controls Parliament through its majority in the House of the People and through its power to have the House dissolved and fresh elections ordered by the President.

Administrative accountability is ensured through legislation, through parliamentary devices like questions, discussions on various motions, committee scrutiny, and through the Minister who actually represents Parliament and controls his department on behalf of Parliament.

***Other Functions*:** Besides, Parliament exercises multifarious functions, for example, in matters like the impeachment of the President, removal of Supreme Court and High Court judges, Comptroller and Auditor-General, Chief Election Commissioner, Presiding Officers of the two Houses etc. (articles 61, 124, 217, 148, 324, 90 and 94; see under relevant chapters).[1]

Anti-Defection Law

The Constitution (Fifty-second Amendment) Act, 1985 amended articles 101, 102, 190 and 191 of the Constitution regarding vacation of seats and disqualification from membership of Parliament and the State Legislatures and added a new schedule (Tenth Schedule) to the Constitution setting out certain provisions as to disqualification on grounds of defection. Originally, the Tenth Schedule *inter alia* provided that:

i. an elected member of Parliament or a State Legislature, who has been elected as a candidate set up by a political party, and a nominated member of Parliament or a State Legislature who is a member of a political party at the time he takes his seat would be disqualified on the ground of defection if he voluntarily relinquishes his membership of such political party or votes or abstains from voting in the House contrary to any direction of such party;
ii. an independent member of Parliament or a State Legislature will be disqualified if he joins any political party after his election;
iii. a nominated member of Parliament or a State Legislature who is not a member of a political party at the time of his nomination and who has not become a member of any political party before the expiry of six months from the date on which he takes his seat shall be disqualified if he joins any political party after the expiry of the said period of six months;
iv. no disqualification would be incurred where a member claims that he belongs to a group representing a faction arising from a split in a party or merger of a party in

1. For further study, see Subhash C. Kashyap, *Our Parliament*, NBT, New Delhi; *Parliamentary Procedure*, Universal, New Delhi, 2006.

another provided that in the event of a split the group consists of not less than one-third of the members of the legislature party and in case of a merger of not less than two-thirds of the members of the legislature party concerned;

v. no disqualification is incurred by a person who has been elected to the office of the Speaker or the Deputy Speaker of the House of the People or of the Legislative Assembly of a State or to the office of the Deputy Chairman of the Council of States or the Chairman or the Deputy Chairman of the Legislative Council of a State, if he severs his connection with his political party;

vi. the question as to whether a member of a House of Parliament or State Legislature has become subject to disqualification will be determined by the Chairman or the Speaker of the respective House; where the question is with reference to the Chairman or the Speaker himself it will be decided by a member of the concerned House elected by it in that behalf;

vii. the Chairman or the Speaker of a House has been empowered to make rules for giving effect to the provisions of the Schedule. The rules are required to be laid before the House and are subject to modifications/disapproval by the House;

viii. all proceedings in relation to any question as to disqualification of a member of a House under the Schedule will be deemed to be proceedings in Parliament within the meaning of article 122 or, as the case may be, proceedings in the Legislature of a State within the meaning of article 212; and

ix. notwithstanding anything in the Constitution, no court will have any jurisdiction in respect of any matter connected with the disqualification of a member of a House.

The Constitution (Fifty-second Amendment) Act, 1985, which has since popularly come to be known as the Anti-Defection Law, has been the subject matter of a controversy from the very beginning. It has been questioned on several grounds *viz.*, that it is violative of the basic structure of the Constitution, that it is beyond the competence of Parliament, and that it gives preference to expediency over principles.

Paragraph 7 of the Tenth Schedule which barred the jurisdiction of the courts was struck down as being *ultra vires* of the Constitution by the High Court of Punjab and Haryana and an appeal against this order was preferred by the Government in the Supreme Court. Several writ petitions challenging the validity and constitutionality of the 1985 enactment were also filed in the Supreme Court and various High Courts. The Supreme Court, on the request of the Government, withdrew and transferred to itself all the writ petitions pending before various High Courts. The Supreme Court[1] found that there were legal infirmities in the passage of the Anti-Defection Law inasmuch as the Constitution Amendment Bill had not been ratified by the requisite number of State Assemblies before being presented for the President's assent. Also, the Speaker's functions under the 10th Schedule called for a judicial determination of issues under the law. The process of determining the question of disqualification could not be considered part of the proceedings of the House and as such was not amenable to judicial review. The Supreme Court struck down Para 7 of the Schedule barring the jurisdiction of Courts and declared that while operating under the Anti-Defection Law, the Speaker was in the position of a tribunal and therefore his decisions like those of all tribunals were subject to judicial review.

Some of the situations that arose do not seem to have been foreseen by those who drafted the 52nd Amendment for outlawing defections. Also, the fact that certain provisions of the Tenth Schedule were found to be amenable to entirely different interpretations by different presiding officers created terrible uncertainty and fluidity in the application

1. *Kihoto Hollohan v. Zachillhu & Others*, AIR 1993 SC 412.

of the law and brought to limelight a number of defects.

At the Union level, two Governments—those of Shri V.P. Singh and Shri Chandra Shekhar—fell in quick succession. Even though Shri Chandra Shekhar formed the Janata Dal(S) Government and won the confidence of the House on a substantive motion, all the members of the ruling Janata Dal(S) were either those who had been expelled by Shri V.P. Singh and declared "unattached" by Speaker Rabi Ray or those against whom show cause notices for disqualification under the Anti-Defection Law had been issued by Speaker Ray in the exercise of his powers under the Anti-Defection Law. The Speaker's action covered all the members of the Council of Ministers headed by Shri Chandra Shekhar. This dragged on until finally on 11 January, 1991 Ray decided to give benefit of doubt to the ruling party and recognised the split as a one time process which began and closed on 5 November. Janata Dal(S) was recognised as a political party with 54 members. The seven members who joined after the date of split were disqualified.

In another case of Janata split, on 7 August, 1992, 20 of the 59 members of the Janata Dal appeared before Speaker Patil physically in one group, at the same time and claimed that they belonged to a group and should be seated separately from the Janata Dal members led by Shri V.P. Singh. Even though eight of these members had been expelled earlier by the Janata Dal leadership in two separate spells, the Speaker allotted them separate seats in the House. They continued to be shown as among the 59 Janata Dal members in all official Lok Sabha records. In his final decision on 1 June 1993. Speaker Patil held that (i) the political parties had no right under the Constitution to expel members from the legislature party so as to take away their constitutional status as members elected on a particular party ticket (Tenth Schedule, Explanation (a) to para 2(1)), and (ii) that the 20 members did not suffer from any disability as on 7 August 1992 and since they had the requisite strength of one-third on that day, they constituted a valid faction of the Janata Dal Parliamentary Party. The Speaker disqualified four of the 20 members on the ground of voluntarily disobeying their party whip. However, the disqualification was to have only prospective effect from the date of the order. Most significantly, the Speaker agreed that the Anti-Defection Law was defective and needed review and reform. He suggested that the task of determining disqualification of members under the Tenth Schedule could better be entrusted to the judges.

It was agreed on all sides that the Tenth Schedule of the Constitution which embodied the Anti-Defection Law had several serious lacunae which had caused tremendous damage to our body politic and that amendments were called for urgently. For instance, several terms like 'political parties', 'split', 'merger' etc. had not been defined. The Tenth Schedule defined a 'Legislature Party' and an 'original political party' in either case with reference to a 'political party' but unfortunately a 'political party' had not been defined. It would be necessary to define a political party and to lay down conditions for its recognition for purposes of the Anti-Defection Law. It was particularly imperative in view of the constitutional provision of Para 3 of the Tenth Schedule to the effect that the breakaway faction following a split would be deemed to be a 'political party' for purposes of Para 2(1).

The Constitution Commission (NCRWC) recommended that all defectors—whether individual or in groups of one-third etc.—should be disqualified for continuing as members. They must resign and seek fresh election and until re-election, they should stand debarred from holding any public office of a minister or any other remunerative political post.

Following the NCRWC recommendation, the Constitution (91st Amendment) Act 2003 amended the Tenth Schedule of the Constitution and inserted a new article 361B to take away the protection from defectors on grounds of split in the party. It disqualified all defectors from membership and made them ineligible for ministership or other remunerative public office till reelection. Also, the number of ministerial posts was limited to 15% of the membership of the Lok Sabha/ Vidhan Sabha. However, the protection under the merger provision still remains.[1]

Parliamentary Reforms

The Constitution Commission (NCRWC) reviewed the working of Parliament for half a century (1950-2000) and *inter alia* recommended:

(i) periodic review of the work of Standing Committees of Parliament,

(ii) setting up of a model standing committee on National economy,

(iii) setting up of a Standing Constitution Committee for a *priori* scrutiny of Constitution amendment proposals.

(iv) discussing major reports of Parliamentary Committees on the floors of the two houses;

(v) parliamentarians throwing themselves open to public scrutiny through a parliamentary 'ombudsman'.

(vi) restoration of domiciliary requirement for Rajya Sabha membership

(vii) codification of parliamentary privileges *inter alia* clarifying that they do not cover corrupt acts like accepting bribe

(viii) more systematic approach to planning legislation, appointment of a Legislation Committee and referring all bills to a departmental standing committee

(ix) the MP LAD Scheme may be discontinued immediately for being inconsistent with the spirit of the Constitution.

---

1. For a commentary on the subject see Subhash C. Kashyap, *Anti-Defection Law and Parliamentary Privileges*, Universal, New Delhi. For further study of Parliamentary Procedure, Privilege Law etc. see Subhash C. Kashyap, *Parliamentary Procedure, Law, Privileges, Practice and Precedents*, Universal Law Publishers, New Delhi, 2006 and________, *History of Parliament of India*, Radha, New Delhi, 2008, 2 Volumes].

13

THE JUDICIARY

PART V, CHAPTER IV, ARTICLES 124-147 AND PART VI, CHAPTER V AND VI, ARTICLES 214-237

Provisions in regard to the judiciary in India are contained in Part V on The Union under Chapter IV titled The Union Judiciary and Part VI on The States under Chapters V and VI titled The High Courts in the States and Subordinate Courts respectively. It is, however important to emphasize that unlike other federal systems, for example, that of the United States, we do not have separate hierarchies of federal and State Courts.

For the entire republic of India, there is one unified judicial system—one hierarchy of courts—with the Supreme Court as the highest or the apex court and as the only arbiter in matters of relations between the Union and the States and the States *inter se.*

THE SUPREME COURT

***Composition of the Court and conditions of Judge's office*:** Article 124 provided for the establishment of the Supreme Court with a Chief Justice and seven other judges. It, however authorised Parliament to increase the number of judges by law. The number as fixed by law [Supreme Court (No. of Judges) Act 1956 as amended in 1986) was 25 in addition to the Chief Justice. It has since been increased to 30 by the 2008 Amending Act. Under article 124(2), Supreme Court Judges are to be appointed by the President

> after consultation with such of the judges of the Supreme Court and of the High Courts as the President may deem necessary.

The proviso to the article says that "in the case of appointment of a judge other than the Chief Justice, the Chief Justice of India shall always be consulted". The only obligation for the Government was to consult the Chief Justice and other judges. Significantly, the appointment was not required to be made 'in consultation' but only 'after consultation'. In actual practice, after receiving the opinion of the Chief Justice, the Cabinet deliberated on the matter and advised the President in regard to persons to be appointed. The President acted on the advice. In case of the Chief Justice, the seniormost judge was usually appointed. The convention, however, was ignored when in the '70s, a couple of Chief Justices were appointed superseding their more senior colleagues.

It was held in *S.P. Gupta v. Union of India* (AIR 1982 SC 149) that consultation must be effective and must imply exchange of views after examining merits, but that it did not mean concurrence. However this case was overruled in 1993 in the *Supreme Court Advocates-on Record Association Vs. Union of India* (AIR 1994 SC 268). In this case, the Supreme Court practically took over the power of selecting the judges for appointment in its own hands. As a safeguard, it mandated the Chief Justice associating two of his seniormost colleagues in the selection process. The procedure for appointment was revised in the light of this judgement in 1994 to the effect that the decisive view in the matter of the appointment of judges shall be that of the Chief Justice of India and in case of a vacancy in the office of the Chief Justice of India, the seniormost judge shall be appointed unless the retiring Chief Justice reported that he was unfit. However, following the government's reservations in regard to certain recommendations made by the Chief Justice in the matter of appointment of judges to the Supreme Court, the matter again became highly controversial and the President made a reference to seek the advisory opinion of the Supreme Court under article 143 of the Constitution. The Court pronouncing its advisory opinion[1] basically confirmed the position in the 1993 judgement but it provided some more safeguards. The Chief Justice had to consult four seniormost judges of the Supreme Court and if two of the four disagreed on some name, it could not be recommended. In effect, decisions were to be taken by consensus where the Chief and at least three of the four had to agree.

The Constitution Commission (NCRWC) recommended appointment of a National Judicial Commission as a machinery for appointment of judges and suggested that retirement age of High Court judges may be increased to 65 years and of the Suprme Court judges to 68 years.

Every judge of the Supreme Court holds office until the age of 65 years. A judge may be removed from his office only by an order of the President passed after an address by each House of Parliament for his removal "on the ground of misbehaviour or incapacity" supported by a majority of the total membership of that House and by a majority of not less than two-thirds of the members present and voting is presented to him in the same session. The procedure may be regulated by Parliament by law (article 124). In the case of Justice Ramaswamy, motion for presenting an address to the President for his removal failed to get the required majority in Lok Sabha.

Contrary to the common belief, there is no provision in our Constitution for the impeachment of a judge. The impeachment is provided for the President and none else.

1. Spl. Ref.No.1 of 1998 on 28 October 1998 [(1998) 7n SCC 739].

Also, there is a fundamental difference between removal procedure and impeachment procedure and between the impact of the adoption of a motion for impeachment and the passing of a motion for presenting an address to the President seeking orders for the removal of a judge. The grounds for the impeachment of the President have to concern 'violation of the Constitution' while an address for removal of a judge has to be on the ground of "misbehavior or incapacity". In case of impeachment, the moment the motion is passed by the two Houses, the President forthwith ceases to be the President. But in case of the motion for removal, it is for the President to consider issuing necessary orders.

Every person appointed as a judge of the Supreme Court, before he enters upon his office, takes an oath before the President or some person appointed in that behalf by him in the form prescribed in the Constitution. The Constitution prohibits a person who has held office as a judge of the Supreme Court from practising law before any court in the territory of India (article 124(6) and (7)).

Judges of the Supreme Court are to be paid such salaries as may be determined by Parliament by law (article 125). This is done by the High Court and Supreme Court Judges (Conditions of Service) Act as amended from time to time. In addition, to salary, the judges are allowed sumptuory allowances, rent free furnished residences, telephone, water, electricity, medical and other facilities exclusive of allowances and privileges like travelling expenses within the country, pension etc.

When the office of the Chief Justice of India is vacant or when the Chief Justice is unable to perform the duties of his office due to absence, the President shall appoint an Acting Chief Justice from among the judges of the Court to perform the duties of the Chief Justice (article 126).

If at any time there is no quorum of judges of the Supreme Court available to hold or continue any session of the Court, the Chief Justice of India is empowered to appoint *ad hoc* judges in the Supreme Court from among judges of the High Courts, having qualifications to be appointed judges of the Supreme Court, for such period as he deems necessary. He can do so only with previous consent of the President and after consultation with the Chief Justice of the High Court concerned. The judge so appointed is duty bound to give priority to the Supreme Court duties. The Chief Justice of India may also invite a retired judge of the Supreme Court or a retired judge of the High Court having the qualification to be a judge of the Supreme Court, to sit and act as a judge of the Supreme Court for such period as he deems necessary. This too can be done with the previous consent of the President and also of the person to be so appointed (articles 127 and 128).

***Power and Jurisdiction of the Court*:** Article 129 provides that the Supreme Court shall be a court of record and shall have all the powers of such a court. Being the highest court of the land, its proceedings, acts and decisions are kept in record for perpetual memory and for presentation as evidence, when need be, in support of what the law is. Being a court of record implies that its records can be used as evidence and cannot be questioned for their authenticity in any court.[1]

Court of record also means that it can punish for its own contempt. But this is a summary power, used sparingly and under pressing circumstances. It does not inhibit genuine and well intentioned criticism of court and its functioning. Fair and reasonable criticism of a judicial act in the interest of public good does not constitute contempt.[2]

The Supreme Court has original, appellate and advisory jurisdiction. Original jurisdiction means the power to hear

1. *Daphtary v. Gupta,* AIR 1971 SC 1132; *Namboodripad v. Nambiar,* AIR 1970 SC 2015.
2. For 'Contempt of Court' see under the chapter on 'Fundamental Rights'.

and determine a dispute in the first instance. The Supreme Court has been given exclusive original jurisdiction which extends to disputes (a) between the Government of India and one or more States (*e.g. State of West Bengal v. Union of India*, AIR 1963 SC 1241) (b) between the Government of India and one or more States on one side and one or more States on the other, (c) between two or more States. However, this jurisdiction shall not extend to a dispute arising out of a treaty, agreement etc. which is in operation and excludes such jurisdiction (article 131). The jurisdiction of the Supreme Court may also be excluded in certain other matters, *e.g.* inter-State water disputes (article 262), matters referred to the Finance Commission (article 280) and adjustment of certain expenses and pensions between the Union and the States (article 290). Recovery of damages against the Government of India cannot be claimed by a State before the Supreme Court under article 131. The article does not cover such ordinary commercial matters between the Union and the States.[1] Also, a dispute to be so brought before the Supreme Court must involve a question, whether of law or fact, on which the existence or extent of a legal right depends.

Under the new article 139A inserted by the 44th Amendment in 1978, the Supreme Court may transfer to itself cases from one or more High Courts if these involve questions of law or of great importance. Also, the Supreme Court may transfer cases from one High Court to another in the interests of justice.

The original jurisdiction of the Supreme Court also extends to cases of violation of the fundamental rights of individuals and the Court can issue several writs for the enforcement of these rights (article 32). It is a unique feature of our Constitution that in principle, any individual can straightaway approach the highest court in case of violation of his fundamental rights.

---

1. *Union of India v. State of Rajasthan* (1984) 4 SCC 238.

The appellate jurisdiction of the Supreme Court extends to civil, criminal and constitutional matters. In a civil matter, an appeal lies to the Supreme Court from any judgement, decree or final order of a High Court if the High Court certifies under article 134A that a substantial question of law of general importance as to the interpretation of the Constitution is involved and the matter needs to be decided by the Supreme Court (articles 132–134).

Considering an appeal under article 133, the Supreme Court held in *P.K. Dave v. People's Union of Civil Liberties* (AIR 1996 SC 2166) that the High Court should refrain from using intemperate language as part of judicial discipline while commenting upon the conduct of another individual particularly when that individual is not before the court.

In criminal cases, an appeal to the Supreme Court shall lie if the High Court (a) has reversed an order of acquittal of an accused person and sentenced him to death, or (b) has withdrawn for trial before itself any case from any court subordinate to its authority and has in such trial convicted the accused person and sentenced him to death (article 134).[1]

Under article 134(1)(c) an appeal against a decision of a High Court can be filed before the Supreme Court if the High Court certifies under article 134A that the case is a fit one for appeal to the Supreme Court. But the proviso to sub-clause (c) lays down that such appeals shall be subject to rules made by the Supreme Court and to such other conditions as the High Court may decide. The grant of the certificate by the High Court for appeals in criminal cases to the Supreme Court depends on an evaluation whether the case involves a substantial question of law and its interpretation on which the Supreme Court is urgently required to pronounce its opinion and whether it would result in grave injustice to the accused if he is denied the opportunity of an appeal to the Supreme Court.

1. *Ram Kumar v. State of M.P.*, AIR 1975 SC 1026; *Padda Narayana v. State of U.P.*, AIR 1975 SC 1252.

Under article 136, the Supreme Court, at its discretion, may grant special leave to appeal from any judgement, decree, determination, sentence or order, in any cause or matter passed or made by any court or tribunal in the territory of India. These powers of the Supreme Court to grant special leave to appeal are far wider than the High Courts' power to grant certificates to appeal to the Supreme Court under article 134. The Supreme Court can grant special leave against judgements of any court or tribunal in the territory, except the military courts, and in any type of cases, civil, criminal or revenue. But, the Supreme Court has itself said that it will grant special leave to appeal only in cases where there has been gross miscarriage of justice or where the High Court or Tribunal is found to have been wrong in law. If the judgement of the court below shakes the conscience and shocks the sense of justice, Supreme Court shall interfere.[1]

Article 137 provides for the Supreme Court having the power to review its own judgements and orders.

Article 143 of the Constitution confers upon the Supreme Court advisory jurisdiction. The President may seek the opinion of the Supreme Court on any question of law or fact of public importance on which he thinks it expedient to obtain such an opinion. On such reference from the President, the Supreme Court, after giving it such hearing as it deems fit, may report to the President its opinion thereon. The opinion is only advisory, which the President is free to follow or not to follow. The first such reference was made in the *Delhi Laws case*, (1951) SCR 747. A recent instance was of President Abdul Kalam seeking (in August 2002) advice of the Supreme Court under article 143 in connection with the controversy between the Election Commission and the

1. *Haripada Dey v. State of West Bengal*, AIR 1965 SC 757; *Matru v. State of U.P.*, AIR 1971 SC 1050; *Ram Saran v. C.T.O.*, AIR 1962 SC 1326; *Muniswamy v. Ranganathan*, (1991) 2SCC 139; *Mahesh v. State of Delhi*, (1991) Cr LJ 1703 (SC).

Government on elections in Gujarat. The issues related to the limits on the powers of the Election Commission under article 324, the impact of article 174 on the jurisdiction and powers of the Commission and whether the Commission could recommend promulgation of President's rule in a State.

The President may also seek the opinion of the Supreme Court, through a similar reference on any treaty, agreement, covenant, engagement, sanad or other similar instrument which had been entered into or executed before the commencement of this Constitution, and has continued in operation thereafter.

Under article 138, the Supreme Court shall have such further jurisdiction and powers with respect to any of the matters in the Union List as Parliament may by law confer. It shall have such jurisdiction and powers with respect to any matter as the Government of India and the Government of any State may by special agreement confer, if the Parliament by law provides for the exercise of such jurisdiction and powers by the Supreme Court. This enlarges the jurisdiction of the Supreme Court and provides it with very special jurisdiction to hear cases of most urgent nature directly and in its original jurisdiction for speedy disposal.

Article 139 lays down that Parliament may by law confer on the Supreme Court power to issue directions, orders or writs in matters not already covered under article 32. Under article 140, Parliament may by law supplement the powers of the Supreme Court. Law declared by the Supreme Court is binding on all courts in India *vide* article 141.[1] But no law can be taken to have been declared where no reasons are given. Also, what is binding is the principle or the ratio of the decision and not findings on facts, opinions

1. *Vineet Narain v. Union of India*, AIR 1998 SC 889; *Dwarikesh Sugar Industries Ltd. v. Prem Heavy Engineering Works (P) Ltd.*, AIR 1997 SC 2477.

or arguments.[1] Decrees and orders of the Supreme Court shall be enforceable throughout India and civil and judicial authorities shall act in aid of the Supreme Court (articles 142 & 144).

For purposes of giving effect to the directions and decisions of the Supreme Court, all authorities, civil and judicial, in the territory of India, have been made subordinate to the authority of the Supreme Court inasmuch as all these are required to "act in aid of the Supreme Court" (article 144). The Supreme Court may from time to time, and with the approval of the President, make rules for regulating generally the practice and procedure of the Court. The officers and staff of the Supreme Court are appointed by the Chief Justice of India or such other judge or officer of the court as he may direct (articles 145 146). Article 147 clarifies that references to interpretation of the Constitution shall cover interpretation of the Government of India Act 1935, Indian Independence Act 1947 etc.

Judicial Review: Judicial review as it has evolved in the United States means the power of the highest court of the land to finally pronounce upon the legality or otherwise of a legislative act in so far as it conforms, or does not conform, to the provisions of the fundamental law, *i.e.* the Constitution of the land. Our Constitution very largely but not entirely follows the U.S. practice in this regard. The Constitution being the fundamental law of the land, every legislative enactment, whether of the Union or that of States must conform to this fundamental law except that in India, after a law is declared unconstitutional, in most cases, the Constitution can be amended to take care of the judicial interpretation and make the law permissible.

Cases are often filed before the Supreme Court by a State

1. *Supreme Court Employees v. Union of India,* AIR 1991 SC 334; *Ramesh v. Union of India,* AIR 1990 SC 560; *C.I.T. v. S.E.W.,* AIR 1993 SC 43; *Krishan v. Union of India,* (1990) 4 SCC 207 (CB).

Government, or by an affected private individual or a party, claiming that in enacting a particular law, the concerned government exceeded its jurisdictional limit with regard to the division of powers under the Seventh Schedule. While reviewing such enactment, the Supreme Court will examine whether jurisdictional limits have been transgressed. Incorporation of a Chapter on Fundamental Rights in the Constitution makes judicial review specially relevant. Article 12 guarantees fundamental rights against all State action. And 'State' under this article has been defined to include the Government and Parliament of India and the Government and the Legislature of each of the States and all local or other authorities within the territory of India or under the control of the Government.

Article 13 declares all laws inconsistent with or in derogation of the fundamental rights to be void to the extent of inconsistency. Up to 1967, the Supreme Court accepted the view that an Act amending the Constitution was not 'Law' in the definition of article 13(2). But, in the *Golaknath case*, the Supreme Court ruled by a majority judgement that an Act amending the Constitution was also 'law' under this definition and therefore subject to judicial review. The Constitution (Twenty-fourth Amendment) Act, 1971 inserted clause 13(4) in the Constitution, laying down that an Amendment to the Constitution is not 'law' under the definition of article 13(2). In the *Keshvanand Bharti case,* the Supreme Court upheld this position.

Article 32 in the Chapter on Fundamental Rights specifically confers the power of judicial review on the Supreme Court. Under this article every citizen has a right to move the Supreme Court by appropriate proceedings for the enforcement of the rights conferred in Chapter III. The Supreme Court can hear the petition in its original jurisdiction. The Supreme Court has been given the power to issue directions, orders or writs in the nature of *habeas corpus, mandamus, prohibition, quo warranto* and *certiorari,* whichever may be appropriate, for the enforcement of any of the rights conferred.

Under article 226, State High Courts have been given similar power, *i.e.*, the power to issue to any person or authority, within its territorial jurisdiction, directions, orders, or writs including writs in the nature of *habeas corpus, mandamus, prohibition, quo warranto* and *certiorari,* or any of them for the enforcement of any of these rights.[1]

***Due Process of Law Vs. According to the Procedure established by Law*:** The U.S. Constitution (Constitutional Amendments) provides that a man may not be deprived of his right to liberty and property except according to due process of law. The Indian Constitution, however, lays down that a man may not be deprived of his rights to liberty except according to the procedure established by law. The due process of law gives wide scope to the Supreme Court to grant protection to the rights of its citizens. It can declare laws violative of these rights void not only on substantive grounds of being unlawful, but also on procedural grounds of being unreasonable. Our Supreme Court, while determining the constitutionality of a law, however was expected to examine only the substantive question, *i.e.*, whether the law is within the powers of the authority concerned or not. It was not expected to go into the question of its reasonableness, suitability or policy implications.

The Supreme Court pronounces its judgement on a specific case through a specific petition. It does not give its opinion or advice on a general reference. Generally, there should be an aggrieved person who petitions the Court to challenge the constitutionality of the statute which has adversely affected his rights. He has to show that he has sustained or is in immediate danger of sustaining some direct injury as a result of the enforcement of the statute, and that the injury complained of is justiciable.

---

1. For a description of writs see under 'The High Courts'.

Public Interest Litigation: In the historic judgement in the Judges' Transfer case, the seven judge Constitution Bench of the Supreme Court held that any member of the public even if not directly involved but having "sufficient interest" can approach the High Court under article 226, or in case of breach of fundamental rights the Supreme Court, for redressal of the grievances of the persons who cannot move the Court because of "poverty, helplessness or disability or socially or economically disadvantaged position". The Court can be approached even through a letter in such a case.[1] After this judgement, it has been open to public minded individual citizens or social organizations to seek judicial relief in the interest of the general public.

In *Bandhua Mukti Morcha v. Union of India* (AIR 1984 SC 803), an organisation dedicated to the cause of release of bonded labourers informed the Supreme Court through a letter that they conducted a survey of the stone quarries situated in Faridabad District of Haryana and found that there were a large number of labourers working in such quarries under "inhuman and intolerable conditions" and many of them were bonded labourers. The petitioners entreated that a writ be issued for proper implementation of the various provisions of the Constitution and Statutes with a view to ending the misery, suffering and helplessness of those labourers. The court treated the letter as a writ petition and appointed a Commission consisting of two advocates to visit these stone quarries, make an enquiry and report to the court on the matter.

In *Lakshmi Kant Pandey v. Union of India,* a writ petition was filed on the basis of a letter complaining malpractices indulged in by social organisations and voluntary agencies engaged in the work of offering Indian children to foreign parents. It was alleged that in the guise of adoption, children of tender age were not only being exposed to a long dreadful

1. *S.P. Gupta v. President of India,* AIR 1982 SC 149.

journey to distant countries at great risk to their lives but also to uncertainty as to their shelter and future. Chief Justice P.N. Bhagwati laid down certain principles and norms to ensure the welfare of the children and directed the Government and various agencies dealing with the matter to follow them ((1987) 1 SCC 667).

In recent years, under what has come to be called judicial activism, the Supreme Court has issued directions to control pollution, to check the evil of child prostitution, to revive a sick company to protect the livelihood of 10,000 employees, to look into the danger to safety in building a dam, to segregate the children of prostitutes from their mothers, to provide insurance to workers in match factories, to protect the Taj Mahal from environmental pollution etc.[1] However, it has been held that non-justiciable political matters cannot be brought before the court under the guise of public interest litigation.[2] *Locus standi* to file a petition depends on the facts as they exist. Even a journalist may file a writ petition if the case falls in the categoty of public interest litigation. On the other hand, if personal interest litigation is sought to be fought as public interest litigation, person instituting such litigation may be made to pay the costs. The Court should not allow an unscrupulous person to vindicate his personal grudge in the garb of public interest.[3]

***Presumption in favour of Constitutionality*:** The presumption is always in favour of constitutionality of an enactment.

---

1. *Subhash v. State of Bihar,* AIR 1991 SC 420; *Vishal v. Union of India,* (1990) 3 SCC 318; *Workers of Rohtas Industries Ltd. v. Rohtas Industries Ltd.,* AIR 1990 SC 491; *Tehri Baandh v. State of U.P,* (1991) 1 UJSC 121; *Gaurav Jain v. Union of India,* AIR 1990 SC 292; *Mehta v. State of T.N.,* AIR 1991 SC 417; *M.C. Mehta v. Union of India,* AIR 1997 SC 734.
2. *Maharshi v. the State,* AIR 1990 All. 52.
3. *Rugmani v. Achutha,* AIR 1991 SC 983; *Bholanath v. State of U.P.* (1990) Supp SCC 151; *Subhash v. State of Bihar,* AIR 1991 SC 420; *Chhetriya Pradushan v. State of T.N.,* AIR 1991 SC 417; *Chetriya Samiti v. State of U.P.* (1991) I SCJ 130.

The burden of providing all the facts and proof against the constitutionality of the statute lies with the petitioners.

***Doctrine of Severability*:** While interpreting the statute, the court has to decide whether the law as a whole or only some parts thereof attract unconstitutionality. The court can declare a law void in part as well, if the facts so warrant.

***Doctrine of Progressive interpretation*:** The Supreme Court, in interpreting the Constitution, has been guided by the doctrine of progressive interpretation *i.e.*, it has taken the ever changing socio legal context in view while interpreting the Constitution.

***Effect of a law declared unconstitutional*:** Under article 141, a law declared by the Supreme Court shall be binding on all courts within the territory of India. Thus, if the Supreme Court declares a law unconstitutional, whether on grounds of legislative competence, or of being violative of fundamental rights, the order shall be binding on law courts in the territory of India. Such law shall be totally ignored and shall not be implemented in subsequent proceedings.[1]

***Independence of the Judiciary*:** In a representative democracy, administration of justice assumes special significance in view of the rights of individuals which need protection against executive or legislative interference. This protection is given by making the judiciary independent of the other two organs of the government and supreme in its own sphere. An independent and supreme judiciary is also an essential requisite of a federal polity, wherein there is a constitutional division of powers between the federal government and governments of the constituent units and a functional division of powers between the executive, legislature and judiciary. Also, an independent and impartial judiciary is an essential requisite for ensuring human rights and protecting democracy. Only an independent judiciary can

1. *Star Co. v. Union of India*, AIR 1987 SC 179; *Assistant Collector v. Dunlop* (1985) 1 SCC 260; *Gourya v. Thakur*, AIR 1986 SC 1440.

act effectively as the guardian of the rights of the individual and that of the Constitution. There are many devices in the Indian Constitution which ensure the independence of the Courts, for example, the constitutional provisions in regard to the appointment and removal of judges, security of tenure, salaries and service conditions, salaries and allowances of judges being a charge on the Consolidated Fund, recruitment and appointment of their own staff by the Supreme Court, debarring the judges of the Supreme Court from practising before any Court in India after retirement, the power to punish for contempt etc.

THE HIGH COURTS

The Constitution provides for a High Court for each State. Parliament may, however establish by law a common High Court for two or more States or for two or more States and a Union territory (articles 214 and 231).

Like the Supreme Court, each High Court is also to be a Court of record and of original and appellate jurisdiction with all the powers of such a court including the power to punish for its contempt (article 215).

Judges of the High Court were appointed by the President after consultation with the Chief Justice of India, the Governor of the State and in case of appointment of all judges other than the Chief Justice, the Chief Justice of the High Court. It was held *in S.P. Gupta v. Union of India* (AIR 1982 SC 149) that all the three functionaries were to be given equal importance in the process of consultation. Thereafter, we had the Supreme Court verdict in the *Advocates-On-Record case* and the advisory opinion.[1]

To be appointed a High Court judge, a person must be a citizen of India with ten years' service in a judicial office or

1. See under the Supreme Court.

ten years' experience as a High Court advocate. On appointment, every High Court judge must take an oath of office. Every High Court judge shall hold office until he attains the age of 62. He cannot be removed from his office except in the manner provided for removal of a judge of the Supreme Court. Further, to ensure the independence of the office of a High Court judge, it is laid down that after being a permanent judge of a High Court, a person shall not plead in any court in India except the Supreme Court or other High Courts. Every High Court judge is entitled to a salary and allowances as may be settled by Parliament by law.

Judges may be transferred from one High Court to another by the President after consulting the Chief Justice of India (article 222). However, the Supreme Court has held that judicial review is necessary to check arbitrariness and that a High Court judge can be transferred only on public interest and that only the judge affected can question it.[1] In the *Advocates case*, the Supreme Court decided that in the matter of transfer of judges as well, the views of the Chief Justice of India will be given primacy and respect, (AIR 1994 SC 266). The President may appoint an acting Chief Justice for a High Court. Also, in case of need, the President may appoint additional and acting judges of the High Court for a period not exceeding two years. The Chief Justice of a High Court may, with the consent of the President, appoint a retired judge to sit and act as a judge (articles 215, 217 224A).

Every High Court shall consist of a Chief Justice and such other judges as the President may deem necessary to appoint from time to time (article 216). Each High Court has powers of superintendence over all the courts and tribunals—other than those set up under any law relating to armed forces—in the area of its jurisdiction (article 227).

Where any High Court is satisfied that a case pending

---

1. *Union of India v. Sankal Chand*, AIR 1977 SC 2328; *K. Ashok Reddy v. Govt of India*, JT (1994) I S C 40.

in the lower courts involves a substantial question of law as to the interpretation of the Constitution, it may withdraw the case and either itself decide it or determine the said question of law and return the case to the Court for determination (article 228).

Every High Court has full control over its staff. The salaries and allowances of the judges and of the High Court staff are all charged on the Consolidated Fund of the State. Appointments of officers and staff of a High Court are made by the Chief Justice of the Court or by such other judge or officer of the Court as he may decide. The terms and conditions of service of the staff and officers of the Court should appropriately be settled by rules made by the Chief Justice and approved by the President (article 229). The jurisdiction of a High Court may be extended to or excluded from a Union Territory (article 230).

Article 226 lays down that every High Court shall have power throughout the territory under its jurisdiction to issue to any person or authority directions, orders or writs including writs of *habeas corpus, prohibition, mandamus, quo warranto* and *certiorari* or any of them for the enforcement of the fundamental rights or for any other purpose. Thus, while the Supreme Court's writ jurisdiction extends only to cases of violation of fundamental rights, the High Courts under article 226 enjoy much wider powers and can issue writs in all cases of breach of any right. This becomes obvious from the use of the term "for any other purpose". The High Court may set aside an illegal order, may declare the law or the right, may order relief by way of, for example, refund of illegal tax etc. Just as the law declared by the Supreme Court is binding on all courts in India, that declared by the High Court is binding on all subordinate courts within the State or within the territory covered by the jurisdiction of the High Court.[1]

---

1. *State of Orissa v. Madan Gopal* (1952) SCR 28; *Rambhadraiah v. Secretary*, AIR 1981 SC 1653; *Desai v. Roshan*, AIR 1976 SC 578; *State of M.P. v. Bhailal*, AIR 1964 SC 1006.

In appeals by special leave against the Patna High Court orders in writ petitions alleging large-scale misappropriation of public funds to the extent of several hundred crores of rupees in the Animal Husbandry Department (Fodder Scam), the Supreme Court directed the High Court to ensure that a fair, honest and complete investigation was completed by the CBI and all persons against whom a *prima facie* case for trial is made out were identified and put on trial in accordance with law. The High Court's jurisdiction extended to examining the manner of investigations and considering the question of extension of time.[1]

It needs to be remembered that the remedy through a writ in cases other than those of violation of fundamental rights is not a normal one and is not expected to be granted as a matter of routine. It is an extraordinary remedy which can be expected in special circumstances and only under the discretion of the Court. Judiciary is not supposed to lay down policy and no court or tribunal can compel the governments to change its policy involving expenditure.[2]

The power to issue writs has been vested in the Supreme Court and the High Courts with a view to ensure quicker justice and early relief to persons whose rights are violated with impunity and who would suffer irreparably if a ready and speedy remedy is not made available without going into avoidable technicalities. There are five well-known writs.

Habeas Corpus literally means a demand to produce the body. It applies in a case where a person is alleged to have been illegally detained. The issuance of the writ means an order to the detaining authority or person to physically present before the Court the detained person and show the

1. *Union of India v. Sushil Kumar Modi*, AIR 1997 SC 314.
2. *Himmat Lal Shah v. State of U.P.*, AIR 1954 SC 403; *Abraham v. ITO*, AIR 1961 SC 609; *Bhopal Sugar Industry v. ITO*, AIR 1967 SC 549; *State of Rajasthan v. Karam Chand*, AIR 1965 SC 913; *Union of India v. Tejram*, (1991) 3 SCC 11; *Kartar Singh v. State of Punjab*, JT (1994) 2 SC 423.

cause of detention so that the Court can determine its legality or otherwise. If the detention is found to be illegal, the detained person is set free forthwith. Since now, after the 44th Amendment, article 21 cannot be suspended even during the proclamation of Emergency, this becomes a very valuable writ for safeguarding the personal liberty of the individual.

While the Supreme Court can issue the writ of *habeas corpus* only against the State in cases of violation of fundamental rights, the High Court can issue it also against private individuals illegally or arbitrarily detaining any other person.

Mandamus is a command to act lawfully and to desist from perpetrating an unlawful act. Where A has a legal right which casts certain legal obligations on B, A can seek a writ of *mandamus* directing B to perform its legal duty. *Mandamus* may lie against any authority, officers, government or even judicial bodies that fail to or refuse to perform a public duty and discharge a legal obligation. The Supreme Court may issue a *mandamus* to enforce the fundamental right of a person when its violation by some governmental order or act is alleged. The High Courts may issue this writ to direct an officer to exercise his constitutional and legal powers, to compel any person to discharge duties cast on him by the Constitution or the statute, to compel a judicial authority to exercise its jurisdiction and to order the Government not to enforce any unconstitutional law.

Prohibition is issued by a higher Court to a lower Court or tribunal and is intended to prohibit it from exceeding its jurisdiction. Writ of *prohibition* is not issued against administrative agencies. It is available only against judicial and quasi judicial bodies.

Certiorari lies against judicial and quasi judicial authorities—courts and tribunals—and means 'to be informed'. When, for example, a tribunal acts without jurisdiction or in excess of it and issues an illegal order, that order can be quashed by a writ of *certiorari*. Such a writ may lie even against an administrative body affecting individual rights.[1]

Quo Warranto is a question asking 'with what authority or warrant'. The writ may be sought to clarify in public interest the legal position in regard to claim of a person to hold a public office. An application seeking such a writ may be made by any person provided the office in question is a substantive public office of a permanent nature created by the Constitution or law and a person has been appointed to it without a legal title and in contravention of the Constitution or the laws.[2]

Besides writs, the High Courts under article 226 may also issue other directions and orders in the interests of justice to the people.[3]

THE SUBORDINATE COURTS

The Governor in consultation with the High Court appoints the district judges. A person who is not already in Government Service should have at least seven years' experience at the bar to become eligible for the position of a district judge (article 233).

Article 233A inserted by the twentieth Amendment Act validated the appointments of and judgements etc. delivered by certain district judges (233A).

Appointment of persons other than district judges to the judicial service of a State shall be made by the Governor in accordance with rules made in that regard. Besides the State Public Service Commission, the High Court has to be consulted in the matter of such appointments (article 234).

The administrative control of the High Court over the district courts and other lower courts is full inasmuch as

1. *Union of India v. Nambudri* (1991) 2 UJSC 302.
2. For public interest litigation see under 'The Supreme Court'.
3. *T.C. Basappa v. Nagappa,* AIR 1954 SC 440.

postings, promotions and grant of leave etc. to any person belonging to the judicial service of a State and holding any post inferior to the post of a judge is vested in the High Court (article 235).[1]

Article 236 is the interpretation clause and explains terms like district judge, judicial service etc. while article 237 empowers the Governor to apply the provisions regarding subordinate courts to any class or classes of magistrates in the State.

Judicial Reforms

Apart from suggesting a National Judicial Commission for the appointment of judges, and increasing the retirement age of judges, the Constitution Commission (NCRWC) *inter alia* recommended:

(i) Adequate training to presiding officers of courts and a systematic assessment of the training needs of judicial personnel at different levels

(ii) Delivery of judgements after the conclusion of the case ordinarily within 90 days

(iii) Award of exemplary costs in appropriate cases of abuse of law

(iv) Preparation of a strategic plan by each High Court for time bound clearance of arrears in courts within its jurisdiction. No case to remain pending for more than a year

(v) Union and State laws to be made for an effective scheme of compensation to victims of crime.

---

1. *Tej Pal v. State of U.P.* (1985) 3 SCC 604; *State of Assam v. Ranga Mohammed*, AIR 1967 SC 903.

14

THE STATES AND UNION TERRITORIES

PART VI, ARTICLES 152–213; PART VIII, 239–240

The Constitution of India contains not only the Constitution of the Union but also a constitution for the States. In fact, with special provisions for some of the individual States, it may be said that there are several State Constitutions within the Constitution of India. Generally speaking, provisions for the States follow the Union pattern. The parliamentary system of Government with a constitutional Head and with ministerial responsibility to the popular House of the Legislature holds equally good at the State level. The real executive power is exercised by the Ministers. 'Satisfaction' of the Governor means the satisfaction of the Council of Ministers.[1]

The State of Jammu & Kashmir, which is an integral part of India, is the only one to have a separate State Constitution of its own. However, several other States enjoy special status and have certain special provisions applicable to only each one of them separately, *e.g.* States of Maharashtra and Gujarat (article 371), Nagaland (371A), Assam (371B), Manipur (371C), Andhra Pradesh (371D & 371E), Sikkim (371F), Mizoram (371G), Arunachal Pradesh (371H) and Goa (371I).

1. *Ram Jawaya Kapur v. State of Punjab,* AIR 1955 SC 549; *Shamsher Singh v. State of Punjab,* AIR 1974 SC 2193.

THE STATE EXECUTIVE

Appointment and Conditions of the Office of the Governor: According to article 153, there shall be Governor for each State. The same person may sometimes be appointed as Governor of two or more States. The Governor is appointed by the President (article 155). The prescribed term of office for a Governor is five years but he holds office at the pleasure of the President (article 156). The pleasure of the President is not justiciable. The Governor has no security of tenure. He may be removed by the President at any time (*Surya Narain v. Union of India,* AIR 1982 Raj. 1).

No person can be appointed a Governor unless he is a citizen of India and has completed the age of 35 years (article 157). Also, the Governor cannot be a member of Parliament or of any of the State Legislatures. If any member is appointed as Governor, his seat in the legislature shall be deemed to have been vacated on the date of assuming the charge of Governor's office. The Governor cannot hold any other office of profit. Every Governor is entitled to free official residence and other emoluments, etc. as may be determined by Parliament by law. In *Hargovind v. Raghukul* (AIR 1979 SC 1109), the Supreme Court held that the office of the Governor was not an office of profit under the Government.

Every Governor and every person discharging the functions of Governor shall take an oath to faithfully execute the office and to preserve, protect and defend the Constitution and the law (article 159).

The Constitution Commission (NCRWC) reiterated the recommendations of the Sarkaria Commission in the matter of appointment of Governors and said that only an eminent, detached figure from outside the State should be appointed Governor after consultation with the Chief Minister.

Governor's Powers and Functions: Under the Constitution, in the discharge of all his functions, with a few exceptions in certain cases, the Governor is to be guided by the aid and advice of the Council of Ministers (article 163).

While both the President of the Republic and the Governor of a State are constitutional heads, there are some fundamental differences between the position of the President and the Governor, *viz.* (i) while the President is elected, the Governor is nominated; (ii) while the President can be removed only by the difficult process of impeachment, the Governor holds office during the pleasure of the President; (iii) while the President is bound by the advice of the Council of Ministers in the discharge of all his functions, in the case of Governors the aid and advice provision applies "except in so far as" the Governor is required to function "in his discretion" (article 163). The 42nd Amendment had amended article 74 to provide that the President "shall" act in accordance with the advice. Such an amendment, however, was not made in the corresponding article 163 applicable to Governors. It has been held that generally the Governor cannot act "except in accordance with the advice of his ministers".[1]

There are certain areas where the Governor may have to use his own wisdom and discretion, *e.g.* in (a) appointing a new Chief Minister in a situation where no single party or leader commands majority support; (b) dismissing a Ministry where it refuses to resign even after losing majority support in the House or after being defeated on a no-confidence motion; (c) dissolution of the Assembly on the advice of a Chief Minister who has lost majority support; (d) determining the royalty for mineral licenses to District Councils in case of tribal areas of Assam, under the Sixth Schedule; (e) advising the President of the failure of the constitutional machinery and to impose President's rule; and (f) giving or withholding assent to Bills, returning a Bill for reconsideration of the House/s or reserving it for the

1. *Sanjeevi v. State of Madras*, AIR 1970 SC 1102; *U.P. Service Commission v. Suresh*, AIR 1987 SC 1953; *Sunit Kumar v. Government of West Bengal*, AIR 1950 Cal. 274.

consideration of the President. Some of the Governors may have to discharge certain special responsibilities also under articles 371 to 371I.

When a Chief Minister of U.P. was dismissed by the Governor after a group of members withdrew their support and the Governor appointed another person as the Chief Minister without a majority test on the floor of the House and the High Court ordered the reinstatement of the former Chief Minister, the Supreme Court ordered a special session of the State Assembly to have a composite floor test between the two contending claimants of Chief Ministership.[1]

Executive Powers: The executive power of the State is vested in the Governor and is to be exercised by him either directly or through officers subordinate to him in accordance with the Constitution (article 154). The executive power of the State is coextensive with its legislative power. Where an item happens to be in the Concurrent List, the executive power of the State will be subject to the powers conferred on the Union by the Constitution or the laws (articles 246 and 162).

The Governor appoints the Advocate-General of the State, the Chairman and members of the State Public Service Commission and the judges of subordinate courts (articles 165, 316, 283 and 284).

The Governor appoints the Chief Minister and other ministers on the advice of the Chief Minister. All the Ministers hold office during the pleasure of the Governor but the Council of Ministers is collectively responsible to the Legislative Assembly of the State. This in practice means that only the person likely to be most acceptable to the House is to be appointed as the Chief Minister and that the Council of Ministers holds office so long as it does not lose the confidence of the House. The 91st Constitution Amendment (2003) places a limit on the number of Ministers that can be

1. *Jagdambika Pal v. Union of India,* AIR 1998 SC 998.
2. *State of M.P. v. Jain,* AIR 1981 SC 2045.

appointed (article 164). The proviso to article 164(1) provided for a Minister of Tribal Welfare who could also be incharge of the welfare of Scheduled Castes and Backward Classes in States of Bihar, Madhya Pradesh and Orissa. The Constitution (94th amendment) Act, 2006 substituted the words "Chhattisgarh, Jharkhand" for the word "Bihar" as there were no Scheduled Areas left in Bihar after the creation of Jharkhand.

All executive action is to be taken in the name of the Governor. The Governor may make rules for the more convenient transaction of business of the State and for allocation of work among the Ministers. A decision of the Council of Ministers does not become operative as a Government order unless expressed in the Governor's name and duly authenticated in accordance with the rules made by the Governor (article 166).

The Constitution (Ninety-first Amendment) Act, 2003 added new clauses (1A) and (1B) to article 164 which read as follows:

(1A) The total number of Ministers, including the Chief Minister, in the Council of Ministers in a State shall not exceed fifteen per cent of the total number of members of the Legislative Assembly of that State.

Provided that the number of Ministers, including the Chief Minister in a State shall not be less than twelve.

Provided further that where the total number of Ministers including the Chief Minister in the Council of Ministers in any State at the commencement of the Constitution (Ninety-first Amendment) Act, 2003 exceeds the said fifteen per cent. or the number specified in the first proviso, as the case may be, then the total number of Ministers in that State shall be brought in conformity with the provisions of this clause within six months from such

---

1. *State of Kerala v. Lakshmikutty*, AIR 1987 SC 331; *B.L. Cotton Mills v. State of West Bengal*, AIR 1967 SC 1145.

date* as the President may by public notification appoint.

(1B) A member of the Legislative Assembly of a State or either House of the Legislature of a State having Legislative Council belonging to any political party who is disqualified for being a member of that House under paragraph 2 of the Tenth Schedule shall also be disqualified to be appointed as a Minister under clause (1) for duration of the period commencing from the date of his disqualification till the date on which the term of his office as such member would expire or where he contests any election to the Legislative Assembly of a State or either House of the Legislature of a State having Legislative Council, as the case may be, before the expiry of such period, till the date on which he is declared elected, whichever is earlier.

Legislative Powers: Under article 171(3)(e) and (5), the Governor may nominate to the Legislative Council of the State—where it exists—one sixth members from among persons having special knowledge or practical experience in respect of literature, science, art, cooperative movement and social service. He may also nominate to the Legislative Assembly a person from the Anglo-Indian community if he feels the community needs representation and is not adequately represented in the Assembly (article 333).

Under article 168, the Governor is a part of the Legislature of the State. He summons and prorogues the two Houses of the Legislature (in case of bicameral Legislatures) and can dissolve the Legislative Assembly of the State (article 174). He addresses the members of the Legislature and may send messages (articles 175 176). Without the Governor's assent, no Bill can become law even after its being passed by the two Houses (article 200).

After a Bill is passed by the Legislative Assembly and the Legislative Council, if any, it is presented to the Governor, presumably with the advice of the Council of Ministers, for his assent to the Bill as passed. The Governor may (i) give his assent to the Bill; (ii) withhold his assent; (iii) reserve the Bill for the consideration of the President or; (iv) except in case of a Money Bill, return the Bill for reconsideration with his message as soon as possible (article 200). There is a fifth possibility which is often not mentioned, *viz.* that of returning the Bill to the Government seeking certain clarifications or information in regard to the Bill and in effect suggesting reconsideration of the advice earlier given by the Council of Ministers for assenting to the Bill (article 167).

If a Bill is returned by the Governor to the Legislature with a message, it will be considered accordingly and if passed again with or without amendments, it will be assented to. Except when the Bill is returned to the Government or reserved for consideration of the President, the Governor may be said to be acting only on the advice of the Council of Ministers in either of the four options. In any case, the exercise of Governor's power in this regard cannot be questioned in a court of law.[1]

Under article 213, the Governor may promulgate ordinances during the period when the House or both the Houses where there are two Houses of State Legislature are not in session. This power corresponds to the power of the President under article 123. The ordinances have the same force and effect as laws passed by the Legislature and assented to by the Governor. Also, they are subject to the same restrictions as laws passed by the Legislature. Thus, the Governor is barred from promulgating an ordinance without instructions from the President (i) if a Bill containing the same provisions would have required President's prior sanction for introduction; (ii) if a Bill containing the same provisions would have been reserved by the Governor for the consideration of the President; or (iii) if a State Act containing the same provisions would have been invalid without the President's assent.

---

1. See, for eg., *Bharat Seva Ashram v. State of Gujarat*, AIR 1987 SC 494.

Every ordinance promulgated by the Governor has to be laid before the State Legislative Assembly (before both the Houses in case of a bicameral State Legislature) and shall cease to operate at the expiry of six weeks from the reassembly of the Legislature or even earlier if a resolution disapproving it is passed. The ordinance may be withdrawn by the Governor at any time (article 213). The notorious misuse of ordinance making powers of the Governor was highlighted in *D.C. Wadhava v. State of Bihar* ((1987) 1 SCC 378). The Bihar Governor promulgated 256 ordinances during 1967-1981. All these were kept going by being repromulgated again and again. The court held that it was "a subversion of the democratic process" and a "fraud on the Constitution". This power is to be most sparingly used only to meet extraordinary situations. It cannot be allowed to be "perverted to serve political ends".

Financial Powers: Under article 202, the Governor is required to cause to be laid before the House or Houses of the Legislature the budget or the Annual Financial Statement. A Money Bill cannot be introduced and a Demand for Grant cannot be moved without the recommendation of the Governor. Even amendments would require recommendation.

Powers of Pardon, etc.: The Governor has been given the power to grant pardons, etc. and to suspend, remit or commute the sentence of any person convicted of an offence against any law relating to a matter to which the executive power of the State extends (article 161). The power, of course, has to be exercised on the advice of the Council of Ministers. In *K. M. Nanavati v. State of Bombay* (AIR 1961 SC 99), the Supreme Court held that it is open to the Governor to grant a full pardon at any time even during the pendency of the case in the Supreme Court, but the Governor cannot so exercise his power of suspension of the sentence for the period when the Supreme Court is seized of the case. The Governor's power of suspension was held to be subject to the rules framed by the Supreme Court.

THE STATE LEGISLATURE

The Legislature of a State consists of the Governor and the Legislative Assembly except that in some States there are two Houses—the Legislative Assembly and the Legislative Council. At present (2009) only Andhra, Bihar, U.P., Maharashtra and Karnataka States have a Legislative Council (article 168). J & K also has two Houses under the State Constitution. It is left to the Legislative Assembly of each State to decide whether to recommend to Parliament abolition of the Council where one exists or to seek establishment of one if none exists (article 169).

The Legislative Assembly of a State shall consist of not more than 500 and not less than 60 members chosen by direct election from territorial constituencies. The Legislative Council shall not exceed one-third of the total membership of the Legislative Assembly of that State subject to a minimum of 40. One-third of the members shall be elected by municipalities, district boards and other local authorities as specified by Parliament by law, one twelfth shall be elected by graduates' constituency, one twelfth by the teachers' constituency, one-third by members of the Legislative Assembly and the remainder, *i.e.* one sixth, shall be nominated by the Governor. Elections to the Council are to be held by the system of proportional representation by single transferable vote (articles 170-171).

The term of the Legislative Assembly shall be five years unless dissolved earlier. The Council shall be a continuing House not subject to dissolution but one-third of its members shall retire every two years (article 172).

In order to be eligible for membership a person must be a citizen of India, must take an oath to the Constitution, must be not less than 25 years of age in case of the Assembly and not less than 30 years in case of the Council (article 173) as on the date of nomination.[1]

1. *Hussain v. Nijalingappa*, AIR 1969 SC 1034.

The house or each house of the State Legislature is from time to time summoned to meet by the Governor who may also prorogue the house or either house and dissolve the Legislative Assembly. The period for which the house/s should meet or the required duration of the sessions is not laid down in the Constitution but the gap between two sessions must be less than six months (article 174).

Article 175 provides for the right of the Governor to address or send messages to the House or Houses of the State Legislature. Under article 176, the Governor is obliged to address the House or the Houses assembled together at the beginning of the first session each year and at the commencement of the first session after each general election to the Legislative Assembly of the State (176). All the Ministers and the Advocate General have a right to speak and take part in the proceedings of the house/s (article 177).

The State Legislature has exclusive jurisdiction to legislate on items in the State List and concurrent jurisdiction in respect of items in List III (articles 245-246).[1]

The position of the Legislative Council in a State is similar to that of the Rajya Sabha at the Union level. This applies *inter alia* to the privileges and immunities of legislatures, disqualification of members, relation between the two Houses, legislative procedure, origin of money bills, etc.

The assembly has a Speaker and a Deputy Speaker elected by the House and having the same position and functions as their Lok Sabha counterparts. The Council, however, also has a Chairman and Deputy Chairman elected by the Council (articles 178 187).[2]

General rules for conduct of business in the Legislative Assembly/Council (articles 188 and 189), provisions regarding disqualification of members, vacation of seats, penalty for unauthorisedly sitting in the house (articles 190

1. See under 'Union-State Relations'.
2. See under The Union Legislature.

193), powers, privileges and immunities for houses of legislatures and members and committees (article 194), salaries and allowances of members (article 195), Legislative procedure including that for passing Money Bills and other Bills (articles 196 200 and 208 212), procedure in financial matters (articles 202 207) are all very similar to corresponding provisions in regard to the Union Parliament. Articles 200 and 201 however, *inter alia* provide for the Governor reserving some Bills for the consideration of the President and then the President assenting to the Bills or withholding asent. Corresponding to the President's power under article 123, the Governor also enjoys power to issue ordinances (article 213) [See under chapter 12 'The Union Legislature'].

UNION TERRITORIES

The Union Territories may be defined as areas directly administered by the Union. At present there are seven Union Territories, *viz.* Andaman and Nicobar Islands, Lakshadweep, Dadra and Nagar Haveli, Daman and Diu, Puducherry, Chandigarh and Delhi (First Schedule). The erstwhile Union Territory of Delhi which had a Metropolitan Council and Executive Councillors has now emerged as the National Capital Territory of Delhi with a legislature and a Council of Ministers (articles 239AA and 239 AB inserted by the sixty-ninth amendment, 1991).

The Parliament may by law provide for the administration of Union Territories. Subject thereto, the administration of Union Territories is to be handled by the President through an administrator appointed by him. The administrator is usually called the Lt. Governor. The President may also appoint the Governor of a neighbouring State as the administrator of a Union Territory. A Governor so appointed shall discharge the functions of the administrator independently of the advice of the Council of

Ministers of the State (article 239). Parliament may by law create for any territory a legislature and a Council of Ministers. Such a legislature and Council of Ministers exist for the Union Territory of Puducherry and for the National Capital Territory of Delhi. The Legislative Assembly in Puducherry may make laws in respect of matters in Lists II and III of the Seventh Schedule in so far as these matters are applicable to the Union Territory. This applies to the Delhi Assembly also but there the legislative and executive powers in respect of public order, police and land and all matters related to these three areas have been retained by the Union to be handled through the Lt. Governor of Delhi. The Union Territory of Andaman and Nicobar Islands has a nominated body in place of a legislature (article 239 A). The administrator of a Union Territory enjoys powers of promulgating ordinances like the Governors of States (article 239B). The President has been empowered to make regulations for peace, progress and good government of all the Union Territories except where a legislature is functioning (article 239A and 240). Parliament may by law constitute a High Court for a Union Territory or declare any Court to be the High Court for its purposes (article 241).

15

UNION-STATE RELATIONS

PART XI, ARTICLES 245–263

Article 1 of our Constitution describes India as a "Union of States". When the British power was established in India it was highly centralized and unitary. To hold India under its imperial authority, the British had to control it from the Centre and ensure that power remained centralized in their hands. A strong central authority was for the British both an imperial and an administrative necessity. The Charter Act of 1833 carried the process of centralization in India to an extreme degree by depriving the Governments of Madras and Bombay of all legislative powers and concentrating them in the Governor-General-in-Council at Calcutta. This act also expressly vested in the Governor-General-in-Council the superintendence, direction and control of the whole civil and military Government of India.

The Government of India Act, 1919, provided for a considerable measure of devolution of authority to the provinces. The Joint Committee on Constitutional Reforms in 1934 observed:

> Notwithstanding the measure of devolution on the provincial authorities which was the outcome of the Act of 1919, the Government of India is and remains in essence a unitary and centralized Government, with the Governor-General-in-Council as the keystone of the whole constitutional edifice.

When the Commonwealth of India Bill came up for discussion in the British House of Commons, the Government spokesman Malcolm Hailey, among other things, significantly said that some kind of federation was inevitable as the ultimate objective to be kept in view. The problems of princely states and of British commercial interests were also raised as grounds for the continuation of a strong central authority under the direct control of the British masters. Both the Simon Commission (1927-29) and the Butler Committee (1927-30) visualized, even though as a distant ideal, a federal Union for the whole of India.

The Government of India Act of 1935 proposed to set up a federal polity in India, with a central government and the Provinces deriving their jurisdiction and powers by direct devolution from the Crown. The Federation envisaged by the 1935 Act never came into being. The Provincial autonomy part of the 1935 Act was put into operation. Since a limited responsible Government was established only at the provincial level, the nationalists naturally asked for more powers for provincial legislatures. The experiment was, however shortlived.

In any case, the country as a whole continued to be ruled under the 1919 Act by a central authority until 1947. And, since under the 1919 Act, there was a central government, a central legislature, a system of central laws etc., even after the new Constitution, the bureaucracy perhaps could not discard the colonial hangover and the use of these terms continued.

When the Constituent Assembly first met in 1946 and early 1947, the idea was to have a federation with a Centre having limited powers. Before the Union Constitution Committee could transact any worthwhile business, the Mountbatten Plan of 3 June 1947 was announced. All hopes of preserving the unity of India vanished and the partition of the country on communal lines became a firm decision. As was expected, a decisive swing followed in favour of a strong Centre. The Union Constitution Committee and the Provincial Constitution Committee decided, at a joint meeting on 5 June, that in view of the 3 June announcement, the limitations imposed by the Cabinet Mission's plan on the form of the constitution no longer existed. Once partition had become a reality, there was no need to appease the Muslim League and restrict the powers of the Union Government. The Union Constitution Committee meeting of 6 June 1947 tentatively decided that the Constitution should be a federal structure with a strong Centre, and that there should be three exhaustive lists with residuary powers vesting in the Centre.

On 5 July 1947, the Union Powers Committee presented a second report to the President of the Constituent Assembly emphasizing that the "soundest framework for the Constitution was a federation with a strong Centre". The report said that the severe limitation on the scope of central authority in the Cabinet Mission's Plan was a compromise accepted by the Assembly much against its judgement of the administrative needs of the country in order to accommodate the Muslim League. The Union Powers Committee was unanimous in its view that it would be injurious to the interests of the country to provide for a weak central authority which would be incapable of ensuring peace, of coordinating vital matters of common concern, and of speaking effectively for the whole country in the international sphere. Meanwhile, 600 and odd princely states were integrated with the emerging Indian Union. As a result, the number of State units in the Indian Union was brought down to manageable proportions.

In the context of these developments, the Drafting Committee decided in favour of describing India as a Union, although its Constitution might be federal in structure. The emphasis on India being a Union was to convey the fact that it was not the result of a compact or agreement between the constituent units but a declaration by the Constituent

Assembly deriving its authority from the one people of India. Further, the conceptualization was clearly intended to convey the federal nature of the polity but with a subordinate position to the States and structural functional balance in favour of the supremacy of the Union. The point was upheld by the Supreme Court in *West Bengal v. Union of India* (AIR 1963 SC 1241).

The predominant concern of the founding fathers as also of the various Commissions and Committees appointed since Independence to consider reorganisation of States or Union-State relations—the JVP Committee, the Dar Commission, the States Reorganization Commission, the Rajamannar Committee, the Sarkaria Commission, etc.—has been that of the unity and integrity of India. The SRC report concluded:

> It is the Union of India which is the basis of our nationality....States are but limbs of the Union, and while we recognize that the limbs must be healthy and strong...it is the strength and stability of the Union and its capacity to develop and evolve that should be the governing consideration of all changes in the country.

Legislative Relations

Article 245 to 255 contain a charter of the distribution of legislative powers between the Union and the States. Parliament may make laws for the whole or any part of India. The Legislature of a State may make laws for the whole or any part of the State. Any State law would be void if it has extra territorial operation unless sufficient nexus can be shown to exist between the object and the State.[1] Laws made by Parliament, however, cannot be questioned on grounds of extra territorial operation (article 245). The Seventh Schedule to the Constitution embodies three lists, *viz.* the Union List, the State List and the Concurrent List consisting

1. *State of Bombay v. RMDC*, AIR 1957 SC 699; *Tata Iron & Steel Co. v. State of Bihar*, AIR 1958 SC 452.

of 97, 66 and 47 items respectively. Even after the changes in the Schedule brought about by Constitution Amendment Acts, the numbers of entries in the three lists have remained the same. Where some entry in full or in part is omitted (*e.g.* entry 33 in the Union List), the omission has been indicated by putting stars (***) and indicating in the footnote the name and number of the relevant Amendment Act. Similarly, where a new entry is added, it is given a supplementary number by alphabets A, B, C, etc. *e.g.* entry 2A in the Union List. Amendments in the three lists have been effected by the third, sixth, seventh, fifteenth, thirty-second, forty-second and forty-sixth amendments. But, the most far reaching changes were made by the seventh and the forty-second amendments.

Article 246 lays down that the Union Parliament would have exclusive jurisdiction to make laws in regard to items in the Union List, the State Legislature would have exclusive power to make laws in respect of items in the State List and both the Union and State Legislatures could legislate in the area of items included in the Concurrent List. In case of any inconsistency between laws made by Parliament and those made by the Legislature of a State in respect of items in the Concurrent List, the Union law shall prevail and the State law shall be void to the extent of inconsistency except where a State law is reserved for the consideration of the President and receives his assent (article 254). In the three fold distribution of legislative powers, residuary powers of legislation have been left with the Union (article 248). Also, Parliament has been given the power to make any law for the whole or any part of the country to give effect to any international treaty, agreement, convention or decision (article 253).

The Union List consists of subjects which are of common interest to the Union and with respect to which uniformity of legislation throughout the Union is essential. Subjects which allow for diversity of interest and treatment are included in the State List and matters in which uniformity of legislation throughout the Union is desirable but not essential are included in the Concurrent List. Although the States are given exclusive powers over the subjects in the State List, there are two exceptions to this general rule. Under article 249, if the Rajya Sabha declares by a Resolution supported by two-thirds of the members present and voting that it is necessary or expedient in the national interest that Parliament should make laws with respect to any matter enumerated in the State List, Parliament is competent to make laws on that matter for the whole or any part of India. Such a resolution remains valid for a year; it can be extended by another year by a subsequent resolution. Any law passed under this provision would cease to be in force within six months after the end of the year.

Again under article 250, Parliament is empowered to make laws on any item included in the State List for the whole or any part of India while a Proclamation of Emergency is in operation. The maximum duration of validity of such laws will be six months after the expiry of the Emergency.

In case of inconsistency between laws made by Parliament under articles 249 and 250 and laws made by State Legislatures, the law made by Parliament shall prevail and the State law shall be inoperative to the extent of repugnancy while the law made by Parliament remains in effect (article 251). Under the Doctrine of Pith and Substance, any jurisdictional conflict between the Union and the State/s in regard to their legislative competence can be settled by the court ascertaining the substance of the matter relating to an item in one list or the other.

According to article 252, two or more State Legislatures by passing a resolution may ask Parliament to make laws on any matter in the State List. Such laws can be extended to other States provided the concerned State Legislatures pass resolutions to that effect.

Administrative Relations

Articles 256 to 263 seek to regulate administrative relations between the Union and the States. It is common in federal systems that the administrative relations between the Union and the States are fraught with difficulties. The Constitution of India seeks to achieve a smooth working relationship between the two levels. It provides that the executive powers of the State Government are to be exercised in such a way as to ensure compliance with the laws made by Parliament. The Union Executive is also empowered to give such directions to a State, as may appear to the Government of India, to be necessary for the purpose.

Article 257 similarly provides that the executive power of every State shall be so exercised as not to impede the exercise of the executive power of the Union and the Union may issue necessary directions in that regard and for protection of railways and maintenance of means of communication of national or military importance. Any extra expenditure incurred by the State for the purpose of fulfilling Central directives is to be reimbursed by the Centre to the State. The provision in Article 261, directing that full faith and credit shall be given to public acts, records and judicial proceedings of the Union and the States in all parts of the Indian territory, adds a lot to the smooth working of Union-State relations. Parliamentary control over Inter-State rivers and provisions for adjudication of any Inter-State water disputes were designed totake away a whole host of possibilities of friction between Union and States and between States themselves (article 262). In fact the Constitution-makers did not want anything to be left to chance; hence the arrangement for Inter-State Councils. Article 263 empowers the President to establish an Inter-State Council to enquire into and advise upon Inter-State disputes and matters of common interest between States or between the Union and the States and make recommendations for better coordination of policy and action.

Under article 258, the President may with the consent of a State Government entrust to that Government or its officers functions in relation to any matter to which the executive power of the Union extends. Similarly, under article 258A the Governor of a State may with the consent of the Union Government entrust to that Government or to its officers functions in relation to any matter to which the executive power of the State extends.[1]

Financial Relations

In regard to the financial relations between the Union and the States too, one can find the general tendency of Indian federalism for centralisation. The Union may be said to be financially more powerful but given the nature of the country's needs for growth through planned economy this may be not only very desirable but entirely necessary. The States, however, have their own resources; the Union provides substantial amounts to the States by way of grants-in-aid, share proceeds of certain taxes, etc. The provision for the appointment of a Finance Commission every five years to examine the distribution of tax proceeds between the Union and States and to determine the principles which should govern the grants-in-aid is patterned on the Commonwealth Grants Commission in Australia and has contributed to the generally smooth financial relationship between the Union and the States.[2]

Union vs. Centre

In the field of Union-State relations, it needs to be specially stressed that a great deal of damage and misinterpretation has been caused as a result of the wrong use of the term 'Centre State' instead of 'Union State'. The Constitution does not use the term 'Centre'; actually 'Central government',

1. For article 356 and proclamation of President's rule in a State, see under Chapter 17.
2. For Financial Provisions see chapter 16.

'Central legislature', 'Central laws' etc. are an unfortunate hang-over from the days of the centralised government during the colonial rule. 'Centre' and 'Union' create very different images and connote concepts very different. 'Centre' is a point in the middle of the circle while 'Union' is the whole circle. The relationship between the Union and the States is that between the whole and the parts and not between the centre of authority and its peripheries.

The Constitution Commission (NCRWC) has recommended:

- River water disputes being important disputes between two or more States and/or the Union, they should be heard and disposed by a bench of not less than three Judges and if necessary, a bench of five Judges of the Supreme Court for the final disposal of the suit.
- Appropriate Parliamentary legislation should be made for repealing the River Boards Act, 1956 and replacing it by another comprehensive enactment under Entry 56 of List I. The new enactment should clearly define the constitution of the River Boards and their jurisdiction so as to regulate, develop all control all inter-State rivers keeping intact the adjudicated and the recognized rights of the States through which the inter-State river passes and their inhabitants. While enacting the legislation, national interest should be the paramount consideration as inter-State rivers are 'material resources' of the community and are national assets.
- In resolving problems and coordinating policy and action, the Union as well as the States should more effectively utilize the forum of inter-State Council.

16

FINANCIAL PROVISIONS AND TRADE ETC.

PART V, CHAPTER 5 AND PARTS XII & XIII,
ARTICLES 148 151, 264–307

COMPTROLLER AND AUDITOR-GENERAL OF INDIA

Financial control of the administration is the bulwark of parliamentary democracy and for exercising financial control an independent audit agency is an essential pre requisite. The Constitution provides for a Comptroller and Auditor-General of India being appointed by the President. To ensure the independence of this office from the executive government of the day, it has been provided that the Comptroller and Auditor-General shall not be removed from his office except on grounds of proved misbehaviour or incapacity, on an address passed by each of the two Houses of Parliament by two-thirds majority of those present and voting and a majority of the total membership of each House being presented to the President in the same manner as applicable to the judges of the Supreme Court under article 124(4). Also, the Comptroller and Auditor-General has been made ineligible for any other office under the Government of India or any State Government. His salary etc. is left to be determined by Parliament by law. The Comptroller and Auditor-General (Duties, Powers and Conditions of Service) Act, 1971, as amended regulates the position. The salary, etc.

of Comptroller and Auditor-General have been equated with the judges of the Supreme Court. The service conditions of those serving in the Audit and Accounts Department and the administrative powers of the Comptroller and Auditor-General are to be laid down by the President by rules framed after consultation with the Comptroller and Auditor-General. The administrative expenses of the office of the Comptroller and Auditor-General are to be charged upon the Consolidated Fund of India (article 148).

The form in which the accounts of the Union and of the States are to be maintained is to be determined by the President on the advice of the Comptroller and Auditor-General. The Constitution left it to Parliament to lay down the duties and powers of Comptroller and Auditor-General in regard to the accounts of the Union and the States (articles 149 and 150). Article 151, however, specifically lays down that the Comptroller and Auditor-General shall submit to the President reports relating to the accounts of the Union and the President shall cause them to be laid before both Houses of Parliament. Similarly reports in regard to the accounts of the States will be submitted to the respective State Governors and shall be laid before the House/s of the concerned legislatures.

FINANCE, PROPERTY, CONTRACTS AND SUITS

Article 265 upholds the salutary democratic principle of 'No taxation without representation' and categorically declares that no taxes can be imposed without the authority of law. Also, it adds, no taxes can be 'collected' except as under the authority of law.

Consolidated Fund: Subject to provision of a Contingency Fund and allocations to the States, all revenues received or loans etc. raised by the Government of India shall constitute a Consolidated Fund of India. Similarly, there will be a Consolidated Fund for each of the States. All other money received by the Union or State Governments shall be credited to the public accounts of the Union or the State concerned. No amount can be withdrawn from the Consolidated Fund without the authority of law. This restriction does not apply to public accounts (Article 266).

Contingency Fund: To meet contingent situations whereunder some expenditure may be required to be incurred emergently, article 267 authorises Parliament and State Legislatures to form their contingency funds. The Contingency Fund is placed at the disposal of Union or State Government (President or Governor) to enable it to make advances for meeting unforeseen expenses pending authorization by the legislature.

Distribution of Revenues between the Union and the States: A scheme for the distribution of revenues between the Union and the States is laid down in articles 268–273. The proceeds of all the taxes levied by the State are fully retained by the concerned States themselves while taxes in the Union List may be in part allotted to the States.

Thus, taxes that belong exclusively to the Union include Customs, Corporation Tax, taxes on capital value of assets, surcharge on income tax, etc. and taxes in respect of matters in the Union List.

Taxes belonging exclusively to the States include land revenue, Stamp Duty on items included in the State List, taxes on passengers and goods carried on inland waterways, lands and buildings, mineral rights, animals and boats, road vehicles, advertisements, consumption of electricity, luxuries, amusements etc., taxes on entry of goods into a local area, State tax tolls, fees in respect of matters in the State List and taxes on professions, trades, etc. not exceeding Rupees 2500 per annum (article 276 and List 2, Seventh Schedule). Stamp duties on Bills of exchange etc. and duties of excise on medicinal and toilet preparations mentioned in the Union List shall be levied by the Union but collected and appropriated by the States and form part of their revenues except in the case of Union Territories (article 268).

Taxes on sale or purchase of goods other than newspapers and taxes on consignment of goods shall all be levied and collected by the Government of India but shall be assigned to the States concerned and distributed among the States as may be decided by Parliament by law. The proceeds attributable to Union Territories, however, shall form part of the Consolidated Fund of India (article 269 as amended by the 80th Amendment during 2000).

There are some taxes and duties in the Union List which are levied and collected by the Union but their proceeds are distributed between the Union and the States. After a Finance Commission has been constituted, Presidential Order in regard to distribution of proceeds from income tax etc. shall issue after considering the Commission's recommendations (articles 270–271).[1]

New article 268A added by the 88th Constitution Amendment provides for levy of taxes on services to be collected and appropriated by the Government of India and the States. New entry 92C inserted in the Union List under the Seventh Schedule reads "Taxes on Services".

Articles 273, 275 and 282 provide for three kinds of grants-in-aid and the circumstances in which these may be extended to the States by the Union. Thus, grants may be given by the Union to the States of Assam, Bihar, Orrisa and West Bengal in lieu of export duty on jute and jute products (article 273). Grants may be given to any State in need as may be deemed essential (article 275). Under article 282, the Union or a State may make a grant for any public purpose irrespective of that purpose being outside the legislative jurisdiction of the Union or State concerned.

Article 274 requires that in case of Bills affecting taxation

1. Article 272 providing for Union excise duties that "may be" distributed between the Union and the States, was omitted *w.e.f.* 9 June 2000 by the 80th Amendment.

in which States are interested, in effect, prior recommendation of the President would be necessary.

The State Legislatures may by law levy taxes on professions, trades, callings or employment. The total amount of these taxes payable by an individual shall not exceed Rs. 2500 per annum. The provision would not affect the power of Parliament to make laws in respect of income from professions etc. (article 276)

Finance Commission: Article 280 provides for the appointment by the President of a Finance Commission consisting of a Chairman and four members every five years. The Commission shall make recommendations to the President in regard to the distribution of proceeds between the Union and the States and to suggest principles which should govern the grants-in-aid to the States from the Consolidated Fund of India. The President shall cause the recommendations of the Commission and action taken thereon to be laid before each House of Parliament (articles 280–281).

Miscellaneous Financial Provisions: Custody etc. of Consolidated Funds, Contingency Funds and moneys credited to public accounts are to be regulated by Parliament and each State Legislature concerned (article 283).

Suitors' deposits and other moneys received by public servants and courts shall be paid into the public accounts of the Union or the State concerned as the case may be (article 284).

Property of the Union shall be exempt from taxation by the States and the property of the States shall be similarly exempt from taxation by the Union (articles 285 and 289).

Articles 286–288 place restrictions as to imposition of tax by the States on consumption or sale of electricity or water and on the sale or purchase of goods outside the State or in case of export or import.

Article 290 provides for adjustments to be made between the Union and State Governments in respect of payment of certain expenses of any Court or Commission and pensions of persons in service before the Constitution. Article 290A provides for certain sums to be paid annually to Devaswom Funds of Travancore and Tamil Nadu from the Consolidated Funds of these States.

Borrowing: The executive power of the Union extends to borrowing upon the Consolidated Fund of India within limits, if any, set by Parliament by law (article 292). A State could also similarly borrow subject to limits set by law by the State Legislature. Government of India, within its borrowing powers, could make loans to any State or give guarantees in respect of loans raised by the State. So long as any of such loans remained outstanding, the State Government could not raise any further loans without consent of Government of India (article 293).

Property, Contracts, Rights, Liabilities, Obligations and Suits: Articles 294, 295 and 296 provide that any property, assets, rights, liabilities and obligations vesting in or accruing to the Government of the Dominion or of any of the Provinces or of any of the Indian States before the commencement of the Constitution shall vest in the Union or the concerned State.

Things of value within territorial waters or continental shelf and resources of the exclusive economic zone shall vest in the Union (article 297).

The executive power of the Union and of each State shall extend to carrying on any trade or business and to acquire, hold or dispose of property and make contracts subject to any law made by the respective legislature (article 298). This article obviously is an independent or additional source of executive power outside article 245. The Supreme Court in *Khazan Singh v. State of U.P.* (AIR 1974 SC 669) held that the power of a State under article 298 to carry on trade etc. extends to carrying on a trade in other States also.[1]

1. Also see *Anraj v. State of Maharashtra*, AIR 1984 SC 781.

All contracts made in the exercise of the executive power of the Union or of a State (i) are to be expressed in the name of the President or the Governor as the case may be and (ii) shall be executed by such officers and (iii) in such manner as may be laid down by him. No personal liability is to attach to the President or the Governor or to the persons executing the contracts etc. (article 299). It clearly follows that article 299 is mandatory and no contracts etc. are valid unless they are entered into strictly in accordance with the requirements of this provision.[1]

The Government of India or of a State may sue or be sued by its name subject to any law made by Parliament or the State Legislature. If the Dominion of India was a party in any suit, the Union of India will stand substituted and if a Province or Indian State was a party it will be substituted by the corresponding State (article 300).

Right to Property: Originally the Constitution had incorporated the right to property as a fundamental right under articles 19(f) and 31. The 44th Constitution Amendment omitted articles 19(f) and 31 with effect from 20 June 1979. Simultaneously, a new article—article 300A—was added to lay down that "no person shall be deprived of his property save by authority of law". Thus, the right to property ceased to be a fundamental right but remained a constitutional right and a legal right. In case of the violation of the right under article 300A, while the Supreme Court's writ jurisdiction under article 32 cannot be invoked, High Court can certainly be approached under article 226. Validity of a law passed under article 300A can be challenged on the ground of no provision being made for payment of compensation for depriving a citizen of his property.[2]

1. *Bihar F.G.F. Cooperative Society v. Sipahi Singh,* AIR 1977 SC 2149; *Mulanchand v. State of M.P.,* AIR 1968 SC 1818; *State of West Bengal v. B.K. Mondal,* AIR 1962 SC 779; *Karamshi v. State of Bombay,* AIR 1964 SC 1714.
2. *Bishamber v. State of U.P.,* AIR 1982 SC 33; *Maneka Gandhi v. Union of India,* AIR 1978 SC 597. Also see under Fundamental Rights.

FREEDOM OF TRADE, COMMERCE AND INTERCOURSE

Article 301 lays down that trade, commerce and intercourse throughout the territory of India shall be free. Parliament may, however, impose by law restrictions in public interest on inter-State trade, commerce and intercourse (articles 301 and 302). Neither Parliament nor a State Legislature can make a law that gives preference to one State over another in the matter of trade and commerce except that Parliament may by law authorise discrimination that may become necessary for dealing with a situation of scarcity of goods in any part of India (article 303).

Regulatory measures or a compensatory legislation imposing tax for facilitating trade cannot be considered violative of the freedom of trade. Both intra State and inte-State trade are covered by the freedom of trade provision. Trade, commerce and intercourse include movement of goods and persons.[1]

Freedom of trade etc. under article 301 is subject to restrictions under articles 302 and 303. Also, under article 304, a State may impose a tax on goods coming from another State if similar goods from within the State are subject to a similar tax so as to ensure that there is no discrimination between the goods from the other State and those manufactured within the State. Restrictions may also be imposed by the State by law in public interest but a Bill for this purpose can be introduced only with the prior sanction of the President. Nothing in articles 301 and 303 shall affect the existing laws and laws providing for State monopolies (article 305).

Article 307 provides for the Parliament appointing an appropriate authority for implementing the provisions of articles 301 to 304.

---

1. *Atiabari Tea Co. v. State of Assam*, AIR 1961 SC 237; *Automobile Transport v. State of Rajasthan*, AIR 1962 SC 406; *State of Bihar v. Harihar Prasad Debuka* (1989) 2 SCC.

The Constitution Commission (NCRWC) recommended that for carrying out the objectives of articles 301, 302, 303 and 304, and other purposes relating to the needs and requirements of inter-State trade and commerce and for purposes of eliminating barriers to inter-State trade and commerce Parliament should, by law, establish an authority called the "Inter-State Trade and Commerce Commission"

17

EMERGENCY PROVISIONS

PART XVIII, ARTICLES 352–360

The term 'emergency' may be defined as 'a difficult situation arising suddenly and demanding immediate action by public authorities under powers specially granted to them by the Constitution or otherwise to meet such exigencies'.

The founding fathers of our Constitution felt that extraordinary situations could arise under which it might not be possible for the normal scheme of the Constitution to function and it might become necessary to suspend the operation of certain parts or provisions to protect the independence and the security of the nation and to safeguard the Constitution and the democratic system.

Dr. Ambedkar claimed that the Indian federation was unique and unlike any other federation inasmuch as in times of emergency it could convert itself into an entirely unitary State. The position was upheld by the Supreme Court in *Gulam Sarwar v. Union of India* (AIR 1967 SC 1335).

Briefly, the Emergency provisions of the Constitution envisage two kinds of emergencies, *viz.* (i) a national emergency under article 352 due to threat of war, external aggression or armed rebellion and (ii) financial emergency under article 360. The third kind of situation, that is, the one under article 356 arising from a failure of the constitutional machinery in any particular State and necessitating

President's rule, though included under the Part on 'Emergency Provisions', may not strictly speaking be considered an emergency situation.

Proclamation of National Emergency

Article 352 provides that if the President, after receiving a written communication of a Cabinet decision, is satisfied that a grave emergency exists whereby the security of India or any part thereof is threatened by war, external aggression or armed rebellion, he may issue a proclamation of emergency for the whole of India or part thereof. He may also issue different proclamations on different grounds. Every Proclamation of Emergency is required to be laid before each House of Parliament, and is to cease to operate at the expiration of one month from the date of its issue by the President unless in the meantime it has been approved by resolutions of both the Houses. However, once approved by Parliament, the Proclamation may continue in operation for six months at a time unless revoked by the President earlier by a subsequent Proclamation. Resolutions approving the Proclamation of Emergency or its continuance have to be passed by either House of Parliament by a majority of the total membership and not less than two-thirds of those present and voting. Also, if the Lok Sabha passes a resolution disapproving the proclamation or its continuance, it shall be revoked forthwith. If notice of a resolution signed by not less than one tenth of the total membership is given to the President/Speaker, a special sitting of the House shall be held within 14 days to consider it.

Article 353 read with article 365 provides that once Emergency is proclaimed, the executive power of the Union extends to giving of directions to any State in regard to the exercise of the executive powers of the State and failure to comply with the directions would constitute enough justification for imposition of President's rule under article 356.

During the operation of Emergency, the legislative

power of Parliament also extends to conferring powers and imposing duties by law on Union authorities in matters not otherwise included in the Union List.

Under article 354, the application of provisions relating to distribution of revenues (articles 268 to 279) may be suitably modified during the period of the operation of Emergency. Article 358 provides for the suspension of the provisions of article 19 during emergencies while article 359 authorises the President to suspend by order the enforcement of all the fundamental rights guaranteed in Part III of the Constitution except the rights of protection in respect of conviction for offences and protection of life and liberty in articles 20 and 21.

The effect of the exercise of powers under articles 358 and 359 is that not only the legislature but also the executive can interfere with the fundamental rights of individuals except those under articles 20 and 21.

Any law passed under articles 358 and 359 in order to be valid must contain a recital to the effect that it is in relation to the Proclamation of Emergency in operation. Also, all such laws shall cease to have effect to the extent of incompetency under the Fundamental Rights as soon as the Emergency ceases or the Presidential order ceases to have effect.

There have been three proclamations of national emergency in India—in October 1962 at the time of the Chinese aggression, in December 1971 in the wake of the war with Pakistan and in June 1975 on grounds of internal disturbance. The first proclamation issued in October 1962 continued till January 1968. The second proclamation issued in December 1971 lasted till March 1977. The thir proclamation issued in June 1975 while the second was still in operation was also revoked in March 1977 with the second. Since the, there has been no proclamation of emergency. During the periods of Emergency, extraordinary powers were assumed by the Union Government under several laws and constitutional amendments passed by Parliament.

There was widespread criticism of the misuse of powers during the period of internal emergency. In the general elections that followed, the ruling Congress(I) under the leadership of Indira Gandhi lost and a Janata Party Government was formed.

Before the 44th Constitution Amendment, state of emergency could be declared under article 352 throughout the entire country only. The Amendment made it possible to cover only a part of the country, as may be deemed necessary, under emergency. Also, the provisions of article 352 were made more stringent in 1978-79 by the Constitution (44th Amendment) Act, 1978 which came into effect from 20 June 1979. To prevent the misuse of emergency provisions, the words 'armed rebellion' were substituted for 'internal disturbance', a written communication of the decision by the Union Cabinet was made an essential pre condition for the issue of a Proclamation by the President, and the entire procedure for emergency provisions was streamlined to ensure dependence on approval of Parliament, particularly of the Lok Sabha. The Amendment made it possible for the President to modify the proclamation without rovoking it subject to approval of Parliament. Thus, the Amendment confined the suspension of article 19 only to situations of war or external aggression, *i.e.*where emergency was proclaimed on internal grounds of 'armed rebellion', freedoms under article 19 could not be taken away. Also, the same amendment laid down that under no circumstances could the enforcement of rights under articles 20 and 21 be denied even during an Emergency.

Several cases involving emergency provisions were decided by the Supreme Court before the 1978 amendment. These dealt with matters arising during periods of the first and second Emergencies proclaimed in 1962 and 1971. The Court upheld the Presidential order suspending the right of a citizen to move the Court to enforce the provisions of articles 21 and 22.[1] In *Makhan Singh v. State of Punjab* (AIR 1964 SC 381) the Court tried to balance the fundamental rights of the citizens with the Emergency provisions and the needs of the security of the State. While conceding that if national security is in peril, individual rights must give way to the State, the Court said:

> How long the Proclamation of Emergency should continue and what restrictions should be imposed on the fundamental rights of citizens during the pendency of the emergency, are matters which must inevitably be left to the executive because the executive knows the requirements of the situation and the effect of compulsive factors which operate during periods of grave crises.

But, the Court also held that it had the power to judge and examine the validity of emergency legislation under which persons were detained with *mala fide* intentions or under excessive delegation of powers to the executive. In another case, the Court upheld the validity of the statute which invested the executive with drastic powers and observed that the power to detain without trial was basically an executive act not subject to judicial review.[2] In *State of Maharashtra v. Prabhakar Pandurang Sanzgiri* (AIR 1966 SC 424), the Court upheld the liberty of a detenu to send his book outside the jail for publication since there was no nexus between the Government order preventing it and the purpose of the enforcement of emergency rules. The stand was reiterated in *K. Ananda Nambiar v. Chief Secretary* (AIR 1966 SC 657) where Justice Gajendragadkar asserted that even during the operation of emergency, in considering the effect of a Presidential order suspending the enforcement of fundamental rights, the order should be strictly construed

1. *Mohan Chowdhury v. Chief Commissioner*, AIR 1964 SC 173.
2. *Sadhu Singh v. Delhi Administration*, AIR 1966 SC 91.

in favour of the citizen's fundamental rights. In *Ram Manohar Lohia v. State of Bihar* (AIR 1966 SC 740), it was held that the order of detention must *prima facie* be proper, that "maintenance of law and order" could not be equated with "maintenance of public order" and that action under Defence of India Rules would be valid only if taken in the "interests of public order" and not merely "in aid of law and order". While protecting the paramount interest of the security of the State during emergency, citizen's rights to freedom could not be taken away without the existence of justifying necessity specified in Defence of India Rules. On this ground, the Court declared a detention "clearly and plainly *mala fide*".[1] In *P.L. Lakhanpal v. Union of India* (AIR 1967 SC 1507), the Supreme Court overruled the decision in the *Sadhu Singh case* and held that principles of natural justice should apply to the decision to review an order of detention. The Court went further in *State of Madhya Pradesh v. Bharat Singh* (AIR 1967 SC 1170) when it said:

> All executive action which operates to the prejudice of any person must have the authority of law to support it, and the terms of Article 358 do not detract from that rule...Article 358 does not purport to invest the State with arbitrary authority to take action to the prejudice of citizens and others: it merely provides that so long as the proclamation of emergency subsists laws may be enacted, and executive action may be taken in pursuance of lawful authority, which if the provisions of Article 19 were operative would have been invalid.

In *Mohd. Yaqub v. State of J&K* (AIR 1968 SC 765), the Supreme Court clearly observed that there was no scope for judicial review to find out any nexus between exercise of power under article 359 and security of India in view of the suspension of the enforcement of fundamental rights in the interests of the security of the State by the President. In *Bhut*

1. *G. Sadanandan v. State of Kerala,* 1966 SC 1925.

Nath v. State of W. Bengal (AIR 1974 SC 806) also, the Court declined to hold the continuance of emergency void. Justice Iyer said that the argument that there was no real emergency fell outside the orbit of judicial control. The position was reiterated in *Collector of Hyderabad v. Ibrahim and Co.* (AIR 1970 SC 1275). The Court said:

> The executive order immune from attack is only that order which the State was competent, but for the provisions contained in article 19, to make. Executive action...which is otherwise invalid is not immune from attack, merely because a proclamation of emergency is in operation when it is taken."

Article 358 made it clear that things done or omitted to be done during emergency could not be challenged even after the emergency was over on the ground of the concerned emergency law having violated article 19.[1]

There appeared to be a considerable shift in the approach of the Supreme Court to cases of violation of Fundamental Rights *vis a vis* emergency provisions arising during the proclamation of internal emergency (1975-1977). Thus, in the *Habeas Corpus case,* the Court refused to interfere in matters of detention of persons as it believed that the intention clearly was to keep preventive detention controlled exclusively by the executive. Detenus could not move any Court for the writ of *Habeas Corpus* if a *prima facie* valid detention order existed.[2]

In *Union of India v. Bhanudas* (AIR 1977 SC 1027) again, the Court held that all rights of personal liberty under articles 19, 21 and 22 could be suspended during national emergency due to Presidential Orders under article 359. Most of these Court verdicts lost validity after the 44th amendment *inter*

---

1. *Makhan Singh's case, op. cit.; Bennett Coleman and Co. Ltd. v. Union of India,* AIR 1973 SC 106; A. *Cooperative Agricultural and Industrial Society Ltd. v. Union of India,* AIR 1976 SC 958.
2. *Additional District Magistrate v. Shivkant Shukla,* AIR 1976 SC 1207.

alia amended articles 352, 358 and 359.

In the *Minerva Mills case,* it was held that the judiciary could act if it was established that the Union Government acted *mala fide* or on irrelevant or no facts. The remedy otherwise could be only political. A matter like the satisfaction of the President is beyond the Court. Only if it was shown that there was, in fact, no satisfaction at all, or the satisfaction was absurd, perverse or *mala fide,* the exercise of power would be unconstitutional. Courts could certainly act under their power of limited judicial review in such a case.1

Proclamation of President's Rule

It is the constitutional duty of the Union to protect its States against external aggression and internal disturbance and to ensure that the Government of every State is carried on in accordance with the Constitution (article 355).

If on receipt of a Report from the Governor or otherwise, the President is satisfied that Government of the State cannot be carried on in accordance with the Constitution or that the constitutional machinery has failed, he may issue a proclamation taking over any of the functions and powers of the State Government including those of the Governor and other State authorities (article 356). The satisfaction of the President, of course, means the satisfaction of the Union Government and President's rule is actually rule by the Union Government. It is important that article 356 is read with articles 355, 256, 257, 353 and 365. This is usually not done. Insofar as article 355 speaks of the duty of the Union to ensure that government of every state is carried on in accordance with the provisions of the Constitution, it is obvious that article 356 is not the only one to take care of a situation of failure of constitutional machinery. The Union can also act in matters of 'external aggression' or 'internal

1. *Minerva Mills v. Union of India,* AIR 1980 SC 1789.

disturbance' under article 355 *i.e.* without imposing President's rule. Article 355 can stand on its own. Also, Union Government can issue certain directions under articles 256, 257 and 353.

It is true that article 356 clearly authorises the President to issue a proclamation imposing President's rule over a State if he is satisfied that a situation has arisen in which the Government of the State cannot be carried on in accordance with the provisions of this Constitution" but a question may be asked when can the President lawfully hold that such a situation has actually arisen. A very specific and categorical answer is contained in article 365 when it says that where a State fails to comply with Union directions (under articles 256, 257 and others) "it shall be lawful for the President to hold that a situation has arisen in which the Government of the State cannot be carried on in accordance with the provisions of this Constitution". It is unfortunate that before rushing to issue a proclamation under article 356, no effort appeared to have been made to ensure that (i) the Union had done all that it could in discharge of its duty under article 355 and (ii) that the State had "failed to comply with, or give effect to" directions. It seems in many cases recourse to 356 has been taken without keeping other provisions in view.

Under the proclamation under article 356, the powers of the State Legislature may become exercisable by or on the authority of Parliament. The State Assembly may be dissolved or kept under suspended animation. The President may take all other steps that may be necessary including suspension of the operation of any constitutional provisions relating to any body or authority in the State except the High Courts. Every proclamation must cease to operate at the expiry of two months unless approved by resolutions of the two Houses. After Parliament's approval also, a proclamation may continue for not more than six months at a time and not for more than a total of three years except in case of a proclamation issued in May 1987 in respect of Punjab which was allowed to continue for five years under the Constitution (68th Amendment) Act, 1991 (Article 356).

During the operation of President's rule under article 356, Parliament may confer the legislative power of the State on the President and authorise him to delegate these powers to other authorities (Article 357).

Article 356, enabling the imposition of President's rule over the States by the Union, has been one of the most criticized and controversial provisions of the Constitution. Under this provision, State Governments have been taken over by the Union on nearly 120 occasions during the last 60 years (1950-2009) *i.e.* on an average twice each year. Opposition members and critics have said that the article has been used, more often than not, for political and partisan purposes by the party in power at the Union level, usually to dismiss State Governments of parties in opposition. In the Constituent Assembly, while replying to the critics of this provision, Dr. Ambedkar had expressed the hope that it might remain a dead letter and might never be used except as a last resort, after everything else failed.

In *State of Rajasthan v. Union of India* (AIR 1977 SC 1361), the Supreme Court held that a proclamation under 356 depends on the subjective satisfaction of the President and the Court could not substitute its own satisfaction for that of the President nor could it, in view of article 74(2), enquire into the advice given to the President by the Council of Ministers. The Court, however, significantly added that if the satisfaction of the President was *mala fide*, based on extraneous or irrelevant considerations or no satisfaction at all, it could interfere. Thus, exercise of President's power under article 356 was brought under judicial review to that extent.

In the *Bommai case*, the Court went much further. It was held (i) that the question of the State Government losing the confidence of the House should be decided on the floor of the House and until that is done the Ministry should not be unseated, (ii) that dissolution of the Assembly by Presidential Proclamation is subject to judicial review, and (iii) that if the court finds that relevant material justifying the proclamation did not exist or that *mala fide* was involved, it may strike it down and restore the Ministry (*Bommai v. Union of India,* JT (1994) 2 SC 215).

The Constitution Commission (NCRWC) has recommended:

(1) Article 356 should not be deleted. But it must be used sparingly and only as a remedy of the last resort and after exhausting action under other articles like 256, 257 amd 355,

(2) In case of political breakdown, necessitating invoking of article 356, before issuing a proclamation thereunder, the concerned State should be given an opportunity to explain its position and redress the situation, unless the situation is such, that following the above course would not be in the interest of security of State, or defence of the country, or for other reasons necessitating urgent action.

(3) The question whether the Ministry in a State has lost the confidence of the Legislative Assembly or not, should be decided only on the floor of the Assembly and nowhere else. If necessary, the Union Government should take the required steps, to enable the Legislative Assembly to meet and freely transact its business. The Governor should not be allowed to dismiss the Ministry so long as it enjoys the confidence of the House. It is only where a Chief Minister refuses to resign after his Ministry is defeated on a motion of no-confidence, that the Governor can dismiss the State Government. In a situation of political breakdown, the Governor should explore all possibilities of having a Government enyoying majority support in the Assembly.

(4) Article 356 should be amended so as to ensure that the State Legislative Assembly should not be dissolved either by the Governor or the President before the proclamation issued under article 356(1) has been laid before Parliament and it has had an opportunity to consider it.

Financial Emergency

The President is authorised by article 360 of the Constitution to declare by a proclamation financial emergency if he is satisfied that the financial stability or credit of India or of any part of its territory is threatened. Such a proclamation may be revoked or varied by a subsequent proclamation. It has to belaid before both Houses of Parliament and ceases to operate at the expiration of two months unless meanwhile approved by resolutions of the two Houses. Once approved by Parliament, unlike proclamations under article 352, it may continue indefinitely until revoked or varied.

During the operation of financial emergency, the executive authority of the Union extends to the giving of directions to any State to observe certain specified canons of financial propriety and such other directions that the President may find necessary or adequate. These directions may include reduction of salaries and allowances of all those serving a State and reserving for the President's consideration all money Bills and other Bills under article 207 after these are passed by State Legislatures. The President may also direct reduction in salaries and allowances of all those serving in connection with the affairs of the Union including judges of the Supreme Court and the High Courts.

Fortunately, thus far, during the last 60 years of the operation of the Constitution, there has been no occasion for the promulgation of Financial Emergency.

18

SERVICES UNDER THE UNION AND THE STATES

PART XIV XIVA, ARTICLES 308–323B

SERVICES

In a modern democratic polity, civil services are an inevitable ingredient of the governmental apparatus. It is, in fact, the non-political and non-elected functionaries who are responsible for carrying on the administration under the direction and control of the elected representatives of the people and in accordance with rules and principles.

Indian bureaucracy or the civil service has been one of the most well-known in the world. In fact, the term 'civil service' was first used for the employees of the East India Company who served in departments other than military. One of the earliest demands of Indian nationalist opinion was to rationalise the structure and functions of the civil service to provide a greater share to Indians in the administration of their country. As a result of increasing pressure and resentment in India, in 1922 the British Government finally bowed to the demand for holding simultaneous Civil Service examinations in India and England. Also, from then on, the Imperial Civil Services (ICS) were to be called the Indian Civil Service (ICS).

The Motilal Nehru Committee report in 1928

recommended the discontinuance of the All India Services until the grant of responsible government to India. During negotiations at the first Round Table Conference, two Indian members of the Services Sub-Committee also called for immediate and total discontinuance of the All India Services. Later, Jawaharlal Nehru and other leaders were highly critical of the ICS. Nehru believed that the whole Government of India was controlled by the ICS. The Indian Civil Service was the backbone of the administration. The ICS were also described as a civilian British army of occupation in India. The ICS officers enjoyed vast powers and authority to take and implement major decisions in administration. They were trained to maintain a distance from the 'natives'. Referring to them as arrogant and overbearing and contemptuous of public opinion, Nehru felt that so long as the spirit of the ICS—the spirit of authoritarianism—pervaded Indian administration and its public services, no new order could be built up. In April 1940 Nehru went so far as to declare that the first and foremost task of the nationalist government would be to abolish the ICS.

The fact remains that at the time of independence, we inherited a well organised framework of All India Services. In addition, there was a network of central, provincial and subordinate services. There were nearly 1000 officers in the ICS, roughly half of them were Indians. Owing to the state of affairs prevailing in the country as well as to avoid creation of any void in the Services, the Interim Government under Nehru promised those who were inclined to continue in the service "the same terms as to scales of pay, leave, pension rights and safeguard in matters of discipline as hitherto". A resolution to this effect was incorporated in the Indian Independence Act, 1947 and finally in the Constitution of India (Article 314 which was repealed in 1972 by the Constitution (28th Amendment) Act.

Sardar Patel's consistent support for the rights and privileges for civil servants was clearly reflected in his speeches in the Constituent Assembly and at other fora. While strongly defending the constitutional safeguards for the civil services, Sardar Patel even threatened to resign if such guarantees were not incorporated in the Constitution. He almost eulogized the achievements of the civil services and asserted that they must get recognition and praise.

The two All India Services, the Indian Administrative Service and the Indian Police Service, were created in 1946 on the British pattern. The attainment of independence and the introduction of the system of parliamentary democracy made the civil services fully accountable to the political executive and the Parliament.

Although matters concerning Government services could be normally regulated by laws and the power to lay down detailed rules for recruitment and conditions of service of the Union and State employees was left to the respective legislatures (*vide* entry 70 of List I and entry 41 of List II), the Constitution-makers deemed it most prudent to assure the services by providing some constitutional guarantees and safeguards in the matter of recruitment, security of tenure, procedure for disciplinary action, etc. In this connection, the Constitution also provided for the setting up of an independent Public Service Commission. The provisions for the Union and State Services applied to the whole of India except the State of Jammu & Kashmir (article 308).

Article 309 provided for the regulation of recruitment and conditions of service of Union and State Government services by appropriate Legislatures subject to the provisions of the Constitution. Until any such laws were enacted, the services were to be regulated by rules made by the President or the Governor as the case may be.

Article 310 laid down the principle that every Government employee—in a defence service or a civil service—held his office during the pleasure of the President or the Governor. It was, however, possible to provide in special cases by contract to pay compensation for early termination of service. Besides, there were special constitutional safeguards in case of certain high functionaries like the judges of the Supreme Court and High Courts, the Chief Election Commissioner, Comptroller and Auditor-General, members of the Public Service Commissions, etc. who could not be removed from their offices except in the manner laid down in relevant articles (124, 217, 317, 324 etc.). Also, separate provisions were made for regulating the recruitment and conditions of service of certain categories of public servants, *e.g.* officers and staff of Legislature Secretariats (articles 98 and 187), employees of the Supreme Court and the High Courts (articles 146 and 299) and persons serving the Indian Audit and Accounts Department (article 148). Article 309 did not apply to them.

Article 311 sought to place certain limitations on the exercise of the pleasure principle in respect of civil servants. Thus, no civil servant could be dismissed or removed by an authority subordinate to the appointing authority and no civil servant could be dismissed or removed or reduced in rank except after an enquiry informing him of the charges against him and giving him a reasonable apportunity of being heard in respect of those charges. The protection was not available to defence employees and even in case of civil employees it did not apply if the penalty was any other than dismissal, removal or reduction in rank. The article, however, made no distinction between a person holding a temporary post and one holding a permanent post.[1]

It has been held that the protection extended by article 311 is only procedural in nature and not substantive. No remedy may lie if all the procedural requirements have been meticulously fulfilled. In the main these requirements are (a) that specific charges must be framed against a civil servant proposed to be proceeded against; (b) the charges must be

1. *Narasimhachar v. State of Mysore*, AIR 1960 S.C. 247; *Parshotam v. Union of India*, AIR 1958 SC 36; *State of Punjab v. Ram*, AIR 1992 SC 2188.

formally conveyed; (c) he must be provided a reasonable opportunity of answering the charges; (d) he must be given an opportunity of defending himself by cross examining the witnesses and adducing all evidence on which he relies; and (e) the decision in the matter must be based on the facts and materials plaçed before the enquiring authority and no materials should be relied upon without the civil servant concerned having an opportunity to examine and explain them. The basic principle is that the enquiry must follow rules of natural justice.[1]

Article 311, it has been held, would not be attracted if there are no penal consequences like loss of salary, allowances or pension accompanying the action against him. Whatever the words used, if these amount to removal or dismissal, the article would apply. If the services are terminated in accordance with the terms of the contract or on superannuation or by way of compulsory retirement as per procedure for the same, article 311 would not provide any protection. In case of reduction of rank also, the test is whether any penal consequences are involved. A person holding a post in a substantive capacity cannot be brought down to a lower post without following the article 311 procedure of enquiry, etc. But, if it is reversion to the substantive post from an officiating one, it is not reduction in rank for purposes of article 311 unless there are any penal consequences.[2]

The Supreme Court has, however held that the Government before deciding to retire a Government employee compulsorily from service, have to consider his entire record including the latest reports.[3]

The enquiry contemplated in article 311 may, however, be dispensed with in certain cases like (a) when the person

1. *Union of India v. Verma*, AIR, 1957 SC 882.
2. *Parshotam v. Union of India*.
3. *State of Orissa v. Ram Chandra Dass*, AIR 1996 SC 2436.

has been convicted on a criminal charge; (b) where the appropriate authority records in writing reasons for the enquiry not being practicable; (c) when the President or the Governor as the case may be is satisfied that in the interest of the security of the State it is not expedient to hold such an enquiry.

All India services are distinguished from Central and State services inasmuch as members of Central services are concerned with only the affairs of the Union and those of State services with State matters while members of the All India services are common to the Union and the States and serve by turns both the Union and State Governments. Two All India services—the Indian Administrative Service and Indian Police Service—are mentioned in the Constitution itself. Article 312 lays down that if Rajya Sabha passes a resolution by two-thirds majority to the effect that it is necessary or expedient in national interest to create one or more all India services, including All India Judicial Service, Parliament may by law provide for such services. Parliament has under this article enacted the All India Services Act, 1951 creating certain all India Services in addition to the IAS and the IPS which had been already created in 1948. Article 312 also empowers Parliament to regulate the recruitment and conditions of service of persons appointed to All India services.

Article 312A inserted by the Constitution (28th Amendment) Act, 1972 empowers Parliament to vary or revoke conditions of service of persons appointed to the Civil Service of the Crown in India before the commencement of the Constitution. Article 313 contains a transitional provision saying that until otherwise provided, all the laws in force applicable to any public service would continue. Article 314 which sought to provide protection to existing officers of certain services was repealed by the 28th Amendment.

PUBLIC SERVICE COMMISSIONS

Article 315 lays down that there shall be a Public Service Commission for the Union and a Public Service Commission for each State. Two or more States may opt for a Joint Commission. On request, the Union Service Commission may also agree to serve all or any of the needs of a State.

The Public Service Commissions are envisaged as independent constitutional institutions not subject to governmental or political interference or control and charged with the responsibility of recruitment and management of public services. All expenses of the Union and State Service Commissions are charged on the Consolidated Fund of the Union or the State concerned (Article 322).

The Chairman and members of the Public Service Commissions are appointed by the President or the Governor as the case may be. As nearly as may be, half of the members must have had ten years' service in the Union or a State Government. Members shall hold office for a fixed term of six years or until the age of 65 in case of the Union and 62 in case of the State Commissions. A Commission member is not removable from his office except in case of insolvency, infirmity of mind or body, on engaging in another paid employment or on being found by the Supreme Court guilty of proved misbehaviour, for having an interest in a Government contract or sharing the profits of any such contract or agreement. Member of a Public Service Commission on expiration of his term of office is ineligible for reappointment to that office (articles 316 317).[1]

Article 318 provides that the terms and conditions of service of a member of the Commission cannot be varied to his disadvantage after his appointment. The President or the Governor as the case may be may determine the number of

1. *U.P. Public Service Commission v. Suresh,* AIR 1987 SC 1953; *Hargovind v. Raghukul,* AIR 1979 SC 1109; *Ref. under 317(1),* AIR 1983 SC 996.

members and staff of the Commission and regulate their conditions of service.

Members of the Commissions are not eligible for any other appointment under the Government.[1] The Chairman of a State Commission can become a member or chairman of UPSC or chairman of another State Commission. A member of the UPSC is eligible to become chairman of UPSC or of a State Commission and a member of a State Commission is eligible to become a member or chairman of UPSC or any State Commission (Article 319).

The functions of Public Service Commissions are:

i. to conduct examinations for appointment to the services of the Union/State;
ii. to make recommendations to the Union/State Government for appointment of persons to its services;
iii. to be consulted in regard to method of recruitment, principles in matters of appointments, promotions, transfers from one service to another, and disciplinary matters of civilian employees;
iv. to advise on any other matter that may be referred by the President/Governor;
v. on request to assist two or more States in regard to schemes for joint recruitment;
vi. to present an annual report to the President/Governor who shall cause it to be laid before Houses of Parliament/State Legislature;
vii. any other function that Parliament/State Assembly may by law assign.

The Supreme Court has held that the function of the Commission is purely advisory and if the Government fails to consult it in any matter specified for consultation, a public servant affected thereby cannot expect a remedy in a court of law under article 320. But where consultation is provided

---

1. *Union of India v. U.D.Dwivedi,* AIR 1997 SC 1313.

for by law or regulation, it will constitute a legal obligation (articles 320 321 and 323).[1]

ADMINISTRATIVE TRIBUNALS

The Constitution (Forty-Second Amendment) Act, 1976 inserted a new part—Part XIVA—and articles 323A and 323B to empower Parliament and State Legislatures to set up by law administrative tribunals for the adjudication of disputes and complaints in all service matters relating to recruitment and conditions of service of public employees. Tribunals may also be set up for certain other matters like taxation, labour and industry, land reforms, elections, rent laws etc. Several such tribunals have since been set up, excluding the jurisdiction of certain level of Courts. Thus the Administrative Tribunals Act 1985 setting up tribunals for resolving service disputes takes away the jurisdication of High Courts while appeal lies to the Supreme Court under article 136 only.[2] In *L. Chandra Kumar v. Union of India* (AIR 1997 SC 1125) it was held that clause 2 (d) of article 323 A and clause 3 (d) of article 323 B are unconstitutional to the extent that they exclude the jurisdiction of the High Courts and the Supreme Court.

Administrative Reforms

The Constitution Commision (NCRWC-2002) considered all those matters in depth and made recommendations of far-reaching importance. These included:

1. The questions of personnel policy including placements, promotions, transfers and fast-track advancements on the

---

1. *State of U.P. v. Srivastava*, AIR 1957 SC 912; *State of U.P. v. Rajasthan*, AIR 1988 SC 162; *Keshav v. U.P. HESC*, (1985) ISCC 671; *Neelima v. State of Haryana*, AIR 1987 SC 169.
2. *Sampath v. Union of India*, AIR 1987 SC 386; *Tamilmani v. Union of India*, AIR 1992 SC 1120.

basis of forward-looking career management policies and techniques should be managed by autonomous Personnel Boards for assisting the high level political authorities in making key decisions.

2. Above a certain level—say the Joint Secretary level—all posts should be open for recruitment from a wide variety of sources including the open market.
3. Officials, before starting their career, in addition to the taking of an oath of loyalty to the Constitution, should swear to abide by the basic principles of good governance.
4. The constitutional safeguards have in practice acted to shield the guilty against swift and certain punishment for abuse of public office for private gain. A major corollary has been erosion of accountability. It has accordingly become necessary to re-visit the issue of constitutional safeguards under article 311 to ensure that the honest and efficient officials are given the requisite protection but the dishonest are not allowed to prosper in office. A comprehensive examination of the entire concept of administrative jurisprudence has to be undertaken to rationalize and simplify the procedure of administrative and legal action and to bring the theory and practice of security of tenure in line with the experience of the last sixty years.
5. The civil service regulations need to be changed radically in the light of contemporary administrative theory to introduce modern evaluation methodology.

19

ELECTIONS

PART XV, ARTICLES 324–329 A

The biggest revolution since the Independence of the country was the adoption of universal adult franchise for elections to the Lok Sabha and the Legislative Assemblies of the States. In a newly independent country with appalling backwardness, dismal poverty and rampant illiteracy, it was an act of faith for the founding fathers to give a vote to every citizen who was not less than 21 years of age (since reduced to 18) and not otherwise disqualified under any law on grounds of non-residence, unsoundness of mind, crime or corrupt or illegal practice (Article 326).

Article 324 provides for a single Election Commission to superintend, direct and control all elections to Parliament and to the State Legislatures and to the offices of the President and the Vice-President. The Election Commission shall consist of the Chief Election Commissioner and such number of other Election Commissioners, if any, as the President may from time to time fix. When any other Election Commissioners are appointed, the Chief Election Commissioner shall act as the Chairman. Until 1989, The Election Commission consisted of the Chief Election Commissioner only. On 16 October 1989 two Election Commissioners were appointed by a Presidential notification. In less than three months, however the notification was revoked and the Election Commission reverted with effrect from 2 January 1990 to being a single member body. It was held by the Supreme Court that it was entirely for the Executive to decide on the need of Election Commissioners other than the Chief Election Commissioner and that the termination of the services of two Election Commissioners on the abolition of the posts was therefore valid.[1] Again, in October 1993 two Election Commissioners were appointed and by an ordinance given the same position and status as the Chief Election Commissioner. Also, the Commission was required to act as a body taking decisions unanimously or by majority. The ordinance challenged unsuccessfully by the Chief Election Commissioner before the Supreme Court, was replaced by the Chief Election Commissioner and other Election Commissioners (Conditions of Service) Amendment Act 1994. It was assented to by the President on 4 January 1994 and given retrospective effect from 1 October 1993.

Article 324 also provides for the appointment of Regional Commissioners at the time of General Elections after consultation with the Chief Election Commissioner. The Chief Election Commissioner cannot be removed from his office except in like manner and on like grounds as a Judge of the Supreme Court and the conditions of his service cannot be varied to his disadvantage after his appointment. Other Election Commissioners, if any, can be removed only on the recommendation of the Chief Election Commissioner.

Article 325 lays down that there shall be one general electoral roll for every territorial constituency for election to either House of Parliament or to the House or either House of a State Legislature. No person is to be ineligible for inclusion in the electoral roll on grounds of religion, race, caste or sex, nor can anyone claim to be included in any special electoral roll for any such constituency on any such ground.

---

1. *Dhanoa v. Union of India*, AIR 1991 SC 1745.

Article 327 vests legislative power in Parliament to make laws relating to all matters concerning elections to either House of Parliament or to the House or either House of a State Legislature, including the preparation of electoral rolls, the delimitation of constituencies and all other matters "necessary for securing the due constitution of such House or Houses".

Article 328 confers powers on State Legislatures to make laws relating to elections to the House, or either House of a State Legislature.

Article 329 seeks to bar interference by courts in electoral matters including (i) the validity of any law relating to delimitation of constituencies or the allotment of seats under article 327 or 328 and (ii) election to either House of Parliament or a State Legislature. The latter can be questioned only by an election petition presented to such authority and in such manner as may be provided by law by the concerned legislature. Under the Representation of the People Act, the power to decide election disputes now vests in the High Courts with a right of appeal to the Supreme Court. Disputes relating to the election of the President or Vice-President are, however, to be settled by the Supreme Court.

Electoral Reforms

During the last six decades, 15 general elections for Lok Sabha and very large number for different State Assemblies have been held. By an large, these have been free and fair and have earned national and international acclaim. But, right from the first general election [1951-52] the need for electoral reforms has been the subject of wide ranging debates. Practically every report of the Election Commission has contained reform proposals and every successive Chief Election Commissioner has applied his mind to this matter. The recommendations of the all party Dinesh Goswami Committee on Electoral Reforms set up in 1990, also found wide support. For its part, the Lok Sabha unanimously passed a resolution on electoral reforms, moved by L.K. Advani, which based itself to an extent on the above Committee's recommendations. The Indrajit Gupta Committee (1998) was most particular about the all party agreement on State funding of elections. The Election Commission reacted to the electoral reform proposals that were sent by the Vajpayee Government for its comments. Also, the Commission made its own proposals.

The Law Commission published a voluminous report containing comprehensive reform proposals. NCRWC made an in-depth study of the problem. Report of NCRWC came at the end of March 2002. Before the government could get over the usual bureaucratic delays and insensitive ways of dealing with reports of such Commissions, the Supreme Court pronounced its judgement on a public interest petition on 2 May 2002. In its operative part, the judgement directed the Election Commission to work out within two months modalities to call for information on affidavit from all candidates seeking election to Parliament or a State Legislature in regard to:

(a) whether the candidate had any conviction, acquittal or discharge on a criminal offence in the past, punishment or fine, if any, imposed;
(b) whether during the six months preceding the nomination, the candidate was accused of any offence punishable with imprisonment for two years or more and charges were framed by a court of law with details thereof;
(c) movable, immovable assets including bank balances etc of the candidate, spouse and dependents;
(d) liabilities, if any, particularly if there are any overdues of public financial institutions or government dues;
(e) educational qualifications of the candidate.

The Supreme Court, *inter alia* held:

> Fair election contemplates disclosure by the candidate of his past including the assets held by him so as to give a proper choice to the voter according to his thinking and

opinion.....If on affidavit a candidate is required to disclose the assets held by him at the time of election, voter can decide whether he could be re-elected even in case where he has collected tons of money.

To maintain the purity of elections and in particular to bring transparency in the process of elections, the Commission can ask the candidates about the expenditure incurred by the political parties and this transparency in the process of elections would include transparency of a candidate who seeks election or re-election. In a democracy, the electoral process has a strategic role. The little man of this country would have basic elementary right to know full particulars of a candidate who is to represent him in Parliament where laws to bind his liberty and property may be enacted.

The right to get information in democracy is recognised all throughout and it is natural right flowing from the concept of democracy.

Under our Constitution, Article 19(1)(a) provides for freedom of speech and expression. Voters' speech or expression in case of election would include casting of votes, that is to say, voter speaks out or expresses by casting vote. For this purpose, information about the candidate to be selected is must. Voter's right to know antecedents including criminal past of his candidate contesting election for MP or MLA is much more fundamental and basic for survival of democracy. The little man may think over before making his choice of electing law breakers as law makers.

The Election Commission referred the Supreme Court Directive to the government (Ministry of Law) on 14 May 2002 for considering necessary action by way of legislation or amendment of Rules regarding nomination papers. The government called an All Party meet to consider the matter on 8 July. Since the two month limit was expiring, the Election Commission on 28 June issued its order which not only called for the information on the lines indicated by the court but also provided for the Returning Officers having the power to reject any nomination on the ground of the candidate not furnishing the required information or giving incomplete information.

The All-party meeting, attended by leaders of 21 parties, as was to be expected, reached a consensus strongly against some of the sought for disclosures in regard to educational qualifications, assets and liabilities etc. and arming the Returning Officers with discretionary powers to reject nomination papers for none or wrong disclosures. After the All party agreement on a draft legislation and all the drama on the issue of an ordinance, the representations made to the President and his returning the ordinance to seek some clarifications, the President finally signed it and the ordinance was issued. The ordinance provided for disqualification of a candidate who had been charge-sheeted in two courts involving the heinous crimes of murder, rape, drug smuggling, kidnapping for ransom, treason, terrorist act leading to death etc. during a period of six months prior to the filing of the nomination.

On 4 October 2002, the Union Cabinet approved amendments to the effect that (1) besides those charged with crimes like murder and rape, those charged under the Prevention of Corruption Act or Prevention of Terrorism Act would also be covered by disqualification, and that (2) disqualification would be for a period of six years from the date of release. Thus the anomaly of a person being able to seek election while serving a prison sentence would be removed.

The Supreme Court put its foot down and reiterated its earlier directives regarding disclosure of full information by the candidates.

The entire question of electoral reforms is embroiled in political controversies and party considerations. The main problems are:

1. the high cost of elections and the question of finding legitimate funds;
2. the role of money, muscle and mafia power and electoral malpractices;
3. the scourge of communalism, casteism, criminalization and corruption;
4. hung legislatures, instable governments and too frequent elections;
5. the large size of constituencies and the question of representative character of legislators when under the first past the post system majority of them are elected by minority of votes cast;
6. absence of ideology-based healthy party system and the prevalence of a large number of parties without any internal party democracy;
7. Non-participation of people in selection of candidates.

While most of the needed reforms may not impact constitutional provisions and may be matters for political consideration, consensus building, legislative action and administrative implementation, all these need to be examined in the context of the scheme of the Constitution, the nature of the polity and proposals for constitutional review.[1]

1. For NCRWC recommendations, see Chapter 25.

20

LANGUAGE PROVISIONS

PART III, ARTICLES 29–30; PART V, ARTICLE 120;
PART VI, ARTICLE 210; PART XVII, ARTICLES 343–351;
PART XXII, ARTICLE 394A AND EIGHTH SCHEDULE

Although there is a separate Part—Part XVII—devoted to 'Official Language', provisions pertaining to language are spread over different parts and chapters of the Constitution.

Protection of Linguistic Minority Rights and Non-Discrimination on Grounds of Religion

Article 29 enunciates the fundamental right of any section of citizens residing anywhere in India to conserve its distinct language, script or culture. No citizen can be denied admission in any educational institution maintained or aided by the State on grounds of language, religion, etc. Article 30 seeks to protect the rights of all minorities—based on religion or language—to establish and administer educational institutions of their choice. The State is enjoined not to discriminate against any educational institution on the ground of its language or religion-based management. (See under the 'Fundamental Rights' chapter).

Article 350A inserted by the Seventh Amendment provides for local authorities in every State endeavouring to extend adequate facilities for instruction in the mother tongue at the primary stage of education to children belonging to linguistic minority groups and for the President issuing necessary directions to any State. The term 'linguistic minority group' has been interpreted to mean a group of people who are in a numerical minority in a State as a whole as distinguished from any particular area or region thereof.[1]

Article 350B provides for the appointment by the President of a special officer for linguistic minorities to investigate matters concerning safeguards for linguistic minorities and to report to the President at such intervals as the President may direct. All such reports may be laid before Houses of Parliament and sent to the State Governments concerned.

Language of Legislatures

Article 120 lays down the official language of Parliament. It says *inter alia* that the business in Parliament shall be transacted in Hindi or in English. The Presiding Officer of either House may, however, permit any member who cannot adequately express himself in Hindi or English to address the House in his mother tongue. Arrangements have since been made in both the Houses of Parliament for simultaneous interpretation of speeches from major regional languages into Hindi and English. In actual practice, however, most of the time, the entire business in either House is carried on in Hindi or English with full facilities of simultaneous interpretation from Hindi to English and *vice versa*.

The corresponding language provision for State Legislatures is article 210. Business in a State Legislature may be transacted either in the official language or languages of the State or in Hindi or in English and the Presiding Officer of a House may allow a member who cannot adequately express himself in any of these languages to address the House in his mother tongue.

---

1. *In re Kerala Education Bill*, AIR 1958 SC 956.

Official Language of the Union

Of the many formidable problems that the founding fathers of our Constitution faced, the question of establishing any one of our languages as a national language or even as an official language of the Union proved to be the most intractable. Finally, under a compromise formula embodied in article 343, Hindi in Devanagari script was accepted as the official language of the Union with the international form of Indian numerals. For a period of 15 years, English was allowed to be continued to be used and even thereafter Parliament could by law provide for the use of English or Devanagari form of numerals for any specified purposes.

Article 344 provided for the setting up of a Commission after five years and thereafter every ten years to make recommendations to the President as to (i) the progressive use of Hindi for official purposes, (ii) restricting the use of English for official purposes, (iii) the language to be used in the Supreme Court and the High Courts, (iv) form of the numerals to be used and (v) any other matter regarding the official language of the Union and the language of communication between the Union and a State or between the States. The Commission was expected to pay due regard to the needs of industrial, cultural and scientific advancement of India and the just claims and interests of the non-Hindi speaking areas in regard to public services.

Article 344 also provide for the constitution of a 30 member committee of the members of the two Houses of Parliament to examine the recommendations of the Commission and to report to the President who could issue necessary directions thereon. Under article 349, no Bill or amendment in regard to language was to be allowed except after consideration of this committee report by the President. The first Official Language Commission was appointed in 1955. It submitted its report in 1956. The report was examined by the Committee of the members of the two Houses of Parliament and its opinion submitted to the President who issued an order on 27 April 1960 constituting a Standing Commission for evolution of Hindi terminology for scientific, administrative and legal literature and the translation of English works into Hindi. Actually, under this order, two Commissions were constituted, one under the then Ministry of Education and the other under the Ministry of Law, to evolve Hindi equivalents. The order *inter alia* provided for continuance of English as the medium of UPSC examinations with Hindi being introduced later as an alternative medium. Parliamentary legislation was to continue to be in English but authorised Hindi translations were to be provided.

As a follow-up of the report of the First Official Language Commission and under article 343, Parliament enacted the Official Language Act, 1963. The Act laid down that even after 15 years, English may continue to be used along with Hindi for all official purposes of the Union and also for transaction of business in Parliament.

Hindi was introduced as an alternative medium for UPSC examinations in certain subjects. Later, candidates were given the option to write their answers in any one of the recognized languages specified in the 8th Schedule.

Regional Languages and Link Language

Article 345 seeks to tackle the issue of the official language for each State and the language for inter-State communication at the governmental level. The legislature of a State may by law adopt any one or more of the languages in use in the State or Hindi for all or any of the official purposes and until that is done, English may continue to be used as hithertofore. The language authorised to be used as the official language of the Union shall be the official language for communication between the States and between a State and the Union. But, two or more States were free to agree to use Hindi for communication between themselves (Article 346).

If a substantial proportion of the population of a State

demand and the President is satisfied, he or she may order that the language used by them may also be officially recognized throughout the State or in any part thereof for such purposes as may be specified.

The 1963 Official Language Act provided that for purposes of communication between the Union and the non-Hindi states, English shall be used and where Hindi is used for communication between a Hindi and a non-Hindi State, such communication shall be accompanied by an English translation.

Language of Higher Courts and Authoritative Texts of Laws etc.

Until Parliament by law provides otherwise, all proceedings in the Supreme Court and in every High Court are to be in English. Also, the authoritative texts of all Bills, amendments, Acts, ordinances, orders, rules, regulations and bye-laws at the Union and State levels have to be in English only. However, the Governor of a State may with the prior consent of the President, authorise the use of Hindi or any language used for any official purposes of the State in the proceedings of the High Court of the State provided that the judgements, decrees and orders must continue to be in English. (Article 348).

The 1963 Official Language Act, provided that Hindi translation of Acts etc. published under the authority of the President shall be deemed to be authoritative and that every Bill or amendment shall be accompanied by a Hindi translation.

The 1963 Act similarly provided for a Hindi translation of State Acts etc. in certain cases. For High Court judgements etc., the Act provided for the optional use of Hindi or other official language subject to the Governor obtaining the prior consent of the President and an English translation accompanying the judgement etc.

Language of Public Grievances

Article 350 made the very significant provision that every person, *i.e.* not only a citizen, was entitled to submit a representation for redress of any grievance to any officer or authority of the Union or a State in any of the languages used in the Union or in the State, as the case may be. Thus, no government department, agency or officer can refuse to entertain a representation on the ground of its not being in the official language.

Development of Hindi

Under Article 351, the Union is duty bound to promote the spread and development of the Hindi language

> so that it may serve as a medium of expression for all the elements of the composite culture of India and to secure its enrichment by assimilating without interfering with its genius, the forms, style and expressions used in Hindustani and in other languages of India specified in the Eighth Schedule and by drawing, where necessary or desirable, its vocabulary, primarily on Sanskrit and secondarily on other languages.

A harmonious reading of the language provisions, particularly of articles 343, 344 and 351, would show that the ultimate goal is the spread and development of Hindi and the gradual switchover to its use for official purposes and as a link language. There is no violation of article 351 if use of English is extended beyond 15 years but the power given to Parliament under article 343 is only to specify the particular purposes for which English may continue to be used by the Union depending upon the progress made by Hindi as the official language.[1] In *Dalavi v. State of Tamil Nadu* (AIR 1976 S.C. 1559), the Supreme Court annulled an order of the State Government sanctioning pension to anti-Hindi agitators. The Court held that the order violated article 351

1. *Union of India v. Murasoli*, AIR 1977 SC 225.

inasmuch as it excited emotion against Hindi instead of promoting it.

Authorised Hindi Text of the Constitution

A new article 394A inserted by the 56th Amendment Act provided for an authoritative text of the Constitution in the Hindi language. An authoritative Hindi text of the Constitution has since been published.

The Eighth Schedule

Besides Hindi, our Constitution also recognizes other languages and the need for their development. The 22 languages of India listed in the Eighth Schedule are: Assamese, Bengali, Gujarati, Hindi, Kannada, Kashmiri, Konkani, Malayalam, Manipuri, Marathi, Nepali,Oriya, Punjabi, Sanskrit, Sindhi, Tamil, Telugu, Urdu, Bodo, Dogri, Maithili and Santhali. The last four were added by the Constitution (92nd Amendment) Act, 2003.

21

AMENDMENT OF THE CONSTITUTION

PART XX, ARTICLE 368

Under article 368 of the Constitution, which is the specific provision dealing with amendment of the Constitution, Parliament is the repository of the constituent power of the Union. The procedure for Constitution amendment, as spelt out in that article, has certain distinctive features which clearly mark out Parliament's constituent capacity from its ordinary role as a legislature. First, an amendment of the Constitution can be initiated only by the introduction of a Bill in either House of Parliament so that the initiative in the matter of constitutional amendment has been exclusively reserved for Parliament. Second, for the most part, the provisions of the Constitution can be amended by Parliament by a special majority, namely, a majority of the total membership and a majority of not less than two-thirds of the members of each House present and voting. It is only in the case of a limited category of constitutional provisions, (*i.e.*, those relating to the Election of the President, Executive power of the Union and States, Judiciary, the Lists in the Seventh Schedule, representation of States in Parliament, provisions of article 368, etc.) that the amendment Bill, having been passed by each House of Parliament with the prescribed special majority, needs to be ratified by the legislatures of not less than one half of the States. Third, on a Constitution

Amendment Bill, as duly passed/ratified, being presented to the President, the President's assent is mandatory and, unlike in the case of ordinary legislative Bills, he has no option to withhold his assent or return the Bill to the House for reconsideration. And, lastly, it is significant that none of the provisions of the Constitution is unamendable inasmuch as Parliament can in any way amend, alter or repeal any provision of the Constitution and such amendments cannot be questioned in any court of law on any ground whatsoever unless they tend to alter or violate what may be considered as the basic features of the Constitution.

Amending Power and Basic Features

During the period 1950-1972, the question of the amendability of fundamental rights came before the Supreme Court in three different cases, namely, *Shankari Prasad Vs. Union of India* (AIR 1951 SC 458); *Sajjan Singh Vs. State of Rajasthan* (AIR 1965 SC 845) and *Golak Nath Vs. State of Punjab* (AIR 1967 SC 1643). Until the Supreme Court decision in the *Golak Nath case*, the law was as follows:

i. Constitution Amendment Acts are not ordinary laws and are passed by Parliament in exercise of its constituent powers as contradistinct from ordinary legislative powers. There is no separate constituent body for the purposes of amendment of the Constitution, constituent power also being vested in 'Parliament'.

   (Later—as late as in 1981—the Supreme Court confirmed that the amending power under article 368 is a constituent power independent of the scheme of the distribution of legislative powers under the Seventh Schedule (*Sasanka v. Union of India*, AIR, 1981 SC 522)).

ii. There is no limitation placed upon the amending power, that is to say, there is no provision of the Constitution which cannot be amended. The terms of article 368 are perfectly general and empower Parliament to amend the Constitution without any exception whatever.

iii. Fundamental Rights guaranteed under the Constitution (Part III) are subject to Parliament's power to amend the Constitution.

In the *Golak Nath case*, the Supreme Court by a 6:5 majority reversed its earlier decisions and held that the fundamental rights enshrined in the Constitution were transcendental and immutable, that article 368 of the Constitution laid down only the procedure for amendment and did not give to Parliament any substantive power to amend the Constitution or any constituent power distinct or separate from its ordinary legislative power, that a Constitution Amendment Act was also law within the meaning of article 13 and as such Parliament could not take away or abridge the fundamental rights even through a Constitution Amendment Act passed under article 368.

In 1973, in *Kesavananda Bharati Vs. State of Kerala* (AIR 1973 SC 1461) the Supreme Court reviewed the decision in the *Golak Nath case.* Ten of the 13 Judges held that article 368 itself-contained the power to amend the Constitution and that 'law' in article 13 (2) did not take in a constitutional amendment under article 368. The law declared in *Golak Nath case* was accordingly overruled. On the question whether the amending power under article 368 is absolute and unlimited, seven Judges, constituting a majority, held that the amending power under article 368 was subject to an implied limitation; a limitation which arose by necessary implication from its being a power to "amend the Constitution". By a majority of 7:6 the Court ruled that "Article 368 does not enable Parliament to alter the 'basic structure' or framework of the Constitution". What constituted the basic structure was, however, not clearly made out by the majority and remained an open question.

Following this decision in the *Kesavananda case*, clauses (4) and (5) were inserted in article 368 by the Constitution (42nd Amendment) Act, 1976, to dilute the limitation of 'basic features' to the amending powers of Parliament. These clauses say that (a) there are no limitations, expressed or implied, upon the amending power of Parliament under article 368(1), which is a 'constituent power', and that (b) a Constitution Amendment Act would not, therefore, be subject to judicial review on any ground. But the applicability of the doctrine of basic structure was reaffirmed by the Supreme Court in *Indira Gandhi vs. Raj Narain* (AIR 1975 SC 2299) and *Minerva Mills Vs. Union of India* (AIR 1980 SC 1789). In the latter case, the Court held clauses (4) and (5) as void, on the ground that this amendment sought to totally exclude judicial review, which was a 'basic feature' of the Constitution. The court further said:

> Since the Constitution had conferred a limited amending power on the Parliament, the Parliament cannot under the exercise of that limited power enlarge that very power into an absolute power. Indeed, a limited amending power is one of the basic features of the Constitution and, therefore, the limitations on that power cannot be destroyed. In other words, Parliament cannot, under article 368, expand its amending power so as to acquire for itself the right to repeal or abrogate the Constitution or to destroy its basic and essential features. The donee of a limited power cannot by the exercise of that power convert the limited power into an unlimited one.

The court, however, did not show where in the Constitution, the power of amendment had been said to be a qualified or limited power except for the procedural requirements laid down in article 368. Be it as it may, the present state of the doctrine of 'basic features' is that so long as the decision in the *Kesavananda case* is not overturned by another full Bench of the Supreme Court, any amendment to the Constitution is liable to be interfered with by the Court on the ground of affecting one or other of the basic features of the Constitution.

In the *Kesavananda case,* Justice Sikri (para 302) had tried to tabulate the basic features of the Constitution as follows:

i. Supremacy of the Constitution
ii. Republican and democratic form of government
iii. Secular character of the Constitution
iv. Separation of powers
v. Federal character of the Constitution.

In the same case, Justice Hegde and Justice Mukherjee included the sovereignty and unity of India, the democratic character of our polity and individual freedom in the elements of the basic structure of the Constitution. They believed that Parliament had no power to revoke the mandate to build a Welfare State and an egalitarian society (para 682). Justice Khanna also said that Parliament could not change our democratic government into a dictatorship or hereditary monarchy nor would it be permissible to abolish the Lok Sabha and the Rajya Sabha. The secular character of the State could not, likewise, be done away with (para 1437).

In *Indira Nehru Gandhi Vs. Raj Narain* (AIR 1975 SC 2299, paras 55 and 213) Justice Chandrachud found the following to be the fundamental elements of the basic structure of the Constitution:

i. India as a sovereign democratic republic
ii. Equality of status and opportunity
iii. Secularism and the freedom of conscience
iv. Rule of law.

The same Judge in the *Minerva Mills case* added the 'amending powers of Parliament', 'Judicial review' and 'balance between the Fundamental Rights and the Directive Principles' to the list of elements basic to the Constitution.

The concept of basic structure was further developed by the Supreme Court and the position that the basic features cannot be altered even by constitutional amendments was further confirmed and more essential features of the basic structure were added in *Waman Rao case* (AIR 1981 SC 271), *Bhim Singhji case* (AIR 1981 SC 234), *S.P. Gupta vs. Union of India* (Transfer of Judges case), AIR 1982 SC 149), *Sampath Kumar's case* (AIR 1987 SC 663) and *Kihoto Hollohon v. Zachilhu* (AIR 1993 SC 412, (1992) ISCC 309); *L. Chandrakumar v. Union of India* (AIR 1997 SC 1125). In *P.V. Narasimha Rao v. State* (AIR 1998 SC 2120), Justice S.C. Agarwal held that "Parliamentary Democracy" is part of the basic structure of the Constitution.

In *Kihoto Hollohon v. Zachilhu,* free and fair elections and sovereign, democratic, republican structure were mentioned among the basic features. In *Subhas v. Union of India* (AIR 1991 SC 631) and *Shiv Kumar v. Union of India* (1992) 2 SCC 428) 'judicial review' was also mentioned as part of the list of basic features. 'Rule of Law' as a basic feature was reiterated in *Indira Sawhney v. Union of India* (1992) Supp (3) SCC 217.

In the *S.R. Bommai case* regarding the dismissal of BJP Governments in Madhya Pradesh, Himachal Pradesh and Rajasthan, Justice Jeevan Reddy and Justice Ramaswamy reiterated that federalism *inter alia* was a basic feature of the Constitution. Justice Ramaswamy held that a democratic form of Government, federal structure, unity and integrity of the nation, secularism, socialism, social justice and judicial review were among the basic features of the Constitution.

In some cases, there is a difference of opinion among the Judges as regards a particular element forming an element of the basic features. For example, Chief Justice Ray did not find it possible to hold the concept of free and fair elections as a basic feature whereas Justice Khanna, in the same case, found this principle to be an element of the fundamental features of the Constitution (*Indira Nehru Gandhi case,* paras 55 and 213). Justice Chandrachud did not subscribe to the view that the Preamble to the Constitution holds the key to its basic structure (para 665). Justice Beg, on the other hand, found that the Court can find the test (of constitutional validity) primarily in the Preamble to the Constitution. The Preamble, he believed, furnished the yardstick to be applied even to constitutional amendments (para 623).

It is thus evident that so far there has been no consensus in this regard among the Judges and no majority judgment is available laying down the features of the Constitution that may be considered 'basic'. The Court has not foreclosed the list of the basic features as suggested by different Judges in different cases. In the *Indira Nehru Gandhi* case, Justice Chandrachud observed that

> the theory of basic structure has to be considered in each individual case, not in the abstract, but in the context of the concrete problem." (Para 2465).

The Basic Features Doctrine of the Supreme Court, in addition to its vagueness and lack of clarity is open to more fundamental objections. Every word of the Constitution should be understood in its normal, natural meaning. In the *Kesvananda Bharti case* itself, the Supreme Court has said that unless otherwise indicated, every word is supposed to have been used in the Constitution in its normal or ordinary connotation and should be given the plain common sense meaning. Unfortunately while interpreting the Constitution and the laws, the Supreme Court does not always do that. The purpose of interpretation is to ascertain the intent of the framers from the words used. We must go by what the Constitution says and not by what judges say it says. We have to first try to read and understand the Constitution and then to critically evaluate what others, including judges, have to say about it. Unfortunately, too little attention is paid to the text of the Constitution and too much emphasis is laid on the case law and the past verdicts of the courts.

Constitution of a country is its foundational law and lays down the basic features of its polity. Every provision of the Constitution is the basic law of the land. Its provisions can hardly be so divided as to make some parts of the Constitution basic and others peripheral. All the three organs of the State—*i.e.* including the judiciary—are responsible to the people. Every act of the Executive, Legislature and the Judiciary has to be tested on the alter of the Constitution and the weal of the people for its validity and legitimacy. None of the three organs is outside the state and none above the people.

The Constitution of India does not contain any provision in regard to basic features. There is nothing to suggest that the Constitution-makers wanted any provisions of the Constitution to be absolutely unamendable. It was certainly not beyond the ingenuity of the founders to provide for it if they wanted it to be so. In fact, all the evidence is to the contrary. It was repeatedly declared in the Constituent Assembly and elsewhere by Nehru, Ambedkar and others that they did not wish to bind the succeeding generations, that, to use Nehru's words, "if you make anything rigid and permanent you stop a nation's growth, the growth of a living, vital, organic people".

If the sovereign people through their representatives cannot bring about desired change, who will? What the Supreme Court has done is to assume to itself a power of veto on all constitutional amendments. Instead of interpreting the amendment clause of the Constitution and declaring the law, the court, in effect, says that it will decide in each case whether to permit Parliament to amend the Constitution. In other words, the constituent power gets transferred from the elected representatives of the people to the judges of the Supreme Court. The Supreme Court is not above the Constitution and laws. It is also accountable to the ultimate sovereigns, the people of India. Just as the power to amend is said to be a limited power only to amend, the Supreme Court's own power to interpret and declare the law cannot be extended to making or rewriting the provisions of the Constitution. To paraphrase differently Supreme Court's own observations about Parliament's amending powers, one is tempted to say:

> Since "the Constitution had conferred a limited" power of judicial review and of interpreting the Constitution only for "doing complete justice" within its "jurisdiction", the Supreme Court cannot "under the exercise of that limited power enlarge that very power into an absolute power". Indeed, limited judicial review "is one of the basic features of our Constitution and, therefore, the limitations on that power cannot be destroyed". In other words, the Supreme Court, under article 32, 141 and 142 cannot expand its power of interpretation so as to acquire for itself the right to amend or prevent amendment to the Constitution on the ground of a self -invented 'basic features' doctrine and thereby in effect destroy the most basic feature of Indian polity, namely the primacy of the people and democracy as a Government of the people, by the people and for the people. It is the people and the Constitution framed by their representatives that have given certain limited powers to the Supreme Court as to other organs. "the donee of a limited power cannot by exercise of that power convert the limited power into an unlimited one".

Since the commencement of the Constitution in 1950 as many as 94 Constitutional Amendments (See Annexure) have been effected under article 368 alone. This has been done in exercise of the Parliament's constituent powers.

The first amendment was found necessary and enacted by the Provisional Parliament itself as early as in 1951, even before the first General Elections to the Lok Sabha and State Assemblies on the basis of universal adult suffrange could be held.

On an average, working out to more than one every seven months, the number of amendments would make our Constitution one of the most frequently amended constitutions in the world. But, that also speaks volumes about the flexibility, dynamism, spirit of accommodating change and tremendous survival potential of our Constitution. We can take legitimate pride in the fact that our Constitution has survived for sixty years while many others during this period floundered and got abrogated, superceded or replaced by military dictatorship or other undemocratic forces. Part of the credit may belong to the amending powers and procedures laid down by the founding fathers.

Besides, a large number of amendments to constitutional provisions were not amendments under Article 368. Certain provisions of the Constitution, *e.g.*, articles 2, 3 and 4 and 169 provide for amendments by ordinary legislation by simple majority in Parliament. Also, many provisions of the Constitution were so worded as to remain valid only until Parliament by law provided otherwise. Thus, in effect, Parliament could substantially modify the position under those constitutional provisions without a formal constitutional amendment being passed. All this would go to show that although a combination of 'rigid' and 'flexible' types, India's Constitution is in large parts more flexible and easily amendable than rigid or diffcult to amend. There has been considerable difference of opinion on whether the power to amend the Constitution has been misused or resorted to too frequently and without justifiable grounds.

Several areas emerged as the most crisis-prone in the scheme of our Constitution during the last six decades. Union-State relations, misuse of powers under article 356 by Governors and the Union Government, reorganisation of States, the relationship between fundamental rights and Directive Principles—from non-enforceability to some primacy and respect for directive principles—the property clause leading to several laws being invalidated by courts, Parliament going in for animated debates and finally ending with right to property being abolished from the category of fundamental rights, the legislature-executive-judiciary interface, privileges of Parliament versus rights of individuals and freedom of the press, appointment of judges—transfer of a decisive voice from the government to the judiciary, President-Prime Minister relationship, the long-drawn debate on decentralization of powers and setting up the Panchayats, Nagarpalikas etc., Election Law and Election Commission—leading to three-member Commission, official language—formula for the continuance of English, reservations for OBCs etc. While some of these matters were sought to be regulated by ordinary legislation or judicial intervention and some remained unresolved, there were others that necessitated constitutional amendments.

Of the 94 constitutional amendments[1] under article 368 effected so far, not all can be considered equally important or of substantial consequence. The more wide-ranging and covering a vast number of provisions were the seventh, the forty-second, the forty-fourth, the seventy-third and the seventy-fourth amendments. Some of the amendments can be divided under four broad heads:

(1) Minor, clarificatory or consequential amendments: For instance, the second amendment removed the upper population limit for a parliamentary constituency from article 81(1)(b); the fifth amendment enabled the President to prescribe a period for the State concerned to convey its views in respect of a Bill referred to it under article 34; the eleventh amendment omitted the unnecessary requirement of a joint sitting for electing the Vice-President and clarified that the election could not be questioned on the ground of there being any vacancy in the electoral college (articles 66 and 71); and the thirteenth amendment inserted a new article 371A to implement the agreement on the creation of the new State of Nagaland.

(2) Amendments to the property clause and restricting other

1. See Annexure.

fundamental rights or giving primacy to Directive Principles: The first amendment amended article 19(2) to place restrictions on the right to freedom of speech in the interests of friendly relations with foreign states, public order etc. To protect agrarian reform measures from being struck down by the courts on grounds of violating the fundamental rights of the landlords, the amendment added the new schedule 9 and the new article 31B. Article 31B provided that Acts and Regulations included in the Ninth Schedule shall not be void on grounds of inconsistency with or violation of any of the fundamental rights under the Constitution. It also clarified the right of the state to implement its scheme of nationalisation in public interest (articles 15, 19 & 31). Articles 85, 87, 174 and 176 were amended to simplify and rationalise convening and proroguing of sessions of Parliament and State legislatures and addresses by the President and Governors. Also, a few minor amendments were made in articles 341, 342, 372 and 376.

In the face of the Supreme Court decisions in regard to acquisition of property and the need for compensation, the fourth amendment sought to restate more precisely the state's power of compulsory acquisition or requisitioning of private property for public purpose and distinguish it from 'deprivation of property'. Also, it was clarified that state monopoly in a particular trade or business did not conflict with the fundamental freedom of trade and commerce (articles 31, 31A, and 305 and the Ninth Schedule).

The seventeenth amendment modified the definition of the term 'estate' in article 31A and included some more State Acts in the Ninth Schedule.

The fortieth amendment added 64 new entries to the Ninth Schedule and substituted article 297 by a new article vesting in the Union all lands, minerals and other things of value underlying the ocean.

The forty-second amendment enacted during the Emergency was thus far the most controversial, comprehensive and far-reaching amendment. It sought *inter alia* to spell out expressly the ideas of socialism, secularism and integrity of the nation in the Preamble, to add a chapter on fundamental duties of the citizens and to make the Directive Principles more comprehensive and give them precedence over fundamental rights. The most objectionable parts of the amendment were those that sought to tilt the balance in favour of the executive by reducing the role of the high courts in the judicial process. Also, the amendment tried to increase the powers of the Union Government and weaken the authority of the States thereby striking at the roots of the federal spirit of the Constitution.The powers of the Prime Minister and the Council of Ministers *vis-à-vis* the President were more clearly stated by laying down that the President had to act in accordance with the advice of the Council of Ministers. The supremacy of the Union Parliament was sought to be asserted particularly in the context of the constituent power in article 368, which could not be subject to any judicial review or other outside control (articles 31, 32A, 39, 39A, 43A, 48A, 51A, 55, 74, 81, 82, 83, 103, 131A, 139A, 144, 145, 150, 166, 170, 172, 192, 217, 225-228A, 257A, 311, 312, 323A, 323B, 330, 352, 353, 356-359, 366, 368).

The forty-fourth amendment sought to remove or correct the distortions brought about during the period of internal emergency. Also, it strengthened safeguards against the emergency provisions and made it impermissible for the executive to continue the Emergency beyond one month without parliamentary approval. Right to property had been the subject-matter of many of the constitutional amendments. The forty-fourth amendment took it away from the category of fundamental rights. The amendment put the right to life and liberty on a secure footing, provided safeguards against the misuse of the Emergency provisions, guaranteed to the media the right to report freely and without censorship proceedings in Parliament and state legislatures (articles 19, 22, 71, 74, 77, 83, 103, 105, 132, 134, 134A, 139A, 172, 192, 194,

217, 226, 227, 257A, 352, 356, 358, 359, 360, 361A, Ninth Schedule).

Several amendments placed fresh lists of statutes on the Ninth Schedule to make them immune to being questioned by courts of law on grounds of contravention of fundamental rights. The list of 13 Acts included in this schedule by the first amendment in 1951 has since grown to as many as 284 Acts. Of these, three entries were omitted by later amendments. The additions have been made by the fourth, seventeenth, twenty-ninth, fortieth, forty-seventh, sixty-sixth, seventy-sixth and seventy-eighth amendments.

(3) *Safeguarding the interests of the Scheduled Castes, Scheduled Tribes and Minorities:* The first, seventh, eighth, twenty-first, twenty-second, thirty-third, fifty-first, fifty-third, fifty-seventh, sixty-second, sixty-fifth, seventy-sixth, seventy-seventh, seventy-ninth, eithty-first, eighty-second and eighty-third amendments all sought to provide better safeguards for the rights and interests of the Scheduled Castes, Scheduled Tribes, Backward Classes and Minorities. Some of these amendments were only to provide for reservations or extend the ten-year period thereof again and again.

(4) *Admission of new territories into the Union:* The tenth, twelfth and the fourteenth amendments were necessitated in order to admit into the Indian Union the erstwhile Protuguese and French possessions in India.

Besides the above categories, several amendments became necessary to implement the schemes of states reorganisation, to put all the states on the same footing and then on linguistic lines (*e.g.*, the seventh amendment) etc. and to honour the agreements with the people in the North-East—the Mizos, the Nagas and others. Two amendments pertained to the admission of the State of Sikkim into the Indian Union.

The fifty-second amendment passed in 1985 outlawed defections by members of Parliament and state legislatures.

The sixty-first amendment reduced the voting age from 21 to 18 years by amending article 326. The most revolutionary and significant constitutional amendments, however, have been the seventy-third and seventy-fourth amendments which have sought to bring power to the people at the grassroots in a more meaningful way by giving some continuity, stability and constitutional status to local self-government institutions—Panchayats and Nagar Palikas.

Of the most recent amendments passed during 2000-2009, the eightieth and the eighty-first amendment acts passed by the two Houses of Parliament were assented to by the President on 9 June 2000. The eightieth amendment amends provisions (articles 269-272) regarding taxes levied and collected by the Union and assigned to or shared with the States. The eighty-first amendment adds a new clause to article 16 to provide for considering unfilled reserved vacancies as a separate class of vacancies not to be included under the present ceiling of fifty percent reservation of vacancies of the year. The eighty-second amendment adds a proviso to article 335 to clarify that it would be in order to provide for reducing the standards of evaluation and requirment of minimum marks for filling by promotion vacancies reserved for Scheduled Castes and Scheduled Tribes in the services of the Union and the States. The eighty-third amendment laid down in clause (3A) added to article 243M that the reservation of seats for Schduled Castes provided under article 243D shall not apply to Arunachal Pradesh.

The Eighty-fourth Amendment amends articles 55, 81, 82, 170, 330 and 332 to provide (a) that reference to 'population of the State' in articles concerning elections to the office of the President and to Lok Sabbha shall continue to mean population as ascertained by the 1971 census until the census after 2026, (b) that until 2026 the allocation of seats in Lok Sabha to the States shall continue to be on the basis of 1971 census but the constituencies within each State may be readjusted on the basis of 1991 census, and (c) that reservation of seats in the Lok Sabha and State Assemblies for SC/ST shall be on the basis of the 1991 census until after 2026.

The Eighty-fifth Amendment amends article 16 to allow provision for reservation in matters of promotion with consequential seniority in services under the State for SC/ST employees.

The Eighty-sixth Amendment (2002) inserts a new article 21A to provide for a fundamental right to education to all children of 6 to 14 years. Also, it substitutes article 45 in the Directive Principles by a new article providing for early child care and education to children below 6 years. By amending article 51A, a new fundamental duty is sought to be added for parents or guardians providing educational opportunities to children between the age of 6 and 14 years.

The Eighty-seventh Amendment (2003) substitutes the figure 2001 for the figure 1991 in the provisos to articles 81, 82, 170 and 330 thereby laying down that the population figures to be taken into account for purposes of readjusting constituencies within each State and for reservation of seats in the Lok Sabha and State Assemblies for SC/ST shall be on the basis of 2001 census.

The Eighty-eighth Amendment (2004) adds new article 268A to provide for levy of taxes on services to be collected and appropriated by the Government of India and the States. It also inserts new entry "92C. Taxes on Services" to the Union List, Seventh Schedule.

The Eighty-ninth Amendment (2003) amends article 338 and adds a new article 338A to provide for two separate Commissions for Scheduled Castes and Scheduled Tribes.

The Ninetieth Amendment (2003) amends article 332 to provide for maintaining the erstwhile representation of the Scheduled Tribes and non-Scheduled Tribes in Assam constituencies included in Bodoland Territorial Areas District.

The Ninety-first Amendment (2003) amends articles 75

and 164, and Schedule 10. It inserts a new article 361B. The amendment places a limit on the number of Ministers. They cannot be more than 15% of the House of the People at the Union level and the concerned Vidhan Sabha at the level of States. Also, it takes away the protection from defectors on grounds of splits and makes defectors disqualified for Membership and ineligible for Ministership or other remunerative political post till re-election.

The Ninety-second Amendment (2004) adds to the Eighth Schedule four more languages *viz.* Bodo, Dogri, Santhali and Maithili to the pre-existing 18.

The Constitution (Ninety-third Amendment) Act, 2005 assented to by the President on 20 January 2006 adds to article 15 the new clause (5) which empowers Parliament to make special provisions for socially and educationally backward classes and for Scheduled Castes and Scheduled Tribes in regard to admission to educational institutions including private aided or unaided institutions other than minority institutions.

The Constitution (Ninety-fourth Amendment) Act, 2006, assented to by the President on 12 June 2006 amends proviso to article 164(1) to substitute the words "Chhattisgarh, Jharkhand" in place of the word "Bihar" since no "Scheduled Areas" were now left in Bihar after the reorganisation in 2000.

An important reason for the frequency of amendments has been the unusually large size of our Constitution. Many matters which are usually regulated by ordinary legislation were included in the text of the Constitution itself under historical constraints or on other grounds. Any modifications therein could, therefore, be done only by constitutional amendments.

While some of the amendments have definitely improved the content and quality of the constitutional document in the context of the changed and changing societal, economic or political needs and some others were either inevitable or consequential for implementation of policy decisions, there were quite a few which were avoidable, unnecessary or motivated by merely political and partisan interest considerations of the ruling majority party. On principle, the Constitution must never be subject to easy amendments by temporary party majorities in legislatures.

The large number of amendments were easily enacted mainly because for the most part of the last 60 years, there was a single dominant party with a large majority. Now, with the era of hung houses and multiparty coalition governments, it may not be easy for various parties to agree on any substantial constitutional amendments and, therefore, it may be extremely unlikely that the erstwhile spate of amendments would continue. The recent Constitution Amendments passed were all of a relatively non-controversial nature in regard to which no political party could afford to disagree.

That there is a growing disenchantment with constitutionalism itself, that norms of civil society are being eroded every day, that the system as a whole seems to be becoming dysfunctional or that basic constitutional reforms and systemic changes seem to be becoming a categorical imperative are all different matters and may call for remedies other than constitutional amendments.[1]

1. Also see under 'Salient Features of the Constitution'.

22

PANCHAYATI RAJ

PART IX AND IX A, ARTICLES 243–243ZG

The Constitution (73rd Amendment) Act, 1992 and the Constitution (74th Amendment) Act, 1992 have added new Parts IX and IX A to the Constitution. Under these two parts, we have as many as 34 new articles—243 to 243ZG—and two new schedules *viz.* schedules 11 and 12. The 73rd Amendment gives constitutional recognition to the Panchayats and the 74th Amendment to the Municipalities. Thus, to the Union and the States, a third tier of governmental instrumentalities has been added.

There is nothing entirely new about the institutions of Panchayats and Municipalities. Both these have existed for long. There were local self-government and Panchayati Raj laws in many parts of India. But, unfortunately these institutions were not able to function satisfactorily for any length of time. Often, they stood superceded. Despite the Gandhian approach of treating the villages as units of polity and Gandhiji's love for Panchayati Raj institutions, Dr. Ambedkar in the Constituent Assembly did not favour them and even said some very harsh things like these being dens of corruption, localism, backwardness etc. Finally, as a compromise or a concession to Gandhi's views, article 40 was included under the non-enforcable Part IV on the Directive Principles of State Policy. It said that the state shall take steps to organise Village Panchayats and endow them with necessary authority "to function as units of self-government".

Hardly any attention was paid to article 40 at the level of Union Parliament until Prime Minister Rajiv Gandhi took serious interest and initiative to bring forward a constitutional amendment. It was, however opposed on grounds of its being an effort to reach the Panchayats directly, bypassing the States. The amended amendment became a reality during Narasimha Rao's time.

The seventy-third and seventy-fourth constitutional amendments made some fundamental changes in our political structure and in the status of local institutions. These institutions acquired constitutional protection. The two amendments provided for the State legislatures making their own laws under the constitutional provisions for establishing Panchayats, Municipalities, etc. and conferring on them such powers and authority as may be necessary to enable them to function as institutions of self-government. In every State, a three-tier system was envisaged. Panchayats were to be established at the Village and district levels and at the intermediate level. States which had a population of less than two million, did not need to have the intermediate level Panchayats.

The important thing was that now Panchayats had to be elected directly by the people in the same manner as members of the popular houses at the Union and State levels were elected *i.e.* through territorial constituencies and on the principle of 'one man one vote'. For a Village Panchayat, the electorate would be the *Gram Sabha* which would consist of those registred in the electoral rolls. These Panchayats cannot remain superceded for long; fresh elections would have to be held within six months of the dissolution of a Panchayat. Secondly, in all panchayats, seats would be reserved for women, Scheduled Castes and Scheduled Tribes. There shall be a fixed five year term for all Panchayats. They shall have their own budget, power of taxation and list of items in their jurisdiction. In their respective areas, the Panchayats shall be able to formulate their own development plans and implement them. Every State shall have a State Election Commissioner for conducting Panchayat elections and every five years a State Finance Commission shall be constituted to take stock of the economic condition of the Panchayats.

Similarly, in the 74th Amendment, there were provisions for the setting up of Nagar Palikas and Nagar Panchayats. In the matter of reservations, elections, power of taxation, formulation and implementation of development projects, constitution of a Finance Commission, fixed term, etc., the provisions were very similar to those in the 73rd Amendment in respect of Panchayats.

Under the distribution of legislative powers between the Union and the States, local government in both rural and urban areas was in the exclusive State List. As it is, all the States—some reluctantly—have passed legislation as required under the new constitutional provisions. Elections to local bodies were held in almost all the States. Also, the 73rd and 74th Amendments do not apply to the States of Meghalaya, Mizoram, Nagaland and Jammu and Kashmir, the Union Territory of Delhi, hill areas in Manipur and Darjeeling in W. Bengal. Also, these do not apply unless extended to Scheduled Areas and Tribal Areas under article 244. The Constitution (Eighty-third Amendment) of the year 2000 has added a clause to article 243M to provide that reservation of seats for the Schduled Castes under article 243D shall not apply to the State of Arunachal Pradesh.

It was hoped that the new Panchayats and Municipalities would begin a new era of real representative and participatory democracy with nearly three and a half million elected representatives—one-third of them women (increased to fifty percent in some States)—involved in the business of governance all over India thereby bringing power to the people where it belonged. As things stood, matters causing some concern were:

(i) The M.P. Local Area Development Scheme (MPLADS) which places at the disposal of every member of Union Paliament a sum of Rupees two crores every year for being spent in his/her area on his/her recommendation on items mentioned in the guide list. There are similar schemes placing funds at the disposal of MLAs at the level of States. All the items on which these large funds can be spent at the discretion of MPs and MLAs are covered by the eleventh and twelfth schedules of the Constitution listing schemes to be entrusted to the Panchayats, Municipalities etc. There is constant clamour and pressure for increasing the amounts under the LADS for M.P.s, MLAs and MLCs.

    The Local Area Development Schemes and the like are tantamount to legislators' foray into the area of executive functions. Secondly, this may seem to be an affront to and a violation of the federal scheme as also of the basic spirit of Panchayati Raj institutions.

(ii) Much can be said for and against the *ex-officio* membership of local Lok Sabha members and M.L.A.s on the district and intermediate level panchayats.

(iii) The ground realities indicate that, for their own reasons, those elected to Parliament and State Legislatures - the M.P.s, M.L.A.s and M.L.C.s - have not taken very kindly to the emerging leadership at the grassroots inasmuch as it may constitute a challenge to their monopoly of political power in the area and develop into new competitive power centres.

(iv) The details of functioning of the Local Government institutions are largely left to the initiative of the State Governments and are to be settled by them. The States have passed vastly varied laws according to their own perception of what and how much can be devolved on the local authorities. While the States naturally want the Union to transfer more of effective legislative, executive and financial powers in wider areas to them, the question is to what extent they would be themselves willing to decentralise further down and share effective power with local self-government institutions. In fact, from the perspective of Chief Ministers and States leadership, it is being argued that the power and jurisdiction of the States are being seriously eroded on the one hand by the Union extending its role and on the other by the local institutions taking over many of its functions and powers. But, so far as the 73rd and 74th Constitution Amendments are concerned, these do not themselves confer any powers as such on Panchayats and Municipalities.

23

MISCELLANEOUS, TEMPORARY AND SPECIAL PROVISIONS

PART XVI, XIX, XXI, XXII, ARTICLES 330–342, 361 367, 369–392, 393-395

SPECIAL PROVISIONS FOR CERTAIN CLASSES

In keeping with its objective of securing social and economic justice to all and establishing economic democracy, the Constitution makes certain provisions to help the weaker sections of the society to come up to the level of the general body of citizens. Thus, the Scheduled Castes and Scheduled Tribes were provided special protection and seats in legislatures and positions in services were reserved for them.

The Constitution does not define the Scheduled Castes or the Scheduled Tribes. These are to be identified by notification by the President in consultation with the Governor of a State in relation to that State. The President has made several orders specifying the Scheduled Castes and Scheduled Tribes in different States. These orders have also been amended by Acts of Parliament under powers given under articles 341–342.

Articles 330–334 as amended from time to time provide for reservation of seats in the Lok Sabha and Legislative Assemblies of States for the Scheduled Castes and Scheduled Tribes and for representation of the Anglo-Indian community for a period of 60 years from the commencement of the Constitution. The number of reserved seats is to be based on the proportion of Scheduled Castes or Scheduled Tribes in the population as per 2001 census figures. Not more than two members of the Anglo-Indian community may be nominated to Lok Sabha and one member to a State Assembly by the President or the Governor, as the case may be, if it is found that that community is not adequately represented in the House.

The Nineteenth Amendment (203) amended article 332 to provide for maintaining the erstwhile representation of the Scheduled Tribes and non-Scheduled Tribes in Assam constituencies included in Bodoland Territorial Areas District.

While there are reserved constituencies, the electorate is the general public, *i.e.* all the voters in the constituency without any distinction of community or caste, etc. There are to be no separate electorates. The reservation of seats was initially intended for a short period of 10 years during which the Scheduled Castes and Scheduled Tribes were expected to forge ahead and get to be at par with the rest of the population. However, every time the period of reservation comes to an end, the Government in its wisdom decides to extend it further by amending the relevant provision of the Constitution (article 334). The latest revision of the provision was made by the 79th Amendment which extended the period to "sixty years", *i.e.* until the year 2010.

Under article 335, the claims of the Scheduled Castes and Tribes are to be taken into consideration while making appointments to public services without sacrificing the efficiency of administration.[1] The Constitution 82nd Amendment Act enacted in September 2000 has, however added a proviso to article 335 to clarify that it would be in order to provide for reducing the standards of evaluation

1. See *Indra Sawhney v. Union of India,* (1992) Supp (3) SCC 217.

and requirement of minimum marks for filling by promotion vacancies reserved for Scheduled Castes and Scheduled Tribes in the services of the Union and the States.

Article 338 and 338A provide for the setting up of two separate national commissions for Scheduled Castes and Scheduled Tribes.

Article 340 empowers the President to appoint a Backward Classes Commission to investigate the conditions of the "socially and educationally backward classes" and to recommend removal of their difficulties and improvement in their conditions. The Supreme Court had held that social backwardness may be due to various reasons including caste, but a classification based solely on caste would not be legal.[1] In the *Mandal case*, the Supreme Court upheld 27 per cent reservation in services for the backward classes, directed the exclusion of the advanced sections or the creamy layer among the backwards from the reservation quota and stressed that the total reservations should not exceed 50 per cent.[2]

Articles 341 and 342 provide for the President in consultation with the State Governor concerned specifying the Scheduled Castes and Scheduled Tribes in respect of each State by publi notification. The notifications cannot be varied except by Parliament by law.

MISCELLANEOUS PROVISIONS

Article 361 seeks to protect the head of the Union (the President of India) and the heads of States (the Governors) from personal answerability before courts of law for any action in discharge of their duties, institution of any criminal proceedings while in office, issuance of any process for arrest from any court and institution of any civil proceedings

---

1. *Janki Prasad v. State of J&K*, AIR 1973 SC 930.
2. *Indra Sawhney v. Union of India*, (1992) Supp (3) SCC 217.

claiming a relief, without giving at least two months notice in writing. The purpose behind the article is to maintain the high dignity and prestige of the Head of the Union or Heads of the States who represent the honour of the Union and of the States. They are the guardians of the Constitution and symbols of authority.

The remedy for wrongdoing at the level of the President is removal from office by a process of impeachment by Parliament under article 61. The Governors of States hold office during the pleasure of the President.

Article 361A was inserted by the 44th Amendment to give protection to publication of proceedings of Parliament and State Legislatures. Proceedings of Legislatures are privileged and cannot be published without the permission of the House concerned. Article 361A says that no person shall be liable to any proceedings—civil or criminal—in any court in respect of the publication in good faith in a newspaper of a substantially true report of any legislative proceeding other than that of a secret sitting. The protection extends to radio broadcasts but does not cover any other publication, *e.g.* in the form of a book, brochure etc.

Article 361B inserted by the 91st Constitution Amendment Act, 2003 makes defectors disqualified from membership and ineligible to be Ministers or to hold any remunerative political post without re-election.

Article 363 bars interference by courts in disputes arising out of treaties, agreements, etc. entered into between the Government of India or its predecessor with the rulers of the princely States.

Article 363A gives constitutional recognition to the abolition of the privileges and privy purses of the princes.

Article 364 provides that the President may by notification exclude major ports and aerodromes from the application of any law.

Article 365 lays down that failure to comply with the directions of the Union may be enough justification for the

President to hold that the Government of the State cannot be carried on in accordance with the Constitution, thereby inviting imposition of President's rule under article 356. (See under the chapter on 'Emergency Provisions' also).

Article 366 is the definition clause and explains the meaning of a number of terms used in the Constitution.

Article 367 is the interpretation clause and says that generally the General Clauses Act shall apply to the interpretation of the provisions of the Constitution, reference to Acts or laws shall cover ordinances issued by the President or the Governor of the State concerned, "foreign state" in the Constitution means any State other than India but the President may by order declare any State not to be a foreign State for particular purposes.

TEMPORARY, TRANSITIONAL AND SPECIAL PROVISIONS

Some of the temporary and transitional provisions were for a fixed period which has already expired. For example, Parliament's power to make laws for matters in the State List under article 369 was for a period of five years only. Similarly, the power of the President in cases of Preventive Detention under article 373 was only for a year.

The most important and politically perhaps the most controversial have been the "temporary provisions with respect to the State of Jammu & Kashmir" in article 370. Under this article, the power of Parliament to make laws for the State of Jammu and Kashmir shall be limited to matters specified in the Instrument of Accession and may extend to any others only with the concurrence of the State.

Articles 371 to 371I contain special provisions in respect of the States of Nagaland, Assam, Manipur, Andhra Pradesh, Sikkim, Mizoram, Arunachal Pradesh and Goa. In each case, the idea is to satisfy the regional, tribal or other susceptibilities and protect the interests of the local people.

Thus, for instance, Acts of Parliament affecting the religious or social practices, customary laws, ownership of land, etc. shall not apply to Nagaland, and the Governor of Nagaland shall have certain special responsibilities.

Article 372 provides for the continuance in force of the existing laws and article 372A empowers the President to adopt the pre Constitution laws to the provisions of the Constitution. Articles 374 to 378A contain temporary provisions in respect of judges of the federal court and High Courts, pending proceedings, Comptroller and Auditor-General and Public Service Commissions before the Constitution, duration of the Andhra Legislative Assembly (inserted by the Seventh Amendment in 1956), etc. Articles 379 to 391 were repealed by the Seventh Amendment in 1956.

Article 392 empowers the President to remove any difficulties in relation to the transition from the Government of India Act 1935 to the provisions of the Constitution and the commencement of the Constitution.

Articles 393-394 provide the short title and the date of commencement of the Constitution. The short title is given as the *Constitution of India.* While some of the articles (5-9, 60, 324, 366, 367, 379, 380, 388, 391-393) came into force immediately (on 26 November 1949), remaining provisions came into force on 26 January 1950 that being the date of commencement of the Constitution.

Article 395 provides for the repeal of the Indian Independence Act, 1947 and the Government of India Act, 1935 etc.

24

WORKING OF THE CONSTITUTION

Need for the Review

The framing and adoption of an acceptable Constitution and political system for a country of India's past, size and nature was no easy task. Our founding fathers gave us an excellent Constitution which has stood the test of time. It envisaged a cohesive and vibrant modern polity with emphasis on democracy, Charter of Fundamental Rights, egalitarianism, secularism and rule of law. With a view to ushering in a socialistic pattern of society, emphasis was laid on planned development. Under successive five year plans, efforts were made to ameliorate the lot of the poor and the downtrodden, build a scientific and technological infrastructure, revolutionise agriculture, diversify industry and raise industrial capacity and output.

There were scores of achievements—integration of some 600 odd states, resettlement of refugees, abolition of zamindari and other land reforms, liberation of Portuguese and French possessions in India, accession of the States of Hyderabad and Jammu and Kashmir, withstanding of several aggressions from our two neighbours, development of a meaningful foreign policy with the cardinal principles of non-alignment and peaceful co-existence (with over a hundred nations at one time accepting India's philosophy and leadership), conducting of fifteen general elections in the largest democracy on earth and peaceful transfer of power more than once from one party to another party or alliance, surviving many pressures, stresses and strains inflicted on our body politic by malevolent forces, both internal and external.

Without going into the details, it can be safely asserted that on the political plane, by far our greatest achievements have been (i) to bring about and maintain the unity and integrity of the nation and the secular character of the polity, and (ii) preserve the system of representative parliamentary democracy, ensuring the freedom and dignity of the individual. When we see all around us, these achievements appear still greater since there are very few nations in the world where really functioning democracy and freedom have survived. Not only are we a functioning democracy, we are also the largest on earth with an electorate of over 700 million people and some 3.2 million elected rulers – from Panchayats to Parliament. It is a fact that—some temporary aberrations notwithstanding—whatever problems we faced, we have solved or sought to solve them within the existing system.

But there is a negative side also. The present is not very exhilarating, particularly when we think of the decline of values in all spheres and all professions, rampant corruption, terrorist activities, the use of money and muscle power in elections, "the politicization of criminals" and "criminalisation of politics", the goings on in some legislatures and the many fissiparous and divisive tendencies like casteism and communalism raising their ugly heads here and there, now and then. The noble aims and objectives enshrined in the Preamble have not been achieved. Instead of being based on some self-sacrifice and motivated by spirit of public service, politics has become a lucrative profession for sharing spoils of office. We have not been able to solve the basic problems of poverty, population, illiteracy, drinking water and development generally.

In any representative democracy, as Dr. Ambedkar had

said, the root concerns are two, *viz.* stability and responsibility. The government that the system throws up should enjoy the strength and stability necessary for the security, development and welfare of the people and those called upon to govern should remain responsible to the people and their representatives.

Our founding fathers had the background of their sad experiences of the arbitrary colonial rule which was neither representative of the people nor responsive to their urges, aspirations and needs. It was not responsible or accountable to any representative body of the people in India. It was natural for the founding fathers to prize 'responsibility' of the executive and accountability of the administration above everything else. They therefore adopted the parliamentary system with its concept of ministerial responsibility. In the Presidential system of Government of the U.S. type, the Executive is known to be more stable inasmuch as the President as the Chief Executive and head of the State is elected for a four year period and cannot be removed except by impeachment. Though not responsible to either House of the U.S. Congress, the Executive in the United States is directly responsible to the people once in four years.

The French have tried to combine different models and establish what may be a parliamentary system of ministerial responsibility with a Presidential system of irremovable Chief Executive superimposed. While the Ministers with the Prime Minister at the head are responsible to the National Assembly, the President is elected by the people for a seven year period and in order to win, he must secure more than 50 per cent votes.

The latest developments in India affecting the economy of the nation, however further underline the need for greater responsibility and accountability of the political Executive and the administrators to the people through the representative institutions. On the other hand, the spectacle of unethically engineered or defection manipulated majorities or of several successive hung Parliaments and State Legislatures and minority Governments and frequent General Elections naturally cause grave concern for stability.

It is obvious that we in India would not like to dilute the element of responsibility. The choice, therefore, is to find ways and means of ensuring greater stability within the existing parliamentary system. It has also to be remembered that what is most important is the stability of the polity, of the democratic system and society and not the stability of the government of the day. All seem agreed that the country can ill afford frequent general elections which, apart from other implications, cost collosal amounts of money. But, in a democracy, stability of the Government may not be the highest virtue.

On 26 January 2010, the Constitution and the Republic of India complete 60 years of their life. In an age when events move and developments take place at the speed of a tropical cyclone, this was not a short period in the life of a nation to take stock of our achievements and failures and attempt a self-appraisal *of the working* of our Constitution and the democratic institutions established thereunder.

Our Constitution is a living, dynamic process, always evolving, constantly in the making through amendments, judicial interpretations, and its actual working. During 1950-2009 it has been amended 94 times (See Annexxure). Wide-ranging amendments followed the Swaran Singh Committee appointed by the Congress to review the Constitution. There have been numerous other amendments which have changed the Constitution without being technically constitutional amendments. Some of the Supreme Court judgements have brought about fundamental changes. In the process, there have been modifications, distortions and reversals of the intention of the framers of the Constitution.

In this scenario, one had to consider whether there was anything wrong in having a look back at our experience of working the Constitution to find out if any of the problems had their source in systemic constraints or in faulty working or improper interpretation of constitutional provisions and if any remedial changes were called for. A case for review was not necessarily a case for constitutional amendments or systemic changes or for altering the basic features of the Constitution.

We had to consider what changes—legal, administrative, or other—were imperative to solve our main national problems. We had to ensure our nation's socio-economic development and quality of life for all citizens, more particularly the deprived sections of society. Areas requiring immediate attention and separate in-depth analysis were those of Union-State relations (decentralization of powers including financial powers to the State and down to the grassroots levels), corruption (ensuring greater probity, integrity and transparency in all walks of life), reforming the political party system and the electoral processes, providing reasonable stability to society and the system without altering the parliamentary system or eroding responsibility and accountability of the government to the people, making the governance clean, efficient, less costly and citizen-friendly.

Various concrete suggestions emerged and were stressed in the earlier editions of this book[1]. Not all of them may be compatible with each other or be fully acceptable. Also, they may not call for any constitutional amendments as such. But, all these may be useful as stimulants to our thinking on constitutional matters and may deserve to be considered. Some of these suggestions may be summed up and recalled here:

---

1. These have been stressed repeatedly during the last 15-20 years. Some of them have been picked up for implementation half-heartedly but almost all of them had found acceptance from the National Constitution Commission (NCRWC).

1. The Lok Sabha or the State Vidhan Sabha—particularly when it is a hung house with no leader commanding clear majority support—should be called upon by the President/Governor to elect its Leader. The person so elected may be appointed Prime Minister or the Chief Minister as the case may be. This will keep the President/Governor above unsavoury controversies.
2. Also, we could provide for a constructive vote of no-confidence in the Council of Ministers. This would make it essential for the House to select a successor simultaneously with the throwing out of the incumbent Prime Minister/Chief Minister.
3. There may be a trend towards developing a system of two major federal parties or alliances. It may be possible for several broadly like minded parties to come together on the basis of a common minimum programme or a national agenda and form a coalition government, with another similar coalition forming the opposition. The emergence of the National Democratic Alliance Government after the thirteenth general elections in 1999 and the subsequent two U.P.A. Governments were pointers in that direction. But, it should not preclude any party on its own occupying in future a predominant position on the basis of popular support to its policies and programmes. The ideal would be a situation of one national party in government and another in opposition.
4. Political parties participating in the democratic processes of a nation's governance must themselves be democratic in their internal organisation. They need to be regulated by law. Party membership must be open to all citizens without any distinction, party elections must be regular, free and fair and sources of party funds must be made public and party accounts must be duly audited and open to public scrutiny.
5. All candidates for elections to houses of Parliament or State Legislatures must be obliged *by law* to make verifiable public declarations of their movable and immovable assets. Those failing to do so or found to have made false

declarations should stand disqualified from being candidates or continuing as members.

Some of the other suggestions offered were:

(a) a three or four tier system of governance with limited direct elections, a strong Union and strong units; the Gandhian bottom up instead of the present top down approach; something like the subsidiarity principle in the European Union and in German polity where maximum power belongs to the grassroot level institutions and only what cannot be handled at the lower level is entrusted to the next higher level;
(b) reforming the electoral system to make it less expensive, more representative and free from money and muscle power;
(c) placing a strict ceiling on the number of ministers and equivalent posts both at the Union and State levels;
(d) disqualifying all defectors from holding any public office;
(e) downsizing the bureaucracy drastically, debureaucratization of development planning and providing a mechanism for compulsory consensus building among people and parties on some basic issues of national concern;
(g) placing a strict ceiling on the borrowing powers of the government and making prior legislative approval necessary;
(h) transferring right to work and to education to the fundamental rights chapter; and
(i) finally, making the Government and the administration clean, corruption free and citizen-friendly through whatever legal, administrative, judicial or other reforms found necessary.

Most of the desirable reforms can be brought about without any amendment in the provisions of the Constitution. A great deal can be done by establishing healthy conventions, suitably reinterpreting the existing provisions of the Constitution, and where necessary bringing about reforms through ordinary legislation. The most important areas of reform in the electoral law and processes and in political parties, for example, need no constitutional changes. If there is political will legislation can be passed to do the needful.

25

NATIONAL COMMISSION TO REVIEW THE WORKING OF THE CONSTITUTION (2000-2002)
AN EVALUATION

The high-level National Commission to Review the Working of the Constitution (also referred to as the Constitution Commission or NCRWC) was appointed by the President on 23 February 2000. Completion of fifty years of the working of the Constitution was considered an appropriate occasion to take stock of the situation, of its successes and failures. The Commission submitted its Report on 31 March 2002.

As the Commission said, its appointment was preceded by "a persistent demand in the civil society" that "the working of the Constitution be subjected to a comprehensive review." The ball was set rolling by two articles in *Times of India* in December 1990 and June 1991 by the present writer *inter alia* suggesting the appointment of a Constitution Commission. A national committee, a seminar jointly organised by 15 All India organisations and an India International Centre project on the Working of the Constitution in 1992-1993, directed by the present writer, also recommended setting up of a Review Commission.

As its name indicated, the brief of NCRWC was to review the working of the Constitution and not to rewrite or review the provisions of the Constitution. A great deal of misunderstanding was caused simply by the Commission being wrongly called by the media "Constitution Review

Commission". The Commission's terms of reference excluded any tinkering with the parliamentary system or the basic structure of the Constitution.

To assess whether the objectives of the great founding fathers, as enshrined in the Constitution, had been fulfilled during the half century (1950-2000), the Commission was expected to act independently and objectively, without fear or favour and in the spirit of serving the best interests of the country and thereby helping the Government and Parliament to consider desirable reforms. It was necessary to examine dispassionately the working of the chief organs of the state—the Legislature, the Executive and the Judiciary. The composition of the 11-member Commission, however, was heavily weighted in favour of the judiciary with as many as four retired judges and four advocates. The sitting and a retired Attorney-General were also members. A journalist, a former Lok Sabha Speaker and sitting M.P., two retired I.A.S. officers—one of them also a former ambassador and the other a former M.P.—and the former Secretary-General of Lok Sabha who was also an advocate and a known constitutional expert completed the picture.

The task of drafting the report was entrusted to the Drafting and Editorial Committee which submitted the full two-volume report on 15 February 2002. The major portion of the final report of the Commission remained the same as it was in the Draft Report. A number of very significant suggestions were approved unanimously and important recommendations made.

Fundamental Rights

Some of the positive and welcome recommendations in regard to Fundamental Rights were for the inclusion of (i) the freedom of the press and other media, (ii) defence of justification by truth in contempt of court cases, (ii) right to rural wage employment for a minimum of 80 days in a year, (iv) right to reasonably speedy and effective justice, (v) right to information, (vi) right to free and compulsory education to all children upto the age of 14 years, and (vii) right to safe drinking water, prevention of pollution, conservation of ecology and sustainable development.

Directive Principles

Under Directive Principles, the Commission commended (i) a strategic plan of action for creating large employment opportunities, (ii) setting up of a National Education Commission every five years, (iii) population control through education and small family norms, (iv) inter-faith and inter-religious harmony and social solidarity (v) machinery for periodical review of the implementation of Directive Principles both by the Union and the States.

Fundamental Duties

The Commission endorsed the recommendations of the Justice Verma Committee to create greater awareness of the constitutional provisions of fundamental duties amongst the citizens through education and media. It suggested the addition of duty to vote at elections, actively participate in the democratic process of governance and pay taxes as fundamental duties of citizens. Also, (i) fostering a spirit of family values and responsible parenthood and (ii) duty of industrial organisations to provide education to children of their employees, were recommended for addition in fundamental duties part of the Constitution.

Judiciary

In regard to the judiciary, initially the Commission took into account the consultation paper, the responses thereto and the views of eminent persons like the former President of India Shri R. Venkataraman and two former Chief Justices of India. According to (Late) Justice Venkataramaiah, in the interpretation placed by the majority of judges on article 124 in the *Second Judges Case*, the text of the Constitution seemed to have been departed from. It neutralised the position of the President and rendered article 74 which required the President to act on the aid and advice of the Council of Ministers irrelevant. The construction made the Supreme Court and the High Courts totally undemocratic. While in a parliamentary democracy the President might be a mere constitutional head when the power was exercised by him on the advice of the Council of Ministers, he could not be asked to play the same limited role where the Chief Justice of India who was not an elected representative advised him. One could not ignore that that could "lead on a future occasion to tyranny in another unexpected place". The meaning given by the Supreme Court to article 124 appeared to be beyond the scope of mere interpretation and virtually amounted to re-writing the constitutional provision.

Justice Verma who had delivered the majority judgement in the *Second Judges Case* himself seemed to have revised his opinion inasmuch he stressed that the intent of the Constitution was not to accord primacy to either the judiciary or the executive as the responsibility of both was to find the most suitable person for appointment and this could best be done by a National Judicial Commission, representing all wings and headed by the Vice-President/ Prime Minister/Chief Justice of India.

The Judiciary, the Legislature and the Executive are all creatures of the Constitution. Their powers and functions are as defined and delimited by the Constitution. It is the Constitution which is supreme and the Constitution is what it is and not what the Supreme Court says or the Parliament wishes it to be. There should not be any attempt to alter the Constitution by an interpretative process by any of the limbs of the state. Power to interpret or declare the law does not include any power to change or make the law. It is a *fortiori* when a question arises as to in which of the limbs, the Constitution has vested the power of appointment of judges. When it involves questions as to whether the power is in the

Judiciary or Legislature or Executive, the approach has to be as observed by the Supreme Court *In Re Special Reference* 1 *of* 1964 [1965(1) SCR 413], Legislators, Ministers and Judges all take oath of allegiance to the Constitution for it is by the relevant provisions of the Constitution that they derive their authority and jurisdiction and it is to the provisions of the Constitution that they owe allegiance.

Perhaps, there is no country in the world whose Constitution provides for vesting the power of appointment of judges of superior courts exclusively in the judiciary itself. In the Commission (NCRWC) there was a general consensus on the mechanism of the National Judicial Commission to ensure that the power of appointment of judges was not exercised arbitrarily either by the executive or the judiciary. The Commission categorically decided in favour of a National Judicial Commission consisting of the Vice-President, the Union Law Minister, the Chief Justice and two senior most judges of the Supreme Court.

Some of the other unanimous decisions of the Commission were to recommend that the retirement age of the Supreme Court and High Court judges should be uniform and it could be 65 years and that the retired judges should not be appointed to any paid positions under the Government. Somehow these recommendations were subsequently dropped or diluted by the Commission and did not find a place in the final report of the Commission even though they were mentioned in the minutes of the meetings of the Commission reproduced in Volume 2 of the report. The final report watered down the principled decision of uniformity in the retirement age of the High Court and Supreme Court judges. It proposed increasing the retirement age of High Court judges to 65 and of the Supreme Court judges to 68. In regard to the National Judicial Commission, the final report dropped the Vice-President and put the Chief Justice as its head thereby seeking to ensure primacy of the judicial wing in the matter of selection of brother judges.

If the independence, primacy and supremacy of the judiciary in its sphere are important—and doubtless these are important—so are the independence, primacy and supremacy of the Parliament in its sphere. After all, Parliament with all its faults is the supreme representative institution of the people. Ultimately, the effort has to be to make all organs of the state more citizen-friendly and people-oriented rather than judge, lawyer, administrator or M.P./ M.L.A. interest-oriented.

According to the minutes of the 11th meeting of the Commission, the suggestions in regard to the judiciary made for being taken up for discussion by the Commission included (i) Intensive training and orientation programmes for the members of the Judiciary at all levels at the time of entry, (ii) refresher courses for upgradation of training and orientation programmes at regular intervals during the service for judicial officers from the lowest to the highest courts, (iii) training camps for lawyers for improving their professional skills and responsibilities, (iv) regulation of fee of the lawyers on the basis of their classification in categories A,B,C, etc., and making cash payment of fees illegal, (v) limits on adjournments in courts, (vi) discouraging unduly lengthy, Ph.D. thesis like judgements, (vii) provision of written arguments, (viii) abolition of the colonial legacy of summer and winter vacations and ensuring a minimum of 220 days of working in a calendar year, (ix) fixed time schedules for clearing the arrears of cases and time bound disposal of current cases. (x) increased use of alternative modes of resolution of disputes with lawyers encouraging out-of-court settlements, (xi) better use of the latest technological devices, and (xii) procedures being made more citizen friendly and courts accountable to people.

Stability and Good Governance

The Commission noted that the last few decades had seen a great deal of political instability. During ten years, there were seven governments and these were unable to provide stable administration and stable policies. The reasons were not far to seek. We adopted the Westminster FPTP model of elections but forgot that it presupposed for its success a two major party system. In a pluralistic society such as ours, some political parties had a vested interest in progressively appealing to narrower and narrowing loyalties. Clearly, if a candidate could win on less than one-third share of the votes polled, he did not need to generate a wider appeal. By making caste and community a factor in political power play, we made the divide even wider and deeper in the Indian society and rendered it nearly impossible for Babasaheb Dr. Ambedkar's vision of a casteless and classless society ever coming true.

The Commission felt that the increasing instability of elected governments was attributable to unprincipled, opportunistic political realignments from time to time and defections and re-defections. The administrative and economic costs of political instability and short-lived governments were enormous and unaffordable. The need for political stability became more pronounced because "in administering any economy in the global context, a reasonable degree of stability of government and strong government is important."

The Anti-Defection Law in the Tenth Schedule of the Constitution was supposed to prevent defections but, in effect, it had become an enabling law for larger defections. As the Commission said "en bloc defections are permitted." Defectors are usually lured with ministerships or other political offices and perquisites "so openly that it really makes a mockery of our democracy." The Commission recommended that all defectors - whether individual or groups - must resign and contest fresh election. They should be debarred from holding any public office of a minister or any other remunerative political post without winning at a fresh election. Also, votes cast by them to topple a government should be treated as invalid.

A significant suggestion repeatedly made by the present writer since 1968 *i.e.* from before the Chavan Committee Report and endorsed by the Commission was in regard to the size of Councils of Ministers. The Commission recommended that the practice of having oversized Councils of Ministers must be prohibited by law. A ceiling on the number of Ministers in any State or the Union government be fixed at the maximum of 10% of the total strength of the popular house of the legislature as provided in article 239AA applicable to Delhi. Also, the practice of creating a number of political offices with the position, perks and privileges of a minister should be discouraged and their number should be limited to 2 per cent of the total strength of the lower house.

The nature of our political system and the resultant politicisation of caste and communal identities had proved to be very divisive of society and disruptive of the national ethos. To cobble up a workable majority to form government, compromises had to be made and ideology or notions of quality of governance took a back seat. It became difficult to take strong measures to curb corruption and provide clean and quality governance. In the end, it was the citizen who was the victim of all the misgovernance.

The Commission found that most of the independent candidates were dummies and only vitiated the sanctity of the electoral process. Only a few – 6 out of 1900 in 1998 and 9 out of over 10 thousand in 1996 – got elected. Such independent candidates should be discouraged and only those who have a track record of having won any local election or who are nominated by at least twenty elected members of panchayats, municipalities or other local bodies spread out in majority of electoral districts in their constituency should be allowed to contest for Assembly or Parliament.

Hung houses happened because the electoral system

was divisive and generated communal and caste-based vote-bank politics. Also, the real cause of instability was concentration of power in the present top-down model of polity. The bottom-up Gandhian model envisaged decentralisation of power with village at the centre and power flowing upward from the grassroots to concentric circles of multi-tier governance and direct elections only at the Panchayat and Nagarpalika levels. The Gandhian model came very close to the subsidiarity principle and advocated that what could not be done at the lower tier only that should be assigned to the next higher tier. NCRWC carefully considered the strong presentations and representations made in support of this Gandhian model but the model was not found feasible "in the present situation." However, the Commission made a strong recommendation for the "immediate discontinuance of the MP LAD scheme as being inconsistent with the spirit of the Constitution in many ways". Apart from other things it trespassed into the areas of local government institutions.

Another suggestion that the present writer had been persisting with for more than a decade and which most directly impacted on the problems of hung legislatures and instability of governments related to the election of the Leader of the House by the Lok Sabha/State Assembly, appointment by the President/Governor of the person so elected as the Prime Minister/Chief Minister and his removal only by a constructive vote of no-confidence. The Commission after due consideration favoured this suggestion.

While any effort to provide that the Lok Sabha/State Assembly should not be subject to dissolution before expiry of its fixed term or that the Council of Ministers should have a fixed term, would be deemed most undemocratic, it is felt that the recommendation of the Commission for the election of the Prime Minister/Chief Minister by the House and his removal only on a constructive vote of no-confidence has tremendous potential to lend the much needed stability to Government. Incidentally, this would not require any constitutional amendment or legislation either.

Presumably on considerations of evolving a less divisive and more unifying political party system for the nation, the Commission unanimously decided that only parties or pre-poll alliances that obtain at least 10 percent of the total votes cast all over the country should be recognised as national parties, and allowed to contest elections to Lok Sabha. Those similarly recognised as State parties or alliances could contest for the houses of the State Legislatures and the Rajya Sabha. This decision was subsequently modified to say 10 per cent all over India or in half the States. Finally, the Commission dropped the percentage requirement altogether and merely recommended that the Election Commission should progressively increase the threshold criterion of eligibility for recognition so that the proliferation of smaller political parties was discouraged. It recommended that only national parties or alliances should be given a common symbol to contest for Lok Sabha. Even this, if accepted and implemented, would be a great advance towards building national unity and stability.

A number of recommendations made by the Commission have impacted national policies and brought about significant even though piecemeal and somewhat half-hearted reforms. To mention a few:

(1) introduction of the minimum rural wage employment guarantee scheme,

(2) amending the Tenth Schedule (Anti-Defection Law) to disqualify group defectors who were thus far protected by the split clause,

(3) making education a fundamental right for children between the age of 6 and 14,

(4) limiting the size of all Councils of Ministers at the Union and State levels,

(5) making defectors ineligible for becoming Ministers or

holding any remunerative public office until re-election.
(6) allowing truth as a defence in contempt of Court Cases,
(7) putting restraints on the borrouring powers of the Union and State governments and expediting the passing of fiscal responsibility law,
(8) making the citizen's right *inter alia* to seek information a fundamental right under the right to freedom of speech and expression, also guaranteeing the right to information specifically by law and giving real substance with the traditional insistence on official secrecy largely discarded to promote transparency and accountability in administration,
(9) introduction of electronic voting machines (EVMs) in all constituencies all over the country for all elections,
(10) use of tamper-proof video and other electronic surveillance at sensitive polling stations,
(11) declaration under law by every candidate at the time of election of his assets making these declarations public and subjected to strict audit,
(12) undertaking intra-State delimitation exercise and rotating the reserved SC/ST seats,
(13) nationwide televising of all important parliamentary debates.

Whatever the Constitution Commission may have done or not done, it did succeed in removing some of the constitutional illiteracy and creating some Constitution consciousness among the people. The Constitution became topical, something that was newsworthy and was being talked about.

Annexure

Table of Constitutional Amendments (1950-2009)

Sl. No.	*Constitution Amendment Act No., Year,*	*Provisions Amended/ Inserted/Replaced*	*Main effect of Amendment*
1	*2*	*3*	*4*
1.	The Constitution (First Amendment) Act, 1951	Articles 15, 19, 31A, 31B, 85, 87, 174, 176, 341, 342, 372, 376 and 9th Schedule	More restrictions on freedoms under article 19 on grounds of maintenance of public order & friendly relations with foreign states, protecting land reform legislation and state's right to carry on any trade, business, industry, service etc. to the exclusion of others.
2.	The Constitution (Second Amendment) Act, 1952	Article 81	Reducing representation in Lok Sabha by omitting the provision of "not less than one member for every 7,50,000 of the population"
3.	The Constitution (Third Amendment) Act, 1954	7th Schedule	Powers to the Union to control the production, supply and distribution of some essential commodities.
4.	The Constitution (Fourth Amendment) Act, 1955	Articles 31, 31A, 305 & 9th Schedule	State's powers of compulsory acquisition of private property and of

1	2	3	4
			providing for state monopoly in certain trade etc. reasserted. Adequacy of compensation not to be questioned. More Acts placed beyond judicial review by being included in the 9th Schedule
5.	The Constitution (Fifth Amendment) Act, 1955	Article 3	Requiring the State Legislatures concerned to give their views under article 3 within a specified period.
6.	The Constitution (Sixth Amendment) Act, 1956	Articles 269, 286 and 7th Schedule	Inter-State sales and purchase tax on trade and commerce (except for newspapers) moved to the Union
7.	The Constitution (Seventh Amendment) Act, 1956	Articles 1, 81, 82, 131, 153, 158, 168, 170, 171, 216, 217, 220, 222, 224, 230, 231, 232, 258A, 290A, 298, 350A, 350B, 371, 372A, 378A, & 1st, 2nd, 4th and 8th Schedule	Implementing the States' reorganisation scheme, ending the Parts A, B and C categories having only 14 States and 6 Union Territories
8.	The Constitution (Eighth Amendment) Act, 1960	Article 334	Extending the reservations in Lok Sabha and State Assemblies for SC & ST and for Anglo-Indians for another 10 years

9.	The Constitution (Ninth Amendment) Act, 1960	1st Schedule	Enabling transfer of certain territories under the Indo-Pak agreement
10.	The Constitution (Tenth Amendment) Act, 1961	Article 240 & 1st Schedule	Including areas of Dadra and Nagar Haveli as a Union Territory
11.	The Constitution (Eleventh Amendment) Act, 1961	Articles 66, 71	Providing that the election of President or Vice-President could not be challenged on the ground of any vacancy in the appropriate electoral college.
12.	The Constitution (Twelfth Amendment) Act, 1962	Article 240 & 1st Schedule	Including Goa, Daman and Diu as a Union Territory
13.	The Constitution (Thirteenth Amendment) Act, 1962	Part XXI	Making special provisions for the State of Nagaland
14.	The Constitution (Fourteenth Amendment) Act, 1962	Articles 81, 240, 239A & 1st and 4th Schedule	Including Pondicherry as a Union Territory
15.	The Constitution (Fifteenth Amendment) Act, 1963	Articles 124, 128, 217, 222, 224, 226, 297, 311, 316, 224A and 7th Schedule	Increasing the age of retirement of High Court Judges and provision of compensatory allowance to judges transferred from one High Court to another, appointment of retired judges to act as judges of High Court and extending the writ jurisdiction of High Courts.

1	2	3	4
16.	The Constitution (Sixteenth Amendment) Act, 1963	Articles 19, 84, 173 and 3rd Schedule	Further restriction on the rights to freedom of speech and expression, to assemble peaceably and without arms and to form associations in the interests of sovereignty and integrity of India, oath or affirmation to be subscribed by candidates seeking election to Parliament and State Legislatures amended to include as one of the conditions that they will uphold the sovereignty and integrity of India.
17.	The Constitution (Seventeenth Amendment) Act, 1964	Article 31A and 9th Schedule	Prohibiting the acquisition of land under personal cultivation unless the market value of the land is paid as compensation. Putting 44 more Acts under the 9th Schedule
18.	The Constitution (Eighteenth Amendment) Act, 1966	Article 3	'State' in article 3 to include Union territory, power to form a new State or Union territory to include the power to do so by uniting a part of a State or Union territory to another.
19.	The Constitution (Nineteenth Amendment) Act, 1966	Article 324	Abolition of Election Tribunals, High Courts to hear election petitions.

20.	The Constitution (Twentieth Amendment) Act, 1966	Article 233A	Validating some appointments of district judges
21.	The Constitution (Twenty–first Amendment) Act, 1967	8th Schedule	Inclusion of 'Sindhi' language in the 8th Schedule
22.	The Constitution (Twenty-second Amendment) Act, 1969	Articles 244A, 275 and 371B	Formation of a new autonomous state of Meghalaya within state of Assam
23.	The Constitution (Twenty-thirdAmendment) Act, 1969	Articles 330, 332, 333, 334	Reservation of seats in Parliament and State Legislatures for Scheduled Castes and Scheduled Tribes as well as for Anglo-Indians for a further period of ten years.
24.	The Constitution (Twenty-fourth Amendment) Act, 1971	Articles 13, 368	To remove all doubts regarding the power of Parliament to amend the Constitution including the Fundamental Rights
25.	The Constitution (Twenty-fifth Amendment) Act, 1971	Articles 31, 31C	Substituting the word 'amount' in place of 'compensation' in the light of the judicial interpretation of the word 'compensation' meaning 'adequate compensation'.
26.	The Constitution (Twenty-sixth Amendment) Act, 1971	Articles 291, 362, 363A, 366	Abolition of the privy purses and privileges of former rulers of princely states

1	2	3	4
27.	The Constitution (Twenty-seventh Amendment) Act, 1971	Articles 239A, 239B, 240, 371C	To provide for certain matters necessitated by the reorganisation of north-eastern states and enabling the promulgation of Ordinances by Administrators of certain union territories
28.	The Constitution (Twenty-eighthAmendment) Act, 1972	Articles 312A, 314	To abolish the special privileges of the members of Indian Civil Services in matters of leave, pension and rights in regard to disciplinary matters.
29.	The Constitution (Twenty-ninth Amendment) Act, 1972	9th Schedule	Including two more (Kerala) Acts in the 9th Schedule.
30.	The Constitution (Thirtieth Amendment) Act, 1972	Article 133	To do away with the valuation test of Rs.20,000 and to provide for an appeal to Supreme Court only on a certificate issued by High Court that the case involves a substantial question of law of general importance and that in the opinion of the High Court, the question needs to be decided by the Supreme Court.
31.	The Constitution (Thirty-first Amendment) Act, 1973	Articles 81, 330, 332	Raising the upper limit for the representation of states in the Lok Sabha from 500 to 525 and reducing the upper

			limit for the representation of union territories from 25 members to 20.
32.	The Constitution (Thirty-second Amendment) Act, 1973	Articles 371, 371D, 371E and 7th Schedule	Giving effect to the provision of equal opportunities to different areas of the State of Andhra Pradesh, the constitution of an Administrative Tribunal with jurisdiction to deal with grievances relating to public services and empowering Parliament to legislate for the establishment of a Central University in the State.
33.	The Constitution (Thirty-third Amendment) Act, 1974	Articles 101, 190 and 9th Schedule	To streamline the procedure for resignation of Members of Parliament and State Legislatures.
34.	The Constitution (Thirty-fourthAmendment) Act, 1974	-	Twenty more land tenure and land reforms laws enacted by various State Legislatures included in the Ninth Schedule.
35.	The Constitution (Thirty-fifth Amendment) Act, 1974	Articles 2A, 80, 81 and 10th Schedule	Conferring on Sikkim the status of an associate State of Indian Union
36.	The Constitution (Thirty-sixth Amendment) Act, 1975	Articles 2A, 80, 81, 371F & 1st, 4th and 10th Schedule	To make Sikkim a full-fledged State of Indian Union and to allot to Sikkim one seat each in the Council of States and in the House of the People.

1	2	3	4
37.	The Constitution (Thirty-seventh Amendment) Act, 1975	Articles 239A, 240	Provision of a Legislative Assembly for the Union Territory of Arunachal Pradesh.
38.	The Constitution (Thirty-eighth Amendment) Act, 1975	Articles 123, 213, 239B, 352, 356, 359, 360	To provide that the satisfaction of President or Governor would not be called in question in any court of law.
39.	The Constitution (Thirty-ninth Amendment) Act, 1975	Articles 71, 329, 329A and 9th Schedule	Disputes relating to the election of the President, Vice-President, Prime Minister and Speaker to be determined by such authority as may be determined by Parliamentary Law. Certain Central enactments also included in the 9th Schedule.
40.	The Constitution (Fortieth Amendment) Act, 1976	Article 297 and 9th Schedule	Vesting in the Union of all mines, minerals and other things of value lying in the ocean within the territorial waters or the continental shelf or the exclusive economic zone of India. Limits of the territorial waters, the continental shelf, the exclusive economic zone and the maritime zones of India to be as specified from time to time. Some more Acts were added to the 9th Schedule.

41.	The Constitution (Forty-first Amendment) Act, 1976	Article 316	To raise the retirement age of Members of State Public Service Commissions and Joint Public Service Commissions from 60 to 62 years.
42.	The Constitution (Forty-second Amendment) Act, 1976	Article 31, 31C, 31D, 32A, 39, 39A, 43A, 48A, 55, 74, 77, 81, 82, 83, 100, 102, 103, 105, 118, 145, 150, 166, 170, 172, 189, 191, 192, 194, 208, 217, 225, 226, 226A, 227, 228, 228A, 257A, 311, 312, 330, 352, 353, 356, 357, 358, 359, 366, 368, 371F, and Parts IVA and XIVA	Specifically including in the Preamble the ideal of socialism, secularism and integrity of the nation, to make the Directive Principles more comprehensive and giving them precedence over Fundamental Rights. Inserting a new chapter on the Fundamental Duties of citizens and special provisions for dealing with anti-national activities, whether by individuals or by associations. Providing for a minimum number of judges for determining questions as to the constitutional validity of laws and for a special majority of not less than two-third for declaring any law to be constitutionally invalid. To reduce the mounting arrears in High Courts and to secure the speedy disposal of service matters, revenue matters and certain

1	2	3	4
			other matters of special importance in the context of socio-economic development and progress, creation of Administrative and other tribunals for dealing with such matters.
43.	The Constitution (Forty-third Amendment) Act, 1977	Article 31D, 32A, 131A, 144A, 145, 226, 226A, 228, 228A, 366	Restoration of the jurisdiction of the Supreme Court and High Courts, curtailed by the enactment of the Constitution (Forty-second Amendment) Act, 1976; omission of article 31D regarding saving of laws in respect of anti-national activities.
44.	The Constitution (Forty-fourth Amendment) Act, 1978	Article 19, 22, 30, 31, 31A, 31C, 38, 71, 74, 77, 83, 103, 105, 123, 132, 133, 134, 134A, 139A, 150, 166, 172, 192, 194, 213, 217, 225, 226, 227, 239B, 257A, 329, 329A, 352, 356, 358, 359, 360, 361A, 371F, 9th Schedule and Chapter IV in Part XII	Right to property omitted as a fundamental right; "armed rebellion" and not merely "internal disturbance" made a necessary ground for proclamation of emergency, preventive detention not to be authorised beyond two months without the decision of the Advisory Board, removing various distortions brought about by the 42nd Amendment.

45.	The Constitution (Forty-fifth Amendment) Act, 1980	Article 334	To extend reservation of seats in Parliament and State Assemblies for Scheduled Castes, Scheduled Tribes as well as for Anglo-Indians for a further period of ten years.
46.	The Constitution (Forty-sixth Amendment) Act, 1982	Article 269, 286, 366 and 7th Schedule	To enable Parliament to formulate by law principle for determining when a consignment of goods takes place in the course of inter-state trade or commerce. To enable the levy of tax on the consignment of goods where such consignment takes place in the course of inter-state trade or commerce. To enable Parliament to specify, by law, restrictions and conditions in regard to the system of levy rates and other incidence of tax on the transfer of goods involved in the execution of a works contract, on the delivery of goods on hire-purchase or any system of payment in instalments. To insert a definition of "tax on the sale or purchase of goods" to include transfer for consideration of controlled commodities, transfer of

1	2	3	4
			property in goods involved in the execution of a works contract, delivery of goods on hire-purchase or any system of payment by instalments, etc.
47.	The Constitution (Forty-seventh Amendment) Act, 1984	9th Schedule	To provide for the inclusion of certain land Reform Acts in the Ninth Schedule.
48.	The Constitution (Forty-eighth Amendment) Act, 1984	Article 356	To provide for continuation of President's rule in Punjab beyond the prescribed limit of one year.
49.	The Constitution (Forty-ninth Amendment) Act, 1984	Article 244 and 5th and 6th Schedule	To give a constitutional security to the autonomous District Council functioning in the State of Tripura
50.	The Constitution (Fiftieth Amendment) Act, 1984	Article 13	Restrictions on fundamental rights extended to members of the force charged with protection of state property, to members of intelligence and counter-intelligence groups of the State, and to those in the telecommunication systems.
51.	The Constitution (Fifty-first Amendment) Act, 1984	Articles 330, 332	Providing reservation of seats for Scheduled Tribes in Meghalaya, Nagaland, Arunachal Pradesh and

			Mizoram in Parliament and to provide similar reservation in the Legislative Assemblies of Nagaland and Meghalaya to meet the aspirations of local tribal population.
52.	The Constitution (Fifty-second Amendment) Act, 1985	Articles 101, 102, 190, 191 and 10th Schedule	To provide that a Member of Parliament or a State Legislature who defects from the party which set him up as a candidate in the election or if an independent member of the House joins a political party shall be disqualified to remain a member of the House unless covered under provision of party splits or mergers.
53.	The Constitution (Fifty-third Amendment) Act, 1986	Article 371G	Preventing application of any Act of Parliament in Mizoram in respect of religious or social practices of Mizos, Mizos' customary law and procedure, administration of civil and criminal practice involving decisions according to Mizos' customary law and ownership and transfer of land unless a resolution is passed in the Legislative Assembly to that effect.

1	2	3	4
54.	The Constitution (Fifty-fourth Amendment) Act, 1986	Article 125, 221 and 2nd Schedule	Increasing the salaries of Chief Justice and Judges of the Supreme Court to Rs.10,000 and Rs.9000 p.m. respectively and of the C.J. and Judges of High Courts to Rs.9000 and 8000 p.m. respectively.
55.	The Constitution (Fifty-fifth Amendment) Act, 1986	Article 371H	To confer statehood on the Union Territory of Arunachal Pradesh and to vest special responsibility on Governor with respect to law and order in the State. The Legislative Assembly of the new State of Arunachal Pradesh to consist of not less than thirty members.
56.	The Constitution (Fifty-sixth Amendment) Act, 1987	Article 371I	To constitute the territories comprised in Goa District of the Union Territory of Goa, Daman and Diu and to provide that the Legislative Assembly of the new State of Goa shall consist of not less than 30 members.
57.	The Constitution (Fifty-seventh Amendment) Act, 1987	Clause 3A in article 332	To provide for reservation of seats in the House of the People for Scheduled Tribes in Nagaland, Meghalaya,

			Mizoram and Arunachal Pradesh for a temporary period until the re-adjustment of seats on the basis of first census after the year 2000.
58.	The Constitution (Fifty-eighth Amendment) Act, 1987	Article 394A and heading of Part XXII	Authorising the publication of an authentic Hindi text of the Constitution and of constitutional amendments.
59.	The Constitution (Fifty-ninth Amendment) Act, 1988	Article 356, 359A	Continuation of President's rule in Punjab upto 3 years.
60.	The Constitution (Sixtieth Amendment) Act, 1988	Article 276	To increase the ceiling of taxes on professions, trades, callings and employment from Rs.250 per annum to Rs.2,500 per annum.
61.	The Constitution (Sixty-first Amendment) Act, 1989	Article 326	Reducing voting age from 21 to 18 years
62.	The Constitution (Sixty-second Amendment) Act, 1989	Article 334	To continue the reservation for the Scheduled Castes and the Scheduled Tribes and the representation of the Anglo-Indians by nomination for a further period of 10 years.
63.	The Constitution (Sixty-third Amendment) Act, 1989	Article 356, 359A	Omitting the special provision re. proclamation of emergency and for continuation of President's rule in Punjab.

1	2	3	4
64.	The Constitution (Sixty-fourth Amendment) Act, 1990	Article 356	To facilitate the extension of the proclamation upto a total period of three years and six months in relation to the State of Punjab.
65.	The Constitution (Sixty-fifth Amendment) Act, 1930	Article 338	In place of the existing special officer for ST & SC, constitution of a National Commission for Scheduled Castes and Scheduled Tribes consisting of a Chairperson, Vice-Chairperson and five other Members.
66.	The Constitution (Sixty-sixth Amendment) Act, 1990	9th Schedule	Including another set of 55 State Acts in the 9th Schedule.
67.	The Constitution (Sixty-seventh Amendment) Act, 1990	Article 356	To further extend the period of proclamation in respect of Punjab to four years.
68.	The Constitution (Sixty-eighth Amendment) Act, 1991	Article 356	To further extend the period of proclamation in respect of Punjab to 5 years.
69.	The Constitution (Sixty-ninth Amendment) Act, 1991	Articles 239AA, 239AB	To provide Delhi with a Legislative Assembly and a Council of Ministers and give a special status to this Union Territory as the National Capital Territory.

70.	The Constitution (Seventieth Amendment) Act, 1992	Articles 54, 239AA	To provide that reference to 'State' in Article 54 and 55 would include the National Capital Territory of Delhi and the Union Territory of Pondicherry for constituting the electoral college for election of the President, to enable the elected members of the Legislative Assemblies of Pondicherry and Delhi to be included in the electoral college.
71.	The Constitution (Seventy-first Amendment) Act, 1992	8th Schedule	To include Konkani, Manipuri and Nepali languages in the Eighth Schedule
72.	The Constitution (Seventy-second Amendment) Act, 1992	Article 332	For making a temporary provision for the determination of the number of seats reserved for the Scheduled Tribes in the State Assembly of Tripura, until the re-adjustment of seats is made on the basis of the first Census after the year 2000.
73.	The Constitution (Seventy-third Amendment) Act, 1993	Article 280, 11th Schedule and Part IX	To insert a whole new Part IX relating to village Panchayats, direct elections to all seats in Panchayats at the village and intermediate level, if any and to the offices of Chairpersons of Panchayats at such levels; reservation of seats for the Scheduled Castes and Scheduled Tribes

1	2	3	4
			in proportion to their population for membership of Panchayats and office of Chairpersons in Panchayats at each level; reservation of not less than one-third of the seats for women; fixing tenure of five years for Panchayats and holding elections within a period of six months in the event of supersession of any Panchayat.
74.	The Constitution (Seventy-fourth Amendment) Act, 1993	Article 280, 12th Schedule and Part IXA	Adding a new Part IXA relating to the Municipalities to provide for among other things, constitution of three types of Municipalities, *i.e.*, Nagar Panchayats for areas in transition from a rural area to urban area. Municipal Councils for smaller urban areas and Municipal Corporations for larger urban areas.
75.	The Constitution (Seventy-fifth Amendment) Act, 1994	Article 323B	To give timely relief to the rent litigants by providing for setting up of state-level Rent Tribunals in order to reduce the tiers of appeals and to exclude the jurisdiction of all courts, except that of the Supreme Court.

76.	The Constitution (Seventy-sixth Amendment) Act, 1994	9th Schedule	To protect Tamilnadu law extending reservation to 69% [18% for SC, 1% ST and 50% OBCs] by including it in the 9th Schedule.
77.	The Constitution (Seventy-seventh Amendment) Act, 1995	Article 16	To continue the existing policy of reservation in promotion for the Scheduled Castes and the Scheduled Tribes by inserting a new clause (4A) in article 16 to provide for reservation in promotion for the Scheduled Castes and the Scheduled Tribes.
78.	The Constitution (Seventh-eighth Amendment) Act, 1995	9th Schedule	To include a number of amending Acts along with a few principal Acts in the Ninth Schedule so as to ensure that implementation of these Acts is not adversely affected by litigation.
79.	The Constitution (Seventy-ninth Amendment) Act, 1999	Article 334	To extend the reservations of seats for the Scheduled Castes and the Scheduled Tribes as well as for the Anglo-Indians in the House of the People and in the Legislative Assemblies of the States for another ten years.
80.	The Constitution (Eightieth Amendment) Act, 2000	Articles 269, 270, 272	To give effect to the new scheme for sharing revenues recommended by the

1	2	3	4
			10th Finance Commission. Under the new scheme of devolution of revenue between the Union and the States, 26 per cent out of gross proceeds of Union taxes and duties is to be assigned to the States in lieu of their existing share in the income-tax, excise duties, special excise duties and grants in lieu of tax on railway passenger fares.
81.	The Constitution (Eighty-first Amendment) Act, 2000	Article 16	To regard unfilled seats reserved for SC&ST as a separate class of vacancies under article 16 to be filled up in any succeeding year or years and not to be considered together with the vacancies of the year in which they were filled up for determining the ceiling of fifty per cent reservation against total number of vacancies of that year.
82.	The Constitution (Eighty-second Amendment) Act, 2000	Article 335	Making provision in favour of the members of the Scheduled Castes and the Scheduled Tribes for relaxation in qualifying marks in any examination or lowering the standards of evaluation for

			reservation in matters of promotion to any class or classes of services or posts in connection with affairs of the Union or of a State.
83.	The Constitution (Eighty-third Amendment) Act, 2000	Article 243M	To provide that no reservation in Panchayats need be made in favour of the Scheduled Castes in Arunachal Pradesh wholly inhabited by tribal population.
84.	The Constitution (Eighty-fourth Amendment) Act, 2001	Articles 55, 81, 82, 170, 330, 332	To provide (a) that reference to 'population of the State' in articles concerning elections to the office of the President and to Lok Sabha shall continue to mean population as ascertained by the 1971 census until the census after 2026, (b) that until 2026 the allocation of seats in Lok Sabha to the States shall continue to be on the basis of 1971 census but the constituencies within each State may be readjusted on the basis of 1991 census, and (c) that reservation of seats in the Lok Sabha and State Assemblies for SC/ST shall be on the basis of the 1991 census until after 2026.

1	2	3	4
85.	The Constitution (Eighty-fifth Amendment) Act, 2001	Article 16	To allow provision for reservation in matters of promotion *with consequential seniority* in services under the State for SC/ST employees.
86.	The Constitution (Eighty-sixth Amendment) Act, 2002	Articles 21A, 45, 51A	To insert a new article 21A to provide for a fundamental right to education to all children of 6 to 14 years. Also, it substitutes article 45 in the Directive Principles by a new article providing for early child care and education to children below 6 years. By amending article 51A, a new fundamental duty is sought to be added for parents or guardians providing educational opportunities to children below the age of 6 and 14 years.
87.	The Constitution (Eighty-seventh Amendment) Act, 2003	Articles 81, 82, 170, 330	To substitute the figure 2001 for the figure 1991 in the provisos to articles 81, 82, 170 and 330 thereby laying down that the population figures to be taken into account for purposes of readjusting constituencies within each State and for

			reservation of seats in the Lok Sabha and State Assemblies for SC/ST shall be on the basis of 2001 census.
88.	The Constitution (Eighty-eighth Amendment) Act, 2004	Articles 92C, 268A	To add new article 268A to provide for levy of taxes on services to be collected and appropriated by the Government of India and the States, to insert new entry "92C. Taxes on Services" to the Union List, Seventh Schedule.
89.	The Constitution (Eighty-ninth Amendment) Act, 2003	Articles 338, 338A	To amend article 338 and add a new article 338A to provide for two separate Commissions for Scheduled Castes and Scheduled Tribes.
90.	The Constitution (Ninetieth-Amendment) Act, 2003	Article 332	To amend article 332 to provide for maintaining the erstwhile representation of the Scheduled Tribes and non-Scheduled Tribes in Assam constituencies included in Bodoland Territorial Areas District.
91.	The Constitution (Ninety-first Amendment) Act, 2004	Articles 75, 164, 361B and 10th Schedule	To amend articles 75, 164 and Schedule 10, to insert a new article 361B, to place a limit on the number of Ministers not to be more than 15% of the House of the People at the Union level and Vidhan

1	2	3	4
			Sabha at the level of States; to take away the protection from defectors on grounds of splits and make defectors disqualified from Membership and ineligible for Ministership or other remunerative political post till re-election.
92.	The Constitution (Ninety-second Amendment) Act, 2004	8th Schedule	To add four more languages *viz.* Bodo, Dogri, Santhali and Maithili to the existing 18.
93.	The Constitution (Ninety-third Amendment) Act, 2005	Article 15	To make a special provision by law for socially and educationally backward classes, SC & STs in regard to admission to educational institutions including private – aided or unaided – institutions other than minority institutions.
94.	The Constitution (Ninety-fourth Amendment) Act, 1951	Article 164	To amend proviso to article 164(1) to substitute the words "Chhattisgarh, Jharkhand" in place of the word "Bihar" as there were now no scheduled areas in Bihar left after the creation of Jharkhand.

For the texts of Constitutional Amendments and their objects and reasons, see Kashyap, Subbash C., *Constitution Making Since 1950: An Overview*, Universal, New Delhi, 2004.

Index

Printed at: Salasar Imaging Systems, Noida

PART IVA

Article 51A

Fundamental duties

It shall be the duty of every citizen of India -

(a) to abide by the Constitution and respect its ideals and institutions, the National Flag and the National Anthem;

(b) to cherish and follow the noble ideals which inspired our national struggle for freedom;

(c) to uphold and protect the sovereignty, unity and integrity of India;

(d) to defend the country and render national service when called upon to do so;

(e) to promote harmony and the spirit of common brotherhood amongst all the people of India transcending religious, linguistic and regional or sectional diversities; to renounce practices derogatory to the dignity of women;

(f) to value and preserve the rich heritage of our composite culture;

(g) to protect and improve the natural environment including forests, lakes, rivers and wild life, and to have compassion for living creatures;

(h) to develop the scientific temper, humanism and the spirit of inquiry and reform;

(i) to safeguard public property and to abjure violence;

(j) to strive towards excellence in all spheres of individual and collective activity so that the nation constantly rises to higher levels of endeavour and achievement;

(k) who is a parent or guardian to provide opportunities for education to his child or, as the case may be, ward between the age of six and fourteen years.